D0162054

THE CAMBRIDGE
COMPANION TO
AUSTRALIAN LITERATURE

This book introduces in a lively and succinct way the major writers, literary movements, styles and genres that, at the beginning of a new century, are seen as constituting the field of 'Australian literature'. The book consciously takes a perspective that sees literary works not as aesthetic objects created in isolation by unique individuals, but as cultural products influenced and constrained by the social, political and economic circumstances of their times, as well as by geographical and environmental factors. It covers Indigenous texts, colonial writing and reading, poetry, fiction and theatre throughout two centuries, biography and autobiography, and literary criticism in Australia. Other features of the companion are a chronology listing significant historical and literary events, and suggestions for further reading. It will be an indispensable reference for both national and international readers.

Elizabeth Webby is Professor of Australian Literature and Director of the Australian Studies program at the University of Sydney. She is the author, editor and co-editor of many books including *The Penguin New Literary History of Australia* (1988), *Modern Australian Plays* (1990), *The Penguin Book of Australian Ballads* (1993), *Australian Feminism: A Companion* (1998) and *The Letters of Walter and Mary Richardson* (2000). For twelve years she was the editor of the influential literary magazine, *Southerly*.

CAMBRIDGE COMPANIONS TO LITERATURE

CAMBRIDGE COMPANIONS TO CULTURE

The Cambridge Companion to Modern German Culture
edited by Eva Kolinsky and Wilfried van der Will

The Cambridge Companion to Modern Russian Culture
edited by Nicholas Rzhevsky

The Cambridge Companion to Modern Spanish Culture
edited by David T. Gies

THE CAMBRIDGE
COMPANION TO
AUSTRALIAN
LITERATURE

EDITED BY
ELIZABETH WEBBY

CAMBRIDGE
UNIVERSITY PRESS

PUBLISHED BY THE PRESS SYNDICATE OF THE UNIVERSITY OF CAMBRIDGE
The Pitt Building, Trumpington Street, Cambridge, United Kingdom

CAMBRIDGE UNIVERSITY PRESS
The Edinburgh Building, Cambridge CB2 2RU, UK
40 West 20th Street, New York, NY 10011–4211, USA
10 Stamford Road, Oakleigh, VIC 3166, Australia
Ruiz de Alarcón 13, 28014, Madrid, Spain
Dock House, The Waterfront, Cape Town 8001, South Africa

http://www.cambridge.org

First published 2000

Printed in China by Everbest Printing Co.

Typeface Sabon (*Adobe*) 10/13 pt.   *System* QuarkXPress®   [BC]

A catalogue record for this book is available from the British Library

National Library of Australia Cataloguing in Publication data
The Cambridge companion to Australian literature.
Includes index.
ISBN 0 521 65122 0.
ISBN 0 521 65843 8 (pbk.).
1. Australian literature – History and criticism.
2. Australia – In literature. I. Webby, Elizabeth. II. Title:
Australian literature. (Series: Cambridge companions
to literature.)
A820.9

ISBN 0 521 65122 0 hardback
ISBN 0 521 65843 8 paperback

CONTENTS

CONTRIBUTORS

MICHAEL ACKLAND is a Reader in English at Monash University. His publications include four editions of nineteenth-century prose and verse and four monographs: *That Shining Band: A Study of Australian Colonial Verse Tradition* (1994), *Henry Kendall: The Man and the Myths* (1995), *Henry Handel Richardson* (1996) and *Damaged Men: The Lives of James McAuley and Harold Stewart* (2000). He is currently researching the place of the grotesque in Australian culture.

MAY-BRIT AKERHOLT is the Artistic Director of the Australian National Playwrights' Centre. She was resident dramaturg at the Sydney Theatre Company for six years and before that, lecturer in drama at NIDA, and tutor in English at Macquarie University. She has translated eighteen plays for the Australian stage, and has published numerous articles about translation, theatre and writing for performance, as well as a study of Patrick White's plays (1988).

DELYS BIRD teaches in the English Department at the University of Western Australia in Australian literary and cultural studies and women's studies and is one of the editors of *Westerly*. She has published on Australian women's writing from the colonial period to the contemporary, and has edited a collection of Elizabeth Jolley's radio plays, *Off the Air* (1995); a book on women and detective fiction, *Killing Women* (1993); and co-edited collections of essays on Elizabeth Jolley's fiction (1991) and Sally Morgan's *My Place* (1992).

DAVID CARTER teaches literature and cultural studies in the School of Humanities, Griffith University, Brisbane, and is President of the International Australian Studies Association. His publications include *A Career in Writing: Judah Waten and the Cultural Politics of a Literary Career* (1997) and a number of edited books, *The Republicanism Debate* (1993), *Outside the Book: Contemporary Essays on Literary Periodicals* (1999) and *Judah Waten: Fiction, Memoirs, Criticism* (1998). He is currently writing a history of twentieth-century magazine publication in Australia.

RICHARD FOTHERINGHAM is Head of the English Department and Reader in Drama at the University of Queensland. His major publications include a study of sport in Australian drama and film (1992), and a biography of the short story writer and playwright Steele Rudd (1995), as well as numerous articles on Australian theatre, film and the performing arts as an industry. He is currently editing two collections of early Australian plays for publication in the Academy Editions of Australian Literature series.

KERRYN GOLDSWORTHY taught Australian literature, women's studies, Victorian literature and creative writing in the Department of English and Cultural Studies at the University of Melbourne for seventeen years; she resigned in 1997 to become an independent scholar and writer. She has edited four anthologies of Australian writing and has written a collection of short stories (*North of the Moonlight Sonata*, 1989) and a monograph on the work of Helen Garner (1996). She was editor of *Australian Book Review* from 1986–87.

DAVID McCOOEY lectures in literary studies at Deakin University (Geelong). He is the author of *Artful Histories: Modern Australian Autobiography* (1996), which won a NSW Premier's Literary Award. He has published widely on Australian poetry in journals such as *Australian Literary Studies* and *Southerly*, and his reviews and poems have appeared in many national and international publications.

PENNY VAN TOORN is a lecturer in Australian literature and Australian studies at the University of Sydney. She is the author of *Rudy Wiebe and the Historicity of the Word* (1995), and co-editor of *Speaking Positions: Aboriginality, Gender and Ethnicity in Australian Cultural Studies* (1995). She has published extensively on postcolonial literatures and theory, focusing particularly on writings by and about indigenous peoples of Australia and Canada.

ELIZABETH WEBBY is Professor of Australian Literature and Director of the Australian Studies Program at the University of Sydney. She has published many books and articles on Australian literature and literary culture. From 1988–99 she was editor of *Southerly*, Australia's oldest literary magazine.

GILLIAN WHITLOCK is Head of the School of Humanities at Griffith University. Her publications on autobiography include *The Intimate Empire. Reading Women's Autobiography* (2000) and an edition of contemporary Australian autobiography, *Autographs* (1996).

CHRONOLOGY

This chronology provides a basic framework of dates in Australian history, together with major literary and cultural events, and selected publications of particular historical or literary significance.

40,000 BC	Aboriginal peoples living on Australian continent from at least this time.
20,000 BC	Rock art in Western Arnhem Land depicts now-extinct animals.
14,000 BC	Tasmania separated from mainland at end of glacial period.
12,000 BC	Archaeological evidence of use of boomerangs for hunting.
1616	Dirk Hartog makes first recorded European landing on Australian continent, in Western Australia.
1642	Abel Tasman lands at Blackman's Bay, Van Diemen's Land.
1703	William Dampier, *A Voyage to New Holland in the Year 1699*.
1770	James Cook lands in Botany Bay, later names and takes possession of New South Wales for Britain.
1788	First Fleet arrives and establishes penal settlement at Sydney and later at Norfolk Island.
1789	Convict production in Sydney of George Farquhar's *The Recruiting Officer*.
	The Voyage of Governor Phillip to Botany Bay.
	Watkin Tench, *A Narrative of the Expedition to Botany Bay*.
1802	George Howe prints first Australian book, the *NSW General Standing Orders*.
1803	Settlement established in Van Diemen's Land, near Hobart.
	First issue of *Sydney Gazette* (1803–42).
1813	First European crossing of Blue Mountains, west of Sydney.
1816	First issue of *Hobart Town Gazette*.
1819	Barron Field, *First Fruits of Australian Poetry*.

1821	First locally produced periodical, the *Australian Magazine* (1821–22).
1824	Penal settlement established at Moreton Bay.
1826	Establishment of Australian Subscription Library in Sydney. Charles Tompson, *Wild Notes from the Lyre of a Native Minstrel.*
1827	Establishment of Hobart Town Mechanics' Institute.
1829	Establishment of Swan River Colony in Western Australia. Henry Savery, *The Hermit in Van Diemen's Land.*
1830–31	Henry Savery, *Quintus Servinton.*
1831	First issue of *Sydney Herald* (still publishing, as *Sydney Morning Herald*).
1833	First settlers arrive in Port Phillip district, later Victoria. Charles Sturt, *Two Expeditions into the Interior of Southern Australia.*
1836	South Australia established as a colony of free settlers. George Bennett, *Wanderings in New South Wales.*
1838	Anna Maria Bunn, *The Guardian.* T.L. Mitchell, *Three Expeditions into the Interior of Eastern Australia.*
1840	Transportation of convicts to NSW ceases. First issue of *Port Phillip Herald* (still publishing as *Herald-Sun News*).
1841	Charlotte Barton, *A Mother's Offering to Her Children.*
1843	Charles Rowcroft, *Tales of the Colonies.*
1844	Louisa Ann Meredith, *Notes and Sketches of New South Wales.* Edward Geoghegan, *The Currency Lass.*
1845	Charles Harpur, *Thoughts: a Series of Sonnets.* Thomas McCombie, *Arabin, or the Adventures of a Colonist in New South Wales.* Mary Vidal, *Tales for the Bush.*
1846	*Moreton Bay Courier* established (still publishing as *Courier-Mail*, Brisbane).
1847	Alexander Harris, *Settlers and Convicts.*
1849	Alexander Harris, *The Emigrant Family.*
1850	First convicts sent to Western Australia. University of Sydney established.
1851	Colony of Victoria gains independence from NSW. Gold discovered in NSW and Victoria.
1852	First mail steamer arrives in Sydney from England. G.C. Mundy, *Our Antipodes.*

1853	Last convicts arrive in Van Diemen's Land.
	Charles Harpur, *The Bushrangers and other poems.*
1854	Eureka Stockade, unsuccessful rebellion of miners at Ballarat, Victoria.
	The Age established (Melbourne, still publishing).
	Catherine Helen Spence, *Clara Morison.*
1855	*Melbourne Punch* established (1855–1929).
	Raffaello Carboni, *The Eureka Stockade.*
	William Howitt, *Land, Labour and Gold.*
1856	Van Diemen's Land renamed Tasmania.
1858	*South Australian Advertiser* established (still publishing).
1859	Queensland becomes a separate colony.
	Henry Kingsley, *The Recollections of Geoffry Hamlyn.*
	Caroline Leakey, *The Broad Arrow.*
1863	Northern Territory separated from NSW.
1865	First issue of *Australian Journal* (1865–1962).
1866	G.B. Barton, *Literature in New South Wales.*
1867	Gold rushes begin in Queensland.
1868	Cessation of convict transportation to Western Australia.
1869	Henry Kendall, *Leaves from Australian Forests.*
1870	Adam Lindsay Gordon, *Bush Ballads and Galloping Rhymes.*
1873	Garnet Walch, *Australia Felix.*
1874	Marcus Clarke, *His Natural Life.*
1876	First issue of the *Melbourne Review* (1876–85).
1880	Bushranger Ned Kelly captured and hanged in Melbourne.
	Bulletin established (Sydney, still publishing).
	Henry Kendall, *Songs from the Mountains.*
	Rosa Praed, *An Australian Heroine.*
1881	Rosa Praed, *Policy and Passion.*
1883	First regular train service between Sydney and Melbourne.
	George Darrell, *The Sunny South.*
1886	Francis Adams, *Australian Essays.*
	Fergus Hume, *The Mystery of a Hansom Cab.*
1887	Ada Cambridge, *Unspoken Thoughts.*
1888	First issue of *The Dawn: A Journal for Australian Women* (1888–1905).
	Rolf Boldrewood, *Robbery Under Arms.*
1889	Jessie Couvreur ("Tasma"), *Uncle Piper of Piper's Hill.*
	Ernest Giles, *Australia Twice Traversed.*
1890	Ada Cambridge, *A Marked Man.*
	Catherine Martin, *An Australian Girl.*

1891	Major shearers' strikes in Queensland, in January and June. Ada Cambridge, *The Three Miss Kings*.
1892	Gold discovered in Western Australia. William Lane, *The Workingman's Paradise*. Price Warung, *Tales of the Convict System*.
1893	Major depression and drought. Francis Adams, *The Australians*.
1894	Women's suffrage attained in South Australia. Henry Lawson, *Short Stories in Prose and Verse*. Ethel Turner, *Seven Little Australians*.
1895	Angus & Robertson publishes A.B. Paterson's *The Man from Snowy River* (10,000 copies sold in first year).
1896	First film made in Australia. Henry Lawson, *While the Billy Boils*.
1898	David Carnegie, *Spinifex and Sand*. H.G. Turner and Alexander Sutherland, *The Development of Australian Literature*.
1899	Steele Rudd, *On Our Selection*.
1901	Australia becomes a federation and first Commonwealth Parliament opened. Miles Franklin, *My Brilliant Career*. Henry Lawson, *Joe Wilson and His Mates*.
1902	Barbara Baynton, *Bush Studies*.
1903	Joseph Furphy, *Such is Life*.
1905	A.B. Paterson, ed., *Old Bush Songs*.
1906	British New Guinea becomes a territory of the Commonwealth.
1908	Commonwealth Literary Fund established. E.J. Banfield, *Confessions of a Beachcomber*. Jeannie Gunn, *We of the Never Never*. Henry Handel Richardson, *Maurice Guest*.
1910	Charles Bean, *On the Wool Track*. Mary Grant Bruce, *A Little Bush Maid*. Mary Gilmore, *Marri'd*. Henry Handel Richardson, *The Getting of Wisdom*.
1911	Louis Stone, *Jonah*.
1912	Louis Esson, *The Time is Not Yet Ripe*. Bernard O'Dowd, *The Bush*.
1913	Christopher Brennan, *Poems*.
1915	Allied landing at Gallipoli in Turkey on 25 April, later commemorated as Anzac Day.

	C.J. Dennis, *The Songs of a Sentimental Bloke.*
1918	May Gibbs, *Snugglepot and Cuddlepie.*
	Mary Gilmore, *The Passionate Heart.*
	Norman Lindsay, *The Magic Pudding.*
1919	John Shaw Neilson, *Heart of Spring.*
1920	Establishment of QANTAS (Queensland and Northern Territory Aerial Services).
1923	Opening of first public radio station in Sydney.
	D.H. Lawrence, *Kangaroo.*
1925	Mary Gilmore, *The Tilted Cart.*
1926	K.S. Prichard, *Working Bullocks.*
1928	Martin Boyd, *The Montforts.*
	Miles Franklin, *Up the Country.*
1929	M. Barnard Eldershaw, *A House is Built.*
	K.S. Prichard, *Coonardoo.*
	David Unaipon, *Native Legends.*
1930	Norman Lindsay, *Redheap.*
	Vance Palmer, *The Passage.*
	Henry Handel Richardson, *The Fortunes of Richard Mahony.*
1931	Ion Idriess, *Lasseter's Last Ride.*
1932	ABC established as national broadcaster.
	Official opening of Sydney Harbour Bridge.
	Kenneth Slessor, *Cuckooz Country.*
1934	Eleanor Dark, *Prelude to Christopher.*
	Brian Penton, *Landtakers.*
	Christina Stead, *Seven Poor Men of Sydney.*
1936	Dymphna Cusack, *Jungfrau.*
	Jean Devanny, *Sugar Heaven.*
	Kenneth Mackenzie, *The Young Desire It.*
1937	K.S. Prichard, *Intimate Strangers.*
1938	Sesquicentenary celebrations: Aborigines' Progressive Association declares 26 January a "day of mourning".
	Xavier Herbert's *Capricornia* wins Sesquicentenary Prize for Fiction.
1939	Expansion of Commonwealth Literary Fund.
	First issue of *Southerly.*
	Kenneth Slessor, *Five Bells.*
	Patrick White, *Happy Valley.*
1940	First issue of *Meanjin.*
	Christina Stead, *The Man Who Loved Children.*
1941	Eleanor Dark, *The Timeless Land.*

Kylie Tennant, *The Battlers*.

1942   Japan bombs Darwin; Japanese submarines in Sydney Harbour.
Gavin Casey, *It's Harder for Girls*.
Eve Langley, *The Pea Pickers*.
Douglas Stewart, *Ned Kelly*.

1943   Kylie Tennant, *Ride on Stranger*.

1944   Ern Malley hoax.
Kenneth Slessor, *One Hundred Poems*.
Christina Stead, *For Love Alone*.

1945   Australian Book Council formed in Sydney.

1946   Children's Book of the Year Award begins.
Martin Boyd, *Lucinda Brayford*.
Judith Wright, *The Moving Image*.

1947   European migration program begins.
M. Barnard Eldershaw, *Tomorrow and Tomorrow and Tomorrow*.

1948   Francis Webb, *A Drum for Ben Boyd*.
Patrick White, *The Aunt's Story*.

1949   Judith Wright, *Woman to Man*.

1950   Menzies' government introduces Communist Party Dissolution Bill.
Frank Hardy, *Power Without Glory*.
Nevil Shute, *A Town Like Alice*.

1951   Dymphna Cusack and Florence James, *Come in Spinner*.
Martin Boyd, *The Cardboard Crown*.

1952   Judah Waten, *Alien Son*.

1954   Establishment of Elizabethan Theatre Trust.
Overland, incorporating *Realist Writer*, begins publication.
Mary Gilmore, *Fourteen Men*.
Vance Palmer, *The Legend of the Nineties*.

1955   First full-year university course in Australian Literature (at Canberra University College).
A.D. Hope, *The Wandering Islands*.
Ray Lawler, *Summer of the Seventeenth Doll*.
Patrick White, *The Tree of Man*.

1956   Olympic Games held in Melbourne.
Regular television transmission commences in Australia.
First issues of *Quadrant* and *Westerly*.
Ethel Anderson, *At Parramatta*.

1957   Patrick White's *Voss* wins first Miles Franklin Award.

1958   National Institute of Dramatic Art established.

Elizabeth Harrower, *The Long Prospect.*
Randolph Stow, *To the Islands.*
1959　R.D. FitzGerald, *The Wind at Your Door.*
Dorothy Hewett, *Bobbin Up.*
1960　First Adelaide Festival of the Arts held.
Alan Seymour, *The One Day of the Year.*
1961　H.M. Green, *A History of Australian Literature.*
Patrick White, *Riders in the Chariot.*
1962　First chair of Australian Literature established at University of Sydney.
Thea Astley, *The Well Dressed Explorer.*
Hal Porter, *A Bachelor's Children.*
1963　Establishment of Australian Society of Authors.
First issue of *Australian Literary Studies.*
Hal Porter, *The Watcher on the Cast-Iron Balcony.*
Randolph Stow, *Tourmaline.*
1964　Donald Horne, *The Lucky Country.*
George Johnston, *My Brother Jack.*
Oodgeroo Noonuccal (Kath Walker), *We Are Going.*
1965　Australian troops sent to Vietnam.
Mudrooroo (Colin Johnson), *Wild Cat Falling.*
Patrick White, *Four Plays.*
Judith Wright, *Preoccupations in Australian Poetry.*
1966　Introduction of decimal currency.
Elizabeth Harrower, *The Watch Tower.*
A.D. Hope, *Collected Poems 1930–65.*
1967　Referendum allows Aboriginal Australians to be recognised as Australian citizens.
1968　Establishment of Australia Council for the Arts.
Alex Buzo, *Norm and Ahmed.*
Joan Lindsay, *Picnic at Hanging Rock.*
1969　Women granted equal pay for work of equal value.
Bruce Beaver, *Letters to Live Poets.*
James McAuley, *Surprises of the Sun.*
Les Murray, *The Weatherboard Cathedral.*
Francis Webb, *Collected Poems.*
1970　Germaine Greer, *The Female Eunuch.*
Patrick White, *The Vivisector.*
1971　Bruce Dawe, *Condolences of the Season.*
David Ireland, *The Unknown Industrial Prisoner.*
James McAuley, *Collected Poems.*

David Williamson, *The Removalists*.

1972 Australian Labor Party wins government and withdraws troops from Vietnam.
Aborigines set up "tent embassy" at Parliament House, Canberra.
Thea Astley, *The Acolyte*.
Dorothy Hewett, *The Chapel Perilous*.
Jack Hibberd, *A Stretch of the Imagination*.
Thomas Keneally, *The Chant of Jimmie Blacksmith*.
Frank Moorhouse, *The Americans, Baby*.

1973 Sydney Opera House opened.
Patrick White wins the Nobel Prize for Literature.
Rosemary Dobson, *Selected Poems*.
Patrick White, *The Eye of the Storm*.

1974 End of the "White Australia" policy, which restricted immigration of non-Europeans.
Thea Astley, *A Kindness Cup*.
Peter Carey, *The Fat Man in History*.
Les Murray, *Lunch and Counter Lunch*.

1975 Dismissal of Whitlam government by Governor-General.
Gwen Harwood, *Selected Poems*.
Xavier Herbert, *Poor Fellow My Country*.
David Malouf, *Johnno*.

1976 Vincent Buckley, *Golden Builders*.
Robert Drewe, *The Savage Crows*.
Les Murray, *Selected Poems*.
Patrick White, *A Fringe of Leaves*.

1977 Foundation of the Association for the Study of Australian Literature.
Robert Adamson, *Selected Poems*.
Helen Garner, *Monkey Grip*.
Kevin Gilbert, *Living Black*.

1978 Sydney Gay and Lesbian Mardi Gras established.
Jessica Anderson, *Tirra Lirra by the River*.
Bruce Dawe, *Sometimes Gladness*.
Christopher Koch, *The Year of Living Dangerously*.
David Malouf, *An Imaginary Life*.

1979 Bruce Beaver, *Selected Poems*.
Randolph Stow, *Visitants*.
Patrick White, *The Twyborn Affair*.

1980 Murray Bail, *Homesickness*.

Robyn Davidson, *Tracks*.
Barbara Hanrahan, *The Frangipani Gardens*.
Shirley Hazzard, *The Transit of Venus*.
Les Murray, *The Boys Who Stole the Funeral*.
1981   Vincent Buckley, *Selected Poems*.
Albert Facey, *A Fortunate Life*.
David Foster, *Moonlite*.
Patrick White, *Flaws in the Glass*.
1982   Thomas Keneally, *Schindler's Ark*.
Olga Masters, *The Home Girls*.
Les Murray, *The Vernacular Republic*.
John Tranter, *Selected Poems*.
1983   Election of Bob Hawke's Labor government.
Beverley Farmer, *Milk*.
Elizabeth Jolley, *Miss Peabody's Inheritance*.
Mudrooroo, *Doctor Wooreddy's Prescription for Enduring the Ending of the World*.
Les Murray, *The People's Otherworld*.
1984   Rosa Cappiello, *Oh Lucky Country*.
Rosemary Dobson, *The Three Fates and other poems*.
Helen Garner, *The Children's Bach*.
1985   Peter Carey, *Illywhacker*.
Jack Davis, *No Sugar*.
Kate Grenville, *Lilian's Story*.
Janette Turner Hospital, *Borderline*.
Louis Nowra, *The Golden Age*.
1986   Michael Gow, *Away*.
Elizabeth Jolley, *The Well*.
Christina Stead, *I'm Dying Laughing*.
1987   Thea Astley, *It's Raining in Mango*.
Laurie Duggan, *The Ash Range*.
Sally Morgan, *My Place*.
Gerald Murnane, *Landscape with Landscape*.
1988   Bicentenary celebration accompanied by strong Aboriginal protests.
Peter Carey, *Oscar and Lucinda*.
John Forbes, *The Stunned Mullet*.
Ruby Langford Ginibi, *Don't Take Your Love to Town*.
Tim Winton, *In the Winter Dark*.
1989   Robert Adamson, *The Clean Dark*.
Mary Fallon, *Working Hot*.

Murray Bail, *Eucalyptus.*
John Forbes, *Damaged Glamour.*
Roger McDonald, *Mr Darwin's Shooter.*
Les Murray, *Fredy Neptune.*
Gig Ryan, *Pure and Applied.*
Archie Weller, *Land of the Golden Clouds.*

1999   Republic referendum held.
Thea Astley, *Drylands.*
Kate Grenville, *The Idea of Perfection.*
Drusilla Modjeska, *Stravinsky's Lunch.*
Les Murray, *Conscious and Verbal.*

2000   Olympic Games held in Sydney.

ELIZABETH WEBBY

Introduction

In 1898, Henry Gyles Turner, a banker and litterateur, and Alexander Sutherland, a schoolteacher and journalist, both from Melbourne, published *The Development of Australian Literature*. This opened with the first of many attempts to provide "A General Sketch of Australian Literature", which devoted forty-seven pages to poetry, about thirty to fiction and eighteen to "general literature": mainly history, biography, and works of travel and exploration. The bulk of Turner and Sutherland's book, however, consisted of biographies of the three Australian writers whom they thought were of greatest significance: poets Adam Lindsay Gordon and Henry Kendall and novelist Marcus Clarke.

Turner and Sutherland's privileging of poetry, inclusion of what we would now call "non-fiction" and exclusion of more popular genres like children's writing and drama established a view of the terrain of Australian literature which was to hold good for at least the first half of the twentieth century. Further introductory accounts were provided by Nettie Palmer in 1924, the American historian and critic C. Hartley Grattan in 1929, and H.M. Green in 1930. In 1961 Green finally followed this up by producing his monumental two-volume *A History of Australian Literature Pure and Applied*. As its title indicates, Green's account was by far the most comprehensive yet to appear, not only discussing the "pure" categories of poetry, fiction and drama, but a very wide range of "applied" works, from newspapers and magazines through to works of philosophy and anthropology. Indeed, for the period it covers – 1789–1950 – Green's is effectively a history of the Australian book and so has proved of continuing value as a work of reference.

To bring some order to this immense range and amount of material, Green used period as well as genre divisions. The periods he chose, and the names he gave to them, reflected the then dominant progressivist model of literary history. So, for Green, to trace the history of Australian literature was to trace an inevitable development from initial "conflict" (1789–1850), through "consolidation" (1850–1890) and "self-conscious nationalism" (1890–1923), to "world consciousness and disillusion" (1923–1950). In particular, his decision to begin a new period with 1890 reflected the then current emphasis on the 1890s as the period when Australian literature changed from being a colonial to a truly national one.

The next substantial critical survey of Australian literature, Geoffrey Dutton's edited collection of essays *The Literature of Australia*, appeared soon after Green's. Published by Penguin Books in 1964, it was clearly modelled on the then very popular paperback volumes of *The Pelican Guide to English Literature*, which Penguin had been publishing since the 1950s. Coincidentally, however, Dutton's Penguin was also remarkably like Turner and Sutherland's earlier work in its approach to Australian literary history: some general survey essays, giving overviews of Australian history and of fiction and poetry, were followed by others mainly on individual authors. As with Turner and Sutherland, too, there was some privileging of poetry, with twelve out of twenty-two chapters being devoted to it, as against seven on fiction and one on drama. While the survey chapters divided at 1920, a chapter devoted to "*The Bulletin* – J.F. Archibald and A.G. Stephens" indicated that the 1890s were still seen as crucial to the development of a national literature.

As an affordable introduction to Australian literature, at a time when it was just beginning to be more widely taught in schools and universities, Dutton's *Literature of Australia* sold very well and a second edition was issued in 1976. The basic structure and many of the chapters remained the same, though changes in the canon of Australian literature over these twelve years saw chapters on novelists Christina Stead and Martin Boyd, and poet Francis Webb, replace earlier ones on nineteenth-century poets, nineteenth-century novelists and the poet R.D. FitzGerald.

Leonie Kramer, whose essay on Henry Handel Richardson had appeared in both editions of Dutton, and who had become Professor of Australian Literature at the University of Sydney in 1968, was the next to plan a history. As editor of *The Oxford History of Australian Literature* (1981), she chose a model closer to Green's than to Dutton's, though without Green's period divisions and with a focus on only the "pure" literary genres of poetry, fiction and drama. For her, it seems, the crucial thing to concentrate on was the aesthetic quality of a work, in order to establish a reliable canon of major authors to be studied in the then burgeoning discipline of Australian literature. By the 1980s, however, structuralist and poststructuralist theories had begun to have an impact on Australian English departments. So *The Oxford History of Australian Literature* received a less than complimentary reception in the changing critical and theoretical climate of the early 1980s.[1]

When Laurie Hergenhan and others began in the mid-1980s to plan a replacement for Geoffrey Dutton's Penguin, to be called *The Penguin New Literary History of Australia*, one of the main problems they faced was how to avoid the elitism of Kramer's history, while working with limitations of both space and time (the work was to be published in the Bicentenary year of 1988) that precluded the detailed surveys made by Green. Part of the solution was to have a lot of fairly short chapters, some of which would be genre-based, some thematic, so allowing a wide range of material to be covered and involving an equally wide range of contributors. All this was to be held together by period divisions, which were to be structural and historical rather than explanatory as were Green's; each period would also have chapters devoted to the then prevailing representations of Australia and Australians, and to the particular material circumstances then affecting the production of Australian literature.

There were also, as in Dutton's Penguin, a few overview chapters, in this case dealing with "Australian Literature and Australian Culture", "Aboriginal Literature", "Australian English", "Australian Humour" and "Forms of Australian Literary History". In the latter, Peter Pierce offered melodrama as the term most appropriate to describe the combative quality of Australian literary historiography since the 1950s. Each major new history, that is, saw itself as taking a very different theoretical approach to that of its immediate predecessor. Kramer's rejected Green's expansive nationalism; the *Penguin New Literary History* reacted against Kramer's elitism.

With the *Oxford Literary History of Australia*, however, which in 1998 replaced Kramer's ill-fated *Oxford History*, the chain appeared to have been broken. As their decision to stay with the term "literary history" implied, its editors, Bruce Bennett and Jennifer Strauss, adopted a fairly similar model to that of the *Penguin New Literary History*. The period divisions were much the same, as was the mix of thematic and genre-based chapters. The major innovations were a greater emphasis on Aboriginal writing and a final chapter on film, television and literature, both reflecting changes in the curriculum since the 1980s.

Planning this *Cambridge Companion to Australian Literature* in the late 1990s, I was faced with the same issues and questions that all these earlier editors had pondered. I had the additional constraint of having to conform to the requirements of a well-established international literary critical series. Only one previous critic had been similarly placed, Ken Goodwin, whose

A History of Australian Literature (1986) appeared as part of Macmillan's "History of Literature Series". Like the contributors to this volume, he needed to keep non-Australian as well as Australian readers in mind, and was similarly limited with respect to space. Accordingly, he used a straight-forward chronological structure, with chapters mainly devoted to periods or decades rather than themes or genres, and with a stress on perceived major writers.

Since this *Companion* will also be read by those whose knowledge of Australia, its peoples and their literatures may be rather slight, as well as by Australian readers, like Goodwin I have adopted a much more conservative structure than that of other recent histories of Australian literature, though one based on genres rather than periods. Like Goodwin's, too, most of this volume is devoted to twentieth-century Australian literature. Although the greater space given to the nineteenth century in the recent Penguin and Oxford literary histories was a very welcome development, reflecting the vast amount of new scholarly research carried out in this area since the 1970s, there was room here for only one chapter specifically devoted to the nineteenth century. Some material from this period, however, is discussed in several of the other chapters. If student preferences at my own university are any guide, contemporary Australian writing is inevitably the area of greatest interest and also, of course, the area where texts are more easily available. Recent multinational takeovers of Australian publishing companies have made it difficult to obtain earlier texts, even of established classics, though many out-of-copyright works can now be found on the internet.[2]

While the chapters in this *Companion* generally follow the usual progression from the past to the present, there are also various contrapuntal movements. Chapter 1, for example, on Indigenous texts and narratives, introduces the whole area, from pre-1788 oral traditions right down to contemporary literature. And though Chapter 2 concentrates mainly on the nineteenth century, it also briefly discusses some twentieth-century developments, especially in the area of writing for children. Conversely, Chapter 3 is mainly concerned with twentieth-century poetry, but opens with a brief survey of colonial verse. Chapter 4 deals with fiction published between 1900 and 1970. But Chapter 5 then goes back to cover the theatrical culture of Australia, understood in the broadest possible way, from 1788 through to 1970. Chapters 6, 7, 8 and 9 discuss contemporary developments in poetry, fiction, theatre and life-writing respectively. And Chapter 10 provides a final overview of the critical perspectives, institutions and ideologies which have most influenced the development of Australian literature, especially during the twentieth century, but also looking back to the nineteenth.

Within this broadly progressive chronological framework, therefore, this *Companion to Australian Literature* aims to introduce, in a succinct and lively way, the major texts and writers, literary movements and controversies, styles and genres that, at the end of the twentieth century, are seen as constituting the subject "Australian Literature". Contributors have attempted to keep a culturally materialist perspective in mind, seeing literary works not only as aesthetic objects produced by gifted individuals but as cultural artefacts inevitably influenced and constrained by the social, political and economic circumstances of their times, as well as by geographical and environmental factors. So, for example, the two chapters dealing with theatre in Australia focus on much more than just the plays written in their respective periods. Both are aware that theatre consists of the plays that people see as well as those that are written, and in Australia the former have mainly come from elsewhere. As well as outlining the development of the theatre industry in this country from 1788 to the 1960s, Richard Fotheringham also considers "theatricality" in a broader sense, as something that frequently occurs beyond the walls of theatres. May-Brit Akerholt, who has been personally involved in many aspects of contemporary Australian theatre, also goes well beyond the play text, discussing significant productions as well as plays, and major actors and directors as well as dramatists. Although there was unfortunately no room in this volume to include a chapter on Australian film, the two chapters on theatre do make reference to film and provide something of an historical context for those interested in it. The Further Reading section also lists some works on film and television, as well as on other areas that could only be touched on here, such as children's literature and journal and magazine publishing.

Terry Sturm's chapter on drama was one of the acknowledged strengths of the 1981 *Oxford History of Australian Literature*. The two chapters in this *Companion* dealing with Australian theatre build on Sturm's work to provide a comprehensive account of this significant area, one lacking in other recent histories. Other particularly innovative chapters here include Penny van Toorn's discussion of Indigenous writing, which draws on her current research to extend the history of such writing back into the nineteenth century, so providing a better basis for understanding contemporary developments. Gillian Whitlock's chapter on autobiography and biography and the intersections between them provides the first extended account of an area that has grown enormously since the 1970s, thanks to changing understandings of identity and subjectivity, and of fiction and non-fiction. And David Carter's chapter on Australian literature and its criticism is the first overview of this important topic since Brian Kiernan's 1974 monograph.

Inevitably, the limited space available for each chapter has meant that many significant genres, writers and works have had to be omitted, especially in the chapters dealing with fiction and poetry. All authors initially wrote more words than their allocation and have been forced to lose many of their favourite and hard-won sentences and paragraphs. All have worked very hard to do the almost impossible – to introduce Australian literature, within its historical, social and cultural contexts, to the interested reader from outside the country, and at the same time to say something new and provocative about their particular genre or area. How well they have succeeded is for others to judge. I am grateful to all of them for agreeing to take on this task and for their good humour and patience during the editorial process. My thanks to Phillipa McGuinness from Cambridge University Press for inviting me to organise this volume and for her encouragement during the process. Also to Peter Debus who helped see it through the Press during Phillipa's absence on maternity leave. As always, Lee Mashman from the University of Sydney has given great assistance in preparation of the manuscript.

The remainder of this introduction provides an outline of the main events of Australian history since the coming of the Europeans in 1788, with a particular emphasis on those most significant for an understanding of Australian literary and cultural history. Together with Chapter 10, it is intended to bookend the intervening discussions of particular genres and periods, but can be skipped by those who are already familiar with this material.

As an island continent in the South Pacific, remote from the main centres of Eastern and Western civilisation, the land mass later to be known as Australia allowed its Indigenous peoples to live for many thousands of years relatively undisturbed by visitors or invaders from outside, and to develop their own unique cultures. There has been much debate among Australian historians as to why, in 1786, the British government decided to dispatch a small fleet of eleven ships, carrying officers, marines and 736 convicted felons, to found a penal settlement at Botany Bay in New South Wales. As the "Great South Land" or "Terra Australis", Australia had figured in European imaginations since at least the second century.[3] From the sixteenth century onwards, a number of Portuguese, Spanish and Dutch ships had come into contact with various parts of the Australian coast and their captains had charted much of it. In 1642, the Dutch explorer Abel Tasman had named the smaller island, later to be rechristened Tasmania, Van Diemen's Land; in 1644, he named part of the west coast of the mainland as New Holland. And from at least the early 1700s, Macassan sailors had visited northern Australia to collect sea-slugs to sell to the Chinese, trading and mixing with the local Indigenous peoples. Finally, in 1770 Captain James Cook arrived to claim the eastern part of the continent for the British Crown and to name it New South Wales. He apparently did so under the impression that there were few Indigenous inhabitants and that, since these few did not use the land in the European sense of cultivating it, they did not own it. Australia was therefore cleared and settled under the legal fiction that it was "terra nullius" or land that belonged to no one, a doctrine not overturned until 1992 and the Australian High Court's landmark Mabo decision.

Both during and after the First Fleet's voyage to Botany Bay, there was much writing of letters and journals, with several of the officers already having an eye on publication. Even those writing to relatives and friends would have been aware that their letters, if they ever did get back to England, would be read by more than one pair of eyes. The early years of settlement were often precarious, as the newcomers struggled to grow crops in unfamiliar conditions. The uncertainty of communication with England added to this, with the wreck of a supply ship meaning that it was June 1790 before the colonists received any news from home. Even as late as 1795, Elizabeth Macarthur could write to a friend that, "By the capture of our ships off the coast of Brazil we were left without any direct intelligence from Europe for twelve months."[4] By then, however, she was also able to write of New South Wales as a place where "The accessories of life are abundant, and a fruitful soil affords us many luxuries." While Elizabeth had the advantage of being married to John Macarthur, a prominent member of the NSW Army Corps, and many were not so privileged, it was clear that the settlement could now be regarded as permanent. In 1797 the Macarthurs bought some of the first Spanish merino ewes to arrive in the colony; the wool industry was to remain one of the cornerstones of Australia's economic prosperity until late in the twentieth century.

As early as 1790, a second settlement had been established at Norfolk Island, 1,000 miles from Sydney, which Cook had noted as a source of supply of flax and pine trees, necessary to keep the British Navy in sails and masts. In 1803 two further settlements were established, apparently from fear of continuing French interest in the region: in Van Diemen's Land, near present-day Hobart, and in Port Phillip Bay, near present-day Melbourne. In 1805, the latter settlement was given up, with both groups uniting to establish Hobart Town. Over the next fifty years, Van Diemen's Land was to experience the virtual wiping out of the Indigenous population with the rapid spread of European settlement and the growth of the wool industry. Given abundant and cheap convict labour, a plantation society was established rather like that in the American South, complete with elaborate, many-columned mansions and a cultured landed gentry. But the fact that Tasmania was also the main provider of places of secondary punishment – where the worst convicts, those who had committed further offences in Australia, were sent – has given Van Diemen's Land, and especially the penal station of Port Arthur, a much darker colouration in the Australian imagination. In 1855, following the end of convict transportation there, the island's name was changed to Tasmania, in an attempt to bury the past. Continuing economic stagnation, however, has meant that more material evidence of Australia's convict, and colonial, past is to be found in Tasmania than anywhere else.

In 1829, following further concerns about possible French interest in Australia, another British settlement was commenced at the Swan River, in what is now Western Australia. The whole of the southern continent had now been claimed by the British. Unofficial settlement of the Port Phillip district was also soon under way, as growing need for new pastures for their sheep led to a two-pronged incursion of squatters, overland from NSW and by sea from Van Diemen's Land. Despite these informal beginnings, the new region was soon prospering and in 1851 was officially separated from NSW to form the new colony of Victoria. In 1836 the province of South Australia had been established as a free, non-convict colony, one much more highly planned and organised than any of the other Australian ones.

Discovery of gold in NSW and Victoria in 1851 began the first large-scale free migration to Australia. Over the next ten years, the population of Victoria grew from 80,000 to 500,000; Melbourne became the largest Australian city, a position it was to hold for most of the nineteenth century. Resentment of harsh administration of the licensing system for gold-diggers led to the only armed rebellion in white Australian history, the short-lived Eureka Stockade, in October 1854. Prosperity brought by the gold discoveries quickened the pace of social and cultural change, especially in Victoria: a university was established in Melbourne in 1853, following the University of Sydney by only a few years. Art galleries, public libraries and museums were also founded, or rehoused in grander buildings. Magazines began to flourish alongside the newspapers that had been a necessary part of colonial commerce since 1803.

While cities expanded, there was also increased movement into the still unsettled areas, especially north into what is now Queensland. Brisbane had been established as the penal settlement of Moreton Bay in 1824 and from the 1840s squatters began to move into and beyond the Darling Downs area. Despite strong resistance from the local Indigenous peoples, towns were established, especially along the north-eastern coastline, and in 1859 Queensland was separated from NSW.

During the 1870s and 1880s, the Australian colonies continued to prosper, fuelled by an increased supply of capital from Britain to construct necessary infrastructure such as roads, railways and the telegraph system. The onset of a major depression in the 1890s changed all this. Capital dried up: wool prices declined and several major banks collapsed. The coming of a seven-year drought in 1895 did nothing to help the faltering pastoral and agricultural industries. Unemployment, strikes and depression did wonders, however, for fledgling unions and socialist political parties and encouraged a growth of nationalism in a population now predominantly Australian-born. The 1890s also saw the beginnings of a local publishing industry as the Sydney firm of Angus & Robertson brought out bestselling editions of the poems and ballads of A.B. "Banjo" Paterson and the stories and poems of Henry Lawson, both of whom had gained a wide readership through the columns of the popular Sydney weekly magazine, the *Bulletin*.

Calls for the Australian colonies to unite, perhaps as a republic, had been voiced since at least the 1840s. They became stronger during the 1890s, leading eventually to the establishment of the Commonwealth of Australia on 1 January 1901, with the former colonies of NSW, Tasmania, Victoria, South Australia, Western Australia and Queensland as the constituent states. The 1890s also saw agitation for female suffrage, achieved first in South Australia in 1894, in the federal parliament from 1901 and the other states over the next four years. While Australian women were among the first in the world to gain the right to vote, the image of the ideal or typical Australian associated with the new nationalism of the 1890s was a decidedly masculine one, whether conceived as pioneer, gold-miner, or bushman. The figure of the soldier or digger was added to this list by the coming of World War I, and particularly events at Gallipoli on 25 April 1915, subsequently enshrined in the Australian calendar as Anzac Day. Through his heroism, Australia was seen to have finally joined the company of nations as an equal, and fully erased the birth stains of Botany Bay and Van Diemen's Land.

In Australia, as elsewhere in the world, the brief euphoria which followed the ending of the war to end all wars was soon followed by the major depression of the 1920s and 1930s. Again, there was widespread unemployment and, while the economic situation was by then over its worst, Australia celebrated the sesquicentenary of white settlement in 1938 in a somewhat subdued vein. Although few were aware of it at the time, the declaration of 26 January 1938 as a "Day of Mourning" by members of the Sydney Aboriginal community was a portent of things to come. In an essay written almost fifty years earlier, in 1890, Henry Lawson had, like most in this period, assumed that the Indigenous peoples of Australia would soon die out, inevitable losers in the evolutionary race.[5] Despite the best endeavours of those who encouraged evolution along its way through massacres, dispossession and, later, attempts to "breed out" the race by removing mixed-blood children from their parents to bring them up in institutions or foster homes, the Aboriginal peoples have survived, even in Tasmania, where it had been assumed "the last Aboriginal Tasmanian" had died in 1876.[6]

During World War II there was another surge in nationalist feeling in Australia, especially when the nation came under direct threat of a Japanese invasion after the attack on Pearl Harbor in December 1941 and the fall of Singapore early in 1942. Between February and June 1942, Japanese planes carried out bombing raids on Darwin, Broome, Wyndham and Townsville and their submarines attacked shipping in Sydney and Newcastle. The arrival of American forces under General Douglas MacArthur, and return of Australian soldiers from the Middle East, helped prevent a large-scale land invasion, as well as marking the shift in Australian military dependency from Britain to America. For many middle-class Australians it was World War II and the fall of Singapore, rather than Federation and Gallipoli, which signalled a decisive cultural shift away from a conception of themselves as Southern Britons to one of themselves as Australians. This shift in consciousness was officially registered by the introduction of Australian citizenship in 1949 – till then, Australians had remained British subjects, even after 1901.

The immediate post-war years saw many other significant changes in Australian society and culture, especially as a result of a government program of assisted mass migration to aid in the task of post-war reconstruction. While initially directed at migrants from Britain, in keeping with the perceived need to maintain Australia's cultural and racial homogeneity, it was soon found necessary to cast the net wider. Between 1946 and 1949, 500,000 migrants arrived; only a third came from Britain, many of the rest were from Italy, Greece and Central Europe. As the notion of a "White Australia", a central government policy since Federation, still held strong, however, non-whites from Africa, Asia and the Middle East remained unwelcome. Many of the newcomers were engaged on large-scale nation-building enterprises, especially the Snowy Mountains Hydro-Electric Scheme in southern NSW.

Helped by this continued influx of new people, the 1950s were a time of great prosperity for those in both the city and the country. They were also a time of growing political and social conservatism. In 1949 the Liberal-Country Party coalition under Robert Menzies took over government, a position it was to retain until 1972. As post-war relations between Russia and the West began to freeze into Cold War positions, Prime Minister Menzies attempted to ban the Communist Party in Australia, an attempt narrowly defeated in a 1951 referendum. Despite this, life in Australia during the 1950s remained fairly conventional. Women were encouraged to return to the home to look after the post-war generation of "Baby Boomers". The typical Australian family was seen as one living in a comfortable three-bedroom suburban home with a Holden car – fully Australian made – in the garage.[7] "Dad" enjoyed time with his mates, went to the footie on Saturday afternoon and to the local RSL or Leagues Club on Saturday night and mowed his lawn on Sunday. "Mum" kept her home spick and span, cooked cakes and dinners from *Women's Weekly* recipes, and made clothes for all the family. Neither was thought to have much in the way of intellectual interests. Those Australians who did want to see the latest overseas movies or plays or read the latest books were often frustrated by lengthy delays in obtaining non-mainstream cultural products in Australia, if not by the still very strict censorship laws. Despite the expansion of universities during the 1950s and the beginnings of government subsidy of the arts with the Australian Elizabethan Theatre Trust in 1954, it was still assumed that Australian artists needed to spend a large period of their career outside Australia to really achieve success. Although the PhD degree had been introduced into Australian universities in 1948, most graduates of promise still preferred to travel to Britain, or increasingly to the USA, to undertake their doctorates.

One of the many cultural figures who were to leave Australia more or less permanently during the 1950s and early 1960s was the actor and writer Barry Humphries. While still in Melbourne, as a member of the Union Theatre Repertory Company, Humphries had developed his signature character, Edna Everage, the "average" Melbourne housewife, who first appeared on stage in 1955.[8] Through Edna, and his other best-known character, Sandy Stone, the returned serviceman, Humphries satirised the bigotry and conformist materialism of 1950s Australia. His criticisms were shared by many other writers and artists of the period, including Patrick White, even though White had made the decision to return permanently to Australia in the late 1940s. In 1956, White wrote an essay, "The Prodigal Son", replying to another by the expatriate writer Alister Kershaw.[9] While, like Humphries, deploring the "exaltation of the average" he found all around him in Australia, White saw it as the writer's duty to contribute to his society rather than live as a permanent exile from it. His novels and plays from the 1950s and 1960s, especially *Riders in the Chariot* (1961), *The Solid Mandala* (1966) and *The Season at Sarsaparilla* (1963), are particularly critical of the closed minds and averted eyes of those living respectably in suburbia. "The average Australian man", hero of so much earlier Australian fiction, is, in *Riders in the Chariot*, shown to be intolerant of difference, as matey larrikinism almost tips over into murder during the fake crucifixion of Himmelfarb. In choosing as his "riders" – his seers and seekers – a Jewish refugee, an Aboriginal artist and two women, White was anticipating three of the major future challenges to old ideas of Australian literature and the "Australian tradition": from multiculturalism, the women's movement and Aboriginal activism. While a fourth, the gay and lesbian movement, may have been the one closest to White's own sense of exclusion, in 1961 it was still not possible to introduce openly gay characters into Australian novels.

During the 1960s the post-war expansion of Australian tertiary education began to have a greater impact on Australian social and cultural life as those born during and after World War II attended university in increasing numbers. While Australian literature was still not widely taught, a chair in the area was established at the University of Sydney in 1962, following a public fundraising campaign led by such literary stalwarts as novelist Miles Franklin. Australian history was by then a well-established university subject, the first full course having been taught at the University of Melbourne in 1946. Manning Clark, who had begun his academic career in the Melbourne History Department, published the first of the six volumes of his major *A History of Australia* in 1962. With the Korean War (1950–53) followed by the war in Vietnam (1962–75), Australians were also becoming increasingly conscious of their situation as a white, Western nation on the edge of Asia. This was heightened by the conservative parties continually playing the card of potential communist threats from red Asian hordes as a way to hold on to political power at successive elections during the 1960s.

The sending of Australian troops to Vietnam in 1965, particularly since it involved using conscripted as well as voluntary soldiers, served to radicalise many elements of the Australian population, especially the young university students liable to be called up, and their families, teachers and friends. Campus "teach-ins" were followed by larger scale moratorium marches: in May 1970 200,000 protesters marched in Melbourne. Opposition to US imperialism in Vietnam was not the only radical movement flourishing on university campuses in the 1960s. The black struggle for equal rights in the USA led to an increased awareness of the operation of racial prejudice in Australia, resulting in criticism of both the White Australia policy and of unequal treatment of Indigenous Australians. In 1965, Charles Perkins, the first Australian Aboriginal to graduate from a local university, led a series of "Freedom Rides", based on American models, to country New South Wales, protesting about discrimination against Aborigines in community swimming pools, hotels and other public places. In 1967, in a landmark referendum, the Australian Constitution was changed, allowing Aboriginals to vote and be included in the census, and giving the Commonwealth government legislative powers over Aboriginal affairs in all states except Queensland.

The 1960s also brought to Australia other influential global "liberation" movements, especially that of feminism or women's liberation, as it was then known. One of the key texts of that movement, *The Female Eunuch* (1970), was, indeed, written by an expatriate Australian, Germaine Greer. While it was to take until the 1980s for the full impact of second wave feminism to be felt in Australian publishing and university curriculums, by the mid-1970s many traditional concepts of Australian history and identity were under challenge, with their masculinist biases exposed by Anne Summers in *Damned Whores and God's Police* (1975) and Miriam Dixson in *The Real Matilda* (1976).

The new writers most concerned to challenge traditional notions of Australian fiction, poetry and drama in the later 1960s and early 1970s were, however, predominantly male. They were united by an awareness of Australia as an urban rather than a rural society, by an interest in breaking taboos over what could be said on stage or printed on the page. Although most were as opposed to American imperialism, as manifested in Vietnam, as to the old colonial dependency on Britain, they now looked to New York or Paris, rather than London, as the cultural centre. For those poets who belonged to the group described as "the generation of '68", this manifested as an interest in the French symbolistes, especially Rimbaud and Baudelaire, as well as in the new American poets. Among the fiction writers, initially working mainly in shorter forms, the "magic realism" of South American writers such as Borges and Marquez was widely read, as well as the more self-referential and formalist experiments of North Americans like John Barth and Richard Brautigan. In the theatre, influences came more from Europe, especially from Samuel Beckett and other practitioners of the absurd, though Betty Burstall's establishment in 1967 of Melbourne's La Mama, a small theatre cum cafe based on one of the same name in New York, was seminal in generating a space for "new wave" playwrights like Jack Hibberd and David Williamson.[10]

One of Williamson's earlier plays, *Don's Party* (1973), provides a handy snapshot of the impact of sexual and women's liberation on the lives of a group of friends gathered to await the results of the 1969 federal election, which most hope will mark the end of two decades of conservative government in Australia. Although the Labor Party was narrowly defeated in 1969, they finally achieved victory under the leadership of Gough Whitlam in 1972, ushering in a brief period when the radical movements of the 1960s had a significant influence on Australian legislation, altering for ever certain earlier key policies. As well as withdrawing Australian troops from Vietnam and recognising the People's Republic of China, the Whitlam government also ended the White Australia policy. With race now no longer one of the criteria for migration to Australia, the last three decades of the twentieth century saw a large-scale influx of people from Asia, especially from China, Vietnam and Korea, with a particular impact on Sydney where most of them settled.

The Whitlam government also made a concerted effort to improve Australia's cultural and intellectual capital. Increased federal funding was provided for both private and state schools, new universities and colleges of advanced education were established and fees for tertiary education abolished. The Literature Board was set up as part of a reorganised Australia Council for the Arts, and substantial funding provided in the way of grants to support new and established writers, and to subsidise the publication of Australian books and literary magazines. The new emphasis on Australianness was also reflected in the replacement of the British Honours system with the Order of Australia and the adoption of "Advance Australia Fair" rather than "God Save the Queen" as the national anthem.

Women and Aboriginals also benefited from Whitlam government reforms. The principle of equal wages for women doing work of equal value to men was enshrined in the statutes and an Office for the Status of Women established. A Racial Discrimination Act was introduced and some recognition given to Aboriginal demands for land rights, especially in the Northern Territory where many Indigenous people were still living on or near to their traditional lands. All these changes, however, alienated many of the powerful, more conservative elements in Australian society who were also concerned about evidence of poor economic management by the Labor government. On 11 November 1975, the Queen's representative, Governor-General Sir John Kerr, dismissed Gough Whitlam and appointed the Liberal Party's leader, Malcolm Fraser, as caretaker Prime Minister of Australia. Parliament was dissolved and in the subsequent general election in December the Liberal-Country Party coalition received a massive swing and achieved government.

Despite the continued outcry by many Labor supporters, who felt the democratic process had been set at naught by one of Australia's last vestiges of colonialism, the Fraser government did not overturn many of the reforms of the Whitlam years, even though "God Save the Queen" again became the national anthem. Aboriginal land rights were granted over twenty percent of the Northern Territory. University tuition remained free and the 1970s saw a large upsurge in the numbers of mature age students, especially women. Equal pay for women spread in the work force, the Family Court was established and femocrats were still influential in government policy development. Growing unemployment and the Fraser government's failure to bring back the economic stability and prosperity of the 1950s and 1960s, however, saw it defeated in the federal election of 1983 by Labor under a new leader, the former trades union supremo Bob Hawke.

Labor continued to hold power in Australia until 1996, even though the economy remained shaky and unemployment and inflation ran rampant during the "greed is good" decade of the 1980s. The key figure of this decade was, however, not a politician but the entrepreneur Alan Bond, who rose from obscurity to become as iconic as the flag used during his successful 1983 campaign for the America's Cup, the boxing kangaroo. In 1987 Bond set up Australia's first private university, named after himself, on Queensland's Gold Coast. Shortly after, as with others who had developed large business empires through a continuous succession of bank loans, the dominoes began to fall and Bond was declared bankrupt; he has since spent time in prison.

The excesses of the 1980s had other impacts on the cultural and intellectual scene in Australia. During 1986 a small fee, called an "administrative charge", was introduced for students in tertiary institutions. Those who saw this as the thin edge of the wedge were proved right; university fees and charges steadily increased during the remainder of the century, helped by a growing emphasis on economic rationalism and "user-pays". In 1989, John Dawkins, the Minister for Education, abolished the so-called binary system of tertiary education, with former colleges of advanced education either amalgamating with older universities, or becoming universities in their own right. At the same time, the Higher Education Contribution Scheme was introduced, which greatly increased fees, but allowed students to defer payment of them until after graduation. During the 1990s there was continuous pressure on universities to generate more of their own income, leading to active recruitment of overseas fee-paying students and eventually to places for full fee-paying locals.

Economic rationalism also reduced the amount of support governments were prepared to give to the cultural industries by way of subsidy. Australia Council grants became harder to get and subsidies to local literary magazines and publishers were reduced. From the later 1980s the Australian publishing scene was significantly altered by a succession of takeovers. The Sydney firm of Angus & Robertson, which had led the way in local publishing since its success with Lawson and Paterson in the 1890s, had become less influential after ceasing to be a family-controlled business in the early 1970s. In 1989 it became part of Rupert Murdoch's HarperCollins conglomerate. Faced with growing competition from electronic and visual media, book publishing became increasingly controlled by the marketing rather than the editorial departments. Writers' festivals, literary lunches and media appearances became an accepted part of the writer's life, with leading novelists like David Malouf resigned to spending as long or longer promoting new novels within Australia and overseas as in writing them. More marginal types of Australian writing – poetry, the short story, academic criticism and history – which had flourished in the 1970s and 1980s under the stimulus of an expanding tertiary sector and increased government subsidy – were now virtually deserted by mainstream publishers. Ironically, the 1990s also saw a vast increase in creative writing classes both within and outside universities. Many more stories and poems were being written, though publication was increasingly done electronically, through small independent presses or at the expense of the author.

Earlier, the so-called Bicentenary of Australia (actually the Bicentenary of the English colony of New South Wales), celebrated in 1988, had been the high point of a couple of decades of nationalist publishing. The Bicentenary authority had, among its other activities, sponsored certain literary works, including the *Penguin New Literary History of Australia* (1988). This was an attempt to reconfigure Australian literary history from a late twentieth-century perspective, taking into account the impact of poststructuralism, postmodernism and postcolonialism with their dismantling of grand narratives and figures of authority, as well as the need to write previously marginalised figures, such as women and Aboriginals, back into the story. Some of the same impulses underlay the twelve-volume *Australians: A Historical Library*, if less exclusively. While the "slice" volumes, dealing in detail with the years 1838, 1888 and 1938, were a product of the new social and cultural history, with its interest in the "ordinary" person and desire to make the previously silenced speak, other reference volumes catered for those who still wanted the authority of traditional histories. And the need to package these commercially sponsored histories in a way that would appeal to the general reader often led to certain disjunctions between the text and the lavish accompanying illustrations.

Two other Bicentenary-sponsored works point to the new directions Australian writing was taking during the last decades of the century: Kate Grenville's *Joan Makes History* (1988) and Ruby Langford Ginibi's *Don't Take Your Love to Town* (1988). Grenville had first come to notice with her Vogel Award-winning *Lilian's Story* (1985), loosely based on the life of noted Sydney eccentric Bea Miles. Lilian, like Bea, refuses to conform to patriarchal strictures on how women should behave, and suffers for it. In *Joan Makes History*, one of the characters from *Lilian's Story* reappears, rewriting significant scenes of Australian history from a feminist perspective. Academic feminists were also rewriting Australia's social and cultural history, most notably in *Creating a Nation* (1994) by Pat Grimshaw, Marilyn Lake, Ann McGrath and Marion Quartly, and *Debutante Nation: Feminism Contests the 1890s* (1993), edited by Susan Magarey, Susan Rowley and Susan Sheridan.

Aboriginal women's autobiography had first made an impact with Sally Morgan's *My Place* (1987), just before the Bicentenary. Morgan's compelling account of her search for the truth about her Aboriginality and her family's history was, it seems, just the book that many Australians had been waiting for. Like Morgan, who had been brought up not knowing she was an Aboriginal, most white Australians had been told little or nothing about Australia's black history. Since the 1970s, through increased Aboriginal activism and the work of historians like Henry Reynolds, more and more has been revealed. Books like Ruby Langford Ginibi's expressed the struggle and sufferings of Aboriginal women as their children were removed from their care, arrested or met untimely deaths, preparing the way for the revelations of the "stolen generations" report in the 1990s. Earlier in the 1990s, the High Court's decisions in the Mabo and Wik cases changed the history of black and white relations in Australia for ever. In the Mabo case the Court ruled that the doctrine of "terra nullius", under which the British Crown had occupied Australia, was invalid, thus finally recognising prior Aboriginal ownership of the land. While the treaty proposed by Bob Hawke has never eventuated, and moves towards a process of reconciliation have slowed following the election of the Liberal-National Party government in 1996, it is no longer possible to ignore the fact of Aboriginal ownership and dispossession.

Acknowledging that Australian history does not begin in 1788, this *Companion* opens with a substantial chapter on "Indigenous texts and narratives" which looks at pre-invasion communication systems and early interactions between Aboriginal peoples and white textual technologies, as well as the more recent growth of Aboriginal literature in English. Later chapters on fiction, poetry, theatre and autobiography also discuss Aboriginal texts and authors wherever appropriate.

NOTES

1 David Carter also discusses these issues in Chapter 10.
2 Many nineteenth- and early twentieth-century Australian texts can be found at http://setis.library.usyd.edu.au/ozlit/.

3 See Alan Frost, "Perceptions of Australia Before 1855" in Laurie Hergenhan, ed., *The Penguin New Literary History of Australia* (Melbourne: Penguin, 1988), p. 93.
4 See Elizabeth Webby, ed., *Colonial Voices* (St Lucia: University of Queensland Press, 1989), p. 95.
5 Henry Lawson, "The New Religion" in Brian Kiernan, ed., *Henry Lawson* (St Lucia: University of Queensland Press, 1976), p. 82.
6 See Lyndall Ryan, *The Aboriginal Tasmanians* (St Lucia: University of Queensland Press, 1981).
7 See Richard White, *Inventing Australia: Images and Identity 1688–1980* (Sydney: Allen & Unwin, 1981), Chapter 10, "Everyman and his Holden", pp. 158–71.
8 Katharine Brisbane, "Barry Humphries", in Philip Parsons, gen. ed., *Companion to Theatre in Australia* (Sydney: Currency Press, 1995), pp. 288–9.
9 Patrick White, "The Prodigal Son", *Australian Letters*, 1.3 (1958), pp. 37–40.
10 Leonard Radic, "La Mama" in Parsons, gen. ed., *Companion to Theatre in Australia*, pp. 320–21.

I

PENNY VAN TOORN

Indigenous texts and narratives[1]

FROM THE BEGINNING: ORAL TRADITIONS

The Aboriginal and Torres Strait Islander peoples of Australia have been telling stories since time immemorial. Although Indigenous oral cultures were once believed to be dying out, it is clear today, in Australia and elsewhere, that many aspects of these ancient cultures have survived in Indigenous communities, and are now thriving as a living, evolving part of contemporary life. Oral songs and narratives are traditionally an *embodied* and *emplaced* form of knowledge. Information is stored in people's minds in various narrative forms which, at the appropriate time, are transmitted from the mouths of the older generation to the ears of the young. Many narratives are connected to specific sites, and are transmitted in the course of people's movements through their country. Certain songs and stories are only transmitted in specific ceremonial contexts, while others circulate in the informal settings of everyday life. For oral traditions to survive, then, "the learning generation" must be in direct physical proximity to "the teaching generation".[2] People must also have access to significant sites in their country, and be free to perform their ceremonies, speak their languages, and carry out their everyday cultural activities.

The arrival of the British at Sydney Cove in 1788 initiated a series of processes which, in various ways and to different degrees in different regions, brought death, displacement, and severe cultural disruption to Aboriginal peoples. Waves of frontier violence and disease decimated Aboriginal populations; welfare authorities took Aboriginal children from their families; missionaries banned traditional languages and ceremonies; and white landholders locked Aboriginal people off their country. Indigenous oral knowledge systems were thus seriously jeopardised or destroyed outright. Few non-Aboriginal people recognised the richness of oral traditions, or considered the possibility that graphic signifying systems such as sand drawings, body scars, paintings, or carvings might be viewed as forms of writing.[3] Most assumed that only literate societies were advanced, civilised and rational, and took orality to be a sign of the backward, primitive and ignorant.

Under adverse political circumstances, then, Indigenous oral traditions have survived and proved extraordinarily resilient and adaptable. In remote communities in central and northern Australia, traditional oral narratives and songs continue to be a primary means of preserving and transmitting knowledge of country, spiritual belief, language, kinship, history and practical skills. Oral narratives may be traditional, semi-traditional or non-traditional. In rural and urban communities, elements of traditional orally grounded knowledge and customs of transmission have survived, although they are seldom recognised as such by outsiders.

The oral tradition incorporates not only a set of songs and stories but also a set of rules and protocols for their transmission. In traditionally oriented Aboriginal societies, information flows may be restricted by differences of age, gender, kinship and affiliations to country. Violations of the dividing lines between secret and public domains of knowledge may incur severe punishments. In some communities, mortuary restrictions prohibit naming deceased persons or repeating songs and stories owned by them. These customs mean that information movements across time and space tend to be highly restricted. It is therefore necessary to consider what happens when these traditional regulative systems come into contact with print and electronic communication technologies capable of recording, multiplying and disseminating information indiscriminately across vast spans of time and space.[4] Technology can indeed help preserve and disseminate traditional oral practices, but it can also act as a force for changing the content of oral narratives and disrupting the customs that traditionally regulated direct oral transmission. Recognising this problem, some communities have devised ways of using introduced media in accordance with their own traditional law.

In certain respects, oral stories and songs are comparable with interactive multi-media. Information is transmitted through *dialogic* transactions in which an *array* of signifying systems operates simultaneously. On formal ceremonial occasions, for example, performers and audience are both participants, and meaning is assigned to words in the context of dance, ritual gestures, ground drawings, carvings and body painting. Similarly, in less formal settings, people might sing songs or recount anecdotes to each other while gathering bush-tucker, weaving baskets or driving along in the car. Oral tradition thus involves far more than a set of spoken stories: it is intricately bound up both with non-verbal communication and with the broader, denser fabric of social and cultural life.

Consequently, when oral narratives are captured in alphabetic writing, translated into English, interpreted in alien cultural contexts and utilised for non-traditional purposes, it is often said that they are reduced to a pale, distorted version of their original form and function. From the time Catherine Langloh Parker published *Australian Legendary Tales* (1896), numerous simplified, sanitised versions of "Aboriginal myths and legends" have been published. Addressing a predominantly non-Aboriginal readership, these texts transform Aboriginal people's living utterances into inert blocks of type on the page, assimilating what may once have been long, complicated, sacred narratives into Standard English fairytales,[5] or new-age mythologies for jaded Westerners seeking to recover the "lost primitive" within. Too often, editors fail to include accurate information about the relevant Aboriginal source-culture, and instead frame the stories to satisfy the psychic and political desires of (predominantly non-Aboriginal) consumers. Although prefatory notes may allege the stories were told by some "last King of the Tribe", readers may never know precisely who "collected" the stories from whom, or under what circumstances. Moreover, if the text editing process is obscured, readers might easily imagine there *was* none, and hence that the words on the page provide a faithful replica of the original oral narrative.

Recently, a number of publications have endeavoured to overcome these problems. Paddy Roe's *Gularabulu* (ed. Stephen Muecke, 1983), *Reading the Country* (1984) by Benterrak, Muecke and Roe, Bill Neidjie's *Story About Feeling* (ed. Keith Taylor, 1989), and *Wandjuk Marika: Life Story* (ed. Jennifer Isaacs, 1995), have each attempted with some success to capture the voice of an oral storyteller on the page. Texts such as these present distinct versions of Aboriginal English, and use special orthographies to represent words from Aboriginal languages and non-standard English pronunciations. The page layouts are designed to indicate the rhythms and pauses of oral utterance. Silences, tone changes, laughter and other non-verbal sounds made by the storyteller are also noted in the text. As well as providing descriptions of the editorial process, these texts give a sense of the dialogic context in which the stories have been told and recorded. Instead of offering a monovocal text which blots "the collector" out of the picture altogether, some of these more recent texts include brief snatches of dialogue between the Aboriginal speaker and the person recording their narratives.

Traditional Aboriginal songs and stories have also been published in literary anthologies. Extracts from traditional song cycles previously translated and published in full by anthropologists have appeared in print in a number of major literary anthologies such as *The Collins Book of Australian Poetry* (ed. Rodney Hall, 1981), *My Country* (ed. Leonie Kramer, 1985), *The Oxford Book of Australian Verse* (ed. Les Murray, 1986), *Two*

Centuries of Australian Poetry (ed. Mark O'Connor, 1988), and *The Macmillan Anthology of Australian Literature* (eds Ken Goodwin and Alan Lawson, 1990). The editors of such anthologies find themselves on the horns of an impossible dilemma. If they omit Aboriginal oral narratives, they perpetuate Eurocentric discriminatory practices, yet if they include these narratives as part of a national Australian literary canon, they attract accusations of cultural appropriation and of assimilating traditional Aboriginal oral narratives into a Western medium and art form.[6]

EARLY ABORIGINAL WRITINGS

The earliest Aboriginal writings in the Roman alphabet were produced by dictation and other collaborative modes. In 1796, Bennelong dictated a letter to Lord Sydney's steward, Mr Phillips, whom he had met while visiting England three years previously.[7] This early letter is a product of the cultural doubleness it so vividly depicts. Bennelong does not adhere to the European epistolary convention of addressing the same interlocutor throughout. It is probable that his departures from the European norm of one-to-one address are not merely "mistakes", but systematic expressions of a different set of assumptions about the context in which verbal communication typically takes place. Bennelong consistently proceeds as though he, and everyone he speaks *about*, are in each other's physical proximity, and can thus be spoken *to* – as is indeed usually the case in relatively small, locally based, oral-tribal Aboriginal societies of the kind in which Bennelong's paradigms of the social world are likely to have developed.

From the late eighteenth century onwards, Aboriginal people were involved in a variety of collaborative modes of textual production. Their words – verbatim or paraphrased, in traditional languages or in English translation – were recorded and published by ethnographers, missionaries, government officials, explorers and historians. On occasions, friendly settlers and designated local guardians of Aboriginal tribes wrote on behalf of Aboriginal groups to government authorities, often quoting or paraphrasing the Aborigines' words. Aboriginal voices thus made their way into texts nominally authored by others. Some Aboriginal people also collaborated with missionaries in translation work. In the 1820s, Biraban, an Awabakal man from the Lake Macquarie area north of Sydney, began working with missionary Lancelot Threlkeld in his translations of the Gospel of St Luke into the Awabakal language.[8] In the 1870s, James Unaipon (father of David Unaipon) worked with the missionary George Taplin translating Ngarrindjeri oral narratives into written English at Raukkan (Point McLeay) in South Australia.[9] In many such texts, it is difficult to identify distinct and separate voice zones, where the so-called "native informant's" voice ends and the putative white "author's" voice begins. It is also the case that Aboriginal people's contributions were not always acknowledged, and that colonial texts ostensibly authored by members of the settler society might more accurately be regarded as having been collaboratively produced.

During the nineteenth century Aboriginal people were also learning to write for themselves, usually at mission schools and on government reserves. The first school for Aboriginal children, Governor Macquarie's Native Institution, was opened at Parramatta in 1815. Individual Aboriginal children were also taken into white people's homes and taught to read and write. For Aboriginal children and their families, schools were both oppressive and potentially empowering institutions. Missionaries and local "protectors" travelled around the countryside rounding up Aboriginal children whom they believed were orphaned or "neglected", and taking them away to be formally educated. Although some parents were genuinely keen to have their children schooled, and were able to retain close contact with them, others were deceived into relinquishing their children "for their own educational good". Schools – and empty promises of schooling – were thus very much part of the history of the stolen generations. Edward Stone Parker, a protector in the Port Phillip District, recorded in 1842 that one Aboriginal leader "complained in his anger that the white fellow had stolen their country and now was stealing their children by taking them away to live in huts, and work, and 'read the book like whitefellows'".[10]

Schools were institutions through which colonial authorities imposed regimes of cultural assimilation, surveillance and bodily discipline on Aboriginal children. While the teachers filled the children's minds with the four Rs – reading, writing, arithmetic and Christian religion – the routines of school life confined the children bodily in one place, doing prescribed activities for certain fixed hours of the day. School inspectors' reports on reserve and mission schools in late nineteenth-century Victoria assessed not only the children's academic progress, but also their hours of attendance, class conduct, posture and manner of holding their writing implements.

As Aboriginal literacy gradually spread, Aboriginal people began writing their own letters, acting as scribes for one another, composing petitions to government officials and writing for newspapers. However, much early Aboriginal writing was done under close surveillance in institutions such as schools and mission establishments, where writing was produced to be read by white authorities. The Aboriginal writers knew their work would be evaluated according to whether it demonstrated not only their mastery of the craft of writing, but also their correct reading and internalisation of European cultural values and Christian beliefs. This kind of writing Mudrooroo has called "writing for the governor's pleasure", and the governor often quite literally had a hand in producing these texts.

The *Flinders Island Chronicle*, the first Aboriginal newspaper, was clearly written "for the governor's pleasure". Published weekly from September 1836 to December 1837, it was handwritten and hand-copied in English by three young Pallawah (Tasmanian Aboriginal) men, Thomas Brune, Walter George Arthur and Walter Juba Martin. Selling for twopence per copy, the paper was intended to "induce Emulation in writing, excite a desire for useful knowledge and promote Learning generally", while also providing a "brief but accurate register of events".[11] Although physically written by the young Pallawah men, the paper was produced under the watchful eye of the Commandant, George Augustus Robinson, who hoped it would promote Christianity and civilisation among the Aborigines. If Robinson did not actually write the *Chronicle*, he had a heavy editorial hand. Proof sheets had to be submitted to him for "correction" before publication. Not surprisingly, the *Chronicle* contains abrupt shifts of style, tone and focus. It frequently extolled the virtues of the Commandant's projects and echoed his Christian exhortations. Yet the Pallawah writers did manage to document aspects of their life on Flinders Island, including details that Robinson might have preferred to suppress. In all likelihood, they subverted the censorship process by adding extra material after Commandant Robinson had proofread the draft copy.

During the nineteenth century, Aboriginal literacy and knowledge of English spread more rapidly among children and young adults than among the older generations. The effect of this pattern of change on traditional Indigenous social hierarchies was varied and complex, because literacy and the English language had the power both to disrupt and to consolidate traditional, orally based Aboriginal gerontocracies. In most traditional Aboriginal societies, secret-sacred knowledge was concentrated primarily among the older, fully initiated men, although women had their own spheres of authority. The most powerful oral tools for communicating with the spirit beings who shaped the world were not disclosed to the uninitiated. Yet literacy and the English language were powerful tools of another kind, tools that enabled Aboriginal people to bargain with a new force that was shaping the world – the white man. As young people of both genders became literate in the English language, their ability to negotiate with colonial authorities gave them power and social status they might not otherwise have acquired. Generally speaking, the distribution of literacy in Aboriginal communities introduced a tendency for power to shift from the older males to the young of both sexes.

Paradoxically, however, writing also worked to consolidate traditional Aboriginal gerontocracies. Although the young had the *technical ability* to write, only the most senior men had the *authority* to negotiate with outsiders on behalf of the community. Thus, when young people acted as scribes for their elders, they not only made themselves more important, they also re-asserted the elders' traditional authority in the community. In many instances, young, literate Aborigines were able to mobilise the authority and reach of the written word in ways that simultaneously defended their communities' political interests, perpetuated traditional social structures, and preserved traditional protocols of communication.

Evidence of this apparently contradictory effect of writing on traditional Aboriginal social structures can be found in documents produced by members of the Kulin nation residing on Coranderrk Reserve near Healesville, north-east of Melbourne. From the 1870s to the 1890s, Wurundjeri leader William Barak organised a series of protests on behalf of the Coranderrk Aboriginal community, against their treatment by certain reserve managers and against plans devised by the Board for the Protection of Aborigines to close the reserve and sell off the land to local white settlers. Barak was a *ngurungaeta* or clan-head of the Wurundjeri people, on whose land Coranderrk was established. His relation to that section of country authorised him to write on behalf of those who lived there. As clan-head Barak had a traditional right and obligation to decide how the Coranderrk land was to be used and who should live there.[12] In all but one of the many petitions written by the Coranderrk people, William Barak's name heads the list of signatories. Barak could not write, but he remained the principal signatory because "A clan-head was … considered the group's rightful representative in external affairs".[13] The order in which the names were listed at the bottom of the petition reflects the resilience of the traditional social structure. The names of the older men (who all sign with crosses) head the list, followed by the younger men (who write their own names), then the older (usually non-literate) women, followed by the younger (literate) women, and finally the children, who write their own names if they are old enough to attend school.

Fragments of historical narrative can be found in these early letters and petitions from the Victorian reserves. Even brief, apparently trivial forms of correspondence, such as requests for train passes, afford vivid glimpses of the difficulties faced by people whose most basic human rights and freedoms were being systematically stripped away. Some of the most moving pieces of writing are by women separated from their children. In April 1884, Margaret Harrison wrote from Ebenezer mission station in north-west Victoria to the Secretary of the Board for the Protection of Aborigines

(BPA), telling him, "my heart is breaking to have them [the children] with me".[14] In May 1885 Lydia Briggs sent a telegram from Echuca in northern Victoria asking the BPA Secretary: "What have you decided about my children?"[15] Women usually wrote to white authorities on their own and their family's behalf, rather than as spokespeople for their community. Although women signed most of the petitions, and occasionally acted as scribes, none acted as principal signatory in the way Barak did. In 1893, Betsy Banfield penned a petition from Barak and thirty other members of the community to Charles Officer, Vice Chairman of the BPA, asking that Coranderrk not be closed down.[16] In all likelihood, Betsy acted as the scribe not only because her handwriting was extremely neat, but because she was the daughter of one of Barak's speakers, Thomas Banfield.

As time went by, however, literate women began to speak for their community, as well as for themselves. A transitional stage in this process can be seen in a letter/petition written in February 1900 by Maggie Mobourne, a resident of Lake Condah Mission Station, to D.N. McLeod, MLA and Vice Chairman of the BPA. Maggie Mobourne made a number of allegations against the mission manager, the Rev. Stahle.[17] Below her signature, a postscript has been added, saying: "We the following corroborate the statements given above", after which the signatures and crosses of eleven Aboriginal residents are added. It appears Maggie Mobourne is principal signatory to this document because it began as a personal letter, not because, like William Barak, she was licensed by traditional Aboriginal law to speak for the community.

As well as writing letters and petitions, Aboriginal people submitted written evidence at official inquiries. In 1881, a Parliamentary Board of Inquiry was established to look into conditions at Coranderrk. Besides giving oral testimony, a number of Aboriginal witnesses brought along written statements, which they – or one of the officials – read out to the commissioners. Aboriginal witnesses thereby gained a small measure of control over the inquiry's agenda, raising issues not addressed in the ordinary line of oral questioning. In written statements prepared beforehand, they were able to speak more freely than was possible when standing up to be questioned in the intimidating atmosphere of the inquiry. They also increased the likelihood that their views would be accurately recorded in the official minutes of evidence.

While government officials used writing as an instrument of colonial administration and control, and promoted Aboriginal literacy as a means of instilling compliance,[18] Aboriginal people used writing as a means of resistance and political negotiation, as well as for personal communications with relatives and friends. Government and mission authorities viewed both kinds of writing with suspicion at times. On some of the Victorian missions and reserves, Aboriginal people complained that their letters were being intercepted, read, and in some cases destroyed by the reserve manager.

Present-day Aboriginal political, historical and autobiographical writing is rooted in the nineteenth-century journalism of the *Flinders Island Chronicle*, in the early letters and petitions to government officials, and in written statements submitted to official inquiries. These non-literary forms of writing continued throughout the twentieth century. Political groups established in the 1920s and 1930s built on these nineteenth-century foundations. As president of the Australian Aborigines' Progressive Association, Fred Maynard wrote letters of protest to the NSW Aborigines' Protection Board. William Cooper, founder of the Australian Aborigines League, compiled a petition to King George V. William Ferguson and John Patten published a manifesto, "Aborigines Claim Citizenship Rights", for the Aborigines' Progressive Association, with Patten going on to establish the APA newsletter, *The Abo Call*, in 1938.

The Abo Call marked a turning-point in Aboriginal politics. The first issue (1 April 1938) identified the paper as "our own paper", and addressed itself expressly "To All Aborigines". Only six editions were published (from April to September 1938), yet *The Abo Call* played a vital role in building a national pan-Aboriginal political constituency. Although based in New South Wales, John Patten published contributions from Aboriginal people in different parts of Australia. He aimed at "rebroadcasting the voice of the Aborigines themselves".[19]

The Abo Call reported on contemporary living conditions on the reserves, and the activities of the Aborigines' Progressive Association, including the bitter rift that developed between the two co-founders, John Patten and William Ferguson. The paper also fiercely contested the dominant white myth of Australia's peaceful settlement, thereby raising white people's awareness and giving Aboriginal readers a shared sense of their own history. By offering glimpses of their common historical experience, *The Abo Call* welded local and regional Aboriginal groups into a national "imagined community", not as a dying race but as a political force with a future. Not everybody approved of *The Abo Call*, however. William Ferguson, co-founder of the APA, disliked the name of the paper, and objected to its having received temporary funding from the right-wing Australia First Movement.

Ferguson had in fact entered into another field of writing. During the middle decades of the twentieth century, Aboriginal writing had remained (as far as we know at present) almost entirely outside the boundaries of the "high literary" genres. Aboriginal writers did not venture into fiction until the third decade of twentieth century, when William Ferguson wrote down the story of "Nanya" as told to him by Harry Mitchell around 1920.[20] Nanya was a young Barkindji clever-man who, "with the full knowledge of doing wrong",[21] eloped into the desert with Mimi, a girl of his own skin or section, whom tribal law forbade him to marry. As a culturally hybrid, multi-generic narrative, "Nanya" is readable in different ways.

Like William Ferguson, David Unaipon combined creative and political writing, and wove Aboriginal and Western narrative elements together. Unaipon, long hailed as Australia's "first Aboriginal writer",[22] was a member of the Ngarrindjeri community at Raukkan (Point McLeay, South Australia), a mission run by the Aborigines' Friends' Association (AFA). Unaipon was a polymath whose interests included physics, mechanical and aeronautical engineering, Latin, Greek and the English sermon. Seeing him as living proof of the success of their own civilising mission, the AFA gave him moral, practical and financial support, sponsoring his public speaking engagements, his scientific demonstrations and his publications.

Unaipon is best known for his booklet, *Native Legends* (c.1929)[23]; his published address, "An Aboriginal Pleads for His Race" (c.1928)[24]; and his autobiographical text, *My Life Story* (c.1951).[25] A diverse array of narrative and discursive traditions intersect in his stories. In "Narroondarie's Wives",[26] for example, Unaipon oscillates between Indigenous-mythic and Western-historical space and time. Biblical, classical, ethnographic, scientific and historical elements are woven into the fabric of a traditional Ngarrindjeri story, which Unaipon tells in formal, educated English interspersed with Ngarrindjeri words. As Eve eats the forbidden fruit of the tree of knowledge in Genesis, Narroondarie's wives eat the Thookerrie, a fish forbidden to women. Like Adam and Eve, Narroondarie's wives

> awoke to their sense of guilt, so the elder said: "Come, let us flee". "But", said the younger, "whither shall we fly? Let us stay and face the wrath of Narroondarie. Stay and be placed back and embodied in a tree-shrub plant ..." "Come!", said the elder, "... we may go into some strange land ..."
>
> So without another word they both gathered a great bundle of grass-tree sticks and carried them to the waterside and bound them together, forming a raft, and they shoved the raft into deep water and sat upon it and paddled across the western side of Lake Albert, and slept at the point near the estate of the late T.R. Bowman.[27]

In passages such as this one, Unaipon's focus, tone and register shift so abruptly that postcolonial hybridity reads like postmodern pastiche.

CONTEMPORARY ABORIGINAL WRITING

The contemporary phase of Aboriginal writing begins in 1964, with the publication of Oodgeroo Noonuccal's (Kath Walker's) first poetry collection, *We Are Going*. This book did not break an Aboriginal silence; Aboriginal people had been writing in the non-literary genres for almost 170 years by this time. Rather, Oodgeroo's writing ended a period of white deafness by bringing a powerful Aboriginal voice into earshot of large, mainstream audiences both in Australia and overseas. The importance of *We Are Going* was that it opened a new channel of transmission that allowed the dominant society to hear what Aboriginal voices had been saying for many years.

Oodgeroo, of the Noonuccal people of Stradbroke Island in Queensland, was publishing most prolifically at a time when Aboriginal activists and issues were beginning to attract considerable attention in the mainstream media. Charles Perkins organised the freedom rides in rural New South Wales in 1965. The Gurindji people went on strike at Wave Hill (Northern Territory) in 1966. The Federal Council for the Advancement of Aborigines and Torres Strait Islanders (FCAATSI) became increasingly influential throughout the 1960s, campaigning successfully in the 1967 referendum to have the federal government assume responsibility for Aboriginal affairs, and to have Aboriginal people counted in the census. In 1972, Aborigines erected the tent embassy on the lawns of Parliament House in Canberra to protest against their lack of land rights and signify their sense of being foreigners in their own land. The emergence of Aboriginal literature in the 1960s and 1970s was part of this entrance of Aboriginal people onto the national political stage.

Oodgeroo, together with Kevin Gilbert, Jack Davis and Colin Johnson (Mudrooroo)[28], were seen as the founders of contemporary Aboriginal literature. Mudrooroo's Aboriginal identity has since been disputed.[29] Even so, he was and still is an influential figure because, from 1965 (when his novel *Wild Cat Falling* was published) to the mid-1990s (when the results of his sister's genealogical research emerged in the mainstream media[30]), his large and diverse body of writings served as an inspiration and rallying point for other Aboriginal writers. Oodgeroo, Gilbert, Davis and Mudrooroo shared a number of common concerns and methods. They called for justice and land rights, challenged racist stereotypes, dismantled exclusionary models of national identity, and corrected biased historical narratives of progress and peaceful settlement. They also insisted on the continuity of past and present. Not only had the past left indelible scars on the present, new wrongs were being perpetrated against Aboriginal Australians every day. "Let no one say the past is dead", urged Oodgeroo. "The past is all about us and within."[31]

Oodgeroo's poetry was an extension of her political work. Since 1960 she had been actively involved in FCAATSI, and often read her poems at rallies. Her poetry effectively documents, analyses and laments the effects of colonialism on Aboriginal people and the land. Some poems call Aboriginal people to action; others directly address "the unhappy [white] race" in angry, accusing, disdainful and sometimes pitying tones. Other poems are more reflective, some looking back to happier times before the coming of the white man.

The early critical reception of Oodgeroo's work warrants close attention today because it exemplifies the kinds of cultural prejudices many Aboriginal writers faced, and continue to face, as they write not only for each other but for "the world of the invader ... a people not one's own ... the conquerors of one's own people".[32] Oodgeroo's major publications – *We Are Going* (1964), *The Dawn is at Hand* (1966) and *My People* (1970) – are reputed to have sold more copies than those of any other Australian poet except C.J. Dennis. Partly because her writing was so popular, it was condemned by sections of the academy. Some critics drew a sharp line between "poetry proper", which transcends its time and place to address universal human concerns, and "mere protest writing", which speaks to its particular historical moment. Dressing their social prejudices in a language of disinterested aesthetic evaluation, they judged Oodgeroo's work to be too narrow and stridently polemical to have any lasting value.

Essentialist beliefs about Aboriginality also shaped early evaluations of Oodgeroo's work. Some critics saw her as too modern to be authentically Aboriginal; others saw her as too old-fashioned and rhetorical to be a proper poet. "Real Aborigines" were stereotyped as traditional song*men* who spoke no English, had never used a pen, and were imprisoned by their ancient traditions. "Real poets", by contrast, were essentialised as avant-garde experimentalists who shunned obvious rhetoric, and broke heroically free of tradition by moulding language transgressively into obscure, indecipherable shapes. On the basis of such assumptions, a politically motivated "Aboriginal poet" – a female one at that – was a contradiction in terms.[33]

Oodgeroo and other Aboriginal writers have faced a linguistic dilemma, which Eva Rask Knudsen has summed up as follows:

Since ... Oodgeroo had her own language stolen from her by white society she must both master the conqueror's standard language to get her message across and avoid the danger of "thinking white" while using it in an environment where every effort to assert an Aboriginal identity is circumscribed by white power.[34]

It is sometimes suggested that "the master's tools will never dismantle the master's house",[35] and that non-radical linguistic practices like those of Oodgeroo, the early Jack Davis and other plain-speaking Aboriginal writers automatically reinforce the very orthodoxies they set out to contest. For historical, financial and political reasons, many Aboriginal writers have little choice but to use the English language in apparently uncomplicated ways. Do they then inevitably subvert their own objectives?

Crucial here is the distinction between assimilation and appropriation. As Bob Hodge has noted, "It's the master's rules, not his tools that are the problem: starting from rule one, that the tools are his and should only be used as and when he directs."[36] Hodge argues convincingly that Oodgeroo used the master's tools in her own way for her own purposes, and suffered no loss of integrity in doing so. Particularly insightful is Hodge's discussion of how Oodgeroo constructs a position for white readers to occupy, a position from which they are at once "implicated in the crimes of the past but also committed to justice for all". Through the act of reading, white readers are reconstructed and "coerced to choose to disidentify with 'typical' Australians while not being offered the choice of supposing it possible to become an honorary Black".[37]

Like Oodgeroo, Kevin Gilbert was often dismissed as too strident and political. A member of the Wiradjuri and Kamilaroi peoples of New South Wales, Gilbert began writing in the 1960s while serving time in prison (as other Aboriginal writers such as Robert Merritt, Robert Walker and Graham Dixon did later). No one could possibly deny that incarceration has had appalling consequences for most Aboriginal prisoners and their families. No one emerges unscathed from that experience. But in prison Gilbert at least had access to books, and time to read, think, write, paint and do linocut work.

Gilbert's first book of poems, *End of Dreamtime*, published in the year of his release, was disowned by him because extensively revised by the editor without Gilbert's permission. A number of other Aboriginal authors have been frustrated by uninvited editorial intervention. Because publishers require books to be financially viable and culturally acceptable to the dominant audience, some Aboriginal authors have had their writings tampered with to satisfy (what publishers and editors think are) white tastes. In 1978, Gilbert published *People Are Legends*, an authorised edition of his early poems. His other major publications include two political books, *Because a White Man'll Never Do It* (1973) and *Aboriginal Sovereignty: Justice, The Law and Land* (1993); a play, *The Cherry Pickers* (written in prison in 1968, and published in 1988); a collection of oral histories, *Living Black* (1977); a poetry anthology, *Inside Black Australia* (1988); and three other poetry collections, *The Blackside* (1990), *Child's Dreaming* (1992) and the posthumously published *Black from the Edge* (1994).

Gilbert's achievements are manifold, and his work has received less attention than it deserves. One of his particular concerns was to correct the historical lie of Australia's peaceful settlement. To this end, some of his poems read the land as a historical document. "Memorials", for example, with its accompanying photographs in *Black From the Edge*, teaches non-Indigenous readers to see the land differently – as a repository of Aboriginal memories in a previously illegible script.

Many of Gilbert's poems are either dramatic monologues, or include sections of direct speech. His poetry, taken as a whole, replicates the effect of *Living Black* in that it allows us to hear a diverse array of Aboriginal voices – male, female, young, old, urban, rural, remote, human and non-human. In "Birth Control For Blacks", for example, an Aboriginal man and woman articulate the opposing racial and gender politics of using the contraceptive pill. The man is all for keeping Aboriginal numbers up; the woman wants a break from pregnancy and child-rearing. Gilbert leaves the question open.

As well as including dialogues in his poems, Gilbert engages dialogically with other texts and writers. His "New True Anthem", for example, replies both to Dorothea Mackellar's classic "My Country" and to Australia's official national anthem, "Advance Australia Fair":

> Despite what Dorothea has said
> about the sun scorched land
> you've never really loved her
> nor sought to make her grand ...
> Australia oh Australia
> you could stand proud and free
> we weep in bitter anguish
> at your hate and tyranny.[38]

Kevin Gilbert and Oodgeroo Noonuccal both passed away in 1993, the Year of the World's Indigenous Peoples. When their first books were published, Aboriginal authors were a rarity. By 1993, Aboriginal writing was a force to be reckoned with, both in the Australian literary scene and the wider sphere of national political life. In poetry, for example, Graham Dixon and Robert Walker wrote out of their prison experiences; Lionel Fogarty and Mary Duroux lamented the loss of their traditional languages; Errol West, Eva Johnson, Margaret Brusnahan and many others put words to the ongoing pain of the stolen children and their families.[39]

A 1998 survey conducted for the Aboriginal and Torres Strait Islander Arts Board of the Australia Council found that fifty-five percent of

Aboriginal authors had written poetry.[40] Unlike novels or plays, poems can be written relatively quickly, and published in local community newsletters and newspapers. Poems are also a good place to experiment with language. The Australia Council study also found that, across all genres, Aboriginal writers were using twenty-seven traditional languages, in addition to Aboriginal Englishes, Kriol and Standard English. A number of Northern Territory poets in Kevin Gilbert's anthology, *Inside Black Australia*, offer poems in their traditional languages, followed by English translations. In her book, *It Just Lies There From the Beginning* (1995), Marjorie Bil Bil, a Marri Ammu woman from Belyuen near Darwin, recorded many of her poems and stories in her traditional languages (she speaks five) and then translated them into English for publication.[41] Eva Johnson, also from the Northern Territory but taken from her mother when she was three, uses a range of different kinds of English, including Aboriginal English, in "A Letter to My Mother":

> I not see you long time now, I not see you long time now
> White fulla bin take me from you, I don't know why
> Give me to Missionary to be God's child.[42]

In terms of both language and content, Lionel Fogarty is perhaps the most radical Aboriginal poet writing today. Descended from the Mulinjari and Gudjela peoples living on Wakka Wakka land at Cherbourg reserve in southern Queensland, Fogarty refers to the English language as "a medium/ that is not mine".[43] Oodgeroo's response to this predicament was to appropriate the imposed language; Fogarty's strategy is to abrogate it. This he does in a number of ways: first, by incorporating traditional Aboriginal words into his poems; second, by using English words that have distinct meanings or connotations in Aboriginal usage (so that a line might remain opaque, or a joke pass unnoticed, to those unaware of the alternative meanings); and, third, by smashing the rules of English syntax and grammar to produce a confrontative "anti-language" that disorients readers and positions them as outsiders.[44] Mudrooroo calls Fogarty "a guerrilla poet", a word-warrior whose strategies shift for each occasion. By keeping his readers off balance, Fogarty exposes us to the full force of his bare-knuckle punchlines. Fogarty is a writer of many voices, a poet with a broad tonal range. In "Little Murri", for example, he gives loving, strengthening advice across the generations to his young grandson.[45] Anger and political outrage emerge in "Consideration of Black Deaths (story)".[46] Amidst the anger and grief, Fogarty also creates laughter. In poems such as "Drunk Cricket Field No. 1", his humour covers the spectrum from slap-stick comedy to witty, cross-cultural word play and absurd postmodern pastiche. A different tone again is heard in "Weather Comes", a powerful, bitterly lyrical poem about poisoned country:

> The weather is wearily
> The winds are webbing
> blowing voices of help
> Sun is lowering its light
> moon is darking its face
> stars is fallen its flight
> rain has rained non stop
> sea waters raised higher
> rivers swallower and
> banks fall apart.
> Trees grow old no more
> Fruits grow wilder no more
> Raw uncleaned smelling
> air goes in the plants soils.
> Ochres shows colours unseen.
> Sand dirt mud soot all look
> different, touch different,
> smell funny.
> We can't hardly believe this
> was once our dreamtime home[47]

The first generation of Aboriginal poets – Oodgeroo, Gilbert and Davis – have left a lasting legacy. Although the Aboriginal descent of Mudrooroo and Roberta Sykes is now in doubt, their contribution must be also acknowledged. Mudrooroo's two poem cycles, *The Song Circle of Jacky* (1986) and *Dalwurra* (1988), were an influential attempt to shape poetry along the lines of traditional Aboriginal song. Similarly, Roberta Sykes' *Love Songs and Other Revolutionary Actions* (1979) inspired a generation of Aboriginal women writers and educated a generation of non-Indigenous readers. In recent years, a new generation of younger, urban, university-educated poets has emerged, including Kim Scott, Lisa Bellear, Anita Heiss and Kerry Reed-Gilbert (daughter of Kevin Gilbert).[48] Their work is grounded, in many respects, in the older protest tradition, yet they write on the basis of their own personal contemporary experiences of alienation, institutionalised racism, and the complex intersections of sexual, racial, class and gender politics.

AUTOBIOGRAPHY AND BIOGRAPHY

One of the most dynamic areas of contemporary Australian writing is Aboriginal autobiography. Autobiography is a story form foreign to traditional Aboriginal cultures. Its beginnings can be found in various modes of formalised dialogue with non-Aboriginal officials and researchers. From early colonial times, Aboriginal people were encouraged to confess their sins to missionaries, testify at official inquiries, and tell their stories to ethnographers and anthropologists. In the middle decades of the twentieth century, theoretical and methodological developments in anthropology and history brought Aboriginal life stories to the fore as a rich information source. Life histories were systematically collected by researchers whose task was made easier by the increasing availability of efficient, portable audio-recording equipment. As soon as lengthy oral narratives could be accurately recorded and transcribed, the stage was set for transforming life-*talking* into life-*writing*, and for thinking of "native informants" as Aboriginal authors.

The process of transforming talk into writing presented a number of problems both practical and political. On the one hand, it was necessary to preserve the integrity of the Aboriginal voice; on the other, readers (predominantly non-Aboriginal) expected certain standards of coherence, conciseness and grammatical correctness. Who might appropriately edit oral narratives for publication? What editorial principles should they use? What orthographic conventions should be observed in the published text? Who, finally, owned the text legally, morally and culturally – the speaker and their community, or the editor, or the publisher, or the reader?

Aboriginal life-writing is thus a highly contested textual territory. Early publications such as *I, The Aboriginal* (1962) and *Lamilami Speaks* (1974) are especially problematic. The title page of *I, The Aboriginal* tells us the book is "by Douglas Lockwood". Yet Lockwood is not "The Aboriginal" referred to in the title; he is the book's non-Aboriginal editor. The Aboriginal "I" is Waipuldanya (also called Wadjiri-Wadjiri or Phillip Roberts). He has been relegated to the role of "native informant" in his own autobiography. Lockwood graciously dedicates the book "with gratitude and affection" to Waipuldanya, the man whose authorial position he has usurped. It would be interesting to know how the book's royalties were distributed, and whether, when *I, The Aboriginal* won the 1962 Adelaide *Advertiser* Festival of Arts Award, the £1250 prize money went to Lockwood or to Waipuldanya.

Since that time a number of Aboriginal men have written or recorded their autobiographies, including Dick Roughsey, Charles Perkins, Jack Davis, Joe McGinness, Jack Bohemia, Wandjuk Marika, Boori Pryor, Warrigal Anderson and Wayne King.[49] But it has been Aboriginal women who have won the largest readership, and perhaps been most successful in building bridges between black and white Australia. As Anne Brewster has noted, Aboriginal women have until recently been less prolific as dramatists, novelists and poets, but since the late 1970s they have dominated in the area of autobiography.[50] The first wave included Margaret Tucker's *If Everyone*

Cared (1977), Ella Simon's *Through My Eyes* (1978), Ida West's *Pride Against Prejudice* (1984), Labumore's (Elsie Roughsey's) *An Aboriginal Mother Tells of the Old and the New* (1984) and Marnie Kennedy's *Born a Half-Caste* (1985). Labumore's story is especially illuminating and unique in a number of respects. Using her own non-standard English, she paints a vivid picture of the Lardil people's bush and mission life on Mornington Island. Labumore's manuscript was edited sensitively and respectfully by Paul Memmott and Robyn Horsman, who outlined and gave reasons for their editorial policies, and were careful to avoid the traps into which earlier editors had fallen.

Sally Morgan's *My Place* (1987) was a watershed publication in being the first Aboriginal-authored bestseller. It was published during the lead-up to the 1988 Bicentenary of British settlement in Australia – or what many Aboriginal people and their friends called the British invasion. Wide media coverage of the Bicentenary provided Aboriginal spokespeople with opportunities to alert the world to Australia's hidden Black history. Popular curiosity about Indigenous views of the past translated into heightened consumer demand for Aboriginal people's personal histories. A number of autobiographies appeared in close succession in the late 1980s and early 1990s. Prominent among them were Ruby Langford Ginibi's *Don't Take Your Love to Town* (1988), Glenyse Ward's *Wandering Girl* (1988) and *Unna you Fullas* (1991), Ellie Gaffney's *Somebody Now* (1989), Doris Pilkington's *Caprice: A Stockman's Daughter* (1991), Mabel Edmond's *No Regrets* (1992), Alice Nannup's *When the Pelican Laughed* (1992) and Evelyn Crawford's *Over My Tracks* (1993). In their different ways, these stories tell of endurance and extraordinary heroism. Like parts of a jigsaw puzzle they create a composite picture of Aboriginal people's historical experience from the 1930s up to the present time.

Speaking in very general terms, it is possible to identify a number of features that distinguish Aboriginal life-writing from traditional Western autobiographical narratives. By and large, Aboriginal autobiographies tend to be less introspective. They often move quickly from event to event in a transparent, perfunctory prose, reminding us perhaps that introspectivity is a luxury enjoyed primarily by leisured elites who assume their thoughts and feelings are important and unique. In the Western tradition, the past is often pictured as faraway, elusive and elaborately mediated, whereas in many Aboriginal autobiographies certain past experiences are so painfully present and immediate that it is extremely stressful for the writer to put their memories into words. Western and Aboriginal autobiographies share a tendency to structure the subject's life story as a journey. In the (male-centred) Western tradition, growing up means leaving the family home behind, and venturing out into the world as a unique, autonomous, self-aware individual. Few Aboriginal autobiographers (of either gender) adhere to this pattern. The Aboriginal subject's journey is usually towards home and traditional country rather than away from it, and growing to maturity means taking one's proper place (or series of places) in the kinship network. If Aboriginal subjects do venture out, they usually maintain strong ties with family and home-place.[51]

Another distinguishing feature of Aboriginal autobiography is that it is more overtly dialogic than its Western counterpart. A number of autobiographical texts have more than one author, for example, Della Walker and Tina Coutts' *Me and You* (1989), Patsy Cohen and Margaret Somerville's *Ingelba and the Five Black Matriarchs* (1990), and Somerville, Dundas, Mead, Robinson and Sulter's *The Sun Dancin'* (1994). Other Aboriginal life-writings have been edited by non-Aboriginal collaborators who remain behind the scenes. Mudrooroo and others have argued that texts produced in this manner are less authentically Aboriginal than those written single-handedly by Aboriginal authors.[52] A problem with this view is that it fails to distinguish between different modes of collaboration. Some Aboriginal writings have indeed been distorted beyond recognition to attract a large readership and conform to Western literary norms and standards. But other, non-exploitative modes of collaboration are possible. Certain Aboriginal authors work by choice with an editorial assistant whose role is to help the author produce a manuscript which, on the one hand, preserves the author's own voice and realises their own intentions yet, on the other hand, allows publishers no excuse for radical editorial intervention.[53] By "in-sourcing" part of the editorial process, Aboriginal writers have maximised their control over the text that finally appears on the bookseller's shelves. Jessie Lennon, for instance, says her book *And I Always Been Moving* (1996) "is my own book out of my own mouth", even though it was recorded and prepared for publication by Michele Madigan.

In recent years, Aboriginal authors have begun writing and/or editing the life histories of family members and friends. Sally Morgan told the story of her grandfather, Jack McPhee, in *Wanamurraganya* (1989). Rosemary van den Berg presented the life story of her father, Thomas Corbett, in *No Options, No Choice!* (1994). Rita Huggins and her daughter Jackie Huggins interwove their distinct and separate voices in *Auntie Rita* (1994), to produce a unique inter-generational dialogue on their family's life. Herb Wharton told the stories of eight Murri drovers in *Cattle Camp* (1994), while in *Follow the Rabbit-Proof Fence* (1996), Doris Pilkington wrote of her mother's and aunt's escape as children from Moore River reserve in Western Australia, and their extraordinary trek home to Jigalong, over

1,500 kilometres to the north. Wayne King devotes almost a quarter of his autobiography, *Black Hours* (1996), to his mother's experience of life as a stolen child, while Jeannie Bell tells Celia Smith's story in *Talking About Celia* (1997). In *Haunted by the Past* (1999), Ruby Langford Ginibi tells her son's life story in a manner that contests the "criminal" stereotype constructed in police and prison records, and engages with the wider issue of Aboriginal incarceration.

Aboriginal autobiographies have entered the public sphere from unexpected directions. One of the most powerful sets of narratives was published in 1997, in the Human Rights and Equal Opportunity Commission report *Bringing Them Home: Report of the National Inquiry into the Separation of Aboriginal and Torres Strait Islander Children from Their Families*. This report included long and short extracts from testimonies by some of the 535 Aboriginal witnesses who gave evidence before the inquiry about their own experiences and those of their families. So great was the power of these stories that the full 700-page report, which retailed at around $60, became a bestseller, as did the abbreviated report, the video and the book of extended testimonies, *The Stolen Children: Their Stories* (1998), edited by Carmel Bird. Along with the data that framed them, the witnesses' stories stimulated intense public interest and political debate on how governments and individuals might redress past wrongs, and contribute to healing and reconciliation in the present. So great was the public interest in the stolen generations' stories that a number of related texts have been published, including Rosalie Fraser's *Shadow Child: A Memoir of the Stolen Generation* (1998), Coral Edwards' and Peter Read's reprint of *The Lost Children* (1997) and Romayne Weare's novel, *Malanbarra* (1997), the story of two children on the run from police who want to take them from their mother.

FICTION

Many Aboriginal writings resist classification within conventional European genre systems. A number of Aboriginal "fiction" writers, for instance, undo the Western commonsense categorical distinction between fact and fiction. They may do this by drawing on their own experiences, by creating historical fictions, and by confronting readers with the double vision of what critics customarily call magic realism. These three strategies form a basis for three strands of Aboriginal fiction, although it must be recognised that these strands may themselves be interwoven in the same text.

For thirty years, Colin Johnson's *Wild Cat Falling* (1965) was viewed as the first Aboriginal novel, his apparently autobiographical work providing a model for other Aboriginal fiction writers. Today, Monica Clare's posthumously published *Karobran* (1978) is regarded as the first Aboriginal novel. *Karobran* is based on Clare's own experiences as a child growing up in welfare institutions and white foster homes in New South Wales. Archie Weller's novel, *Day of the Dog* (1981), and short story collection, *Goin Home* (1986), included people and events typical of those he knew growing up in East Perth, but also used motifs derived from gothic romance. While John Muk Muk Burke's *Bridge of Triangles* (1994) draws on his early life growing up in New South Wales, Herb Wharton's novel *Unbranded* (1992), and story collection *Where Ya' Been, Mate?* (1996), spin wonderful, funny yarns out of his hard life as a Queensland drover. And in his beautifully crafted novel *True Country* (1993), Kim Scott makes "stepping off points for the imagination" out of people and situations encountered during his time as a teacher at Kalumburu in the far north of Western Australia.[54]

Parts of Scott's *True Country*, and other novels such as Sam Watson's *The Kadaitcha Sung* (1990), Alexis Wright's *Plains of Promise* (1997) and Archie Weller's *Land of the Golden Clouds* (1998), might be called magic realist. Yet magic realism exists only in the eye of the beholder. What looks, to the European eye, like a clash between two worlds or two discursive orders might in fact seem perfectly coherent, normal, and non-anomalous from a different cultural perspective. While magic realism allegedly dismantles European perceptual conventions,[55] it is observable as a distinct practice only to modern Western minds in which fact and fantasy, history and myth, the plausible and the unbelievable, are customarily situated as binary opposites. Traditional Aboriginal cultures had different ways of classifying stories. What Westerners call magic realism might be seen, from a different cultural viewpoint, as a self-consistent story form.

A number of Aboriginal novelists have concerned themselves with re-writing history. They contest the myths of heroic exploration and peaceful settlement that, for many years, were disseminated through the school system. Mudrooroo's novels, *Long Live Sandawarra* (1979), *Doctor Wooreddy's Prescription for Enduring the Ending of the World* (1983) and *Master of the Ghost Dreaming* (1991), formed a nucleus around which a tradition of Aboriginal historical fiction developed. Eric Willmot's *Pemulwuy* (1987) seized the moment of the Bicentenary to tell of the organised resistance by the Eora, Dharuk and Tharawal peoples to the British invasion of what is now the Sydney region. Willmot's daughter, Haidi Willmot, rewrote the story for young readers in her novel *The Castles of Tuhbowgule* (1992). Like Pemulwuy, Richard Wilkes' Nyoongar leader, Bulmurn (in the 1995 novel of the same name), had magical powers and was reputed to be impossible to kill. Yet while Pemulwuy was a real person, Bulmurn was a fictional character based on a number of Nyoongar leaders including Midgegooroo, his son Yagan, Yellangona, Mundy, Waylo and Banyowla. Kim Scott's second novel, *Benang: From the Heart* (1999), takes a different path through Western Australian history. Focusing on a family in which, in keeping with official assimilation policies, white men married several generations of Nyoongar women, Scott brilliantly elucidates the social and psychological repercussions of "breeding out the colour".

Recently, a number of Aboriginal women writers have moved into fiction, a genre previously dominated by men. Alexis Wright's *Plains of Promise* (1997) and Melissa Lukashenko's *Steam Pigs* (1997) have raised questions about domestic violence and sexual exploitation within the Aboriginal community, as well as between Aboriginal and non-Aboriginal people. Sue Wilson, the Murri heroine of Lukashenko's *Steam Pigs*, must decide whether to stay with her abusive, working-class Aboriginal man or accept asylum from her white, university-educated, feminist friends. While many writers have noted the gender-specific nature of racial oppression, younger novelists like Melissa Lukashenko, Alexis Wright and Kim Scott are focusing on the complex, politically ambivalent situations that arise when differences of gender, sexuality and class cut across lines of racial and cultural difference.

CHILDREN'S WRITING

During Wandjuk Marika's term as Chairman of the Aboriginal Arts Board of the Australia Council, he presided over the publication of a ground-breaking book – *The Aboriginal Children's History of Australia* (1977). Using written and painted contributions from Aboriginal children from forty-nine schools around Australia, *The Aboriginal Children's History* included Dreaming stories, oral histories of the "Old Time", accounts of visits of the Macassans, the arrival of whitefellas and life on the missions and cattle stations, the diversity of contemporary Aboriginal historical experience, and the children's continuing ties to country and culture in the present day. As Wandjuk Marika pointed out in his introductory remarks, as well as being a book that "awakened Aboriginal children ... to an awareness of this identity and pride in their past", it also "speaks in a language that will be understood by children and adults throughout the world".[56]

Since the 1970s, an array of different kinds of children's books has been produced by Aboriginal writers and illustrators. Some are designed as educational resources for use in schools. As well as helping to develop literacy in both English and Aboriginal languages, these texts familiarise Aboriginal children with their traditional cultural heritage and/or introduce non-Aboriginal children to aspects of traditional Aboriginal culture. Daisy Utemorah, for example, has published a number of traditional stories about birds and animals for early readers in English. Lionel Fogarty's children's book *Booyooburra: A Story of the Wakka Murri* (1993), illustrated by Wiradjuri artist Sharon Hodgson, reproduces spoken Murri English on the page to evoke a local oral context of storytelling in Wakka Wakka country. The story is associated with a specific site on the Cherbourg Reserve, and addresses itself to children familiar with that place: "You know the big rocks and the big waterhole in Cherbourg old yard where the reservoir hill that feeds the settlement with water is? That's where this story comes from." For children acquiring literacy in more than one language, a number of multilingual children's books have been published by local and regional presses. Ross and Olive Boddington collaborated with the Yamaji Language Centre in Western Australia to produce *The Budara Story* (1996). This book tells the story of Budara the healer in both Wajarri and English, and provides a guide to pronunciation and word lists for translation exercises.

Aboriginal illustrators have helped produce some outstanding children's books. Bundjalung artist Bronwyn Bancroft has illustrated Oodgeroo's 1992 edition of *Stradbroke Dreamtime*, Sally Morgan's *Dan's Grandpa* (1996), and Percy Mumbulla's *The Whalers* (1996).[57] Paintings and line drawings by Kukatja artist Lucille Gill play a central role in the award-winning book *Tjarany/Roughtail: The Dreaming of the Roughtail Lizard and Other Stories Told by the Kukatja* (1992). Produced collaboratively by Gill with Gracie Greene (who told the stories in Kukatja) and Joe Tramacchi (who translated them into English), this book serves a wide array of educational purposes. The story is told both in Kukatja and English; extensive background information about the Kukatja language and kinship system is supplied; and readers are instructed in the process of seeing and understanding Lucille Gill's superb paintings.

CONTESTED IDENTITIES

Unlike writers from dominant ethnic groups, Aboriginal and other non-Anglo-Celtic Australian writers have been required to prove their authenticity and put their cultural identity on display. Knowing the particulars of their Aboriginal descent, identifying as Aboriginal, and being accepted as such by an Aboriginal community, most Indigenous authors have little trouble satisfying the three criteria of Aboriginality defined by the federal government. However, a small number of writers called themselves Aboriginal either knowing they were *not* of Indigenous descent, or thinking they *may* have been Aboriginal without being able to establish their ancestry or define their position within a specific kinship network. These writers have found themselves at the centre of media controversies about political correctness and affirmative action, and of academic debates over whether "identity" is best conceptualised as a stable essence or a mutable, contingent construct.

In the context of the many literary hoaxes and frauds of the 1990s, journalists have variously linked Mudrooroo, Roberta Sykes, Archie Weller, Leon Carmen ("Wanda Koolmatrie") and Streten Bozic ("B. Wongar") together as fakes.[58] Yet it is crucial to distinguish between the circumstances under which these individuals identified as Aboriginal. Mudrooroo, Weller and Sykes have not been able to establish Aboriginal ancestry, yet after suffering racial abuses on the basis of other people's assumption of their Aboriginality, they positioned themselves socially and politically as Aboriginal. By contrast, Bozic and Carmen voluntarily adopted false Aboriginal pen-names for their own respective purposes, knowing full well they had no Aboriginal ancestry.

According to Mudrooroo's elder sister, who researched the family's history, Mudrooroo's mother was white, and his paternal grandfather was probably of African-American descent.[59] Whether Mudrooroo ever believed he was Aboriginal is not entirely clear. His former wife asserted in 1996 that "his belief in his Aboriginality is sincere and life-long".[60] In 1997, however, Mudrooroo claimed that he was first "textualised" as Aboriginal in 1965 in Mary Durack's introduction to *Wild Cat Falling*, and that at the time he felt he "had to go along with" that official designation.[61] Irrespective of whether, or when, Mudrooroo came to believe he was Aboriginal, his older brother maintains: "If you were a coloured kid or an Aboriginal kid, you all sat in the same bench. These experiences make you a Nyoongah."[62]

Archie Weller bases his claim to Aboriginality on his memories of growing up with Aboriginal kids and sharing police persecution,[63] and on his belief that he and his paternal great-grandmother look Aboriginal.[64] Weller's efforts to trace his great-grandmother's history have so far proved inconclusive.[65] However, his brother maintains: "If you grew up in a West Australian country town and you think you are Aboriginal and people think you are Aboriginal, you bloody well are."[66] The Dumbartung Aboriginal Corporation have invited Weller to go through their protocols, presided over by Nyoongah elders, for establishing Aboriginal identity, but like Mudrooroo he has so far declined. Robert Eggington insists on the importance of the Dumbartung protocols to identify those who illegitimately use "resources earmarked for our community".[67]

Roberta Sykes too was presumed by others to be Aboriginal. In the first volume of her autobiography, *Snake Cradle* (1997), she discloses her uncertain paternity, but recalls that at school in Townsville she was called "boong", "black gin" and "Abo". At seventeen she was gang-raped by four white men, one of whom stood up at his trial and shouted, "What the hell – she's an Abo! She's just a fucking boong!"[68] Sykes has clearly suffered with Aboriginal people, and fought alongside them politically. Her long-term involvement in Aboriginal politics, often at considerable cost to herself, seems to have shielded her from much of the acrimonious media criticism levelled at Mudrooroo, and to a lesser extent at Weller.

Mudrooroo, Weller and Sykes are to be distinguished from Streten Bozic ("B. Wongar") and Leon Carmen ("Wanda Koolmatrie") who, while adopting Aboriginal pen-names, were never *involuntarily* interpellated as Aboriginal. Bozic, a Serbian who came to Australia in 1960, published several novels in Australia and overseas under the name "B. Wongar" before being unmasked by Robert Drewe in 1981.[69] While B. Wongar's identity is well known in Australian literary circles, he is presumed in Europe and America to be an Aboriginal writer,[70] and has sales numbering over a million copies worldwide.[71] Bozic maintains he does nothing wrong in writing as an Aboriginal. In the name of creative freedom, he asserts his right to write "stories about anything".[72] This freedom does not equate, however, to a right to write *as anyone*. As Ben Saul has argued, "Individual rights must always be balanced against collective ones: in this case, the right of indigenous communities to have some control (or degree of autonomy) over their cultural representation."[73] At the time Bozic assumed the Wongar persona, there was little glamour or financial reward to be gained from identifying as Aboriginal (and indeed the size of such benefits is often overestimated today). As a refugee, Bozic might be seen as epitomising the common non-Indigenous desire to indigenise oneself, or root oneself spiritually in a land in which one feels alien.

The most cynical appropriation of Aboriginal identity was perhaps that of Leon Carmen. In 1994, the Aboriginal publishing house, Magabala Books, published an autobiographical novel, *My Own Sweet Time*, ostensibly written by a young expatriate Aboriginal woman, Wanda Koolmatrie. The novel was shortlisted for the 1996 NSW Premier's Awards, and won the Dobbie Award for a first novel by a woman writer. When "Koolmatrie's" agent, John Bayley, offered Magabala a second novel manuscript in 1997, the publisher asked to meet the author. Bayley confessed that Wanda Koolmatrie did not exist and that the books had been written by a non-Aboriginal man, Leon Carmen.[74] Carmen and his agent justified this deception by arguing that in the current climate of political correctness and affirmative action, manuscripts by women and ethnic minority writers were far more likely to be accepted for publication than those of middle-aged white males.[75] Like Streten Bozic, Carmen asserted his right to individual creative freedom, claiming that "black people I've known aren't likely to get

excited" about his imposture.[76] Yet creative freedom does not extend
to claiming false authorial identities, or breaching the implicit contract
that autobiographic genres establish between writers and readers. And
Aboriginal people *did* get excited about Carmen's deception. Bundjalung
author Ruby Langford Ginibi called him a "bloodsucker",[77] and Anita
Heiss' poem, "Leon Carmen", labelled him "a liar, a fraud, an imposter"
who has "left a black mark on the soul of Aboriginal Literature".[78]

THE POLITICS OF READING

Aboriginal writers have achieved considerable success in recent years.
Aboriginal-authored texts have won major literary prizes. Publishers such as
Magabala Books, Fremantle Arts Centre Press, University of Queensland
Press, Allen & Unwin and Hyland House have healthy Aboriginal lists.
Aboriginal-authored publications are reviewed in major newspapers and
journals, and have been incorporated into school and university curricula.

Some have argued that mainstream interest in Aboriginal writing has been
won at too high a cost, and that Aboriginal writers must be wary of con-
ceding too readily to the dominant society's tastes and cultural values – a
difficult thing to avoid when Aboriginal people make up just two percent of
the potential national readership, and when the publishing industry is
dominated by non-Aboriginal people.[79] The politics of addressing mainstream audiences are highly ambivalent. On the one hand, when Aboriginal
writers attract the attention of mainstream audiences, they effectively hold
those readers in their power. If they are writing *about* the dominant society,
they are also asserting the power of the observing subject over the observed
object. On the other hand, Aboriginal writers are also subjecting themselves
to outside judgement, thus placing themselves within the audience's sphere
of influence. To compel mainstream readers to listen, for example, they may
find they have to use a language and a story form that their readers
understand and like. The danger for Aboriginal writers, then, is that they
jump out of the frying pan, only to land in the fire: they break out of the role
of the mute, named object, only to be confined to the role of the circumscribed speaking subject, writing once again "for the governor's pleasure".[80]

This power imbalance between Aboriginal writers and non-Aboriginal
consumers is certainly a cause for concern. To address the problem effectively, however, it is perhaps wise to look beyond the spectacular metaphor of one monolithic cultural block absorbing, crushing, or imprisoning
another. This metaphor leaves out of account the mutability and internal
heterogeneity of the relevant interest groups – namely, the Aboriginal literary
community, the national and international readership, and the publishing

industry that mediates between them. Occasionally, elements within these groups negotiate outcomes that genuinely satisfy all parties. They open up new sets of options, new paths forward that others may follow in their own attempts to work through, or around, potential conflicts of interest. Aboriginal manuscripts are indeed being reproduced, disseminated and interpreted in institutional settings dominated by non-Aboriginal people. Yet there is often some degree of play within and between institutions; and there are moments when the power of dominant societies and cultures can be deflected, annulled, or appropriated. Cracks and blind spots exist in most contemporary systems of cultural and financial domination. The trick is to find them, form alliances in them, and negotiate ways forward through them towards a more just and equitable future. Some Aboriginal writers, for instance, have harnessed market forces to their own political agendas; others are using non-commercial publishing channels to reflect critically on their own cultural subordination. Some publishing houses are recruiting Aboriginal editors and advisors in an effort to proceed in a culturally sensitive and respectful manner. And some non-Aboriginal readers are trying to unlearn old habits, assumptions and values so that, eventually, they might learn to read, not as "governors who must be pleased", but as receptive, well-informed listeners in an equitable cross-cultural dialogue.

NOTES

1 A note on terminology: Indigenous Australians use a range of terms to refer to themselves. Many call themselves "Aboriginal people", especially when invoking their shared history and national political solidarity. Others object to the term "Aboriginal" because (a) it was imposed on them by the British, an invading foreign power, (b) it obscures the multiplicity and diversity of Indigenous Australian societies and cultures, and (c) it fails to distinguish the Indigenous peoples of Australia from those of other parts of the world. Many prefer to identify themselves by their language group, for example, Bundjalung, Wiradjuri, Bidjara, Larrakia or Arrernte. Regional terms are also used, for example, Koori (in New South Wales and Victoria), Murri (in Queensland), Nunga (in South Australia), Pallawah (in Tasmania) and Nyoongah (in Western Australia). Non-Aboriginal people may be called "whites", "whitefellas", or "gubba", "watjela", "migloo" and "balanda". In this chapter, I use the terms "Aboriginal people" or "Indigenous Australians" when speaking generally. Regional and language-group names are used when the focus is more specific. If this practice causes offence, I sincerely apologise, and welcome comment. To refer to non-Aboriginal people, I use "non-Aboriginal", "white", or "Anglo-Celtic", depending on the context and whose point of view is implicitly being invoked.

2 Peter Read in Coral Edwards and Peter Read, eds, *The Lost Children* (Sydney: Doubleday, 1989), p. xii.

3 Different views as to what counts as writing can be found in Walter J. Ong, *Orality and Literary: The Technologizing of the Word* (London: Methuen,

1982); Nancy D. Munn, *Warlpiri Iconography: Graphic Representation and Cultural Symbolism in a Central Australian Society* (Ithaca, NY: Cornell University Press, 1973); and Carol Cooper, "Traditional Visual Culture in South-East Australia" in Andrew Sayers, *Aboriginal Artists of the Nineteenth Century* (Melbourne: Oxford University Press, 1994), pp. 91–109.

4 See Eric Michaels, *Bad Aboriginal Art: Tradition, Media and Technological Horizons* (Minneapolis: University of Minnesota Press, 1994).

5 In 1953, Henrietta Drake-Brockman selected and edited stories from Catherine Langloh Parker's 1896 and 1898 volumes, and published them as *Australian Legendary Tales*, illustrated by Elizabeth Durack. The book won the 1954 Children's Book of the Year Award.

6 Mudrooroo has adopted both positions on this question. See Colin Johnson [Mudrooroo], "White Forms, Aboriginal Content", in Jack Davis and Bob Hodge, eds, *Aboriginal Writing Today* (Canberra: AIAS, 1985), pp. 21–33; and Mudrooroo, *Milli Milli Wangka: The Indigenous Literature of Australia* (Melbourne: Hyland House, 1997), pp. 22–32.

7 Reproduced in Isabel McBryde, *Guests of the Governor – Aboriginal Residents of Government House* (Sydney: Friends of the First Government House Site, 1989), p. 25.

8 John Harris, *One Blood: 200 Years of Aboriginal Encounter with Christianity* (Oxford: Lion, 1990), p. 53.

9 Harris, *One Blood*, p. 367.

10 E.S. Parker, Report 1 January 1842 to 31 August 1843, quoted in M.F. Christie, *Aborigines in Colonial Victoria 1835–86* (Sydney: Sydney University Press, 1979), p. 126.

11 "Prospectus", 10 September 1836, quoted in Michael Rose, ed., *For the Record: 160 Years of Aboriginal Print Journalism* (Sydney: Allen & Unwin, 1996), p. 3.

12 See Diane Barwick in Laura E. Barwick and Richard E. Barwick, eds, *Rebellion at Coranderrk* (Canberra: Aboriginal History Inc., 1998), p. 9.

13 Barwick, *Rebellion*, p. 9.

14 Australian Archives, Victorian Office, Series B 313/1, Item 122.

15 Australian Archives, Victorian Office, Series B 313/1, Item 27.

16 Australian Archives, Victorian Office, Series B 313/1, Item 221.

17 Maggie Mobourne to D.N. McLeod, 27 February 1900, facsimile reproduction in Jan Critchett, *Untold Stories: Memories and Lives of Victorian Kooris* (Melbourne: Melbourne University Press, 1998), p. 242.

18 Cf. M.F. Christie, "Aboriginal Literacy and Power: An Historical Case Study", *Australian Journal of Adult and Communication Education* 30.2 (July 1990), pp. 116–21.

19 Quoted in Rose, ed., *For the Record*, p. 30.

20 William Ferguson, "Nanya", in Jack Davis *et al.*, eds, *Paperbark: A Collection of Black Australian Writings* (St Lucia: University of Queensland Press, 1990), pp. 175–96; Simon During, "Broaching Fiction: A Short Theoretical Appreciation of William Ferguson's *Nanya*", *Cultural Studies* 9.1 (1995), pp. 161–68.

21 Ferguson, "Nanya", p. 179.

22 See John Beston, "David Unaipon: The First Aboriginal Writer (1873–1967)", *Southerly* 3 (1979), pp. 334–50.

23 David Unaipon, *Native Legends* (Adelaide: Hunkin, Ellis and King, n.d. [c.1929]).
24 David Unaipon, "An Aboriginal Pleads for His Race", in *Australian Aborigines, Photographs of Natives and Address* (Adelaide, c.1928).
25 David Unaipon, *My Life Story* (Adelaide: Aborigines' Friends' Assocation, n.d. [c.1951]).
26 David Unaipon, "Narroondarie's Wives", in Davis *et al.*, eds, *Paperbark*, pp. 19–32.
27 David Unaipon, in Davis *et al.*, eds, *Paperbark*, pp. 23–4.
28 During the later 1980s and early 1990s, Colin Johnson made a series of name changes, first to Mudrooroo Narogin, then to Mudrooroo Nyoongah, and finally to Mudrooroo.
29 For further discussion of the question of Aboriginal identity in relation to Mudrooroo and other writers, see the section headed "Contested identities" later in this chapter.
30 See, for example, Victoria Laurie, "Identity Crisis", *Australian Magazine*, 20–21 July 1996, pp. 28–32; Patsy Millett, "Identity Parade", *Bulletin*, 27 August 1996, pp. 74–5.
31 Oodgeroo, "The Past", in Kevin Gilbert, ed., *Inside Black Australia* (Melbourne: Penguin, 1988), p. 99.
32 Mudrooroo Narogin, *Writing From the Fringe* (Melbourne: Hyland House, 1990), p. 148.
33 See for example, Anon., Review of *We Are Going, Australian Book Review* (May 1964), p. 143; Andrew Taylor, Review of *The Dawn is at Hand, Overland* 36 (May 1967), p. 44.
34 Eva Rask Knudsen, "From Kath Walker to Oodgeroo Noonuccal? Ambiguity and Assurance in *My People*", in Adam Shoemaker, ed., *Oodgeroo: A Tribute* (St Lucia: University of Queensland Press, 1994), p. 111.
35 Audre Lord, *Sister Outsider* (New York: Crossing Press, 1984), p. 112.
36 Bob Hodge, "Poetry and Politics in Oodgeroo: Transcending the Difference", in Adam Shoemaker, ed., *Oodgeroo*, p. 68.
37 Hodge, "Poetry and Politics" in Shoemaker, ed., *Oodgeroo*, p. 75.
38 Kevin Gilbert, "The New True Anthem", in Gilbert, ed., *Inside Black Australia*, pp. 197–8.
39 Graham Dixon, *Holocaust Island* (St Lucia: University of Queensland Press, 1990); Robert Walker, *Up Mate, Not Down!: Thoughts From a Prison Cell* (Adelaide, 1987); Errol West, "There is no one to teach me the songs", "Misty mountains tell me", "Sitting, wondering, Do I have a place here?"; Eva Johnson, "A Letter to My Mother"; Mary Duroux, "Dirge for a Hidden Art", and "Lament for A Dialect", in Gilbert, ed., *Inside Black Australia*; Lionel Fogarty, *Kargun* (Coominya, Qld.: C. Buchanan, 1980), *Yoogum Yoogum* (Melbourne: Penguin, 1982), *Murrie Coo-ee* (Spring Hill: C. Buchanan, 1983), *Kudjela* (Spring Hill: C. Buchanan, 1983), *Ngutji* (Spring Hill: C. Buchanan, 1984), *Jagera* (Coominya: C. Buchanan, 1989), *New and Selected Poems: Munaldjali, Mutuerjaraera* (Melbourne: Hyland House, 1995).
40 "Writers Have Their Say", *Koori Mail* 189 (18 November 1998), p. 15. My thanks to Ruby Langford Ginibi for bringing this report to my attention.

41 Marjorie Bil Bil, *It Just Lies There From the Beginning: Aboriginal Poems and Stories from the Top End* (Alice Springs: IAD Press, 1995).

42 Eva Johnson, "A Letter to My Mother", in Gilbert, ed., *Inside Black Australia*, pp. 24–5.

43 Lionel Fogarty, "Tired of Writing" [1982], in *New and Selected Poems*, p. 109.

44 Mudrooroo refers to Fogarty's "anti-language" in his introduction to Fogarty's *New and Selected Poems*; see also also Bob Hodge and Vijay Mishra, *Dark Side of the Dream* (Sydney: Allen & Unwin, 1990), pp. 205–208.

45 "Little Murri: Be a Murri before an Australian", in *New and Selected Poems*, pp. 42–3.

46 In *New and Selected Poems*, p. 18.

47 In *New and Selected Poems*, p. 38. Thanks to Lionel Fogarty and Hyland House for permission to reproduce this extract from "Weather Comes".

48 Kim Scott has published in various literary journals and anthologies; Lisa Bellear, *Dreaming in Urban Areas* (St Lucia: University of Queensland Press, 1996): Kerry Reed-Gilbert, *Black Woman Black Life* (Kent Town, S.A.: Wakefield Press, 1996); Anita Heiss, *Token Koori* (Sydney: Curringa Communications, 1998).

49 Dick Roughsey, *Moon and Rainbow* (Sydney: A.H. & A.W. Reed, 1971); Charles Perkins, *A Bastard Like Me* (Sydney: Ure Smith, 1975); Jack Davis, *A Boy's Life* (Broome: Magabala Books, 1991); Joe McGinness, *Son of Alyandabu* (St Lucia: University of Queensland Press, 1991); Jack Bohemia and Bill McGregor, *Nyibayarri, Kimberley Tracker* (Canberra: Aboriginal Studies Press, 1995); *Wandjuk Marika: Life Story*, as told to Jennifer Isaacs (St Lucia: University of Queensland Press, 1995); Boori Pryor, *Maybe Tomorrow* (Melbourne: Penguin, 1998); Warrigal Anderson, *Warrigal's Way* (St Lucia: University of Queensland Press, 1996); and Wayne King, *Black Hours* (Sydney: Angus & Robertson, 1996).

50 Anne Brewster, *Literary Formations* (Melbourne: Melbourne University Press, 1995), p. 41.

51 A range of issues and patterns evident in non-Western women's life-writing is explored in Sidonie Smith and Julia Watson, eds, *De-Colonizing the Subject: the Politics of Gender in Women's Autobiography* (Minneapolis: University of Minnesota Press, 1992); see also Anne Brewster, *Aboriginal Women's Autobiography* (Sydney: Sydney University Press, 1996).

52 See Mudrooroo, *Milli Milli Wangka*, pp. 184–5.

53 From mid-1995 to mid-1997 I worked in this capacity with Ruby Langford Ginibi on *Haunted by the Past* (Sydney: Allen & Unwin, 1999).

54 See the Author's Note in *True Country* (Fremantle: Fremantle Arts Centre Press, 1993).

55 See Stephen Slemon, "Magic Realism as Post-Colonial Discourse", *Canadian Literature* 116 (Spring 1988), pp. 9–23; Bill Ashcroft, Gareth Griffiths and Helen Tiffin, *The Empire Writes Back* (London & New York: Routledge, 1989), pp. 149–50.

56 See front cover flap and Introduction, *The Aboriginal Children's History of Australia* (Adelaide: Rigby, 1977).

57 *The Whalers* is based on one of many stories Percy Mumbulla told to Roland Robinson in the 1940s and 1950s.

58 See for example, Helen Daniel, "Double Cover", *Age*, 31 August 1996, p. 9; Bill Perrett, "Questions of Identity", *Sunday Age*, 17 August 1997, p. 8; Peter Craven, "To be young, gifted and black", *Australian*, 16 March 1997, p. 38; Richard Guilliatt, "Black, white & grey all over", *Sydney Morning Herald*, 11 April 1997, p. 13; Debra Jopson, "Now a black writer confesses: I can't prove that I'm Aboriginal", *Sydney Morning Herald*, 24 April 1997, p. 1. For a comprehensive analysis of the media debate on Aboriginal literary "frauds", see Ben Saul, "Aboriginality and the Politics of Panic", BA Hons Thesis, University of Sydney, 1999. My thanks to Ben Saul for permission to draw on his research in the writing of this section.

59 Victoria Laurie, "Identity Crisis", *Australian Magazine*, 20–21 July 1996, p. 29.

60 Thomas Johnson, quoted in Roger Martin and Shaun Anthony, "Family adds fuel to literary fire", *West Australian*, 27 July 1996, p. 15.

61 Mudrooroo, "Tell Them You're Indian", in Gillian Cowlishaw and Barry Morris, eds, *Race Matters: Indigenous Australians and "Our" Society* (Canberra: Aboriginal Studies Press, 1997), pp. 262–3.

62 Quoted in Terry O'Connor, "A question of race", *Courier-Mail*, 28 March 1998, p. 24.

63 *In Search of Archie*, ABC TV, 1998.

64 Debra Jopson, "Now a black writer confesses …", *Sydney Morning Herald*, 24 April 1997, p. 1.

65 *In Search of Archie*, ABC TV, 1998.

66 Debra Jopson, "Writer's black ancestry stranger than fiction", *Sydney Morning Herald*, 24 April 1997, p. 6.

67 Robert Eggington, *In Search of Archie*, ABC TV, 1998.

68 Roberta Sykes, *Snake Cradle* (Sydney: Allen & Unwin, 1997), p. 320.

69 Robert Drewe, "Solved: The Great B. Wongar Mystery", *Bulletin Literary Supplement*, 21 April 1981.

70 Ben Saul, "Aboriginality", p. 52.

71 *A Double Life*, SBS TV, 1997.

72 Streten Bozic, in Ray Willbanks, *Speaking Volumes – Australian Writers and Their Work* (Melbourne: Penguin, 1992), p. 208.

73 Ben Saul, "Aboriginality", p. 55.

74 Andrew Stevenson and Ava Hubble, "Award-winning Aboriginal author outs 'herself' as white male", *Courier-Mail*, 13 March 1997, p. 1.

75 Andrew Stevenson and Ava Hubble, "A hoax called Wanda", *Advertiser*, 13 March 1997, p. 1.

76 Quoted in Stevenson and Hubble, "A hoax called Wanda", p. 1.

77 Quoted in Debra Jopson, "Uproar over hoax Aboriginal Writer", *Sydney Morning Herald*, 14 March 1997, p. 3.

78 Anita Heiss, "Leon Carmen", *Australian Short Stories* 60 (1997), p. 32.

79 See Bruce McGuinness and Denis Walker, "The Politics of Aboriginal Literature", in Davis and Hodge, eds, *Aboriginal Writing Today*, pp. 43–54.

80 See Penny van Toorn, "Discourse/Patron Discourse: How Minority Texts Command Attention from Majority Audiences", *SPAN* 30 (April 1990), pp. 102–115; and Mudrooroo Narogin, *Doin Wildcat* (Melbourne: Hyland House, 1988).

2

ELIZABETH WEBBY

Colonial writers and readers

The English colonisation of Australia from 1788 coincided with a vast increase within the parent culture of both general literacy and the ready availability of reading matter. By the end of the nineteenth century, almost all of the white adult population of Australia could read and write, with the Australian colonies making up one of the major overseas markets for English publishers. By 1900, too, Australian readers were beginning to develop something of a taste for writing about Australia and about themselves. Though the local publishing industry was still printing very few books, the many newspapers and magazines, which had flourished since the 1860s in particular, regularly serialised novels by Australian authors, as well as printing poems, short stories and essays. Through the pages of the Sydney *Bulletin*, established in 1880 to rapidly become Australia's most popular magazine, writers like Banjo Paterson and Henry Lawson became well known. When, in the mid-1890s, volumes of their poems and stories were issued by the fledgling publishing house of Angus & Robertson, they sold in their thousands. Certain works of the earlier novelists Marcus Clarke and Rolf Boldrewood, which had also been serialised locally before achieving book publication in Britain, remained popular thanks to their adaptation for the stage. But for much of the nineteenth century, and indeed afterwards, Australian readers were mainly interested in books by English authors and Australian authors were largely dependent on the English publishing industry. This chapter will trace some of the major changes in what people read and wrote in Australia from 1788 to 1901, with a particular focus on non-fiction, fiction, poetry and writing for children.

REPRESENTING A NEW WORLD

Those who arrived in Sydney Cove in 1788 were confronted with a land-scape, fauna and flora, as well as an Indigenous population, quite unlike any they had previously experienced. Some of these novel creatures, such as the

black swan, seemed quite literally to belong with notions of Australia as the
Antipodes, the "upside-down country", which, in the words of the early
poet Barron Field,

> ... would seem an after-birth,
> Not conceiv'd in the beginning
> (For GOD bless'd His work at first,
> And saw that it was good),
> But emerg'd at the first sinning,
> When the ground was therefore curst;[1]

Even things that looked more familiar, or homely, could on closer inspection
turn out to be quite the reverse. Hence the early establishment of the trope
of Australia as the disappointing or deceptive land. This is found, for
example, in the accounts of early settlement by writers otherwise as different
as George Worgan, a naval surgeon on the First Fleet, and Thomas Watling,
a convict artist who arrived in 1791.[2]

From the beginning it was clear that there would be a ready market in
England for accounts of New South Wales, or Botany Bay as it was still
generally called, even though the settlers had soon moved from that
location, after discovering that James Cook's account of it had been too
glowing.[3] Worgan refers to the journals being kept by some of his fellow
officers, David Collins and Watkin Tench, implying a certain rivalry in their
efforts to be the first to describe the new country and its inhabitants for
English readers. Tench won and, both then and subsequently, his accounts
have also been the clear winner with readers. His *Narrative of the Expedition to Botany Bay* (1789) and *A Complete Account of the Settlement
at Port Jackson in New South Wales* (1793) were the first international
Australian bestsellers, and as recently as 1996 a version of Tench's journals
edited by the natural history writer Tim Flannery under the title *1788* also
sold very well, this time in Australia. Besides a great eye for detail and a
ready curiosity and sympathy, Tench has a lively and relatively modern
descriptive style, which helps to ensure his continued appeal to readers.

During the first decades of the nineteenth century, as more and more of
the new land was explored, accounts of expeditions into the interior became
the next source of interest for readers, in Australia as well as Britain. As
Oxley, Sturt, Leichhardt, Mitchell and others returned from successful, or
more often unsuccessful, attempts to find a supposed great inland sea or
cross the continent in one direction or another, they wrote up their journals
for publication in London. The styles of their accounts were as varied as
their journeys, influenced by their different educational, or national, backgrounds. But all were eagerly read, in Australia in particular by those who

wished to follow in the explorers' tracks in search of pastures new. By the 1830s the convict-built roads had sufficiently penetrated the wilderness to allow scope for the non-professional traveller. Captain William Dumaresq, writing about his trip over the Blue Mountains for the Sydney newspaper the *Australian* in 1827, noted that, "when we come to think of the interior, we know no more of it than we do of the moon".⁴

By the 1840s women were also beginning to supply accounts of life in Australia for the British market; one of the earliest, and liveliest, was Louisa Ann Meredith, who had been a published author in England before marrying and travelling to Australia. Her *Notes and Sketches of New South Wales, During a Residence in that Colony from 1839 to 1844* was published in London in 1844. Meredith's forthright criticisms of the social pretension and lack of real culture she found in Sydney assured her work a less than joyous reception there, though it went through several editions in Britain.

After transportation of convicts to New South Wales ceased in the early 1840s, there was a growing need to boost its attractions to potential English immigrants. As well as numerous emigrant handbooks, several novels were published, seen by a later critic as being little better than "books of travel in disguise".⁵ Charles Rowcroft's *Tales of the Colonies* (1843) was, however, extremely popular in its day and contains much lively writing as well as helpful hints to prospective colonists. Its portrait of the English settler Crab, forever complaining about the ways in which the new land does not measure up, forever threatening to return home, but never actually leaving, introduces one of the most common nineteenth-century Australian comic types, the unhappy new chum. In the twentieth century, Crab was to reappear as the "whingeing Pom", the English migrant for whom Bondi Beach is not a patch on Blackpool.

Alexander Harris' *The Emigrant Family* (1849) attempted to disguise its cautionary tale of how not to manage a colonial station within a fairly conventional plot of villainous overseers, marauding Aborigines and damsels in distress. Its unusual choice of a Negro as villain perhaps allowed for some justification of the racial prejudice so clearly being exercised against the original owners of the land. Harris was also one of the first to introduce the "native", or white Australian-born, bushman hero in Reuben Kable and his currency lass sister Mary. It was Harris' supposedly autobiographical *Settlers and Convicts* (1847), however, that most caught the attention of those historians of the 1950s concerned with establishing a nationalist Australian tradition and identity. Harris' assumption of a working-class persona and his praise of bush mateship appeared to strongly endorse the "Australian" legend; later research has shown that Harris was much better educated than he pretended.⁶ To a large extent, *Settlers and*

Convicts was fiction, an early endorsement of Australia as the "working-man's paradise".

The discovery of gold in New South Wales and Victoria at mid-century led to a renewed interest in Australia from publishers, readers and writers. Among those attracted to Australia by the gold were several English writers, including the poet "Orion" Horne, and William Howitt, whose *Land, Labour and Gold; or, Two Years in Victoria* (1855) remains one of the most readable accounts of this tumultuous period. In observing the often out-rageous behaviour of lucky diggers, as they lit their pipes with banknotes and made hasty marriages, Howitt reinforced the idea of Australia as a country of the new "Hairystocracy", where old class restrictions were being broken down. For ladies, this often translated into an extreme difficulty in obtaining servants, resulting in their having to do more domestically than merely arranging the flowers and the menus, and hence to later doubts about whether Australian women really deserved to be called "ladies".

In the later decades of the century, once the excitement of gold had died down, travellers were forced to go further afield in search of exotic subject matter for their readers in Europe. Explorers and others began to venture into central and northern Australia, and the notion of the "real" Outback, or the "Never Never", was introduced into Australian literature. The ill-fated Burke and Wills expedition of the early 1860s provided much material for history painters, sculptors and poets, not to mention later historians, if no memorable writing of its own. Ernest Giles, however, undertook some further epic journeys during the 1870s and eventually succeeded in crossing the central desert westwards from South Australia, as described in *Australia Twice Traversed* (1889), one of the late classics of Australian exploration.

In his 1957 novel *Voss*, Patrick White contrasts and compares the physical journeys of his male explorers with the mental travelling of Laura, who remains in Sydney. A similar contrast can be experienced if one turns from the exploration accounts of Giles and others to the private letters and diaries kept by those, mainly women, who often did not travel a great deal within Australia, though had certainly undergone adventures to get there, and continued to experience novelties unknown to their English correspondents. While some of this material had long been known and used by historians, and some had been published as far back as the 1930s, the growing interest in women's writing since the 1980s has resulted in many more letters and diaries being made available to readers and so attracting scholarly and critical attention.[7] A significant recent publication is Lucy Frost's edition of *The Journal of Annie Baxter Dawbin, 1858–1868* (St Lucia: University of Queensland Press, 1998). This makes available some of the material in the thirty-two notebooks used by Annie Baxter Dawbin to record her Australian experiences between 1834, when she arrived in Tasmania as the young bride of an army officer, and 1868, when she travelled to New Zealand with her second husband. In between she had lived on stations in the New England region of New South Wales and in Victoria, as well as spending time in Melbourne, everywhere making good use of her sharp eyes and even sharper wit. Other important nineteenth-century letter writers and diarists include G.T.W.B. Boyes, Rachel Henning, Louisa Clifton, Elizabeth Macarthur and Annabella Boswell.[8]

AUSTRALIAN READERS: BOOKS, MAGAZINES AND NEWSPAPERS

While some books came to Australia with the First Fleet, they remained in fairly short supply until regular importations began in the 1820s. As early as February 1828, however, one of several short-lived local magazines, the *Austral-Asiatic Review*, was enthusing, "The British nation is characteristic-ally designated '*a reading People*'; and wherever they spread themselves – however distant from their native land circumstances may carry them – their native attribute remains rather increased than diminished." During the first half of the century Sir Walter Scott was the literary author whose works were most advertised as available in Australia, followed by Shakespeare and Byron. Around fifty copies of works by Scott were advertised for sale in Australia during the 1820s, as compared with 140 during the 1830s, and 1,600 in the 1840s. The enormous increase between the last two decades reflects not only the substantial increases in Australia's white population but the improvements in printing technology which helped make books cheaper as the century progressed.

By mid-century it was possible to buy the latest English releases only four to six months after they had appeared in London and at not much greater prices. By the end of the century, with copyright acts finally in place, Australian readers formed a very significant source of income for British publishers. "Colonial editions", for sale only in Britain's overseas colonies, allowed Australian booksellers to obtain popular British books at heavy discounts. While this no doubt kept local readers happy, Australian writers and publishers were less advantaged. Royalties on cheap colonial editions were, of course, considerably reduced, while local publishers found it impos-sible to compete with such cheap imported books. Hence most nineteenth-century Australian literary works continued to be published in Britain; local publication usually meant publication at the author's expense or, at best, by obtaining subscriptions from friends and relatives, as happened with Charles Tompson's collection of youthful poems, *Wild Notes from the Lyre of a Native Minstrel*, published in Sydney in 1826.

From early on, writers complained of other problems, such as Australian readers' prejudice against local productions. On 21 January 1828, for example, a correspondent using the pseudonym "Candid" wrote to the editor of the Sydney newspaper the *Monitor* about the lack of response to another magazine, the *South-Asian Register*: "The South-Asian is really a *good work*; and people have only to get rid of the vulgar local prejudice that, because written at Botany Bay it must by consequence be bad – they have only to get rid of this prejudice, to believe so." While this prejudice was a long time dying, and may still not have completely disappeared, commercial interests ensured that local newspapers flourished from almost the beginning of settlement. And, if it was their columns of advertisements that ensured these papers' success, almost from the beginning their pages were also open to local writers. Initially these were chiefly poets and essayists, but as the century wore on short story writers and novelists were also published. After the gold rushes had brought vast increases in population, especially to Melbourne, it also became possible for some local magazines, mostly closely modelled on popular English ones, to gain a foothold. *Melbourne Punch* (1855–1929), the most successful of numerous attempts to copy this London institution, gave employment to many local comic writers and poets, such as Henry Kendall, as well as to cartoonists. The *Australian Journal* (1865–1962), modelled on the *London Journal*, provided forty pages of small print for sixpence, concentrating on fiction by local as well as English and American authors. While best known today as the original home of Marcus Clarke's classic novel of the convict system, *His Natural Life*, serialised from 1870–72, many women writers also appeared in the *Australian Journal*. One of the most significant and prolific of them was Mary Helena Fortune, whose detective stories were a regular feature of the *Australian Journal* for over forty years. No doubt they would have proved equally popular with English readers but Fortune appears not to have had the contacts then essential if an Australian author was to achieve publication in Britain.

As already mentioned, the first locally published Australian bestseller was Banjo Paterson's *The Man from Snowy River* (1895) which sold ten thousand copies in the first year. Paterson, Henry Lawson, Steele Rudd, Edward Dyson, Price Warung and others who had established their names via the columns of the *Bulletin*, had now a substantial local readership, enabling the Sydney firm of Angus & Robertson to publish some of them successfully in book form. Most novels, however, continued to appear from British firms; Miles Franklin's *My Brilliant Career* (1901) was twice rejected by Angus & Robertson before being published in Edinburgh by Blackwoods. Franklin was able to enlist the help of Henry Lawson, who was going to London to further his career, to find a publisher, though at the cost of numerous changes to her manuscript. Like many Australian writers before and since, her work was adapted to the supposed demands and prejudices of non-Australian readers, who were assumed to form the bulk of its audience. Ironically, in Franklin's case more copies of *My Brilliant Career* were sold in Australia than in Britain; as these were colonial editions, however, her royalty cheque was correspondingly smaller.

SOME EARLY POETS

Any sort of royalty cheque would have been welcome to Australian poets, who more often found themselves paying for the publication of their poems, rather than gaining financially from them. Hence, while a great deal of verse appeared in the pages of nineteenth-century Australian newspapers and magazines, few of these writers were able to achieve publication in a more substantial form. The first volume of poems to be printed in Australia, Barron Field's very slender *First Fruits of Australian Poetry* (1819), was published at his own expense and circulated only to friends, who included Wordsworth and Charles Lamb. The mock-heroic title was part of the gentlemanly joke – as were the two poems on such unlikely topics as "The Kangaroo" and "Botany Bay Flowers". Some hostile local readers, however, refused to laugh; the author of "Review of Judge Field's Poetry", published in the *Sydney Gazette* on 25 November 1826, was especially annoyed by Field's playful claim to be the first "Austral harmonist". To him, this title belonged to Michael Massey Robinson, "the poet-laureate under Macquarie's Administration, a gentleman who has really produced a number of truly poetical pieces". Robinson was an educated ex-convict who, like others of his class, was taken under the wing of Governor Macquarie. His official paeans to the past and present glories of Great Britain and the future greatness of Australia, not to mention the goodness of his patron, were delivered as part of the celebrations of the King's and Queen's birthdays each year. They were as lacking in intentional humour as Field's poems were in seriousness, and are now mainly of historical interest as part of Macquarie's attempt to create a more "civilised" Sydney.

Like the review which praised them, Robinson's poems had originally appeared in the pages of the *Sydney Gazette*, as well as being issued separately by its printer, George Howe, presumably for distribution as part of the royal birthday celebrations. Since 1804, some original poetry had been published in the *Gazette*, which first appeared on 5 March 1803, and nearly all later Australian newspapers followed this tradition, often featuring a "Poet's Corner". While most of the verses published in newspapers and in the usually short-lived literary magazines were no better than one might expect, and dealt with such poetic staples as love and death, some do give amusing glimpses of colonial life not often to be found elsewhere. Even before the beginnings of newspaper publication, there had been a tendency to use verse as a means of exposing or satirising perceived abuses of power by local officials. Manuscript verses, called "pipes" because they were apparently rolled up and left in various conspicuous places around the town, are known from the late eighteenth century.[9] Once alternative, non-government controlled newspapers began to appear in the 1820s, they provided a ready home for similar satires against the governor and others. One of the most prolific, and outspoken, writers of this type of political satire was Laurence Halloran, another ex-convict, who died in 1831, apparently in the midst of writing "a violent piece of poetry against the Governor".[10]

None of Halloran's published satires, however, dealt with his experiences as a convict. Though there are many extant ballads and other verses about convicts and the Australian convict system, some of which have circulated widely since the folk music revival of the 1950s and 1960s, very few of these were actually written by convicts. One of the best known, "Botany Bay", which begins "Farewell to Old England for ever" and has a rousing chorus of "too-ral, li-addities", was not even written until 1885, although it was based on an earlier broadside ballad, "Justices and Old Bailey".[11] Broadside ballads, so called because they were sold as individual sheets, printed on one side only, were a highly popular genre in the eighteenth and early nineteenth centuries. Hundreds were printed in London, Dublin and other British towns and many of these would have circulated in Australia during the convict period, though none seems to have been printed here.[12] Some poems on convict themes were published in early Australian newspapers though again most of them would not have been written by convicts. The moving "The Exile of Erin, on the Plains of Emu", for example, first published in the *Sydney Gazette* in 1826, was the work of the Rev. John McGarvie, a Scottish clergyman.[13]

One convict who did write ballads and satires about the convict system was Francis MacNamara, also known as "Frank the Poet".[14] While one poem by him was published in the *Sydney Gazette* in 1840, most of his work remained in manuscript until fairly recently. Some of the better-known and more stirring convict ballads, such as "Moreton Bay" and "Jim Jones at Botany Bay", have been attributed to MacNamara, though there is no firm evidence for this. His chief work is not a ballad but a long satirical poem in rhyming couplets, "The Convict's Tour to Hell". Here the persona, called Frank, gets his revenge on all of those who had persecuted him in life by consigning them, literally, to the Devil:

Who is that Sir in yonder blaze
Who on fire and brimstone seems to graze?
'Tis Captain Logan of Moreton Bay
And Williams who was killed the other day
He was overseer at Grosse Farm
And done poor prisoners no little harm
Cook who discovered New South Wales
And he that first invented gaols
Are both tied to a fiery stake
Which stands in yonder boiling lake.

Frank himself, however, is invited to join colleagues such as the bushranger Jack Donohue in Heaven, before finally awakening to find "'twas but a dream".[15]

CHARLES HARPUR

The most significant nineteenth-century Australian poet, Charles Harpur, the son of Irish convicts, was also an accomplished writer of satirical poetry, though neither in his own time nor today has that formed a substantial part of his reputation. Much of his satirical verse appeared only in newspapers, often anonymously, or remained unpublished. Harpur clearly did not intend to include it in the material he obsessively rewrote and copied in the hope that he would finally achieve book publication in Britain. But his satirical verse makes up an important part of Harpur's output, showing his versatility as a poet as well as his continued commitment to radical causes.

At almost the opposite pole from his often crude and hard-hitting satirical poems are Harpur's love poems, especially the series of sonnets initially addressed to "Rosa", in reality to Mary Doyle whom Harpur was to court from 1842 until her family eventually agreed to their marriage in 1850. (Penniless poets have never been particularly desirable sons-in-law!) As with most of Harpur's other significant poems, his inability to publish these sonnets in any more lasting form than the pages of newspapers resulted in much rewriting and revising. Ironically, the volume that finally appeared in 1883, at the instigation of his widow, many years after Harpur's death, was heavily and poorly edited by another hand. Part of the subsequent neglect of Harpur's poetry can be attributed to his work being known only in this very corrupt form until after World War II. In 1948 C.W. Salier published a small collection of the Rosa sonnets, and in 1963 the poet Judith Wright published the first study of his work.[16]

Harpur is now securely established as Australia's leading nineteenth-century poet. In part this is because of the great variety of different styles in which he worked – he wrote long epic poems on Biblical and classical topics, such as "The Witch of Hebron", in addition to work discussed here. He was, also, however, the first writer to attempt to deal seriously with local realities, producing tragedies and epics at a time when it was generally assumed that Australian material was unsuitable for works in the higher literary genres. Others who wrote tragedies in Sydney in the 1830s and 1840s – and there were more than one might have expected – set them in ancient Rome or at least in old England. In 1835, Harpur surprised the editor of the *Sydney Monitor* newspaper by turning up with a blank verse tragedy called "The Tragedy of Donohoe". Though Edward Smith Hall was regarded as a radical, and had spent time in prison for printing anti-government critiques, even he could not accept Jack Donohue, a local bushranger also celebrated in the ballad "The Wild Colonial Boy", as a tragic hero. In later revisions, Harpur sensibly made his protagonist a generic rather than a specific bushranger.[17]

Harpur's two best-known poems are "A Midsummer Noon in the Australian Forest" and "The Creek of the Four Graves". The shortness of the former, along with its capturing of a typically Australian scene – the hush that falls over the bush in the middle of a very hot day – made it a standard anthology piece, even in its corrupt state. "The Creek of the Four Graves", extensively rewritten by Harpur in ways which clearly demonstrate his wish to emphasise its epic qualities, tells a common enough tale of a pioneer and some of his men going out "to seek / New streams and wilder pastures", only to be attacked, and most killed, by Aborigines. Egremont, the master, survives by hiding in a convenient hole in a creek bank; the Aborigines attribute his disappearance to some legend of their own about the creek. It, however, is not of interest to the poet; what he depicts is the creation of a European Australian legend, as signified by the men's graves now giving a name to the formerly nameless (to Europeans) creek. Harpur's poem therefore shows the way in which the Australian landscape was possessed imaginatively as well as materially, with "the grave in the bush" remaining a potent image for many later writers and artists.[18]

LATER POETS

A further significance of Charles Harpur was his influence on a later poet, Henry Kendall, who, together with Adam Lindsay Gordon, was once regarded as Australia's pioneer poet. Kendall was, in his turn, influential on another important later poet, Christopher Brennan. Just as Harpur had shown Kendall that it was possible to be a poet in Australia, and that it was even possible to write serious poems, as well as ballads and comic verse, on local subjects, so reading some of Kendall's poems performed the same service for Brennan.[19] Kendall was for many years known mainly for his lyrical celebrations of the Australian bush, his more mellifluous lines appealing more strongly to the late nineteenth-century ear than Harpur's often craggier ones. "Bell Birds", a tribute to this distinctive bush singer, was learnt by heart by generations of Australian schoolchildren, though largely forgotten today. Like Harpur, Kendall also wrote a great deal of satirical verse, and prose, as he struggled to earn a living from journalism. He also attempted longer poems on non-Australian topics, as these were at the time seen as forming a large part of what it meant to be a poet, even though neglected by most later readers.[20]

Adam Lindsay Gordon, the only Australian poet to be honoured with a plaque in Poets' Corner in Westminster Abbey, is also now known by only a handful of his works. Like Kendall and Harpur, he attempted long poems on non-Australian subjects, such as the ballad-style *The Feud*, set in Scotland and heavily influenced by Sir Walter Scott. It is Gordon's Australian ballads, however, that are found in anthologies today, especially "The Sick Stockrider", for long also a recitation favourite and seen as a precursor to the bush ballads of the 1890s. In "The Sick Stockrider", another variation on the popular "grave in the bush" theme, a dying bushman looks back over his life, nostalgically recalling adventures with "comrades of the old colonial school" when

> 'Twas merry in the glowing morn, among the gleaming grass,
> To wander as we've wandered many a mile,
> And blow the cool tobacco cloud, and watch the white wreaths pass,
> Sitting loosely in the saddle all the while.[21]

As with Harpur's "The Creek of the Four Graves", Gordon's poem performed important nation-building work by celebrating the recent Australian past in terms and genres which helped legitimise possession of the land through the performance of heroic deeds and, ultimately, by literally becoming part of it in death.

HISTORICAL AND ADVENTURE FICTION

In "The Sick Stockrider" one of the narrator's past adventures involved "a glorious gallop after 'Starlight' and his gang", possibly the inspiration for the name of the mysterious hero of Rolf Boldrewood's classic bushranging adventure story *Robbery Under Arms* (1888). Gordon's poem, of course, is very much on the side of law and order, as was an earlier novel which clearly also influenced Boldrewood's, Henry Kingsley's *The Recollections of Geoffry Hamlyn* (1859). As its title indicates, Kingsley is also concerned with legitimation, like Gordon using an older, if not yet dying, narrator who looks back on a more heroic past, in this case involving the restoration of the fortunes of an old English family through a successful pastoral venture in Australia. Unlike Gordon, Kingsley does acknowledge the fact of Aboriginal dispossession, though the actual massacre takes place off-stage and the squatters' main enemies are an escaped convict turned bushranger, and his gang.

As well as providing ready made villains for early adventure novels like *Geoffry Hamlyn*, the convict system was also dealt with more directly in many colonial novels.[22] The first novel to be published in Australia was *Quintus Servinton*, printed in Hobart in 1830–31 and written by the convict Henry Savery. This was a fairly thinly disguised autobiographical account of crime and punishment but one with a much happier ending than was to be Savery's own. While Servinton's wife stands by him in his trials, and he is eventually restored to her and to freedom, Savery's own wife was apparently unfaithful and eventually left him. After being reconvicted of forgery he died in prison at Port Arthur.

It is less easy to discern an autobiographical impulse behind another early novel apparently written by a convict, *Ralph Rashleigh*, though when this was first published in 1929 it was assumed to be non-fiction and appeared in a heavily edited version. Colin Roderick, who published the full manuscript for the first time in 1952, has argued that it is the work of a convict named James Tucker, who arrived in Sydney in 1827 and later spent time at penal stations in Emu Plains and Port Macquarie, where he wrote some plays as well as this novel. Certainly, *Ralph Rashleigh* does contain a very lively account of the convict theatrical performances given at Emu Plains in the 1820s. Later Ralph, whose surname is one of the few moralistic features of the text, is captured by bushrangers, resentenced to Newcastle where he is treated brutally and flogged, and escapes to live for some years with an Aboriginal tribe. Whoever he may have been, the author of *Ralph Rashleigh* seems to have been more interested in telling an entertaining tale, replete with all the elements readers might have expected to find in a story set in convict days, than in either presenting his hero as a wronged innocent or using the convict system to reflect more generally on life.

While some later authors, such as Eliza Winstanley in *Her Natural Life* (1876, reprinted 1992), also do little more than draw on readers' continuing fascination with convict doom and gloom, two important novels, Caroline Leakey's *The Broad Arrow* (1859) and Marcus Clarke's *His Natural Life* (1874), develop broader themes.[23] *The Broad Arrow*, originally published by Leakey under the pseudonym "Oline Keese", draws on the five years she spent in Tasmania with her sister, between 1848 and 1853. Although long overshadowed by Clarke's novel, which it clearly influenced, *The Broad Arrow* has recently been re-read by feminist scholars in terms of its portrayal of a strong and passionate woman trapped within patriarchal social structures, which the penal system makes even more punitive and brutal than usual. As is apparent from her subtitle – *Some Passages in the History of Maida Gwynnham, A Lifer* – Leakey's heroine is sent to Van Diemen's Land for the term of her natural life. Like Clarke's Rufus Dawes, she is innocent of the crimes for which she is convicted, though not totally innocent – she has allowed herself to be seduced and so by nineteenth-century standards is a "fallen woman". Leakey's strongly evangelical Christian beliefs also prevented her from taking the same stance as Clarke: Maida must eventually die, but die in a state of Christian resignation and repentance.

Clarke in contrast presented in *His Natural Life* something in the nature of a scientific experiment: is it possible for humanity, for civilisation, to survive without religious belief? In the original, and much longer, version of *His Natural Life* serialised in the *Australian Journal* from 1870–72, Clarke used an alchemical frame-story to suggest the nature of his experiment: will a naturally good man become corrupted if placed in an overwhelmingly evil and negative environment? To test this he subjected an innocent man, Richard Devine, to the worst hell then imaginable on earth – as convict Rufus Dawes he is forced to endure the Australian, more especially the Tasmanian, convict system. In addition to the disgrace of his fall in class position and social standing, the horror of having to associate with brutes like Gabbett, the cannibal, and be subjected to the not so petty tyrannies of brutal officers like Maurice Frere, Clarke puts Devine/Dawes through a series of trials in which every one of his good acts backfires on him, until he feels totally alienated and abandoned. Yet even then Dawes continues to act unselfishly: despite his brutalised convict exterior he is still Devine. So Clarke demonstrates that humanity does not need religion to keep it from degenerating into savagery, a view frequently argued, especially by clergy-men, at this time of increasing religious doubt. The two main clergymen in the novel are presented as far from admirable. The Rev. Meekin is sent up as an effeminate fop for whom the Christian faith is a mere profession, some-one who has no insight into the sufferings of his fellow men, and no ability or desire to help them. The Rev. North, although treated more sympathetic-ally, and powerfully presented through his own journal entries which allow the reader direct insight into his tormented mind, is an alcoholic and a potential adulterer and, in the revised version, even guilty of the robbery for which Devine is convicted.

Many of Clarke's contemporary readers, however, were unable to accept his positive view of human resilience; they felt that a man subjected to the horrors of Van Diemen's Land could never reclaim his place in society. Clarke was therefore persuaded to carry out an extensive revision of his novel before it appeared as a book, in the process not only shortening it considerably but reluctantly killing off Rufus Dawes. While most subsequent critics have preferred the revised version, as more unified and more tragic, it is also a much more pessimistic work, one in which children suffer for the sins of their parents, rather than, as in the earlier version, redeeming them. Whereas the serial version of *His Natural Life* had presented post-gold rush Australia as a land transformed, a place to make a new start, in the revised version it remains at the charcoal stage.

With *Robbery Under Arms* (1888), the best known of Rolf Boldrewood's many novels, there are also many differences between the book and serial, originally published in the *Sydney Mail* in 1882–83. Here, however, there was none of Clarke's careful if sometimes agonising revision. Most cuts were made by Boldrewood before the novel's one-volume republication by Macmillans in 1889; some had been made earlier, accidentally, but were never picked up. There are also quite a few errors in the novel's chronology, no doubt the result of Boldrewood writing it a few chapters at a time, while the serial was already under way. Despite its more than occasional crudenesses, however, the 1889 version of *Robbery Under Arms* was a bestseller in both England and Australia. In part this may be because Boldrewood cannily decided to have three heroes for the price of one: there is the novel's narrator, Dick Marston, the rebellious currency lad given to arguing about equality with those of more conservative beliefs; there is his much more lovable younger brother, Jim; and there is Captain Starlight, the mysterious aristocratic Englishman, leader of their bushranging gang. There are also bad bushrangers, to set the "good" ones in relief, and rather a lot of moralising, as required by the standards of the day. But above all there is a vast amount of hard riding through the bush and frequent good deeds in the way of saving lives and damsels otherwise in distress. Boldrewood often uses imagery drawn from card games and from the theatre to suggest that, for his heroes, bushranging is little more than fun and games for bigger boys. At other times, it is presented as an almost legitimate activity via comparisons with soldiering and other masculine professions. An element of bravado is very strong, especially with Starlight, and much of the novel's action is concerned with great feats of daring and accomplishment, as when Starlight's horse Rainbow wins the Turon Cup.

While *Robbery Under Arms* no doubt became a bestseller largely because it is an exciting novel to read, its wider significance for Australian literature lay in Boldrewood's pioneering use of a colloquial first person narrator, and hence of the Australian vernacular as a literary style. As the New Zealand writer Frank Sargeson once pointed out, he did this a year or two before Mark Twain published *Huckleberry Finn* (1884), though Twain and other American writers had of course been using vernacular narrators for some time before this.[24] The young Henry Lawson was one of those who read *Robbery Under Arms*, or had it read to him, as it was running in the *Sydney Mail* in 1882–83.[25] And many passages of *Robbery Under Arms* would, if read out of context, be assumed to be by Lawson. Because of its influence on Lawson, and through him on all those writers seen as following in the Lawson tradition, *Robbery Under Arms*, though usually dismissed by nationalist critics because of its romance elements and aristocratic English hero, must be seen as one of the seminal works of nineteenth-century Australian literature.

HENRY LAWSON AND THE SHORT STORY

The construction by later nationalist literary critics and historians of the 1890s as the decade when Australian literature first "came of age" has had many unfortunate consequences for the work of earlier writers, relegating them to the status of the immature or merely imitative. It has also led to a misleading separation of the work of Henry Lawson from that of his predecessors. Like all authors, Lawson did not write in a vacuum; like all authors he was influenced by the political and literary currents of his time. Two well-known works, "Some Popular Australian Mistakes" (1893) and "The Union Buries Its Dead" (1893) are in part exercises in debunking the fictional clichés that had already attached themselves to tales of the bush:

> I have left out the wattle – because it wasn't there. I have also neglected to mention the heart-broken old mate with his grizzled head bowed and great pearly drops streaming down his rugged cheeks. He was absent – he was probably "Out Back".[26]

What is being sent up here, of course, is style as much as content – the adjectival cliché of "the great pearly drops" as well as the clichéd flora. This story was first published in the Sydney newspaper *Truth* as "A Bushman's Funeral – A sketch from life" and it is important to recognise the journalistic origins of much of Lawson's best work. The Sydney magazine the *Bulletin* (1880–), where much of Lawson's earlier fiction appeared, was one of the first in Australia to follow the precepts of the "new journalism" of the period – shorter paragraphs, shorter sentences, shorter items all round – and some of this greater emphasis on simplicity and snappiness of style can be seen in Lawson's work of the 1890s. Some of it, however, was already present in earlier descriptive journalism, such as A.J. Boyd's "Old Colonials" series, first published in the *Queenslander* in 1875–76. The fairly simple vocabulary and syntax, and attempt to capture a working-class speaking voice, seen in sketches like "The Shepherd" and "The Fencer", clearly look forward to Lawson.[27]

Most of Lawson's best earlier stories could, like "The Union Buries Its Dead", be described as "sketches from life". That is, they have very little in the way of plot, are usually quite short and give the impression of artlessness, achieving their effects from carefully chosen, vividly realised detail. Often the "sketch" analogy is even more deliberately employed, as in the opening of "In a Dry Season": "Draw a wire fence and a few ragged gums, and add some scattered sheep running away from the train. Then you'll have the bush all along the New South Wales Western line from Bathurst on."[28] As this opening paragraph suggests, this story, like "The Union" and others based on Lawson's 1892–93 trip to Bourke and "the real Out Back", might be classified as travel sketches; the slightly earlier "The Drover's Wife" and "The Bush Undertaker" are character sketches of already well-established bush types. Unfortunately for Lawson, it seems to have been just these close links with journalism, the lightness of touch so different from the standard heavily plotted story of his time and earlier, which led contemporary critics to fail to fully recognise the true originality and achievement of his stories and sketches. Reviewing Lawson's first major collection, *While the Billy Boils* (1896), for the *Bulletin* on 29 August 1896, A.G. Stephens observed that

> Lawson might conceivably have written many of his fragmentary impressions into a singly plotted, climaxed story which would make a permanent mark. Or if even he had contrived a set of characters to pass from chapter to chapter, as Mark Twain manages, and hung his matter on their pegs, his result would have been stronger.[29]

Lawson apparently took this criticism to heart and attempted to write more "plotted" stories, which inevitably turned out to be less distinctive than the best of his earlier work, and rather more like those being written by many others at the time. His four interlinked stories tracing the highs and lows in the relationship of Joe and Mary Wilson are, it is true, among his masterpieces. Here he was able to develop themes and characters in the way that Stephens had recommended, but "Joe Wilson's Courtship" (1901) also marked the peak of Lawson's achievement, although he was to live and publish for another twenty or so years.

Another *Bulletin* story writer, Arthur Hoey Davis, who published under the pseudonym Steele Rudd, did contrive "a set of characters to pass from chapter to chapter". Two of them, Dad and Dave, after countless re-embodiments in adaptations for stage, radio and both large and small screens, not to mention appearances in numerous dirty jokes, have become Australian folk heroes, their literary origins usually long forgotten. One of Rudd's stories, "Starting the Selection", appeared in the *Bulletin* in April 1895; it and later stories proved highly popular with readers, so much so that the *Bulletin* itself published them in volume form in 1899 as *On Our Selection*. Rudd's earlier stories resemble some of Lawson's selection sketches in presenting a generally rather sardonic view of the trials and tribulations of the small-time farmer with a large family and little money. From the very first, however, there was a much broader comic note, the first paragraph of "Starting the Selection" concluding: "It was a scorching hot day, too – talk about thirst! At every creek we came to we drank till it stopped running."[30] As this suggests, the oral tradition of comic exaggeration is strongly felt in all of Rudd's work, though only in some of Lawson's. Success meant that the more realistic and experiential aspects of his stories were increasingly abandoned in favour of broad and generally physical jokes: dreadful things keep happening to both man and beast and everyone laughs.

The stories of another *Bulletin* writer of the 1890s, Price Warung, followed a very different path. Like a much earlier writer, John Lang, he focused on the convict period in Australia. Lang's stories, though almost contemporaneous with what he was describing, were initially titled "Legends of Australia"; like Charles Harpur, he seems to have felt that the only way to deal with Australian material was to give it a spurious historicity. When the first part of the "Legends" was published in Australia in 1842, it received a generally hostile response from local reviewers; Lang subsequently left for India and all his other fiction was published outside Australia, including the collection of stories *Botany Bay: or, True Tales of Early Australia* (1859) for which he is now best known. Though Price Warung's stories were also based on actual events and real-life characters, their tone was much more sardonically ironic than Lang's. In keeping with the *Bulletin*'s then strongly republican, anti-British stance, Warung's portrayal of the convict system stresses its corrupt and brutal administrators and commandants and their mistreatment of prisoners, so reinforcing the view given earlier by Marcus Clarke. Warung's stories, though still regularly anthologised, never met with the popular success of Lawson's and Rudd's. By the end of the nineteenth century most Australian readers preferred to forget the past, especially if they suspected they might have convict ancestry: the battles to be celebrated were those against the bush rather than the System.

WRITING FOR CHILDREN

As well as the ballads of Banjo Paterson and the stories of Lawson and Rudd, the 1890s produced another highly successful work which has continued to be read by successive generations: Ethel Turner's novel *Seven Little Australians* (1894). Like most Australian novels of this time, it was published in England where, indeed, Turner had been born twenty-four years earlier. It is, however, almost as "offensively Australian" in tone as Joseph Furphy's *Such is Life* (1903), insisting on the distinctiveness of an Australian childhood and challenging the imperialist and masculinist tone of most other children's fiction of the period. Turner's heroine, Judy Woolcot, is an archetypal Australian girl: fond of physical activity, high-spirited, rebellious, a younger version of some of the heroines found in slightly earlier novels by Rosa Praed and Catherine Martin. She is, however, spared their dilemmas over choice of marriage partner; while Turner differs from other 1890s writers in setting her story on the outskirts of Sydney, she still manages to arrange for Judy to be killed by a falling tree at the novel's climax. Clearly, Turner could not imagine Judy, anything but a dutiful daughter, becoming a dutiful wife, but neither was she able to take the further step and, like Miles Franklin a few years later, imagine her turning her back on an eligible man. Turner was to write many more novels, but was like Miles Franklin at least in never quite repeating the success of her first.

Novels written specifically for children, as distinct from traditional folk and fairy tales or novels originally written for adults but later handed down, were, of course, still quite a new thing in the nineteenth century. The first children's books to be published in Australia were spelling, grammar and other textbooks. The first children's book to be written and published here, *A Mother's Offering to Her Children* (1841), was equally didactic in intent, if rather more sophisticated in form. By Charlotte Barton, mother of the novelist Louisa Atkinson, it used the popular form of a dialogue between a mother and her children to impart useful information about history, geography, natural history and so on, including some Australian examples and stories.

While Turner presented Australian difference primarily through characterisation and attitude, other children's writers both before and after her fell back on the more easily realised distinctiveness of flora and fauna and of life in the bush. Both Ethel Pedley, in *Dot and the Kangaroo* (1899), and May Gibbs, in her various "Gumnut Baby" tales such as *Snugglepot and Cuddlepie* (1918), however, also used their anthropomorphised animals and flowers to present early messages on the need to conserve the Australian environment. Norman Lindsay, author of another children's classic, *The Magic Pudding* (1918), produced in part as a relief from the horrors of World War I, also dressed his koalas and bandicoots in the fashions of the time, but his message was a rather more anarchic one of eternal struggle for the good things of life. In contrast, Mary Grant Bruce's popular "Billabong Series" of novels, beginning with *A Little Bush Maid* (1910, published in London after serialisation in the Melbourne *Leader*), confirmed for both English and Australian readers a vision of Australia as a bush paradise, where men were mates and women helpmates, both always ready to come to the service of the Empire whenever needed.[31]

Since the end of World War II especially, writing for children has been one of the most successful areas of Australian literature and many others have emulated Ethel Turner and Mary Grant Bruce in attracting large audiences both at home and abroad. While imaginative picture books featuring Australia's unique animals remain highly popular, as witnessed by the success of Mem Fox and Julie Vivas with *Possum Magic* (1983), authors now address a wide range of concerns and work in a variety of genres, from the grim realism of much young adult fiction through to science fiction and fantasy. Books by John Marsden, though often seen as too confronting and controversial, regularly top the bestseller lists; other highly popular contemporary children's writers are Nadia Wheatley, Gillian Rubenstein, Robin Klein and Garry Crew.

FICTION BY WOMEN

While women writers have, in Australia as elsewhere, always been dominant in the less elitist literary genres, especially children's writing, their contribution to nineteenth-century Australian fiction was for many years disregarded, or dismissed as "colonial" – inauthentic, imitative, and overly concerned with romance. We now know that the second novel to appear in Australia, *The Guardian* (1838), was written by a woman, Anna Maria Bunn. Like Barron Field's *First Fruits*, *The Guardian* was privately printed in Sydney, and never offered for sale. We do not know why Mrs Bunn wrote it; perhaps to take her mind off the unexpected and untimely death of her husband George in 1834. *The Guardian* contains many signs of its colonial origins, such as frequent references to local material, including to one of Field's "Botany Bay flowers", the fringed violet. It is, however, set in Ireland and its plot is a violently gothic mix of thwarted love, mysterious gypsies, incest and retribution. As well, there are many comic episodes, and today the novel is of most interest for its hybrid quality and its indications of what women were reading in Australia in the 1830s.

By the 1840s, the bush was already firmly established as the setting for Australian fiction. Mary Vidal's *Tales for the Bush* was initially published in Sydney in eight monthly parts, each priced at sixpence, before being issued in book form in 1845. As there were two later London editions and an 1850 translation into Dutch, Vidal's extremely didactic tales, full of moral lessons on the need to keep the Sabbath holy, be respectful to one's superiors, uncomplaining and temperate, were clearly popular with contemporary readers. Certainly, they were well received by local reviewers, the *Australian* for 23 May 1844, for example, commenting: "This well got-up little serial increases in public favor. The fourth number is before us, and fully sustains the reputation of its predecessor."[32] After returning to England in 1845, Mary Vidal published several novels, including two set in Australia, *The Cabramatta Store* (1850) and *Bengala; or Some Time Ago* (1860; reprinted 1990).

The first of Louisa Atkinson's several novels, *Gertrude the Emigrant* (1857), was also initially published in parts in Sydney, with illustrations by the author herself. Atkinson has gained some attention more recently as the first Australian-born woman novelist but her accounts of bush life, though containing a great deal of valuable historical material, lack the wit and humour found in the novels of Catherine Helen Spence, for long believed to be Australia's first woman novelist. Spence's best-known work remains her first, *Clara Morison* (1854), subtitled "A Tale of South Australia During the Gold Fever", one perhaps added by her British publisher to cash in on the then intense interest in the Australian gold discoveries. Although Spence's plot of an orphaned governess who overcomes many trials and temptations to eventually marry her squatter lover might initially suggest an Antipodean rewriting of *Jane Eyre*, *Clara Morison* is both more realistic and in its own way more radical than Charlotte Bronte's gothic romance. Clara, unable to find work in Adelaide as a governess, prefers to suffer a decline in class status and become a servant rather than accept other more dubious offers, such as marriage with a stranger. While perhaps reflecting current and continuing concerns over the class position of the colonial lady, who often could not afford to emulate the English ideal, the white-handed lady of leisure, *Clara Morison* also endorses women's capacity for both practical and intellectual work. This was to remain one of Spence's major concerns and, later in life, having given up novel writing for journalism as more likely to provide an audience for her ideas, she was one of the leading figures of the women's suffrage movement in Australia.

As there was no way her novel could achieve publication in Australia, except at her own expense, Spence entrusted the manuscript of *Clara Morison* to a friend travelling to Britain. It was eventually published in

Edinburgh, though with significant cuts, made without Spence's consent. Other Australian writers of the second half of the nineteenth century experienced similar difficulties in getting their novels published. If they remained in Australia, it was possible to gain fairly extensive publication in local magazines and newspapers but much more difficult to move to book publication without themselves physically moving to Britain. Of the major women writers, only Ada Cambridge was able to combine regular local newspaper serialisation of her fiction with subsequent book publication in Britain.

The work of the very prolific Mary Helena Fortune, for example, until recently remained buried in the columns of the *Australian Journal*, a popular fiction magazine published from 1865 to 1962. Publishing under two pseudonyms, "W.W." for her detective fiction, much of it using a male persona, and "Waif Wander" for her historical novels, comic stories and journalism, Fortune supported herself by her writing for some forty years. The actress Eliza Winstanley also turned to fiction writing in the 1850s, editing the London periodicals *Bow Bells* and *Fiction for Family Reading* after she became too old to play the roles which had established her name in Australia in the 1840s and later in London.

Ada Cambridge, whose fiction and poetry have attracted increasing attention over the past twenty years, published her first Australian serialised novel in 1875. Though for many years dismissed as a mere romance writer, Cambridge uses the romance formula to question and ironise the position of women, the institution of marriage and, frequently, the conventions of romance itself. In *A Marked Man* (1890), Richard Delavel repents his hasty marriage to an intellectual inferior but is never allowed to fully enjoy the fruits of a more companionable relationship; there is, however, a suggestion that the next generation will be wiser and happier in their choices. The later *Sisters* (1904) contrasts the marriages of the four Pennycuik girls. One weds an older man for money, is unfaithful and doomed to unhappiness; another is forced into an unwanted marriage with a clergyman: after his death, she finally feels "clean" again (like other women of her time, Cambridge saw marriage without love as no better than prostitution). A third sister marries beneath her, but lives contentedly, with many children; the most beautiful of them all eventually marries her long-lost sweetheart, only to find him now a valetudinarian. This is a novel which most definitely does not endorse the "happy ever after" scenario, demonstrating, along with most of Cambridge's others, that the concerns of many colonial women writers were not all that different from those of later ones like Miles Franklin.

Although the novels of the prolific Rosa Praed lack Cambridge's wit and delicate irony, they remain equally interesting for their franker treatment of female desire and examination of the dilemma of the colonial girl. Early novels such as *Policy and Passion* (1881) show naive Australian heroines strongly attracted to the sophisticated Englishman, a situation reversed in the later *Lady Bridget in the Never-Never Land* (1915; reprinted 1987) where Praed uses the more stereotypical "Crocodile Dundee" scenario of visiting lady and virile bushman. *The Bond of Wedlock* (1887; reprinted 1987), one of the first of Praed's novels to be set wholly in London, also presents a naive heroine who, along with her equally naive husband, is no match for the wily and wealthy Sir Leopold D'Acosta (Praed's names are often significant). Marriage to an Englishman with literary connections, and expatriation after 1876, allowed Praed a ready access to British publishers, at the expense of neglect by later Australian readers and critics.

Some of Praed's concerns are also to be found in the work of "Tasma" (Jessie Couvreur), another who married a European and spent much of her later life outside Australia. "Tasma's" *The Penance of Portia James* (1891), for example, is like *The Bond of Wedlock* in contrasting the lot of a woman trapped in an unsatisfactory marriage with that of another who lives a freer, bohemian lifestyle. Catherine Martin's *An Australian Girl* (1890) also features a heroine who finds herself tied to a less than perfect man, in this case one who drinks too much as well as being her intellectual inferior (though virile and wealthy). Here, however, the novel endorses Stella's decision to stay in her marriage, in part because her now reformed husband is an Australian and the text shares some of the burgeoning nationalism characteristic of the 1890s as well as an interest in socialist politics, usually only associated with male writers of the realist school.

As one sees from Desmond Byrne's *Australian Writers* (1896), one of the earliest critical studies, in the 1890s the Australian fiction canon was made up of equal numbers of male and female writers: Ada Cambridge, Rosa Praed and "Tasma", as well as Henry Kingsley, Marcus Clarke and Rolf Boldrewood. (In contrast, Byrne singles out only one poet, Adam Lindsay Gordon, for detailed treatment.) While 1901 marked a complete political break between colonial Australia and the new federated nation, culturally there was not so much difference. Most Australian readers still read many more works by English authors than by Australian; most Australian novels were still published overseas. This situation would continue until well after World War II. Later critics like Vance Palmer characterised writers such as Boldrewood and Cambridge as colonial on the strength of their overseas publication as much as their use of romance formulas. But, as their novels were in both cases originally run as serials in Australian newspapers, it is not correct to assume they were written with English rather than local readers in mind. Ironically, most of Palmer's own fiction had London imprints, as did that of other leading "nationalist" writers like Katharine Susannah Prichard, Eleanor Dark and M. Barnard Eldershaw. Until after World War II, local publishers like Angus & Robertson preferred to concentrate on more popular fiction and non-fiction, such as the travel writing of Ion Idriess and the detective fiction of Arthur Upfield. For them, there was a wide readership in both Australia and elsewhere, since by the 1930s Australian readers had finally come to appreciate at least some of the writing done locally.

NOTES

1 "The Kangaroo", *First Fruits of Australian Poetry* (Sydney: George Howe, 1819).
2 See extracts from Worgan and Watling in Elizabeth Webby, *Colonial Voices* (St Lucia: University of Queensland Press, 1989), pp. 10 and 12.
3 See Watling, in Webby, *Colonial Voices*, p. 12.
4 Webby, *Colonial Voices*, p. 151.
5 Frederick Sinnett, "The Fiction Fields of Australia", originally published in the *Journal of Australasia* in September and November 1856; reprinted in John Barnes, ed., *The Writer in Australia* (Melbourne: Oxford University Press, 1969), p. 17.
6 See *The Secrets of Alexander Harris* (Sydney: Angus & Robertson, 1961).
7 The poet Hugh McCrae in 1934 edited the letters and diaries of his grandmother Georgiana McCrae for publication as *Georgiana's Journal*. Recent research has shown a high degree of intervention and invention by him, and this material is currently being re-edited for publication in the Academy Editions of Australian Literature series.
8 See Dorothy Jones, "'Letter Writing and Journal Scribbling'", in Debra Adelaide, ed., *A Bright and Fiery Troop – Australian Women Writers of the Nineteenth Century* (Melbourne: Penguin, 1988), pp. 15–28.
9 See Elizabeth Webby, "Pipes and Odes: Literature and Music", in James Broadbent and Joy Hughes, eds, *The Age of Macquarie* (Melbourne: Melbourne University Press, 1992), pp. 88–100.
10 George Allen to the Rev. Horton, 7 April 1831, Mitchell Library.
11 See Philip Butterss and Elizabeth Webby, eds, *The Penguin Book of Australian Ballads* (Melbourne: Penguin, 1993), pp. 172–3.
12 For further information see Cliff Hanna, "The Ballads: Eighteenth Century to the Present", in Laurie Hergenhan, ed., *The Penguin New Literary History of Australia* (Melbourne: Penguin, 1988), pp. 194–209.
13 See Butterss and Webby, eds, *Australian Ballads*, pp. 74–5.
14 The fullest account of MacNamara and his work can be found in John Meredith and Rex Whalan, *Frank the Poet* (Melbourne: Red Rooster Press, 1979).
15 The full text can be found in Butterss and Webby, eds, *Australian Ballads*, pp. 48–53.
16 The most complete edition currently available is Elizabeth Perkins, ed., *The Poetical Works of Charles Harpur* (Sydney: Angus & Robertson, 1984). Perkins is preparing a full scholarly edition of Harpur's poems for the Academy Editions of Australian Literature series.

17 See Charles Harpur, *Stalwart the Bushranger*, ed. Elizabeth Perkins (Sydney: Currency Press, 1987).

18 See Elizabeth Webby, "The Grave in the Bush", in Dennis Haskell, ed., *Tilting at Matilda* (Fremantle: Fremantle Arts Centre Press, 1994).

19 See Christopher Brennan, "Some Makers of Australia" (1927), in Terry Sturm, ed., *Christopher Brennan* (St Lucia: University of Queensland Press, 1984).

20 For further discussion see Michael Ackland, *Henry Kendall: The man and the myths* (Melbourne: Melbourne University Press, 1995).

21 In Brian Elliott, ed. *Adam Lindsay Gordon* (Melbourne: Sun Books, 1973), p. 109.

22 For a more detailed discussion of convict fiction see Laurie Hergenhan, *Unnatural Lives* (St Lucia: University of Queensland Press, 1983).

23 While later reprints of Clarke's novel usually appear under the title *For the Term of His Natural Life*, this was first used in 1882, after his death, so has no authorial validity; critics now prefer to use the original, shorter title.

24 See Frank Sargeson, review of World Classics edition of *Robbery Under Arms*, *Landfall*, 4 (1950), pp. 262–65.

25 Henry Lawson, "A Fragment of Autobiography", in Colin Roderick, ed., *Henry Lawson, Autobiographical and Other Writings, 1887–1922* (Sydney: Angus & Robertson, 1972), p. 193.

26 John Barnes, ed., *The Penguin Henry Lawson Short Stories* (Melbourne: Penguin, 1986), p. 43.

27 Reprinted in Elizabeth Webby, *Colonial Voices*, pp. 264–67.

28 John Barnes, ed., *The Writer in Australia*, p. 37.

29 Reprinted in Colin Roderick, ed., *Henry Lawson Criticism, 1894–1971* (Sydney: Angus & Robertson, 1972).

30 Steele Rudd, *On Our Selection*, 1899 (Sydney: Angus & Robertson, 1992).

31 For further discussion of Bruce and Turner, see Brenda Niall, *Seven Little Billabongs* (Melbourne: Melbourne University Press, 1979).

32 See also reviews in *Australian*, 20 February and 18 March 1844; *Sydney Record*, 24 February, 9 and 30 March 1844; *Weekly Register*, 24 February 1844.

3

MICHAEL ACKLAND

Poetry from the 1890s to 1970

Australian verse, throughout much of the nineteenth century, occupied an uncertain place in a predominantly utilitarian society. Foreign models and publications dominated the limited local market, while a virtual absence of patronage left poets exposed to the vagaries of government service, or the endless demands "imposed by sheep, on an indifferent run in a bad season".[1] Nevertheless, colonial writers were keenly aware that many national literatures were relatively recent formations. They knew that the liberation of the German states from Napoleonic France coincided with a rich literary efflorescence, and recognised how Irish aspirations for independence were accompanied by promising endeavours to awaken the Harp of Erin. These were heartening examples, but they in no way lessened the trials caused, in the words of one poet, by an "exotic culture which dwarfs or destroys all home sympathies, and surrounds its possessor with the bleak atmosphere of local indifference".[2] Calls for political and literary self-reliance culminated in the emergence of popular balladists in the 1890s, when poetry reflected and helped to shape growing national sentiment. By the 1920s, however, this creative impulse was largely exhausted. Nationalists were again underlining the need for "some sort of civilization ... to be built up in Australia if we are not to remain a meaningless jumble of creeds, cliques, classes",[3] and by the 1930s the interlinking of literature and nationhood was complicated by formalistic considerations. Modernist literary trends had been slow to make a major impact locally, and a generation of fledgling poets, born mainly during or in the aftermath of World War I, attempted to reconcile international movements with the quest for personal and national authenticity. Their efforts in the 1950s and beyond contributed decisively to the emergence of a local literature, and lent to Australian verse a resonance and self-assurance, anchored unselfconsciously in either local or overseas settings, which had been largely beyond the grasp of their predecessors.

Feeding into, though not always apparent in the work of 1890s balladists, is a colonial verse tradition concerned with justifying, and with particularising, the act of white settlement. From the outset, established poetic forms were adapted to rewrite the seizure of *terra australis* by Hanoverian England as the altruistic fulfilment of God's decree. Whether in the odes of the unofficial poet laureate of the first settlement, Michael Massey Robinson, or in "Australasia", a panegyric on the local course of empire by William Charles Wentworth, the continent is described as an unenlightened, uncultivated and silent anomaly before the European coming confirms it in its proper place in a Providential plan. Complementary if less explicit acts of appropriation were performed by settler poems which sought to assimilate the unknown and unfamiliar. Incidents of station life, the loss of loved ones or minutely observed accounts of travel through bush landscapes, once enshrined in verse, provided evidence of a burden willingly assumed and of a determination not to relinquish what had been so dearly won. So did celebrations of exploration or laments – with titles like "The Last of His Tribe" or "Aboriginal Death Song" – on what was perceived as the irreversible decline of the original inhabitants. Even locally-born white poets, opposed to the English establishment, were concerned with earning a right to the land. Most notably Charles Harpur, in ambitious verbal canvases such as "The Creek of the Four Graves" and "The Bush Fire", depicted the colony as a new stage on which Edenic possibilities could unfold, if humankind managed to be true to its God-given potential. His successor, Henry Kendall, assimilated key elements of the Romantic heritage to celebrate the splendour and mystery of the bush in works such as "Bell Birds", "Orara" and "To A Mountain".

For female poets the going then, as later, was considerably tougher. If Harpur and his peers complained of the difficulty of finding time for composition between bread-winning tasks, for women in a one or two-room hut with the constant demands of children, housekeeping and helping to raise as well as cook the next meal, it was exceptionally difficult. With more settled conditions, however, and a steady increase in the female population through schemes aimed at correcting the initial gender imbalance, educated, highly articulate women gained increasing literary prominence as well as an acute awareness of local pressures to conform. Catherine Martin, who abandoned poetry for prose, projected their dilemma in gruesome terms as a surgical procedure overseen by a Jesuit: "When I came to myself my body was still on the plank, but my head had been cut off, and was in a waste-paper basket … the Doctor was examining my heart, which was lying on a rough delf plate". The upshot of her free-thinking waywardness is a heart "natural to a reptile".[4] Ishbel's dream, although ostensibly inspired by the question of "whether emotion is primarily a cerebral process", reflects the suppression, as well as the severance, of thought and feeling demanded of women.

Nevertheless, dissent persisted, and women's verse, from being primarily an extension of their accepted role as promoters of moral works, became an outlet for radical ideas. Emma Anderson had dramatised her sex's impasse decades before in a fine long poem, "The Shadow of the Past", published posthumously in *Colonial Poems* (1869). There male oppression, coupled with the destructiveness of love and marriage for females, is foregrounded by Helen, in response to the tragic fate of her mother and sister. She forswears wedlock and dedicates herself to preparing a different future for her younger sister, May, before achieving a late reconciliation with her father. The mid-1870s saw significant and sometimes subversive collections of poetry by Ada Cambridge, Emily Manning and Martin. But they also resorted to meliorating stratagems or subterfuge when dealing with controversial issues. Manning, for instance, was careful to couch her questioning of Providence in "The Balance of Pain" as a dialogue between a faith-inspired wife and her querulous, physically deformed spouse. Cambridge concealed her critique of women's predicament in a world dominated by male codes and brute power behind ballad motifs popularised by Sir Walter Scott. Amputation, in short, assumed many forms.

Its effects were abetted by the marketplace. By and large, radical works, whether written by men or women, failed to act as a leaven on later poets. Harpur's verse, published only piecemeal during his lifetime, appeared posthumously in a severely bowdlerised edition, which deleted his metaphysical speculation and republican effrontery. Other poets appeared in limited editions which attracted little more than coterie attention, and reviewers missed how romance or Old World subjects commented obliquely on current issues. Such complexities were neither welcomed nor looked for in a colonial author. Nationalist sentiment on the eve of Federation made it easy to view poems set in other ages or climes as anachronistic or irrelevant. They were often derided for an alleged lack of innovation and maturity, or as regrettable reflections of homesickness, inferior to Adam Lindsay Gordon's "Galloping Rhymes", which seemed direct precursors of the popular, myth-making verse of the 1890s.

POETS OF THE 1890s

The 1890s saw a flowering of popular ballads, promoted, both then and afterwards, as authentic records of Australian experience. Many were published first in the Sydney *Bulletin*, the self-appointed organ of national consciousness, whose democratic credo included the tenet that every man had at least one sketch or poem worthy of committing to paper. Its literary editor, A.G. Stephens, projected Australia as a new realm capable of inspiring works worthy of comparison with those of antiquity:

[W]hat country can offer to writers better material than Australia? We are not yet snug in cities and hamlets, moulded by routine, regimented to a pattern. Every man who roams the Australian wilderness is a potential knight of Romance; every man who grapples with the Australian desert for a livelihood might sing a Homeric chant of victory, or listen, baffled and beaten, to an Aeschylean dirge of defeat. The marvels of the adventurous are our daily common-places. The drama of the conflict between Man and Destiny is played here in a scenic setting whose novelty is full of vital suggestion for the literary artist.[5]

His call to "live Australia's life and utter her message" was answered by a host of male balladists: pre-eminently by A.B. ("Banjo") Paterson and Henry Lawson, destined to become household names, as well as by Barcroft Boake, E.J. Brady, Will Ogilvie and others who tapped aspects of the frontier myth. Public images were shaped to conform to this blueprint. The best male poet of his generation, John Shaw Neilson, was described as a naive bushman inspired by chance encounters with the landscape. The finest female poet, Mary Gilmore, was praised for celebrating the pioneer ethos, to the detriment of less orthodox works and her concern with the lot of her sex. Gilmore's career, at least, was reconcilable to Stephens' conception of quintessential local experience as man pitted against the environment. This usually precluded women, much as he diminished their literary contributions. Cambridge's writing he described as only accidentally Australian, "her men and women might be staged anywhere"; for him, women's "work has (naturally) neither the mass nor the quality of the men's work".[6]

In spite of the acknowledged need for origination and the diversity of subjects treated, most of the 1890s ballads reveal common values and presuppositions which set them apart from Continental precedent. When German writers like Achim von Armin, Clemens Brentano, Joseph Görres and Jacob Grimm began to collect and write ballads a century earlier as the basis for a national literature, they could draw on a rich heritage stretching back to the Middle Ages. From this emerged a vision of an aristocratic and brotherly community prepared to pursue martial deeds, of shepherds and lovers amid woods and streams, and of nature as a benign force infused with a sense of mystery and faith. These writers saw themselves as spokespersons for the "Volk", the German people – an entity which had no equivalent in the southern colonies. Here local settings became a crucial if superficial indicator of Australianness, while writers took their lead not from European balladry, but from colonial oral tradition. It was spiced with satire and refractory attitudes towards establishment values, and coloured by a sense of suffering and hardship. These became hallmarks of the 1890s ballads. In them, irrespective of whether Lawson is portraying the lot of the urban poor or Paterson celebrating emancipated life in the bush, the focus is resolutely secular, mundane and materialistic. The balladist is the matter-of-fact recorder of the daily given, be it humorous or tragic, not a prober of metaphysical depths who evokes uncanny or mystical presences. The mood is belligerently male and democratic, categories and antagonists are clear-cut. Poems destined to achieve wide popularity, like Paterson's "The Man from Snowy River" or "Waltzing Matilda", affirm indomitable resolve, improvisation and a single memorable act, as if more were scarcely admissible against overwhelming odds. The chief actors are anonymous examples of a New Man being forged by unique circumstances, and hence prototypes of a "Volk" yet to be tested, recognised and applauded on the international stage – a belief which made Paterson a willing war correspondent and his countrymen volunteers for the Great War.

This popular masculine self-imaging came at a time of intense gender debate, and effectively relegated women to a complementary, passive or invisible role, one opposed by female activists, among whom were notable poets. Woman, in the burgeoning nationalist literature of the day, is portrayed as a domestic mainstay, a repository of moral values and a guarantee of racial superiority, but rarely as initiator or agent. She, like the land in earlier imperial pageants, is a potential helpmate whose fulfilment demands impregnation, as well as a marker which assures stability and legitimises white encroachment: "In the huts on new selections, in the camps of man's unrest, / On the frontiers of the Nation, live the Women of the West".[7] This, like many aspects of the bush myth, reflects male nostalgia rather than a colonial society agitated by demands for easier divorce, universal suffrage and wider career or educational opportunities for women. Men dreamt of outback freedom while women campaigned for male responsibility towards their dependants – though at the risk of social ostracism. This groundswell of protest against gender inequalities informs *Unspoken Thoughts* (1887), Cambridge's most outspoken contribution to the woman question. A *livre composé* before Brennan began his own more celebrated composition in 1891, it was similarly "the sublimation of a whole imaginative life and experience into a subtly ordered series of poems",[8] which affords a moving progress from a realm shrouded in metaphoric night to a scarcely imaginable future. Heterosexual norms are attacked and her generation summoned to courageous action, of which she provides a foretaste by condemning socially sanctioned prostitution in wedlock in favour of unions based on mutual consent and natural attraction:

> Thy love I am. Thy wife I cannot be,
> ... Some want, some chill, may steal 'twixt heart and heart.
> And then we must be free to kiss and part.[9]

Cambridge's dissent, however, remained within the bounds of expediency, and the volume appeared anonymously. She continued to follow an outwardly orthodox course, married to an Anglican minister, and only years later reissued more temperate versions of these poems under her own name in *The Hand in the Dark* (1913).

Two locally born poets whose lives had been directly shaped by the social turmoil preceding Federation were more forthright: Louisa Lawson and Mary Gilmore. The former, after experiencing the trials of married life on the New South Wales goldfields, moved to Sydney in 1883 with a young family to support, and was soon involved in radical circles. In 1888 she founded Australia's first feminist newspaper *The Dawn*, hoping to render at last audible "the whispers, pleadings, and demands of the sisterhood".[10] Lawson's *"The Lonely Crossing" and Other Poems* (1905) was a further attempt to give voice to a broad spectrum of women's concerns; however, these are now often coloured by a cumulative weariness like that of the persona who dreams in vain of release through death: "The sound of the stockwhip away on the hill. / Ah, God! It is day, and I'm suffering still!"[11] These compositions, unlike the *Short Stories in Prose and Verse* of her son Henry, published by the same *Dawn* press in 1894, were destined for oblivion, as was two-thirds of her verse, which remained in manuscript. Mary Gilmore, at the outset at least, knew her place with regards to literature. In 1903 she confirmed to A.G. Stephens her commitment to the roles of wife and mother, over "the temptation" to "give way to writing & to dreams of writing" which might lead "to the neglect of other things manifestly more right to do".[12] This acquiescence sat uneasily with an enterprising spirit who had given up teaching to join in 1896 the socialist utopia founded by William Lane in Paraguay, and her first collection, *Marri'd and Other Poems* (1910), moved well beyond women's conventional domestic concerns to explore passion and social inequalities.

J.S. NEILSON AND CHRISTOPHER BRENNAN

In another sign of things to come, stock nationalist formulas were already a dead letter in the work of the two most original pre-war poets, Christopher Brennan and John Shaw Neilson. By different routes, each became a precursor of Australian modernism. Brennan, after breaking off his training for the priesthood, pursued academic studies in Berlin, taught comparative literature at Sydney University, and followed eagerly the development of French symbolism. In 1897 he sent his work to Mallarmé, who was quick to acknowledge their poetic affinity, or their common "parenté de songe".[13] Neilson's meagre formal education was supplemented by eclectic reading and the encouragement of A.G. Stephens, whose outspoken nationalism did not close him off from international trends. In the works of Brennan and Neilson, the portrayal of local givens is subordinate to more pressing, and often spiritual concerns, though with strikingly different results. The limpid statement and provocative simplicity of Neilson's verse are far removed from Brennan's complexly interwoven, at times abstruse texts. Their poetic visions may be summarised in terms current among their Sydney successors in the late 1930s as the difference between a symbolism which in its supreme moments knows and conveys a tangible sense of a higher presence, and one which still convolutely searches.

Brennan's composition peaked with the appearance of *Poems* (1913), thereafter he and modernism stalled in Australia. The summation of two decades of painstaking work, the collection grew from the same malaise explored in 1891 in his MA thesis entitled "The Metaphysics of Nescience", and in the poem which appeared as its envoi, beginning "Farewell, the pleasant harbourage of Faith". *Poems* commences with the mental journeyings of a surrogate quester, who looks in vain for fulfilment in love or for lasting answers. Next it focuses on the source of his frustration, dubbed Lilith, after the rejected first-mate of primal Adam. Part of a long tradition of misogynistic iconography, stretching from the Whore of Babylon through Pope's Dulness to the *fin de siècle* fascination with the *femme fatale*, Lilith encapsulates all that allures and baffles the finest hopes of humankind:

> All mystery, and all love, beyond our ken,
> she woos us, mournful till we find her fair:
> and gods and stars and songs and souls of men
> are the sparse jewels in her scatter'd hair.[14]

Against this embodiment of "all horror" and "the round of nothingness", the poet evokes the "final grain of deathless mind, / which Satan's watch-fiends shall not find".[15] The lines recall, of course, Blake's deathless moment expanding into eternity and undetectable by "Satan's watch-fiends", and they foreground at once Brennan's belatedness and his spiritual bankruptcy. Ultimately for him there was no saving grace discernible in society or the heavens, and the individual mind proved to be a very fragile bark indeed. Dismissed from his post for adultery and succumbing to alcoholism, his squalid end was far removed from that of the similarly impecunious Blake, who reputedly died blessed by visions of angels.

Closer to the English Romantic in manner and genius was Neilson, who created his own subtly resonant symbolism in response to humanity's fallen condition. The fear-inspiring Presbyterian heritage of his childhood, coupled with mutability and social injustice, forms the dark side of his vision. His version of Eden is linked with such standard images as childhood, spring or radiant light, stripped of cloying accretions and presented with an often faultless sense of rhythm:

> The bird is a noble, he turns to the sky for a theme,
> And the ripples are thoughts coming out to the edge of a dream. (p. 138)[16]

Restored to primal vigour, Neilson's bird of the imagination is one of a cluster of symbols for an untainted and ever accessible godhead, as opposed to the warped creed of his youth when God, "terrible and thunder-blue", was recognised to be the author of an "ungracious scheme" (p. 95). Grace is rediscovered in epiphanic moments or in deity naturalised, thinking "like a beautiful tree" (p. 95). To this the creation affords constant egress, while the poet or such surrogates as a bird or an unworldly musician are repositories of visionary truth:

> The fiddler was a handless man
> That could not sow or reap:
> He did not know the care of kine
> Or the many ways of sheep.
>
> Of water-birds he played and boats
> And the white legs in a stream,
> Of hot love in the market-place
> And the spinning of a dream. (p. 77)

What Harpur and Kendall had adumbrated through scarcely tangible entities, like brooding midsummer or invisible but audible birds, Neilson articulates in poems of haunting originality such as "The Orange Tree" or "The Gentle Water Bird". He is fully aware of their place in a perennial endeavour to resurrect paradisal potential in the midst of cyclical pain – "Long I dispute, old is the argument" (p. 139).

The range of the man who spoke of being "assailed by colours / By night, by day" (p. 79) is deceptively straightforward, his artistry understated. Behind finely honed simplicity lies uncompromising effort. The brief forty lines of "The Orange Tree", for instance, required four years of labour, and Neilson, while performing manual tasks, is reported to have busied his mind at times by seeking an apt word or rhyme. The results are frequently arresting lines: "Surely God was a lover when He bade the day begin / Soft as a woman's eyelid – white as a woman's skin" (p. 60). Determined, as he put it, to "outgeneral Reason" (p. 48), he could draw on a startlingly Expressionistic palette, which dominates whole poems like "The Smoker Parrot", or teases thought in passing asides: "He will keep all the sweet colours lavender blue / But he goes seeking the colours eyes never knew"

(p. 108). The same poet exposed the nexus between institutionalised faith, wealth and empire, savaged a "changeless Heaven, / ... with a furious Law" (p. 98), and anticipated ecological concerns: "You cut the flower into the heart, your axe is at the tree" (p. 132). Yet Neilson, too, fell victim to incomprehension. How, it was asked, could a humble labourer produce subtle and thematically complex works? For decades, his work appeared mainly in ephemeral publications, although Stephens and other admirers brought out *Heart of Spring* (1919), *Ballad and Lyrical Poems* (1923), *New Poems* (1927) and *Beauty Imposes* (1938). His *Collected Poems* was published in 1934, yet only in the wake of World War II, more than fifty years after Neilson had resolved to become a poet in 1893, was he recognised by one of Australia's most cosmopolitan poets as a kindred spirit, "employ[ing] the idiom of a refined and bookish culture; [his] rhymes are studied and of epicene delicacy".[17]

EARLY TWENTIETH-CENTURY VERSE

More influential than Neilson in their day were proponents of aesthetic and prophetic verse. The former were represented by bohemian poets such as Victor Daley and Hugh McCrae, who avoided the distinctive flora and fauna of bush balladry in favour of a part dream, part Arcadian realm. Escapist and nostalgic, their poetry was a precursor of the Vision School which developed around Norman Lindsay in the 1920s. Lindsay was an eclectic hater, whose favourite targets included puerile nationalism, conformity and the post-war lure of modernism. Equated with infection, modernism was labelled by him and his acolytes "a freak, not a natural growth", rooted in this "age of speed, sensationalism, jazz and the insensate adoration of money".[18] His antidote, as spelt out in the manifesto *Creative Effort: An Essay in Affirmation* (1919), was a vitalist credo. Poets, like Kenneth Slessor and R.D. FitzGerald, were encouraged to explore energy, beauty and sexuality courageously, to achieve true life through art. And what better place for this secular renaissance of the spirit than untainted Australia? Antithetical to Lindsay's aesthetic credo was the call of Bernard O'Dowd for verse engaged with the issues of the day – for a "Poetry Militant" to replace the waning power of theologians. Dubbing poetry "the final flower of the human intellect", he followed Stephens in summoning local "poets of the dawn ... to chart the day and make it habitable".[19] They were to cut through the delusions of commercialism and provide ideas to guide the leaderless mob. These concepts had considerable impact, whereas his verse was later remembered unkindly as "a *cloaca maxima* into which has flowed all the ideological drivel of the nineteenth century".[20] Its blunt assertions, jingling rhymes and sterile abstractions served as a warning to later generations of the dangers of making poetry subordinate to ideology:

Invention, Industry, Unrest,
The Spirit of your age –
I bring all standards to the test,
All formulas re-gauge.[21]

Both Lindsay and O'Dowd countered post-war disillusionment, but their nationalist programs retarded the assimilation of poetic modernism in Australia.

For female poets during the first decades of the twentieth century, literary creativity was usually a less central preoccupation, though it was often infused with their determination not to accede to the universal, normative claims of male viewpoint, as in the brief career of Lesbia Harford. Like her contemporary Zora Cross, Harford was vitally concerned with women's issues. Cross, for instance, wrote celebratory sonnet sequences on hetero-sexual love and her unfolding response to motherhood, and lived openly in a de facto relationship. But her for the time frank, unconventional thoughts pale beside Harford's, much as Cross' well-crafted verse appears mellifluous beside Harford's sparse, essentialist lines. These repeatedly contrast male concern with control and technical knowledge with women's liberating openness to natural drives. From the public library to the lover bearing down "like the sky, / Insistent that you love me" (p. 103),[22] Harford asserts her sex's right to passion and independence: "I think my own thoughts / In my woman's head" (p. 70). Gender, to her, marks irreconcilable difference. In a poem of 1917 this is conveyed through a couple's diverging points of view during a seaside walk: her attraction to immediate, intimate colour, her affirmation of "inchoate beauty ... / Plurality essential" (p. 93), his "alien sense of beauty, line / Preferred to colour, distance to the near" (p. 92). As a writer, Harford put aside metaphysical speculation to focus on diurnal reality and "some human need" (p. 129). Above all, she is a poet of love and sexual desire, whose self-avowed mission was to prolong rapture through verse. To do this faithfully, she believed, required her to "render it barely" (p. 65), as in "Grotesque" (1918):

My
Man
Says
I weigh about four ounces,
Says I must have hollow legs.
And then say I,
"Yes,
I've hollow legs and a hollow soul and body.
There is nothing left of me.
You've burnt me dry". (p. 96)

Maintaining that "I take my poetry very seriously, and am in no hurry to be read",[23] Harford was free to project neglected aspects of female experience, from menstruation to schoolgirl crassness or a machinist's romantic dreams, from lesbian to marital passion, when

> Pat wasn't Pat last night at all.
> He was the rain,
> The Spring,
> Young Dionysus, white and warm,
> Lilac and everything. (p. 118)

The intimate honesty of her verse is rare, its uncluttered truths enduring. A weak heart cut short one of Australia's boldest post-Federation poetic trajectories, while the manuscript status of most of her verse ensured that it failed to influence succeeding generations who repeated her struggle against ingrained conventions.

Not all female poets between the wars suffered the same neglect. A number produced sensitive occasional pieces which earned well locally and overseas, so that Mabel Forrest could state that, contrary to popular opinion, "my personal experience has been that poetry *does* pay".[24] The one major writer who fitted neither category was Mary Gilmore. *Marri'd and Other Poems* was followed by *The Passionate Heart* (1918) and five further volumes, ending with *Fourteen Men* (1954). Prose reminiscences like *Old Days, Old Ways* (1934) made her a national figure, and related scenes in her poetry were highly praised for having "crystallized ... the hard, brave, sad, proud lives of the men and women of the frontier – the pioneers ... To these, Mary Gilmore has given deathless recognition."[25] Certainly many poems affirm the Anzac tradition or go little beyond the *Bulletin*'s bush ethos, while others, as in *The Rue Tree* (1931), are cloyingly devout. But there remains a major body of work which is robust, complex and was seminal for later writers, particularly in its exploration of sexual difference and its reappraisal of Aboriginal culture. Repeatedly a male viewpoint, which associates transformation with severance, death or instability, is contrasted with a female view of continual process and renewal. This is variously represented by nature, the earth or water, as in "Change" (p. 117).[26] There a man deserted by past gods is enclosed in a limbo of misery until his childlike fear is allayed by the maternal sea. Similarly, even apparently destructive elemental forces can be envisaged as "burst[ing] in seed far sown" (p. 116), or the pain of a woman's death sublimated in the beautifully waxing moon (p. 93). Familiar with Aborigines from her childhood, Gilmore presented their culture in *The Wild Swan* (1930) and *Under the Wilgas* (1932) as strong and valuable before the arrival of predatory colonists:

> What others played I know not; we,
> In self-contained content, tradition-learned,
> Dwelt in a world whose olden flame
> Beside our humbler hearth-fire burned. (p. 76)

In her verse the markers of imperial myths are recast, white settlers arraigned. "We who destroyed denied tribal law / We had not wit to read" (p. 70). Or as she noted in private: "In regard to the blacks the white man said they had no intellect but only instinct. But at what level was the intellect that saw no further than this?"[27]

Not consisting merely of "touchingly simple heart-notes, home-throbs" as O'Dowd maintained,[28] her verse represents, as she claimed, commitment to the "narrow way" of truth (p. 118), even if this was unpalatable to many contemporaries. The poet's social conscience never died, nor did her lust for living, although a number of works reflecting this were winnowed from her *Selected Poems*. Courage for her, in a poem of that name, is exemplified by the bravest act of one of her sex who "forsook one love had proved / Lest from his height, him, love had moved". Yet sympathy is also extended to a speaker who confesses: "I hid my eyes lest I should see / How little his heart took thought of me".[29] Diverse in response but always intensely human, Gilmore remains hard to enrol under any single banner. She can describe positively "The nun in every woman born", as well as counterbalance nurturing with passional longing in a refrain ("And all thy body aches remembering me") or in verse headed "Of Women":

> You who wrought me ill,
> You who brought me grief,
> You I remember with anger like flame,
> Do I hate you? How can I tell.
> Only I know that at sound of your name
> I tremble like a leaf;
> Only I know, when I hear your voice on the air,
> My heart like a wound
> Is broken there![30]

And the same hunger informs her life-affirming vision:

> ... Wonder is dead? O fool,
> Wonder can never die:
> Not while, within a pool,
> A man can see the sky![31]

These largely forgotten works, together with frequently anthologised ones like "Eve-Song", amply demonstrate Gilmore's credo: "Life is the unappeased, / Is passion, is desire" (p. 220). By the 1950s she had demonstrated the high public standing a woman poet could attain, opening up fields to be later exploited by Judith Wright and others. The Jindy-worobaks would attempt to fulfil her call for a distinctive national literature "using the aborigines, their lore, and native customs and words" (p. 308), while her verse and programmatic statements anticipated later developments aimed at making poetry simple, direct and resonantly true.

KENNETH SLESSOR AND MODERNISM

Although Norman Lindsay fulminated against modernism and the local press mocked its excesses, contamination could not be avoided, nor the global mood of disenchantment, captured by T.S. Eliot in *The Waste Land* (1922), shut out. R.D. FitzGerald, true to Lindsay's vitalist credo, could "postulate, beyond everyday life, opportunity or duty to create out of art and poetry a parallel world of action and beauty".[32] Similarly, his verse summoned readers "to be up and about and moving and ever upon quest / of new desires of the spirit", while the same determined affirmation led him to discern in Kenneth Slessor's poems a "frustration [which] may well be evidence on occasion of a state of enduring effort unsatisfied".[33] For Slessor, however, and for a generation born during the Great War whose adolescence was marked by the Depression, suburban uniformity and social unrest, disillusionment with former moral and aesthetic norms was real. Harold Stewart, in lines he later repudiated, greeted a new poetic age:

> Out of the ugly sensual now
> From the hard cold dry real
> Abstract the strict difficult beauty
> Which only the moderns feel.[34]

Slessor, savouring the lights, smells and harshness of Sydney's William Street, echoed these sentiments: "You find it ugly, I find it lovely" (p. 42).[35] Similarly, Stewart's contemporary, James McAuley, acknowledged the great debt of his generation to Eliot, having discovered in the American's *Poems 1909–1925* what he had sought until then in vain – verbal precision, emotional restraint and an explanation of his own deep malaise. To these fledgling modernists, Eliot's example confirmed not the need for free verse, but for artistic excellence achieved through sustained discipline, which would become a hallmark of their careers. Slessor, too, reminded his audience, in theory supported by commensurate works, that "the traditions of the present are the experiments of the past; to rest on them is to deny a future" (p. 155). In the 1930s the battle over the future direction of Australian verse was rejoined with renewed fervour.

Slessor described composition as "a pleasure out of hell" because of the psychological and intellectual effort it cost him.[36] His major creative period spanned two decades, beginning with *Thief of the Moon* (1924) and *Earth-Visitors* (1926) (clearly influenced by Lindsay's aesthetic), peaking with *Cuckooz Country* (1932) and *Five Bells* (1939), and tapering off during his period as an official war correspondent. A highly skilled prosodist and brilliant imagist, Slessor used art to keep nihilism at bay, and this struggle is often refracted in the canon of *One Hundred Poems*, which he brought together in 1944. His abiding unease, together with its Romantic origins, is spelt out in "Stars". As so often in the works of Heinrich Heine, to which he was attracted, Slessor undercuts the stereotyped lover's rhapsody to the night sky by shifting brusquely to a Pascalian vision of ultimate emptiness now firmly anchored in the southern firmament: "I saw the bottomless, black cups of space / ... tunnels of nothingness, / The cracks in the spinning Cross" drawing him towards "Infinity's trap-door, eternal and merciless" (pp. 10–11). Against this onrush he offers lasting works of imagination. Their recurring early type is engraving, cutting with burin and acids into metal plates to create the intaglios of Albrecht Dürer, the burning words of Marco Polo, or the *oeuvre* of Rubens: a fortress "cut and won / From darkness" (p. 31). Yet his *One Hundred Poems* (1944) opens with a telling image of inevitable defeat. The effects of passing immortals, Slessor's "Earth Visitors", are strictly transient: "In daylight, nothing, only their prints remained / Bitten in snow". Similarly, although occasional personae may dream of bucolic forgetfulness ("Till, charged with ale and unconcern, / I'll think it's noon at half-past four!" [p. 33]), acute anguish is their typical lot: "Vilely, continuously, stupidly, / Time takes me, drills me, drives through bone and vein" (p. 35).

Slessor's corpus recasts obsessively the mind's struggle against imminent annihilation. Rarely is a moment's respite conceded, such as the imagined art world of Dürer's room in "Nuremberg", where "Clocks had been bolted out, the flux of years / Defied" (p. 6). More usually, time moves on grimly, decimating human dreams, its passage marked by tombstones, fading photographs or mechanical contrivances. Art alone, which embodies individual longing and remains in interpretative flux, can escape temporal limitations – a paradox which lies at the heart of Slessor's acknowledged masterpiece from the late 1930s, "Five Bells". Far more than an elegy to his drowned friend Joe Lynch, the poem is a meditation on time which the author likened in a later note to an Arabian fairytale. There a man plunges his head into a basin of magic water to live a whole lifetime in a few moments before returning to his unchanged existence. The analogy highlights the co-existence of diverse conceptions of time, as well as the capacity of art to create and make accessible another order of reality. Water in "Five Bells", however, like the mutable creation, is destructive. They "pour to one rip of darkness" (p. 44). The magic is provided by the poet's imagination which, as in *The Waste Land*, shores fragments of memory against impending eclipse: Joe's physical appearance, his mental bric-à-brac, compositions in faint ink – "all without use, / All without meaning now" (p. 46). Nevertheless, their spare evocation endures beyond physical decay in a work which foregrounds intransigent loss coupled with the creative leap it can foster.

> I felt the wet push its black thumb-balls in,
> The night you died, I felt your eardrums crack,
> And the short agony, the longer dream,
> The Nothing that was neither long nor short;
> But I was bound, and could not go that way,
> But I was blind, and could not feel your hand. (p. 47)

Although the speaker acknowledges his own impotence, and so takes his place in a long line of Slessor protagonists who "beat the sides of emptiness" (p. 43), complete defeat is averted through art, or as the poet put it elsewhere: "Man's heaven is the place he builds / By thoughts imagined and things done. / ... Who dream of nought to nothing go" (p. 31). Short of a later, Eliot-like conversion, further poetic statement after "Five Bells" would have been supererogatory. Slessor wrote little but light verse during his remaining years; meanwhile, a younger generation of poets moved well beyond his tentative assimilation of modernism and his uneasy truce with meaninglessness.

POETS OF THE 1930s AND 1940s

"Five Bells" was published at a time when the Australian poetic scene was riven by declamatory, rival groups. The days of the *Bulletin*'s greatness and its power to set norms for local verse were long past. Small circulation, and often shortlived, magazines were broadening forums for debate and poetic publication, as well as underpinning distinctive schools. Of these, the three most significant were the Jindyworobaks, the Angry Penguins and the radical student poets publishing in the resurgent university magazine *Hermes*. Each group denounced a complacent, materialistic society, and offered its own formulas for invigorating the moribund state of local poetry. Like Gilmore in her verse on Aboriginal life, the leader of the Jindy-worobaks, Rex Ingamells (1913–55), was stirred to action by pioneering anthropological studies such as W.B. Spencer and F.J. Gillen's *The Native Tribes of Central Australia* (1899), reissued in 1927 as *The Arunta*. The name of Ingamells' group derived from a native word supposed to mean to annex or join, and underscored his aim to wed white and black traditions to produce a unique Australian civilisation. Again belated Romanticism informed a nationalist program. Imagining that the Aborigines had adapted to and absorbed an unchanging environment, Ingamells held that their language and thought were a special expression of climatic and physical conditions. The spirituality lacking in the West was rediscovered in the outback, and the Indigenous word identified with a suggestive magic which Ingamells hoped to replicate in his own verse:

> Far in moorawathimeering,
> safe from wallan darenderong,
> tallabilla waitjurk, wander
> silently the whole day long.[37]

Such "Jindyworobosh" was duly satirised; however, the movement re-actualised debate on Indigenous culture, and promoted local talent in its annual anthologies. Nor was its leader blind to international perspectives, recognising prophetically that "some of the greatest Australian literature yet to be may have no local colour at all. Its settings may be in China or Mars."[38]

The major proponents of modernist verse were less tolerant. Max Harris, quoting the above stanza from Ingamells' "Moorawathimeering", mocked the "aboriginalising" of English and put forward a counter program based on Surrealism and the New Apocalyptic movement. Determinedly avant-garde in his comportment and compositions, Harris sought to shock local philistines with works like *The Vegetative Eye* and "The Pelvic Rose", which combined stream of consciousness with sexual throbbings: "But now the vision changes and the rose is blown, / petals spiralling the labia to the light / … flame writes the epic horror, fiercely states / 'through the ages the old old man masturbates'".[39] Unlike Harris, who maintained a constant flow of printed provocation, *Hermes* depended on the changing aptitudes and attitudes of the student body at Sydney University. Nevertheless, it became a crucial testing ground for modernism, beginning in 1933 with the editorship of Howard Daniel who asserted: "Show me the undergraduate interested in poetry who has no adequate knowledge of modern verse and I will show you a man who has not adjusted to his environment."[40] By the late 1930s the magazine was attracting talents as diverse as James McAuley, Amy Witting, Dorothy Auchterlonie (later Green), Harold Stewart and Donald Horne. A.D. Hope, lecturing at the nearby Sydney Teachers College, added to the manuscript poetry in circulation, while making his mark as a deadly reviewer. Dubbing the Jindyworobaks "the Boy Scout School of

Poetry", he underscored the contradictions inherent in a project which sought self-understanding in a culture "still more alien and remote".[41] He was even more scathing about the Angry Penguins' pretensions, subjective outpourings and semi-digested borrowings when reviewing *The Vegetative Eye*. "Mr Harris is morally sick and discusses his symptoms with the gusto of an old woman showing the vicar her ulcerated leg." The resulting work, according to Hope, was "a Zombie, a composite corpse ... animated by psychological Voodoo", which deserved to have a stake driven through its decadent heart.[42]

Intense rivalry between the Sydney poets and the Angry Penguins, based in Adelaide and Melbourne, climaxed in the celebrated Ern Malley hoax. The brainchild of McAuley and Stewart, Ern was supposedly a deceased motor mechanic whose sister Ethel, much to her surprise, found manuscript poems among his personal effects. Unable to judge their worth, she sent them to the supremo of Australian modernism, Max Harris. His verdict was generous to a fault. Describing Malley as "one of the most outstanding poets we have produced here", and asserting "the perfection and integrity of his verse", Harris devoted the June 1944 issue of *Angry Penguins* to the *oeuvre* of this antipodean Chatterton. The plot was exposed on 18 June in the Sydney tabloid *Sunday Sun*, which ensured that the hoax reached a wide reading public. On 25 June it recounted how the poems had been composed one afternoon by the two Sydney poets, using free association interleaved with material drawn from random sources, to create works of patent nonsense. Their overriding aim, according to the *Sunday Sun*, was to demonstrate that the Angry Penguins were "insensible of absurdity and incapable of ordinary discrimination", leading them to present repeatedly as "great poetry" work which "appeared to us to be a collection of garish images without coherent meaning and structure; as if one erected a coat of bright paint and called it a house". Harris countered that the works contained much better material than its authors knew, and debate on their merits continues to this day.

The Ern Malley poems represented a watershed in their creators' work, and arguably in Australian verse. Their rapid composition was made possible by a long apprenticeship in modernism, as well as by internalised material that came to the surface once spontaneous writing commenced. So, too, did actual emotional and mental states which, despite contrived nonsense or disjunctions, lend Malley's work a surprising coherence. At times the wilful disruption of otherwise comprehensible verse is delayed too long, as in "Petit Testament", or even disparate elements, like a pamphlet on controlling mosquitoes, become part of a larger mosaic, an *objet trouvé* recontextualised with the playful humour of contemporary art in "Culture as Exhibit":

> "Swamps, marshes, borrow-pits and other
> Areas of stagnant water serve
> As breeding-grounds ..." Now
> Have I found you, my Anopheles!
> (There is a meaning for the circumspect)
> Come, we will dance sedate quadrilles,
> A pallid polka or a yelping shimmy
> Over these sunken sodden breeding-grounds!
> We will be wraiths and wreaths of tissue-paper
> To clog the Town Council in their plans.
> Culture forsooth! Albert, get my gun. (p. 94)[43]

Individual poems are also tantalisingly self-reflexive. "We are as the double almond concealed in one shell", confesses the speaker of "Colloquy with John Keats" (p. 97). "Palinode" highlights the Sydney tradition of literary parodies, and the opening lines of "Baroque Exterior" read like a witty prophecy of the hoax's impact: "When the hysterical vision strikes / The facade of an era it manifests / Its insidious relations" (p. 93). As Ern conceded, in words that applied to the hoaxers who until then had not published a volume of verse, it was "something to be at last speaking / Though in this No-Man's-language appropriate / Only to No-Man's Land" (p. 100).

POETS OF THE 1950s

One of the most positive and enduring legacies of the hoax was to free Australian verse from dogmatic models and create an environment in which eclectic talents could flourish. Certainly the popular press revelled in this debunking of modernist obscurity, while the crushing of Harris' claims to be the doyen of Australian poetry created a gap eventually filled by Hope and McAuley, who were receptive to a broad range of local compositions in the post-war decades. It was a period which elicited extreme responses. Hope could lash contemporary critics and poetasters in *The Dunciad Minor* (1950), as if Australia were about to witness a reinstatement of Dulness' empire, whereas its abundant literary activity moved Francis Webb to insist: "surely nowhere save perhaps in the Middle Ages has there been such an efflorescence of poetry as this here in Australia ... All homage to the Brennans, Slessors, McCraes, Lawsons, who fathered this. And joy to this no-hoper who is actually a tiny little atom of it."[44] *A Drum for Ben Boyd* (1948) and *Leichhardt in Theatre* (1952) by this alleged no-hoper, however, aroused considerable attention with their innovative diction, born of his perception that "truth itself is a mass of stops and gaps", and their obvious determination, shared with his personae, to grapple audaciously "with the outskirts of the unknown".[45] One of the earliest to recognise Webb's talent was the *Bulletin*'s literary editor, Douglas Stewart, whose own work extended both the vernacular tradition of Adam Lindsay Gordon and his elevation of suffering into a potential sign of greatness: "every man ... / Dreams, and nearly triumphs, and is always defeated, / And then, as we did, triumphs again in endurance".[46] Popular verse forms were also being rethought by David Campbell in *Speak with the Sun* (1949) and *The Miracle of Mullion Hill* (1956). There, realising that "faced by a woman, our balladists mounted a horse", Campbell repeopled their settings with diverse races, sexes and bush fauna, and asserted the power of individual vision to comprehend nature, not simply to record it: "The Murray's source is in the mind / And at a word it flows".[47] In the same period Rosemary Dobson, in the finely sculptured poems of *In a Convex Mirror* (1944), *The Ship of Ice* (1948) and *Child with a Cockatoo* (1955), began her meditations on time framed by European art and legend, searching "for something only fugitively glimpsed; a state of grace which one once knew, or imagined, or from which one was turned away".[48] In practical terms, this diversity was underpinned by grants from the Commonwealth Literary Fund, reinvigorated and expanded in 1939, and by the willingness of the major local publishing house, Angus & Robertson, to print commercially unviable but distinguished literature. It supported the early endeavours of most of these writers, and helped ensure, as one contemporary put it, that the 1950s were "years of poets".[49]

Alec Hope, after a slow, uncertain start, became an imposing commentator on local letters, and Australia's most important verse satirist. His first collection, *The Wandering Islands* (1955), was followed by a further ten volumes, ending with *Orpheus* (1991). The savagery of his pen was at times difficult to reconcile with his studied air of imperturbability; however, Vincent Buckley scented "strange bogeys deep in his psyche" and Harold Stewart was drawn to that "lovely man, Hope. Nice and nasty!"[50] Spurning the self-applauding insularity of Australian literary circles, Hope aligned himself with European creative traditions. Here was authoritative precedent, as well as myths and esoteric details to reanimate with contemporary relevance, as he set out allegedly "nobly, without crank or quirk or / Default, to show it as it is, / And through his art to bring to birth / New modes of being on the earth" (p. 190).[51] Evidence of the first part of this program fulfilled against "the great Un-culture" (p. 199) abounds in early works like "Australia", "Sportsfield" and "The Brides". These challenged nationalist platitudes and exposed the base instinct underlying popular rituals, as when nubile young women are described in terms of man's favourite toy:

He will find every comfort: the full set
Of gadgets; knobs that answer to the touch
For light or music; a place for his cigarette;
Room for his knees; a honey of a clutch. (p. 82)

Hope's work, however, is seldom free of crank or quirk. Its sexual obsessiveness helped earn him the sobriquet "phallic Alec", and a hostile reception from feminists – although like his satiric alter ego Old Hairy, the copulating king of the baboons, he would doubtless claim that this reflected as much his race's as his own preoccupation with "Fuck, fight, food, fleas; you know, the four great F's" (p. 258). Nor did Hope found "new modes of being", unless this be understood more generally as "reviv[ing] / In men the creative energies by which they live" (p. 60). Though resourceful and unrelenting in attack, his scepticism, ploughed like salt into the soil of his vanquished targets, rarely promises to aid regrowth. And his inveterate self-defensiveness, abetted by wit and tripping metres, defuses, almost trivialises, incidents of enduring interest, like the sundering of lovers in "The Judgement" or the poet's encounter with the numinous in "A Letter from Rome". Yet although his saving vision often amounts to little more than vague echoes of past assurances ("Another providence begins, / The Word withdraws but never fails" [p. 199]), his advocacy of poetic craftsman-ship inspired a later generation of poets, such as Bruce Dawe, who found it stood out "like Ayers Rock in the vast plain of nonsense written about verse, here".[52]

JAMES McAULEY AND HAROLD STEWART

Equally opposed to free verse were Ern Malley's progenitors who, after World War II, joined the many writers questing for a new faith and new directions. As "reconstruction" became the catch-cry of the day, they sensed a return to reconstriction, and sought solutions outside the dominant Anglo-Saxon heritage. Influenced by the teachings of Traditionalists such as René Guénon, who preached that the West had departed from the great spiritual truths embodied in Oriental as well as primitive cultures, their gaze moved to the Asia-Pacific region. Stewart focused on Sino-Japanese civilisation. McAuley became professionally and emotionally involved in Papua New Guinea. There he discovered "a world where the inexorable organic rhythms were insistent", and eventually "a 'school of sanctity' for some", or as he put it in verse: "Land of apocalypse, where the earth dances, / The mountains speak, the doors of the spirit open, / And men are shaken by obscure trances" (p. 98).[53] Complementing these intellectual shifts, the compositions of both men turned away from what McAuley dubbed the

"Magian heresy", or the modernist raising of the poetic word into a surrogate religion, and tried ostensibly to make verse the expression of timeless truths instead of subjective experience. This change is evident between Mcauley's initial collection *Under Aldebaran* (1946) and *A Vision of Ceremony* (1956). The first brings together a variety of symbolist and discursive works written over two decades, including scathing reflections on his native land, then in the grip of severe censorship:

> Knowledge is regarded with suspicion.
> Culture to them is a policeman's beat;
> Who, having learnt to bully honest whores,
> Is let out on the Muses for a treat. (p. 40)

The second collection bears witness to his 1952 conversion to Catholicism, by attempting to revitalise and individualise the teachings of Rome. The effects were not always happy, nor the reception positive. As McAuley recognised: "Christ, you walked on the sea, / But cannot walk in a poem, / Not in our century" (p. 242). Ensuing volumes of verse were less doctrinaire. *Captain Quiros* (1964) provided a parable of the modern world bereft of defining principles in its portrayal of an ill-fated Spanish mission to establish a terrestrial paradise in the Pacific. In *Surprises of the Sun* (1969) McAuley broke through to the lyrical simplicity and unarmoured, confessional mode which he had previously esteemed but shied away from. Poems subtitled "On the Western Line" evoke unsparingly the emotional deprivation of his childhood, when "small things" "cut like a saw" (p. 246). Other pieces, like "In the Huon Valley", anticipate the starkly clear depictions, redolent with natural and life experience, which rendered so moving his final collections – *Time Given* (1976), *Music Late at Night* (1976) and *A World of Its Own* (1977), written with the knowledge that he had terminal cancer.

Stewart, even more radically than McAuley, turned his back on prevailing codes in the post-war decades. An extremely shy gay caught in a fiercely homophobic society, concealment, subterfuge and increasing isolation from a community which disdained all that was dearest to him marked his life and work. His sexual predilection is only hinted at in his verse, as when the Greek goddess of dawn is recast as a youth of striking physical beauty in "The Annunciation" (1940). Instead he aspired towards impersonality in *Phoenix Wings* (1948) and *Orpheus and Other Poems* (1956), collections dominated by mythically convoluted and aesthetically refined works which reviewers damned as vacuous. In addition, both volumes contained pioneering pieces on Eastern themes – scenes from a proposed longer work set in China, entitled *Landscape-Roll*, that was only completed in the 1990s. Unlike usually superficial local endeavours to encapsulate Oriental lore, such as Judith Wright's "Eight-panel Screen" which reduces Taoism to "Patience and the endless way" (p. 272),[54] even Stewart's early work reveals a thorough immersion in Asian cultures. There precise, supple diction, typical of his later years, is used to dramatise central tenets, as well as more general truths: "Here cares and creditors no more infest / The house of mind. Its poverty is rest. / Possessing nothing, I am not possessed".[55] Throughout the 1950s and 1960s he was slowly building on a war-time insight that Asia offered new possibilities for an English-language poet: "these are not mere fertilizing interests & agents but the very medium through which I realize myself … What Greece has been, from the Renaissance on, to English poets, Ancient China & the East in general are to me. I am most at home in their art & ideas, most myself, when effacing my self in those times & places & people."[56] Its first major fruits were two collections of haiku which sold tens of thousand of copies worldwide: *A Net of Fireflies* (1960) and *A Chime of Windbells* (1969). In 1966 Stewart moved permanently to Japan where he wrote his masterpiece *By the Old Walls of Kyoto* (1981). A 138-page epic depicting his spiritual pilgrimage in the ancient capital of Japan, it is undoubtedly the finest long poem written by an Australian, and according to Hope the greatest poem produced in English this century. Here finally Rex Ingamells' vision of transnational verse was fulfilled, but by a man whose withdrawal ensured that his life's work remained largely unread in what he termed "darkest Woz".

JUDITH WRIGHT

What McAuley and Stewart sought outside Australia, Judith Wright found and celebrated in her native New England. A prolific writer and activist, Wright has long been a notable public figure, particularly prominent as a champion of ecology and Indigenous rights. Her fame, however, rests largely on eleven collections of verse published over four decades, beginning with two outstanding volumes, *The Moving Image* (1946) and *Woman to Man* (1949). These contain or foreshadow her major concerns, and proclaim a deep kinship with the continent's rhythms and destiny: the landscape has become "part of my blood's country" (p. 20). Much as Patrick White invigorated and spiritualised the often humdrum prose of Australian realist fiction, so Wright recast local subjects, plumbing them for timeless truths, and stressing the need for unison with the land. Whereas the generic bullock-driver depicted by Kendall plodded along at the level of his dusty beasts, Wright's bullocky, his mind having become a conduit for the elements, achieves prophetic status. Embraced by the heavens and earth, he eventually becomes one with the countryside, a bone which feeds not impedes, much as his apocalyptic dreams contribute to rendering this potentially the Promised Land. Similarly, "Remittance Man" and "Soldier's Farm" afford variations on the Coming Man depicted by Henry Lawson in "Middleton's Rouseabout". His Andy is "a country lout", without opinions or "any 'idears'",[57] and so is able to gain a local dominion of uncertain worth. Wright's sons of the soil are equally feckless and devoid of larger vision. Nonetheless, they are celebrated for participating fully, if unthinkingly, in life, and the proof of their election is a final unity with the country which transcends personal defeats and even death:

> He asked for nothing but the luck to live,
> so now his willing blood moves in these trees
> that hold his heart up sunwards with their arms.
> The mists dissolve at morning like his dreams
> and the creek answers light as once his eyes;
> and yet he left here nothing but his love. (p. 11)

The poet is he or she who takes this empathy a step further, identifying with and consciously voicing the land – a daring act presented repeatedly within the tradition of wise, visionary madness which transforms the prisoner's straw "into flowers of wonder" (p. 4), or reveals the temporal, according to the Platonic epigraph prefixing Wright's first collection, as "a moving image of eternity".

Underlying these individual pieces, and reinforced by the experience of World War II, was a profound conviction that humankind had taken a wrong turn, and that it was the poet's task to provide healing alternatives. *The Moving Image* closes with the words: "Our dream was the wrong dream / our strength was the wrong strength" (p. 24). It opens with the assertion that "yet, the lovelier distance is ahead" (p. 3), and a programmatic statement:

> I am the maker. I have made both time and fear,
> knowing that to yield to either is to be dead.
> All that is real is to live, to desire, to be,
> till I say to the child I was, "It is this; it is here.
> In the doomed cell I have found love's whole eternity". (p. 4)

Like Gilmore, Wright makes benign love her lodestar. It alone assures possession, offers compensation for pain, and underpins all relations as well as her faith that life's passage is ultimately good. The punitive lesson of Genesis, for example, is rewritten in "The Garden" in terms of affirmative knowledge by depicting an aged Eve who has been comforted, not blighted, by a long existence. Though to the empirical eye she may appear a "scarecrow, bag of old bones" (p. 38), to the speaker's heart she represents fulfilment and refinement in an endless cycle which encompasses both death's black hand and regeneration: "all that we meet and live through, gathers in our old age / and makes a shelter from the cold, she says" – a point underscored by the closing vignette of her with snake and butterfly, traditional symbols of natural transformation and transcendence. The central metaphor for Wright's belief in nurturing continuity is the tree, deep-rooted and prolific. A mother murmurs to her child: "I am the earth. I am the root, / I am the stem that fed the fruit, / the link that joins you to the night" (p. 31). Then dreamers are haunted by knowledge of "The burning wires of nerves, the crimson way / from head to heart, towering tree of blood" (p. 41), at the same time as roots reach deep under the house to regions as mysterious as those perfumed by native plants, whose dust-like pollen signifies eternal renewal: "no land is lost or won by wars, / for earth is spirit" (p. 141). Such a vision, and the verse which conveys it, are ultimately an act of faith, in keeping with Wright's belief that we "have choice or power to make us whole again" (p. 10), or, in terms which Harpur would immediately have recognised, that mankind can still either make or mar this God-given planet.

WOMEN POETS OF THE 1960s

Although Wright and Dobson brought out collections regularly over many years, a number of poets were still impeded by the conflicting dilemmas that dogged Gilmore's early years. Typically their careers are marked by a long hiatus between juvenilia and published works, or by a late rise to literary fame reflecting the postponed unfolding of potential. *Kaleidoscope* (1940) by Dorothy Green was followed decades later by *The Dolphin* (1967). The first collections of Gwen Harwood, Dorothy Hewett and Kath Walker/ Oodgeroo appeared in the 1960s, and for Amy Witting literary recognition came only in the late 1980s. Low self-esteem, augmented by the soaring reputations of male peers, was difficult to overcome, as was the realisation, according to Witting, that proven intellectual capacity in a female was about as appealing as facial hair to the opposite sex. Also, well into the 1960s literary circles, no less than public bars, were men only preserves, with women largely confined to the lounge-bar roles of polite applause and ego-flattering compliance. This fostered indignation and a transgressive dimension in their writings. Harwood's reminiscences recall the world of Jane Austen. Home came first. Poetry books were read propped over the sink amid the suds, composition carried on in her head. "I can work on a 50-line poem without pencil and paper, a skill I developed when in domestic turmoil … I keep all that out of the way; a secret vice, like drinking with bottles in the wardrobe. I hid my poems in odd places", and even from her daughter.[58] The resulting frustration appeared in works published under the pseudonym Miriam Stone, like "Suburban Sonnet: Boxing Day" and "Burning Sappho". There the poet-persona rages silently against her refractory child ("Inside my smile a monster grins / and sticks her image through with pins"), or against the sexual demands of her partner: "In my warm thighs a fleshless devil / chops him to bits with hell-cold evil". These sentiments were progressively excised from Harwood's selected works, as she created a less troubled surface above complex depths.[59] "It says in the Coverdale translation of the Psalms that the lions wait upon God for their meat. I've always felt particularly drawn to the lion and its image – the king of beasts ... It is much easier for a woman to disguise that kind of ferocity than it is for a man."[60] And, it might be added, much more expected, although the older women whose poetic emergence coincided with the social protest of the 1960s produced works guaranteed to arouse controversy.

The verse of Hewett and Walker has a directness and frankness rarely seen in local women's poetry before the emergence of Judith Wright. Both were committed activists, Hewett to Communism and Walker to the struggle for Indigenous rights, as seen when she resumed her traditional name of Oodgeroo of the Noonuccal in 1988 in protest against Australia's Bicentenary celebration, or in her three volumes, *We Are Going* (1964), *The Dawn is at Hand* (1966) and *My People* (1970). Viewing poetry as a means of protest and education, Oodgeroo is, as a communal singer, constantly aware of the need to provide an alternative, readily transmissible version of history to her people: "They brought you Bibles and disease, the liquor and the gun: / With Christian culture such as these the white command was won" (p. 62).[61] Her usual models are oral, laced with commonsense and a distinctive brand of humour, as when she mockingly contrasts a primitive past with modern progress ("No more message-stick; / Lubras and lads / Got television now, / Mostly ads"), to end with the latest scientific advance:

> Lay down the woomera,
> Lay down the waddy.
> Now we got atom-bomb,
> End everybody. (p. 33)

Hewett, no less than Oodgeroo, assumed the burden of literary self-empowerment, and in her selected works from the 1960s collections *What about the People!* (1961), *Windmill Country* (1968) and *Late Night Bulletin* (1969) focuses on female sensibility and experience. In keeping with her self-portrait as a latterday "Eve, spitting the pips in the eyes of the myth-makers" (p. 73),[62] earthy realism enlivens her descriptions of passionate heterosexual relationships, or abrupt shifts of register unsettle reader-expectations in ambitious works like "Go Down Red Roses" or "Window on Sydney". At a time when Hope was preaching classical control, Hewett was seeking innovative solutions to provide new perspectives, whether with Whitmanesque lines that encompassed life's plenitude, seen at their best in the moving saga of generations "Legend of the Green Country", or with a volume of poetry conceived in its entirety as a challenge to patriarchal conventions, such as *Rapunzel in Suburbia* (1976). In the face of neglect or hostile reviews, she chose neither the silence nor the submission of her colonial precursors, but boldly, as she put it after reviewing crowned canonical figures, to "abdicate a throne, / And piddle in a gutter of my own" (p. 141).

Harwood's work is less easy to categorise, oscillating between engagement and evasion, mask and apparently direct utterance, metaphysical meditation and social satire. The titles of her first collections betrayed nothing of this range – *Poems* (1963), *Poems/Volume Two* (1968), *Selected Poems* (1975), followed by the arrestingly titled *Lion's Bride* (1981) and *Bone Scan* (1988). Notoriety came quickly in 1961 as a result of a mini-hoax perpetrated against that former bastion of Australian bush tradition, the *Bulletin*. To it she submitted two well-crafted sonnets about the medieval lovers Abelard and Eloisa, whose first letters formed the acrostics "So long Bulletin" and "Fuck all editors". Its duped editor, Donald Horne, who had applauded the Ern Malley hoax, later launched a piqued attack on "lady poets" who let their "fantasies" run riot to "satisfy their own special humour".[63] This sexism and attempted condescension were not lost on Harwood, who had found that compositions under male pseudonyms such as Walter Lehmann ("author" of the sonnets) and Francis Geyer received considerably more positive responses from magazine editors than did work by a Tasmanian housewife and mother of four. Publication under pen-names continued afterwards, as did the creation of distinct personae or characters, such as Professors Eisenbart and Kröte. Both are to some extent comic alter egos. Kröte, like his creator, is strongly drawn to music. Eisenbart is an acclaimed member of the Academy, in the tradition of Goethe's Faust or Thomas Mann's Gustav von Aschenbach in *Death in Venice*. He shares their perpetual struggle to integrate the calls of intellect with those of life, upon which art depends for its material, and which entails a menacing openness to sexual desire as well as death. Consequently, in "Early Morning" Eisenbart is figuratively slain by "shafts" of sunlight, whose physical counterpart is the coupling in which he has just indulged, or he succumbs to Tadzio's avatar in "Ganymede", with Harwood suggesting through a prehistoric tableau that art's freeze-frame is the only form of reproduction which can hope to be spared time's unrelenting blade:

> A painting from the Lascaux caves
> hangs reproduced above their bed:
> bird-masked beside his wounded prey
> an ithyphallic hunter dead. (p. 34)[64]

No Eisenbart for whom symbols afford a straightforward "sublime affirmation" (p. 41), Harwood explores humanity's troubled predicament caught between reason and impulse, conviction and unknowing, parturition and death. A recurring early correlative for this situation is the dolphin, traversing water and air, knowing love and grief, experiencing "the strong / leaping of spirit through a temporal sea" (p. 9), while this state is repeatedly explored in *Poems/Volume Two* (1968) in works such as "Littoral" and "New Music". Their common theme is the need to plumb depths, or to shift beyond appearances to enduring truths, projected often through the time-honoured symbol of light. In "Littoral" the speaker acknowledges the imperative to:

> suffer, and change, and question all,
> wrestle with thought and word, and bind
> my speech to earth's own laws to win
> the heart's true life at last. (p. 71)

Here the truths of the heart and spirit are synonymous, involving a movement "past the span / of human hands and human skill / to affirm *what is*" (p. 71). Love is one potential key to this leap. Music is another, and even fallible words, with the poet ideally grasping truth in the midst of constant change. Mankind's present condition, however, is figured as darkness, just as it is pointedly a child who experiences the ideal realm of music, where "joy transcends / all temporal need, where the heart understands / unquestionable shapes of truth, and mends / its mortal wounds".[65] For an adult, as one persona remarks, "great questions all have wavering answers" (p. 193). Clearer avowals of faith are usually mediated by other voices, like John Ruskin's, who found "in clouds a deep, calm presence / 'which must be sought ere it is seen / and loved ere it is understood'" (p. 181). Repeatedly Harwood senses it, but sees at best its translucent effects. Her awareness of the boundaries of language and knowledge, of unfulfillable longings and constraints, permits no ultimate vision, but this does not prevent artistic creation based on trust and aspiration, the counterpart of her unsparing self-image as "a skinful of elements climbing / from earth to the fastness of light" (p. 100).

In Harwood's verse, as in the best work of her contemporaries, Australian poetry succeeds at last in being firmly anchored in the regional and personal, yet international in its appeal. She, like Wright, McAuley and the succeeding generation of poets headed by Les Murray, found nature "radiant as mystery still" (p. 7), and registered a new sense of Australia as habitat, shared precariously but richly with various eco-systems, a sense unavailable even to colonial visionaries. With the passing of time the gaze of poets has moved closer to objects and daily life, whereas their perspective has lengthened and diversified. Australian verse is no longer identifiable by the scent of wattle or the crack of the stock-whip, nor even by Standard English. Poetry is now composed not only in the vernacular, but after the 1960s in diverse migrant tongues. Similarly, mass communication and travel have eased the crippling intellectual limitations felt by writers born during the first decades of the twentieth century, and in 1969 Wright and McAuley headed a group of local poets bound for New Delhi to showcase Australian verse. Only a long-term expatriate like Harold Stewart, biased by decades of neglect, could still rail well into the 1990s at the unmitigated shallowness of "Oz kulcha", for him summed up by "The Australian Trinity":

> First, as our National Hero, we adore
> Godfather Kelly, Ned who fought the law.
> Next, to our Equine Saviour we give thanks:
> His Godson, Phar Lap (murdered by the Yanks).
> Last, as our culture's Bard of Kitsch, we boast
> Of Ern L. Malley, our Unholy Ghost.[66]

This mental image derived largely from the 1930s, when poetasters could dash off verse declaring "'Tis not for fame and glory I write, / But just because my heart is light", and end collections with a hackneyed flourish: "And because we love this land of the 'roo, / So readers all, adieu, adieu".[67] By the 1960s banal parochialism had given way to engagement with American and European trends, and the male lions of the pride were having to reckon with strong, versatile female rivals. The days of the bushman poet had long been numbered, those of the international conference performer had only just begun.

NOTES

1 Harpur letter to N.D. Stenhouse, 2 July 1859, reprinted in Michael Ackland, ed., *Charles Harpur: Selected Poetry and Prose* (Melbourne: Penguin, 1986), p. 158.

2 From "The Poems of Thomas Davis" (1871), reprinted in Michael Ackland, ed., *Henry Kendall: Poetry, Prose and Selected Correspondence* (St Lucia: University of Queensland Press, 1993), p. 168.

3 Vance Palmer, "The Spirit of Prose" (1921), quoted in Katherine Gallagher, "Shadows and Silences: Australian Women Poets in the Twenties and Thirties", in David Brooks and Brenda Walker, eds, *Poetry and Gender: Statements and Essays in Australian Women's Poetry and Poetics* (St Lucia: University of Queensland Press, 1989), p. 88.

4 *The Old Roof-Tree: Letters of Ishbel to her Half-Brother Mark Latimer (August–January)* (London: Longman, 1902), p. 193.

5 From Introduction to *The Bulletin Story Book* (1901), reprinted in Michael Ackland, ed., *The Penguin Book of 19th Century Australian Literature* (Melbourne: Penguin, 1993), p. 249.

6 From "Australian Literature 1" (1901), reprinted in Leon Cantrell, ed., *A.G. Stephens: Selected Writings* (Sydney: Angus & Robertson, 1978), pp. 84 and 88.

7 George Essex Evans, "The Women of the West" (1906), reprinted in Ackland, ed., *19th Century Australian Literature*, p. 171.

8 From "Studies in French Poetry 1860–1900" (1920), reprinted in A.R. Chisholm and J.J. Quinn, eds, *The Prose of Christopher Brennan* (Sydney: Angus & Robertson, 1965), p. 329.

9 "An Answer", reprinted in Ackland, ed., *19th Century Australian Literature*, p. 209.

10 Louisa Lawson, "About Ourselves", reprinted in Ackland, ed., *19th Century Australian Literature*, p. 275.

11 "Lines Written During a Night Spent in a Bush Inn", reprinted in Ackland, ed., *19th Century Australian Literature*, p. 173.

12 W.H. Wilde and T. Inglis Moore, eds, *Letters of Mary Gilmore* (Melbourne: Melbourne University Press, 1980), p. 30.

13 Letter of 16 September 1897, quoted in Robin B. Marsden, "New Light on Brennan", *Southerly*, 31 (1971), p. 131.

14 "Lilith", reprinted in Terry Sturm, ed., *Christopher Brennan* (St Lucia: University of Queensland Press, 1984), p. 73.

15 "Epilogues", reprinted in Sturm, ed., *Christopher Brennan*, p. 100.

16 Page references to Neilson are to Cliff Hanna, ed., *John Shaw Neilson: Poetry, autobiography and correspondence* (St Lucia: University of Queensland Press, 1991).

17 A.D. Hope, "Paradox and Parable", *Southerly*, 4 (1945), p. 43.

18 Lionel Lindsay, *Addled Art* (London: Hollis and Carter, 1946), p. 15.

19 "Poetry Militant: An Australian Plea for the Poetry of Purpose" in *The Poems of Bernard O'Dowd: Collected Edition* (Melbourne: Lothian, 1944), pp. 3 and 9.

20 From "The Grinning Mirror" (1956), reprinted in Leonie Kramer, ed., *James McAuley: Poetry, essays and personal commentary* (St Lucia: University of Queensland Press, 1988), p. 73.

21 "Vulcan" in *The Poems of Bernard O'Dowd*, p. 118.

22 Page references to Harford are to Drusilla Modjeska and Marjorie Pizer, eds, *The Poems of Lesbia Harford* (Sydney: Angus & Robertson, 1985).

23 Letter to Percival Serle, 12 June 1926, quoted in Jennifer Strauss, "Stubborn Singers of Their Full Song: Mary Gilmore and Lesbia Harford", in Kay Ferres, ed., *The Time to Write: Australian Women Writers 1890–1930* (Melbourne: Penguin, 1993), p. 129.

24 A. Gore-Jones, "Writing and the Woman. Interview with Mrs. M. Forrest", *Australian Woman's Mirror*, 3 March 1925, p. 13.

25 Donald C. Cameron, Foreword to *Battlefields* (Sydney: Angus & Robertson, 1939).

26 Page references to Gilmore are to Mary Gilmore, *Selected Verse* (Sydney: Angus & Robertson, 1969).

27 A signed, handwritten note inside the front cover of a copy of *Under the Wilgas* (Melbourne: Angus & Robertson, 1931), Rare Books Collection, Monash University.

28 "Poetry Militant", *The Poems of Bernard O'Dowd*, p. 14.

29 From, respectively, *Under the Wilgas*, p. 109, and "The Song of Banna", *The Passionate Heart* (Sydney: Angus & Robertson, 1918), p. 115.

30 From, respectively, "The Comforter", *The Rue Tree* (Melbourne: Robertson and Mullen, 1931), p. 19; "Fuegian", *The Passionate Heart*, p. 141; and *Under the Wilgas*, p. 138.

31 "In the Park", *The Rue Tree*, p. 53.

32 From "Kenneth Slessor" (1971) in Julian Croft, ed., *Robert D. FitzGerald* (St Lucia: University of Queensland Press, 1987), p. 53.

33 From "Long Since ..." (1934) and "Kenneth Slessor", Croft, ed., *Robert D. FitzGerald*, pp. 46 and 54.

34 "Instructions to Contemporaries", Harold Stewart Papers, NL MS 8973/13/4 (NL identifies a collection held in the National Library, Canberra).

35 Page references to Slessor are to Dennis Haskell, ed., *Kenneth Slessor: Poetry, essays, war despatches, war diaries, journalism, autobiographical material and letters* (St Lucia: University of Queensland Press, 1991).

36 From "Writing Poetry: the Why and the How" (1948), quoted in Adrian Caesar, *Kenneth Slessor* (Melbourne: Oxford University Press, 1995), p. 64.

37 "Moorawathimeering" in Brian Elliott, ed., *The Jindyworobaks* (St Lucia: University of Queensland Press, 1979), p. 11.

38 From *Conditional Culture* (1938), reprinted in Elliott, ed., *The Jindyworobaks*, p. 230.

39 Alan Brissenden, ed., *The Angry Penguin: Selected Poems of Max Harris* (Canberra: National Library of Australia, 1996), p. 14.

40 *Hermes*, Trinity Term, 1933, p. 9.

41 From "Culture Corroboree" (1941), reprinted in Elliott, ed., *The Jindyworobaks*, pp. 248–9.

42 "Confessions of a Zombie", *Meanjin*, 3 (1944), p. 48.

43 Page references to Malley's poems are to John Tranter and Philip Mead, eds, *The Penguin Book of Modern Australian Poetry* (Melbourne: Penguin, 1991).

44 Letter to Gwen Harwood, 2 April 1964, cited in Introduction, Michael Griffith and James A. McGlade, eds, *The Poetry of Francis Webb* (Sydney: Angus & Robertson, 1991), n.p.

45 "A Drum for Ben Boyd", Griffith and McGlade, eds, *The Poetry of Francis Webb*, pp. 43 and 54.

46 *The Fire on the Snow* (1944) in Douglas Stewart, *Selected Poems* (Sydney: Angus & Robertson, 1992), p. 54.

47 David Campbell, *Selected Poems* (Sydney: Angus & Robertson, 1986), from Preface to 1973 Edition and "Soldier's Song", p. 10.

48 Rosemary Dobson, *Selected Poems* (Sydney: Angus & Robertson, 1973), Preface, p. xiii.

49 The title of Chapter IX in Vincent Buckley, *Cutting Green Hay: Friendships, movements and cultural conflicts in Australia's great decades* (Melbourne: Penguin, 1983).

50 *Cutting Green Hay*, p. 157, and Stewart, letter to Horne, 11 November [1939], Horne Papers, ML MS 3525, MLK 2132, Mitchell Library, Sydney.

51 Page references to Hope are to A.D. Hope, *Collected Poems* (Sydney: Angus & Robertson, 1972).

52 Letter to Hope, 13 January 1969, quoted in Kevin Hart, *A.D. Hope* (Melbourne: Oxford University Press, 1992), p. 51.

53 "My New Guinea" (1961), reprinted in Kramer, ed., *James McAuley*, pp. 22 and 29. Page references to McAuley's poetry are to his *Collected Poems* (Sydney: Angus & Robertson, 1994).

54 Page references to Wright are to her *Collected Poems: 1942–1970* (Sydney: Angus & Robertson, 1971).

55 "A Flight of Wild Geese" in Stewart, *Phoenix Wings: Poems 1940–6* (Sydney: Angus & Robertson, 1948), p. 43.

56 Letter to H.M. Green, 17 April 1943, NL MS 3925.

57 Ackland, ed., *19th Century Australian Literature*, p. 263.

58 Barbara Williams, *In Other Words: Interviews with Australian Poets* (Amsterdam: Rodopi, 1998), p. 56.

59 The previous quotations are a good example of this. "Burning Sappho" appeared first in the *Bulletin*, 23 June 1962. When reprinted in *Poems/Volume Two*, the lines beginning "In my warm" were omitted, as was the whole poem from her *Selected Poems*.

60 Jenny Digby, *A Woman's Voice: Conversations with Australian Poets* (St Lucia: University of Queensland Press, 1996), p. 61.

61 Page references to Oodgeroo are to *My People* (Milton: Jacaranda Press, 1990).

62 Page references to Hewett are to her *Collected Poems* (Fremantle: Fremantle Arts Centre Press, 1995).

63 "The Hoax that Misfired", *Bulletin*, August 1961, quoted in Alison Hoddinott, *Gwen Harwood: The Real and the Imagined World* (Sydney: Angus & Robertson, 1991), p. 88.

64 Page references to Harwood are to her *Selected Poems* (Sydney: Angus & Robertson, 1990).

65 "Four Impromptus: II", in Harwood, *Poems/Volume Two* (Sydney: Angus & Robertson, 1968), p. 40.

66 Letter to Milton Moon, 5 November 1992, NL MS 8973/16/32.

67 From the conclusion to Alice Beck, *"Bonny Yathroo" and Other Australian Verse* (London: Stockwell, 1934).

4

KERRYN GOLDSWORTHY

Fiction from 1900 to 1970

AROUND FEDERATION

In the last decade of the nineteenth century as Australia moved towards Federation, fiction writers began to depart from the generic conventions of romance and melodrama, and from the construction of the reader as essentially a British consumer looking for exotic and colourful tales of the colonies. Writers like Henry Lawson, Miles Franklin and Joseph Furphy were more interested in depicting what was "Australian" from an insider's point of view; the Australian landscape and ideas about the Australian "national character" moved to the foreground in fiction around the turn of the century.

This, at least, is how things appear to be. The truth is more complicated: in this as in all eras, the kind of fiction that had the best chances of survival, in both the short and the long term, was the kind encouraged by editors and publishers. As Susan Sheridan and others have argued, during this period women writers of "romance" fiction were edged out of the Australian picture by writers whose work addressed more overtly the issues around nationhood.[1] Barbara Baynton, if anything an anti-romance writer, survived this particular cut but still had her work heavily edited, the better to fit prevailing ideas about what it ought to be. In turn-of-the-century Australia where editors and publishers were scarce, the few who did exist had disproportionate power over what sort of literature would be published, read and valued in its own society. An obvious example is the legendary A.G. Stephens of the *Bulletin*, an inspired and heavily interventionist editor, later a publisher, with strong views about what Australian literature was and ought to be.

Most of the best-known fiction from this period – some of Henry Lawson's Joe Wilson stories, Miles Franklin's *My Brilliant Career* (1901), Barbara Baynton's stories, and Joseph Furphy's *Such is Life* (1903) – was written before the Federation date of 1 January 1901 but only appeared in book form after it, as though somehow Federation had given it form and permanence, or had found its expression in a literature preoccupied with questions of nationality. Two publications in the Federation year of 1901 – *Joe Wilson and His Mates* and *My Brilliant Career* – illustrate this in different ways.

Henry Lawson was a writer of established reputation at the height of his powers, not yet in the personal and professional decline into which he later sank, but already a writer from whom a certain kind of style and content, and certain kinds of opinions, had come to be expected. By 1901 when he published *Joe Wilson and His Mates* he was already "being Henry Lawson", and his name had already come to be associated with what was "Australian". Some of the qualities that endured for many years in the received version of the national character were those exemplified by and celebrated in the Joe Wilson stories, as in Lawson's work generally: mateship, class (but not race or gender) egalitarianism, and a kind of laid-back stoicism. Lawson's stories and characters have been a major influence in the construction of that traditional "national identity" that only the last few decades have begun to dismantle, an identity reflected by historian and former South Australian Premier John Bannon in his essay on the Australian federal movement: "Federation ... is a pedestrian process marked by exclusion: of the workers, of women, of indigenous people, of Asians, of non-English speaking Europeans."[2]

But one irony in the publication of what was in many respects such an "Australian" book was that Lawson was in England, where he hoped to stay, having gone there in the first place because of the lack of opportunity for writers in Australia; many of the stories in *Joe Wilson and His Mates* were actually written in London. One aspect of these stories that does give them a "colonial" flavour is what John Barnes calls "an obvious awareness of a foreign audience in Joe Wilson's explanations – an aspect of the Joe Wilson stories that some Australian readers find irritating".[3] Still, Lawson regarded his two-year stay in London as, in his own phrase, the "high tide" of his creative life, and most literary critics and historians agree; the stories in *Joe Wilson and His Mates*, along with those in the earlier *While the Billy Boils*, are regarded as his finest achievement.

Joe Wilson and His Mates consists of two sections: "Joe Wilson", containing a sequence of four linked stories narrated by the main character, and "Joe Wilson's Mates", a further fourteen stories which include the classics "The Loaded Dog" and "Telling Mrs Baker". The four Joe Wilson stories – "Joe Wilson's Courtship", "Brighten's Sister-in-law", "Water Them Geraniums" and "A Double Buggy at Lahey's Creek" – provide when taken as a unit the most sustained example we have of Lawson's skills in narrative and characterisation, as well as in the representation of the effects of environment on character and events; a central theme of this sequence is the strain that the hardship of bush life has placed on Joe's marriage.

Joe gets a long entry to himself in *The Oxford Companion to Australian Literature*, which observes that this sequence of stories "has been justly admired for its controlled presentation of the process of alienation and disintegration wrought by the experience of bush life".[4] It's interesting to note, however, that Lawson – like Furphy, and indeed like Franklin – consistently presents "the bush" as good for mateship but bad for marriage; masculine bonds are strengthened by adversity in the bush, but marriage ties are weakened by it.

It was Lawson who wrote a preface to another book published in this same Federation year: Miles Franklin's *My Brilliant Career*. This first novel by an exuberant nineteen-year-old combined romance, anti-romance, thinly veiled autobiography, and a robust and sentimental nationalism that is echoed in Lawson's preface. Because turn-of-the-century Australian national-ism was so profoundly masculinist in its values and expression, the book's feminism is at strident odds with its nationalism, and the fact that neither Franklin nor her narrator-heroine Sybylla Melvyn seems aware of this is one of the things that gives the narrative its frenetic, slightly incoherent feel.

Lawson solves this problem in his preface by dismissing one half of it, failing utterly to understand the dilemmas of a girl who might (in any era, much less that one) want agency and independence as well as love, in a remark that has in recent times been derisively quoted by a variety of feminist critics: "I don't know about the girlishly emotional parts of the book – I leave that to girl readers to judge; but the descriptions of bush life and scenery came startlingly, painfully real to me, and ... as far as they are concerned, the book is true to Australia – the truest I ever read."[5]

My Brilliant Career is in fact deeply ambivalent about "bush life and scenery"; Sybylla's view of both, always heavily imbued with either positive or negative emotion, often seems mainly a projection of her own state of mind. This ebullient novel is a long monologue dramatising a number of inner conflicts: between love and ambition, desire and propriety, stasis and motion, and not least between Sybylla's love of Australia ("I am proud that I am an Australian, a daughter of the Southern Cross, a child of the mighty bush") and her desire for the cultural life of cities and of other countries.[6] With its stress on the female dilemma of Love versus Art and the benefit of insights provided by second-wave feminism, Gillian Armstrong's 1979 film of this novel – and the brilliant performance of Judy Davis as Sybylla – went a long way towards making sense of a semi-autobiographical character whose emotions and motivations the young Franklin clearly did not properly understand herself.

The third of these "Federation" books is one of the great masterpieces and challenges of Australian literature: Joseph Furphy's *Such is Life*. This sprawling, opaque and very funny novel, initially purporting to comprise a randomly chosen week from the diary entries of the narrator Tom Collins (though this plan is quickly abandoned), was at once a late experiment in realism and a very early anticipation of postmodern techniques of fragmentation, allusion, pastiche and authorial self-consciousness. As with *Joe Wilson and His Mates* and *My Brilliant Career*, its rural setting helped to reinforce "the bush" as an essential element in Australia's idea of itself; but unlike either of the other two books it was not an immediate hit with the reading public. It was so original, so far ahead of its time and so demanding of its readers that it was not until 1944, after decades of tireless promotion by Furphy admirers like Miles Franklin, Kate Baker, A.G. Stephens and Vance Palmer, that Furphy's reputation began to grow.

Such is Life was also, in its conception and execution, a conscious and deliberate rejection of one pre-Federation mode of writing: the masculine adventure version of the nineteenth-century romance, as typified by the work of Henry Kingsley and Rolf Boldrewood. *Such is Life* has been called "Furphy's parody of romance"[7] and described as "significant for the part it played in turning Australian fiction away from the colonial romance".[8]

Furphy's famous description of it in 1897 – "temper, democratic; bias, offensively Australian" – was, minus the "offensively", adopted as the motto of the radical journal *Overland* on its inception in 1954.[9] With its rejection of colonial modes and values and its overt, aggressive nationalism, *Such is Life* seemed well timed on its publication in 1903 to reflect the birth, two years earlier, of Australia as an independent nation.

HISTORICAL FICTIONS

Australian fiction writers through the twentieth century have returned again and again to the historical novel as a form of nation-building, of alternative history writing, of expiation for colonial guilts, or of comment on their own times. Obviously there are no rules about how far in the past a novel is required to be set before it qualifies as an "historical novel"; the question is more one of genre and intention. Most of the historical novels published during the period covered by this chapter seem driven by a mythopoeic impulse in the wake of Federation, a drive to tell stories about the country that construct it as a nation, and to move it away from the inchoate colonialism of its origins by returning to them and exploring the process of nation formation. In historical fiction before 1970, the methodology in most cases was a comparatively simple form of either psychological or social (sometimes socialist) realism, and the three aspects of nineteenth-century Australian history concentrated on were convicts, pioneers and gold.

Dorothy Green's book on Henry Handel Richardson discusses gold as a central symbol in *The Fortunes of Richard Mahony* (1930), and it may well, as she argues, symbolise the "spiritual wholeness" that Mahony seeks and fails to find.[10] It also, however, represents the greedy, venal, get-rich-quick mentality on which much of nineteenth-century Australian society was built, a mentality powerfully represented both by Mahony's financial ruin when the share market collapses and by the opening scene where a prospector is buried alive by a vengeful and anthropomorphised landscape.

The Fortunes of Richard Mahony was originally published in three volumes – *Australia Felix* (1917), *The Way Home* (1925) and *Ultima Thule* (1929) – and republished after some minor editing as a trilogy in 1930. In a thoughtful 1928 journal entry Nettie Palmer reflects on the first two volumes and the possibilities of the third, which she knows is shortly to appear:

> A re-reading of "The Way Home" has sent me back to the first volume, and I'm surprised at the way I missed so many of its implications ... I certainly didn't see its significance for this country.[11]

The Fortunes of Richard Mahony is certainly a book about gold, about wealth and about nation-building; the Ballarat gold rush of the 1850s is its initial focus, and Richardson offers a vivid recreation of the time and place, and the politics of both. But what has earned this trilogy an enduring place in the history of Australian fiction is the complexity and breadth of its various concerns. It is also about marriage and money, about restlessness and dislocation, about emigration and the meaning of "home", and, undeniably, about death – and the relation death might have to nationality. In the tragic and drawn-out decline of Richard Mahony and the final image of his isolated grave, the closing mood of the trilogy anticipates the end of Patrick White's *Voss*: "If you live and suffer long enough in a place," says Judd – the convict and sole survivor of the expedition, a fact which is itself a pungent comment on White's own view of the nation's foundations – "you do not leave it altogether. Your spirit is still there."[12]

Katharine Susannah Prichard's "goldfields trilogy" – *The Roaring Nineties* (1946), *Golden Miles* (1948) and *Winged Seeds* (1950) – deals with the goldfields of Western Australia, the developing mining industry, and the industrial strife that inevitably resulted. Gold here is simply a symbol of wealth, an occasion for class struggle and industrial strife. Prichard's trilogy, a vast mass of historical detail, is seen by critics of varying political opinions as important mainly for the way it marks a stage in her declining career; the poet, playwright, novelist and ex-fellow-Communist Dorothy Hewett argues that after the suicide of Prichard's husband in 1934, "the sensuousness, the sexual energy [had] drained out of her writing, leaving only the husk of schematic politics to sustain her".[13] But in both trilogies – as in the first Australian "goldfields" novel, Catherine Helen Spence's *Clara Morison* (1854) – the labour/capital dichotomy hovers over the narrative, and comparisons are drawn implicitly or otherwise between the madness of gold greed and the dignity of work.

Katharine Susannah Prichard's first novel *The Pioneers* (1915) was in the romantic and triumphalist mode of the nineteenth century, with the pioneering spirit overcoming various adversities to make a better life. The prize-winning, critically acclaimed and financially successful *A House is Built* (1929) was also a first novel, by Marjorie Barnard and Flora Eldershaw writing in collaboration as "M. Barnard Eldershaw". *A House is Built* views the nineteenth-century nation-builders from a very different angle, concentrating on trade and the city, where a Sydney family establishes a business, a fortune and a dynasty. This novel offers a critique of the period by focusing on the restricted lives of nineteenth-century middle-class women denied access to or agency in public life. Barnard and Eldershaw were using the genre of the historical novel partly to reflect the dilemma of middle-class women in their own time, still largely denied the right to work and independence.

Five years after the publication of *A House is Built* another very different and much blacker version of the rural "pioneer" novel appeared in Brian Penton's *Landtakers* (1934). Like *A House is Built*, this novel uses a nineteenth-century narrative to explore ideas and theories about Australia in Penton's own time; it examines the effects of the Australian landscape and historical conditions on the European sensibility. *Landtakers* was the first of what was to be a trilogy, though in the event there was only one published sequel, *Inheritors* (1936); this followed the fortunes of the family descended from the original central character, Derek Cabell. A detailed account of the third novel, which exists in typescript, can be found in Patrick Buckridge's biography of Penton, where he places it in the context of the first two:

> The focus of this novel, as of the previous two in the trilogy, is on the effects of the Australian environment on the lives and mentalities of its European inhabitants. The main shift of emphasis here is that where *Landtakers* was chiefly concerned with the moral and psychological effects of the struggle with the land on the pioneers of the first generation, and *Inheritors* with the social, political and economic effects of this original struggle in the second generation, this third volume concentrates on the intellectual and artistic effects, both of the violence and corruption of the earlier generations, and also of the sheer distance of Australia from the centres of European culture.[14]

The message of the Penton trilogy was that Australia's pioneer history was not heroic but brutal and corrupting, and that Australian history and literature had rewritten it in whitewash. "[T]he romantic portrait of heroism and respectability," says Ken Goodwin, "is created, falsely, by Cabell's son only in retrospect ... Penton's thesis is that white Australian society has never escaped its convict origins, its early struggle for existence".[15]

Miles Franklin's most successful pioneering novel was another family saga and prize-winner with the ambiguous title *All That Swagger* (1936). The word "swagger" is used here as a noun, as Franklin explained: "*All That Swagger* simply means the bravado of the bravura days – a little dash, a little extra virility which carried them through hardship and loneliness."[16] Franklin's choice of an Irish rather than an English pioneer hero enables her to sidestep the more problematic issues raised by the history of Australia's relationship with England and the implications of that for her own national-ism and egalitarianism. She published a sequence of six other "pioneer" novels under the pseudonym "Brent of Bin Bin" between 1928 and 1956, described by several critics as a "family chronicle", but Marjorie Barnard voiced majority critical opinion, then as now, when she wrote to Jean Devanny that Franklin "has reached the top of her form in *All That Swagger*".[17]

The inclusion under this heading of Xavier Herbert's *Capricornia* (1938), set only thirty-four years earlier than its publication date, raises some questions about what constitutes an "historical novel". *Capricornia*, set in the Northern Territory at the turn of the century, is chiefly a narrative of race relations; its purpose is to investigate and comment on some of the past social values and practices from which twentieth-century Australian society evolved. As a comment on the country's origins it has features in common with *Landtakers* and *All That Swagger*, combining the picturesque sprawl of the latter with the dark vision of the former.

So the pioneer experience was politicised by Penton and again by Herbert, in novels published during an increasingly political decade. It was left to Patrick White in *The Tree of Man* (1955), a post-war novel about new beginnings, to psychologise, privatise and poeticise the pioneer experience, using the irresistible trope of the innocent couple in an Antipodean Garden of Eden. The obvious problem with this novel, reading it at the end of the century, is that it uses this powerful metaphorical framework at the expense of Australia's original inhabitants, virtually writing them out of the country's history.

But during the period covered by this chapter, any sense of historical responsibility and inherited guilt, as manifested in the literature, was still mainly focused on Australia's convict past. Brian Penton in *Landtakers* and its sequels argues that Australia's convict past is of central importance to the development of its national character; R.D. FitzGerald's poem "The Wind at Your Door" (1958) was, and remains, one of the most brilliant and complex articulations of historical complicity and inherited responsibility in Australian literature. This preoccupation with the "convict stain" was also explored by Judith Wright in her essay "The Upside-Down Hut" (1961). "The fact of Australia's convict-settlement origin," she says,

> has a deep meaning in our twentieth-century consciousness … It symbolizes a kind of split in our collective mind that is as important today as it ever was … [T]he basic themes are still the same. They were what Australia had to offer – the two themes of exile and of hope; and they remain the inner argument of almost all important writing done here, however they may be elaborated or disguised.[18]

Many Australian fiction writers during this period made use of Australia's convict history in their characters, plots and themes, notably Penton, Eleanor Dark and Patrick White. The earliest of these was William Gosse Hay, whose novels were chiefly entertainments: elaborately plotted historical romances in the nineteenth-century style, the best known being *The Escape of the Notorious Sir William Heans* (1919). Comparatively few earlier twentieth-century novels, however, addressed the convict era, or the convict system, directly as their central subject. Two notable exceptions, published within ten years of the FitzGerald poem and the Wright essay when the complex issue of inherited historical responsibility was clearly preoccupying Australian writers, are otherwise very different novels: Hal Porter's *The Tilted Cross* (1961) and Thomas Keneally's *Bring Larks and Heroes* (1967).

The Tilted Cross, like *The Escape of the Notorious Sir William Heans*, is set in Tasmania in the 1840s and uses, in Porter's elaborate style, antipodean metaphors of inversion to structure this moral fable about injustice and the abuse of power. *Bring Larks and Heroes*, set in the very early days of the penal colony in New South Wales, is more realist and less mannered, but both Porter and Keneally flirt with and skirt around the image of hell and damnation as the idea behind the transportation of convicts. Like Porter, Keneally makes use of the antipodean trope in his investigation of the British use of Australia as a place of punishment: both novels' patterns of imagery rely on the idea that injustice will inevitably prevail in a place where all the stars and seasons feel upside down and wrong.

There remains a number of historical novels that do not fit into any of these categories but represent major milestones in the fiction of this period. Eleanor Dark's trilogy – *The Timeless Land* (1941), *Storm of Time* (1948) and *No Barrier* (1953) – concentrates at first on the relationship between one white and one black man, Governor Phillip and Bennelong, later expanding to recount the fortunes of two pioneer families and several subsequent governors of New South Wales.

The Timeless Land was one of the early detailed examinations in fiction of contact history, and certainly one of the most sympathetic thus far to the situation of Aboriginal people. One early scene, in which the arrival of the First Fleet in 1788 is described from the point of view of the Aboriginal people watching it from the cliffs, is a landmark moment in Australian writing. While the legitimacy of representing Aboriginal points of view in white writing is and should be debatable, it is still extraordinary for a novel of this period to begin with an account of black subjects and white objects, the watchers and the watched.

Published in 1941, the same year as *The Timeless Land*, Ernestine Hill's bestselling *My Love Must Wait* incorporated both the "convict" and the "explorer" elements of Australia's nineteenth-century history. In this, her only novel, Hill fictionalises the life of explorer Matthew Flinders while remaining faithful to her detailed researches of his life and achievements. Patrick White's *Voss* (1957), the other most notable "explorer" novel of this period, is based on the much more mysterious and shadowy figure of Ludwig Leichhardt and makes imaginative use of the diaries of another explorer, Edward John Eyre. White uses the Leichhardt and Eyre material as a means to an end; one of the subjects this book explores is the relationship between history and myth, between hard evidence and metaphysical experience.

Ethel Anderson's *At Parramatta* (1956), published the year before *Voss*, joins in its departure from prevailing realist modes, and shares some of its settings, but in other ways could not be more different. This eccentric and highly original collection of linked stories was so different both from White's work, and from the realist, social realist, and socialist realist writing that otherwise dominated the fiction of the period, that it found no real context and sank out of sight. The elaborate, sometimes even fantastic style with which it evokes the period is reminiscent of Porter's in *The Tilted Cross* – which it also resembles in its sharp observations of class structure and abuses of power in colonial society; as Carole Ferrier has pointed out, "the boundaries between the socialist realists and the others, in hindsight, are often much less clear cut than they have been drawn".[19]

Nancy Cato, also a poet, has been publishing historical fiction since the 1950s; her best-known work is the "Murray River" trilogy – there is obviously something about history, possibly its size and untidiness, that brings out the trilogy in fiction writers – originally published as *All the Rivers Run* (1958), *Time, Flow Softly* (1959) and *But Still the Stream* (1962) and reissued in one volume as *All the Rivers Run* (1978), which in turn was adapted for a TV series screened in 1983.

Clearly there are a number of sub-genres being occupied and agendas being followed in the historical writing of this period. What these sometimes very different books have in common, however, is their concern with how the past becomes the present, and what lessons reside for the latter in the former.

WRITING THE WARS

"War literature" in Australian fiction covers a lot of territory, geographical and otherwise. The best-known Australian novel of World War I is Leonard Mann's *Flesh in Armour* (1932); others include Frederic Manning's *The Middle Parts of Fortune: Somme & Ancre 1916* (1929) and Frank Dalby Davison's *The Wells of Beersheba* (1933).[20] The novels and stories of World War II were more plentiful and more varied in their approach. Army memoirs, autobiographies and other non-fictional responses abounded; the best-known novel dealing directly and exclusively with the war experience of violence in an unfamiliar landscape is T.A.G. Hungerford's *The Ridge and the River* (1952), based on the Australian campaign at Bougainville.

Martin Boyd, writing after World War II, revisited both wars in two of his best novels. *Lucinda Brayford* (1946) is among other things a sustained attempt to represent the motives and experience of a conscientious objector, and can be usefully compared in this respect to Kylie Tennant's *The Joyful Condemned* (1953). Boyd's *When Blackbirds Sing* (1962), the fourth novel of the Langton tetralogy and set during World War I, chronicles the "difficult" Dominic's passage from soldier to pacifist.

Fiction writers dealing with World War II were more inclined to write, so to speak, around the war; a surprising number of novels concentrate on the effect of the war on women. Nevil Shute's *A Town Like Alice* (1950) focuses on a group of female POWs captured by the Japanese in Malaya; Dymphna Cusack and Florence James' *Come in Spinner* (1951), set in Sydney in 1944, concentrates on the lives of women left at home, as do Tennant's *Tell Morning This* (1967)[21] and Xavier Herbert's *Soldiers' Women* (1961) – albeit from radically different points of view; Herbert's book is an odd mixture of moralism and masculinism.

Two other novels dealing at some length with constructions of masculinity in the context of World War II provided a literary education for a generation of Australian schoolchildren in the 1960s: George Johnston's *My Brother Jack* (1964) and Randolph Stow's *The Merry-Go-Round in the Sea* (1965), both autobiographically based, are also written "around" the war.

WOMEN AND FICTION

In 1928 the editor of the *Bulletin* offered, for the best novel manuscript submitted, a prize of a hundred pounds and the promise of subsequent publication. There were 540 entries; the prize was shared between *Coonardoo* (1929), by the already well-known and established Katharine Susannah Prichard, and *A House is Built* by M. Barnard Eldershaw. A prize intended to honour one winner had in fact been shared among three, and all of them were women.

In spite of the prize, neither novel could find an Australian publisher and both were published in England the following year; this typified an ironic pattern of the period, during which the writers most concerned to establish and consolidate a serious national literature were precisely those who had the most trouble getting their work published at home.[22] The issue of whether to publish in Australia or overseas has been a vexed one for Australian fiction writers for the whole of this century; writers in the late 1990s are rightly concerned that their books will be difficult to market overseas if initially published in Australia; writers a century earlier were advised by Henry Lawson, in the absence of publishing opportunities, "to go steerage, stow away, swim, and seek London, Yankeeland or Timbuctoo".[23]

Drusilla Modjeska's *Exiles at Home: Australian Women Writers 1925–1945* (1981) used some of the energies generated by second-wave feminism to put a new spin on the history of Australian fiction. Women, says Modjeska,

> were writing and publishing in large numbers in the thirties and they were able to give each other comfort and support. They were politically active, they were often angry and they made sure their presence was felt as writers and as women. Their remarkable history and the broader tradition that stretches beyond them has been undervalued and obscured.[24]

Two of these writers, Marjorie Barnard and Flora Eldershaw, produced in 1938 a collection of critical essays in Australian fiction that still make engaging and instructive reading today, and give a reliable guide to which writers were seen as most important in 1938.[25] *Essays in Australian Fiction* contains essays on – in this order – Henry Handel Richardson, Katharine Susannah Prichard, Frank Dalby Davison, Vance Palmer, Leonard Mann, "Martin Mills" (Martin Boyd), Christina Stead and Eleanor Dark.

Gender balance, in 1938, was probably the last thing on Barnard and Eldershaw's minds, and is something this book achieved as a matter of course. But by 1981, when *Exiles at Home* was published, the only two Australian women fiction writers whose work was consistently included in anthologies, university courses, general literary histories and the like were

Henry Handel Richardson and Christina Stead. Richardson's *The Fortunes of Richard Mahony* and Stead's *The Man Who Loved Children* (1940) and *For Love Alone* (1944) were Australian literature's canonical texts in the "fiction by women" category. Both writers left Australia as young women; Richardson made one brief return visit, and Stead returned home only in her sixties, after the death of her husband.

It may have been the very "internationalism" of these two that made their work appealing to the Australian cultural gate-keepers and taste-makers of the time; whatever, their predominance tended to obscure the work of their stay-at-home contemporaries, and the value of the latter seems to have been recognised more by historians – *Exiles at Home* began life as a PhD thesis in History – than by literary critics. "However unconventional one's taste or ranking", wrote historian Geoffrey Serle about Australian writing between the two world wars, "it would be almost impossible to deny that most of the best novelists were women."[26]

Serle, writing in 1973, finds it necessary to use words like "unconventional", "impossible" and "deny" in order to frame the claim, as though he feels he must apologise for this strange fact. After listing his female "front rank" among fiction writers of the 1920s and 1930s – Henry Handel Richardson, Eleanor Dark, Christina Stead, Katharine Susannah Prichard, M. Barnard Eldershaw, Kylie Tennant and Miles Franklin – he observes their mostly precarious financial independence with apparent approval:

> Some of them had the income-security of marriage. But the great majority were "career-women". Moreover, unlike female novelists historically, most of them were distinguished by their breadth, social involvement and far-reaching militancy.[27]

There are some begged questions here; more than one of these women, for example, had a husband or partner who was more of a liability than otherwise. The dismissive comment about "female novelists historically", with its unspoken assumption that the public sphere provides superior subject matter, is standard for a male (or indeed female) observer in 1973. But what is impressive about this observation is what it acknowledges as crucial: not only that their material circumstances had considerable bearing on how, and how much, these women managed to write, but that those circumstances were largely determined by their gender. What Serle does *not* see, however, is that for most women writers any advantage of financial security bestowed by marriage has always been offset by the time it takes to run a household and bring up a family. Perhaps of more relevance than their marital status to their productivity as writers is the fact that of the eight women (counting two for "Barnard Eldershaw") in Serle's "front-rank" list, only three had children.

But there are, of course, twentieth-century women writers who pre-date these. Barbara Baynton, whose best-known book *Bush Studies* (1902) was published the year after *My Brilliant Career*, was a great deal less concerned with "Australianness"; gender relations in the context of a relentlessly harsh and sinister bush landscape are a central theme of her work. Women in Baynton's stories are the victims of their menfolk and the landscape: trapped, exploited, deceived, bereaved, humiliated, raped and murdered. Maternity seems the only positive value to be found in her work and even that is represented, in stories like "The Chosen Vessel" and "A Dreamer", as rendering women especially vulnerable to horrible experiences.

The combination of the way that environment brutalises character in Baynton's stories with their near-absence of any sense of moral order suggests, as Henry Handel Richardson's work was shortly also to do, the influence of nineteenth-century European naturalism. Two of Baynton's contemporaries, Henry Lawson and Steele Rudd, represent the bush in their short stories quite as harshly as Baynton does in hers, but Rudd's bush is essentially an occasion for comedy – increasingly so after his first collection of stories, *On Our Selection* (1899) – while Lawson's is a place that makes his characters more intensely themselves, for better or worse. While their characters also find it a struggle, neither, unlike Baynton, writes the bush as a place that brutalises and destroys its inhabitants.

Henry Handel Richardson's *The Fortunes of Richard Mahony*, like almost all her other fiction, concerns itself intimately and in great detail with the relationships between men and women; Mary and Richard Mahony's is one of the most detailed and memorable marriages in Australian literature. Richardson's other fiction explores not marriage but rather, in a way, its opposite: the disjunctions and discontinuities between sexual desire and social arrangements.

Her first novel, *Maurice Guest* (1908), is a disturbing study of obsessive, destructive sexual and romantic love. In her second, *The Getting of Wisdom* (1910), a precocious, "difficult" schoolgirl is obliged to do some preparation for, and gain some understanding of, the different possibilities for woman-hood in a late-colonial Australian city: a life of art and the intellect, or a life of socio-sexual orthodoxy, characterised by dishonesty, cupidity and hypocrisy.

The Getting of Wisdom also sounds a theme that reverberates through some of Richardson's other fiction: it engages, frankly for its time, with the subject of lesbian love, figured largely as a possible escape from the horrors of orthodox courtship and marriage. Some of her short stories, notably "Two Hanged Women", "The Wrong Turning" and, more obliquely, "And Women Must Weep", treat similar issues.

Nineteen twenty-nine, the year the third and final volume of Richardson's trilogy was published, ushered in a period of extraordinary productivity and quality in Australian fiction, especially fiction by women. Throughout the 1930s and even through World War II, in spite of such basic material constraints as paper shortages, a generation of Australian women writers, working in a network of support and friendship that included its elder stateswoman Miles Franklin and, as a central figure and facilitator, the influential critic and essayist Nettie Palmer, continued to produce fiction reflective of their times.[28]

While this generation of women writers was concerned with questions of women's freedom and autonomy, their feminist concerns were put to one side as the threat of fascism and world war became more real. Of Miles Franklin and her lifetime of work and writing in feminist causes, Modjeska says

> when she died in 1954 she did so disappointed ... In that anti-feminist decade she looked in vain for the next generation of young women to take up the cause. Twenty years earlier she had watched the women who were writing become diverted, in her view, from an early promise of feminism into the broad left anti-fascist struggles.[29]

After Franklin the oldest member of this group was Katharine Susannah Prichard. The general critical consensus on Prichard is that her best fiction was produced in the period between what were perhaps the two most far-reaching events of her life: her joining of the Communist Party of Australia as a founding member in 1920, and the suicide of her husband in 1934. Though she published her first novel in 1915 and her last in 1967, the novels *Working Bullocks* (1926), *Coonardoo* (1929) and *Intimate Strangers* (1937), and the short story collection *Kiss on the Lips* (1932), are regarded as her most significant and most successful work.

From *Black Opal* (1921) onwards, political concepts in general and an ongoing critique of capitalism in particular were central to Prichard's practice as a fiction writer. With Jean Devanny's *Sugar Heaven* (1936), Prichard's novels began an impressive sequence of women's fiction about working life, including novels as diverse as Eve Langley's *The Pea Pickers* (1942), Kylie Tennant's *Ride on Stranger* (1943), Dymphna Cusack and Florence James' *Come in Spinner* (1951) and Dorothy Hewett's *Bobbin Up* (1959).

The best-known novel of M. Barnard Eldershaw is the extraordinary futuristic dystopia published in censored form as *Tomorrow and Tomorrow* in 1947 and republished with its full text and original title, *Tomorrow and Tomorrow and Tomorrow*, in 1983. Marjorie Barnard and Flora Eldershaw were two of the most influential members of the Australian literary community in the period between the wars. Not only did they manage a successful and sustained collaboration on a series of novels, a number of short stories and an impressive and influential collection of literary criticism, but they were active "women of letters" in the development of a literary infrastructure within Australia. Both gave lectures and wrote reviews and essays on Australian literature, and Barnard published a number of historical studies; both were high-profile members of the influential Fellowship of Australian Writers during the 1930s. Maryanne Dever's theory as to how these two – or any – women could have gained this amount of cultural authority goes some way towards explaining the predominance of women in Australian writing generally during this whole period:

> While access to hegemonic intellectual positions might conventionally be viewed as crucial to the formation of cultural authority, it was in some respects less fundamental to the authority exercised by Barnard and Eldershaw ... The "amateur" or non-professional status granted the field of Australian literature arguably limited competition for its colonisation which may in turn have allowed women to establish themselves in the practice of it without significant opposition.[30]

Eleanor Dark, born in the year of Federation, was the youngest member of this loose and heterogeneous group. While her interests both in social justice of various kinds and in the psychological state of the individual are visible from first to last in her fiction, there was a steady progression outwards, so to speak, from a preoccupation with the characters' interiority and the psychological realism of early novels like *Prelude to Christopher* (1934) and *Sun Across the Sky* (1937) to the overt concern with public life, group welfare and political developments in her later work, notably *The Little Company* (1945) and the *Timeless Land* trilogy. Dark's feminism is also a force in her fiction; her first novel *Slow Dawning* (1932) was specifically concerned with the problems of autonomy and agency in a young woman's personal and professional life.

Christina Stead, a year younger than Dark, left Australia as a young woman in 1928 and did not return permanently until 1974. Almost all of her fiction was written and published in Britain, Europe or the United States, and Australian settings feature in only two of her twelve novels – *Seven Poor Men of Sydney* (1934) and *For Love Alone* (1944) – and a few of the stories in the first of her three short story collections, *The Salzburg Tales* (1934). *The Man Who Loved Children* (1940) also draws heavily on her Sydney childhood and uses autobiographical material transplanted to a Washington setting at the request of her publishers.

Like most of her Australian literary contemporaries, Stead was politically committed, sometimes active, on the Left; like them, too, she was oppressed and to some degree silenced by the reactionary political climate of the early 1950s. In later life she refused to claim any affinity or sympathy with feminism or feminists, but, as with Dark, the question of women's agency and autonomy is central to her fiction.

Stead's two best-known novels, *The Man Who Loved Children* and *For Love Alone*, represent among other things the struggle of a daughter to free herself from the household and values of an oppressive father. Each also chronicles a destructive sexual (or rather, in both cases, para-sexual) relationship, Sam's with his wife Hetty in *The Man Who Loved Children*, and, in *For Love Alone*, Teresa's with Jonathan Crow; Teresa survives, Hetty does not. Two later books with progressively less likeable heroines, *Letty Fox – Her Luck* (1946) and *Miss Herbert (The Suburban Wife)* (1976), also consider the problems for women in addressing the questions of what to believe and how to live, and in meeting their needs for what Jonathan Crow calls "Bread and work and love, the poor man's trinity."[31]

Other notable women writers publishing in the middle decades of the century included Dymphna Cusack, Kylie Tennant and Ruth Park, all of whose best-known work is set in or around Sydney and deals with – among other things – social injustice and the plight of the poor, especially of poor women. Cusack and Tennant in particular confronted the problems of women and the consequences of sexual freedom; Cusack's first novel *Jungfrau* (1936) compared the lives of three young women friends who take different personal and professional paths. *Jungfrau*, Tennant's *Ride on Stranger* (1943) and Cusack and James' *Come in Spinner* (1951) all involve unwanted pregnancies, abortion and death.

The conservative, repressive social and political atmosphere of the 1950s, and the recognition by both Right and Left that literature was a powerful political force, resulted in a complex literary history during that period which has been examined in detail, from various angles, by a number of contemporary critics.[32] Katharine Susannah Prichard, still a member of the Communist Party, wrote to Miles Franklin in 1950 that she feared their friendship would be a problem for Franklin on the latter's imminent visit to Perth: "The Menzies blunderbus [sic] may make it awkward for you to be with me … I don't want to embarrass my friends." Franklin, referring to Menzies' proposed Communist Party Dissolution Act, replied characteristically: "Mr Menzies would be one of the chief reasons I'd like to stay with you … I have said to Henrietta, if it (the Bill) were to go through, she and I might be taken up for having you as a friend."[33]

The two most significant women novelists to emerge in the 1950s and survive as writers into the 1960s were Thea Astley and Elizabeth Harrower. The nature of Australian society in the 1950s and the difficulty of life for those who could not accept its values are represented in two oddly similar novels by these women, Harrower's *The Long Prospect* (1958) and Astley's *A Descant for Gossips* (1960), both of which align malice and stupidity with conservative suburban values in the same way that Patrick White's *Riders in the Chariot* (1961) was shortly to do. Both novels are powerfully claustrophobic; *The Long Prospect* in particular details the way that material conditions in general and housing arrangements in particular render any kind of personal freedom or privacy almost impossible, and the restrictive material conditions of people's lives seem analogous to the repression of ideas. Harrower published several other novels of which the best known is *The Watch Tower* (1966), a horrifying story of a marriage which again demonstrates how easily women could become trapped in unbearable life situations during that period.

Harrower stopped publishing fiction in the 1960s, but Thea Astley's has been one of the most solid, enduring and distinguished careers of any Australian novelist. By 1970, even with five novels already published, including two – *The Well Dressed Explorer* (1962) and *The Slow Natives* (1965) – winners of the Miles Franklin Award, and as the only female fiction writer in the country to win consistent critical attention and praise throughout the sixties, Astley still had most of her achievement, success and recognition ahead of her.

REALISMS

"In Australian criticism since the 1940s," says David Carter, "the term 'social realism' has overlapped with 'socialist realism'. But while the latter is derived from an explicit theory, the former is rather the result of a *lack* of theory."[34] But Jennifer Strauss offers a definition of social realism, citing some of the work of Frank Dalby Davison as exemplifying what she calls "the strict definition of social (rather than socialist) realism: non-lyrical, non-judgmental, concerned with the lives of 'ordinary' people".[35]

The work of a number of other writers has been traditionally thought of as social realism, a mode that dominated Australian fiction from the 1930s till the end of the 1950s, when the so-called "metaphysical" fictions and/or stylistic complexities of White, Porter, Astley and Stow began to compete with social and socialist realism for the attention of readers and critics. As well as Vance Palmer, Tennant and M. Barnard Eldershaw, others whose work is generally categorised as social realism include Leonard Mann,

Gavin Casey, Alan Marshall and the neglected Margaret Trist, whose best stories are among the most memorable Australian fiction of the 1940s and anticipate the work of Olga Masters forty years later.

Those writers generally identified as socialist realists were mostly active members of the Communist Party: Prichard, Devanny, John Harcourt, Judah Waten, Frank Hardy and Hewett. Apart from Prichard, each of these writers' names tends to be strongly identified with his or her best-known novel: Harcourt's *Upsurge* (1934), Devanny's *Sugar Heaven*, Hardy's *Power Without Glory* (1950), Waten's *Alien Son* (1952) and Hewett's *Bobbin Up*.

One writer whom critics seem shy of assigning to either camp is John Morrison, one of the most highly regarded Australian short story writers of this period and indeed of this century. Morrison's stories of urban working life on the waterfront and other sites fit Strauss' description of social realism, but some also feature what Carter calls "radical documentary".[36] Most of Morrison's stories clearly reflect his socialist beliefs but do not engage directly with political rhetoric.

ABORIGINAL REPRESENTATIONS

Before 1970 the only Australian novel by a writer then identified as Aboriginal was Mudrooroo's *Wild Cat Falling* (1965), published under his "white" name Colin Johnson. The representation of Aboriginal people in fiction was left almost exclusively to white writers during this period, and shifts in attitude, from the simplest kind of colonial racism to the complexities of contemporary identity politics, can be tracked in fiction as the century progresses. Katharine Susannah Prichard and Xavier Herbert are usually seen in Australian literary history as the two writers who broke new ground in their fictional representations of Aboriginal people, though the representations of race relations in the two novels in question, *Coonardoo* and *Capricornia* respectively, have been searchingly re-examined by some contemporary literary critics.[37]

In two novels by Rosa Praed, *Fugitive Anne* (1902) and *Lady Bridget in the Never-Never Land* (1915), Aboriginal people are used as material for the romance plot; in both novels, the course of a troubled marriage between white characters is determined by events in the lives of their Aboriginal counterparts. Catherine Martin's *The Incredible Journey* (1923), with its heroic and devoted Aboriginal mother, implicitly claims that maternal love transcends racial difference, while at the same time constructing racial difference as clear-cut and absolute. Susan Sheridan argues that this novel is a "breakthrough" text in its representation of Aborigines, saying it is "the only colonial woman's text of this period that I can find in which the

Aboriginal woman is central to the narrative and is constructed as a subject in her own right".[38]

There is, from about this point on, a steadily more complex, sympathetic and disquieted attitude to Aboriginality apparent in Australian fiction, where there are two frequently recurring subjects. One is black/white sexual and emotional relations; the other is the nature of the Aboriginal relationship to the land, with its central importance to Aboriginal culture and its implications for the white descendants of a settler culture.

The earliest fiction writer to treat both of these subjects was the English biologist, writer and adventurer E.L. Grant Watson, who wrote six novels and several short stories with Australian settings, after an anthropological expedition into north-western Australia in 1910–11 that profoundly changed his life. "Out There" (1913) is an "eternal triangle" story of a white man, an Aboriginal woman and a white woman, a story in which the values of Aboriginal culture are valorised in a way that makes it extraordinary for its time. Grant Watson's novel *The Desert Horizon* (1923) engages with the problems for a settler culture in Australia's north-west and, again, affirms the value of Aboriginal attitudes and relationships to the land.

Such determined foregrounding of Aboriginal values, as Susan Sheridan has pointed out in an otherwise mainly negative reading of the representation of Aboriginality in Katharine Susannah Prichard's *Coonardoo*, is one of the things that made it undeniably a progressive novel for its time:

> What distinguishes this novel in literary terms is Prichard's attempt to represent Coonardoo's point of view from time to time, and to present it as specifically Aboriginal, by inscribing the culture's language and practices as a valid and coherent perspective.[39]

As Sheridan also notes, however, Coonardoo is constructed and her fate determined by white male desire, and the novel remains essentially focused on white male subjectivity; Coonardoo's role is that of mediator between white men and the land. A later novel, Mary Durack's *Keep Him My Country* (1955), operates on the same logic, as Sheridan indicates; both novels, she says, are based on "the idea that the white man's desire for the Aboriginal woman would, if honoured, place him in a proper spiritual relationship to the land". She argues that in neither of these novels

> is there any doubt that the white man who loves the land/woman will still be its owner and user ... Thus the fantasy of reciprocal inter-racial love becomes a kind of justificatory myth for white settlement.[40]

In *Capricornia*, Xavier Herbert is concerned, like Grant Watson, with the failure of Europeans to understand or come to terms with the land; *Capricornia* is also an indictment of the way Aboriginal people have been dealt with on personal, legal and political levels in the Northern Territory and, by extension, in Australia generally. Like most of the twentieth-century fiction dealing with race relations, it reveals deep anxieties about miscegenation, though in a different way from colonial fictions; one of its central concerns is with the fate of mixed-race children abandoned or brutalised, and with their status and fate in both Aboriginal and white society. In his introduction to the 1990 edition of this novel, Mudrooroo reads *Capricornia* as "an allegory of an Australia that refuses fundamental change".[41]

Published either side of *Coonardoo*, two novels by Vance Palmer – *The Man Hamilton* (1928) and *Men are Human* (1930) – both also treat the subject of interracial sexual relations; the stillbirth of the "half-caste" baby in *The Man Hamilton* anticipates the horrible death of Norman Shillingsworth's infant son in *Capricornia* ten years later, and carries the same symbolic suggestion. Palmer's own extreme disquiet on the subject of interracial sex and his construction of it as exclusively a matter of white male subjectivity are apparent in both novels. His problems in getting *Men are Human* published give some indication of how radical *Coonardoo* was for its time: "the disastrous experience with *Coonardoo* shows us that the Australian public will not stand stories based on a white man's relations with an Aborigine", wrote the *Bulletin*'s S.H. Prior, after having given Palmer's novel third prize in the competition won by *Coonardoo* and *A House is Built*; "There is no chance, I suppose of your whitewashing the girl?"[42] Nettie Palmer shed some light on this in a letter dated 9 August 1929; the *Bulletin*, she said, had received

> such barrels of letters from people who read *Coonardoo* with a microscope and were not used to reading anything literary at all, and they've let themselves be scared stiff by those letters.[43]

As the century progressed, novels on the theme of interracial sexual relations and the fate of mixed-race individuals became progressively more complex and less racist. They include Gavin Casey's *Snowball* (1958), Leonard Mann's *Venus Half-Caste* (1963), and Dymphna Cusack's *Black Lightning* (1964). Two novels published in 1961, Nene Gare's *The Fringe Dwellers* and Patrick White's *Riders in the Chariot*, examine the liminal status of the so-called "half-caste" in post-war Australian society.

White gives his character Alf Dubbo the physically squalid living conditions and terminally unhealthy state of Gare's fringe dwellers but also a central role as an artist with a rich spiritual life, suggesting that white Australia should look to Aboriginal values and skills as a way of redeeming itself – a suggestion that seemed a great deal more radical in 1961 than it does now. Another novel suggesting the same thing is Randolph Stow's *To the Islands* (1958), in which the missionary Heriot uses what he has learned from Aboriginal spiritual life to deal with his own racial guilt; while this novel represents Aboriginal spiritual values as superior to Christian ones, including the nature of relationship to the land, an unsympathetic reading might see it as a story of guilt expiated through a neat act of cultural appropriation from its own object.

Peter Mathers' extraordinary experimental novel *Trap* (1966), its narration polyphonic and its chronology anticipating the structure of the World Wide Web, is perhaps the most subversive novel in this category. The eponymous central character, a mixed-race agitator, troublemaker and anarchist, proves in the end to be descended also from white Australian aristocrats and capitalists; the policy of assimilation intended to "breed out" Aboriginality proves to have had the opposite effect, and the Aboriginal character moves from the margins to the centre of power.

Some of the most extraordinary writing on Aboriginality before 1970, however, occurs in the detective novels of Arthur Upfield, in which all of these topics are canvassed neither in the social realist mode of Palmer and Prichard nor the "metaphysical" mode of Stow and White, but rather within the conventions of the detective-fiction genre. Among other things, Upfield may have been the first Australian writer to reverse the usual form of interracial sexuality and create a white female character as a desiring subject; one of his characters is a white woman who confesses with her dying breath that the father of her baby is the Aboriginal King Henry: "so magnificent a man that I became as putty in his hands".[44]

Despite the fact that his writing is sometimes "bordering on eugenics ... in a way that is more than characteristic of the period, particularly in its account of the appearance and behaviour of mixed-race individuals",[45] the message implied by Upfield's detective character was that the mixed-race individual, endowed with the best qualities of both black and white, was superior to either. Upfield's detective, the suggestively named Napoleon Bonaparte (Detective Inspector in rank and "Bony" for short) has unique problem-solving skills and uses them in the cause of justice. The question of land and its significance is addressed as well: "Upfield insists that neither the whitefella policeman nor the blacktracker alone can crack the crimes of the Outback," says Kay Torney,[46] and Stephen Knight adds that "only Bony really has control of its distances and its mysteries; equally it is very common for the ending of the book to involve the land somehow as an agent of revelation or even of vengeance".[47]

Stephen Knight sees in the character of Bony "a fictional resolution to the uneasy presence of the Aboriginal in early stories ... [embodying] both realisation and containment together".[48] This comment recalls a remark of Susan Sheridan's about *The Incredible Journey*: "Here again is the classic ambivalence of colonial discourse, the simultaneous affirmation and disavowal of likeness."[49] "Realisation and containment", "affirmation and disavowal": the history of white writing on Aboriginality throughout this period is marked by such ambivalences, and looks, with hindsight, like one long effort to hold two opposing ideas in the mind at the same time.

PATRICK WHITE

In 1973, when Patrick White was sixty-one, he won Australia's first Nobel Prize for Literature. Between 1935 and 1989 he published eleven novels, a collection of poems and stories, a novella, eight plays, two collections of short stories, a full-length autobiography and two collections of autobiographical and polemical essays and reflections. But his reputation was made by, and rests on, his novels. His work dominated Australian literature for three decades, and his influence continues to go wide and deep in the work of contemporary Australian writers.

The first detailed critical overview of White's work appeared in the June 1956 issue of *Meanjin*, whose editor Clem Christesen had observed the publication of *The Tree of Man* by commissioning a full survey of White's work to date. The result was a long essay by Marjorie Barnard entitled "The Four Novels of Patrick White", discussing *Happy Valley* (1939), *The Living and the Dead* (1941), *The Aunt's Story* (1948) and *The Tree of Man* (1955).[50] White was delighted. "A great many people have become excited over *The Tree of Man*," he wrote to Barnard, "but it is the first time anyone has shown that I have been working towards it over the last twenty years."[51] It is instructive to look at Barnard's essay in the light of Simon During's recent book on White: the two critiques bracket the trajectory of White's Australian reputation, consolidated by Barnard's essay and just beginning to fade forty years later when During's book appeared.[52]

Until the publication of *The Tree of Man* and its aftermath, White's fiction, while well received in the United States and to a lesser extent in Britain, had fared less well in Australia. The most famous negative Australian comment was made in A.D. Hope's review of *The Tree of Man*; Hope, as an academic, classicist, actively anti-modernist poet, perhaps inevitably called White's writing "pretentious and illiterate verbal sludge".[53] Not only his style but also his subject matter was regarded as suspect by realist writers and rationalist critics who found White's mysticism unpalatable or worse.

Happy Valley is set in an Australian valley where nobody is happy; *The Living and the Dead*, set entirely in England, shows some of the themes, motifs and stylistic devices of White's later work. In his third novel, *The Aunt's Story*, White began to demonstrate the complexity of his vision, give play to his originality, and extend his range. The novel explores two kinds of disintegration, with the fragmentation of Theodora's consciousness into madness paralleled by the destruction of Europe during World War II.

The two novels White published in the 1950s established his reputation internationally and marked its turning point in Australia. White in later years liked to emphasise the negative reactions of critics like Hope, so rendering invisible the positive responses of those like Barnard. *Voss* (1957) springs from the same mythopoeic impulse as *The Tree of Man* and returns, albeit indirectly, to the subject of World War II in the characterisation of its eponymous megalomaniac German explorer. *Voss*, too, elicited mixed reactions from Australian critics; it was largely in response to these that White wrote his 1958 manifesto, "The Prodigal Son". "I was determined to prove," he said, in a remark that was to implant itself firmly in Australian literary history, "that the Australian novel is not necessarily the dreary, dun-coloured offspring of journalistic realism."[54]

With the publication of *Riders in the Chariot* in 1961, White began to be seen as one of the country's great artists, constructing a nation and its social history in his writing, and suggesting possibilities for a spiritual dimension to life in a relentlessly secular country. In a similar vein of protest or resistance, *Riders in the Chariot*, with its racially assorted four main characters – "an orthodox refugee intellectual Jew, a mad *Erdgeist* of an Australian spinster, an evangelical laundress, and a half-caste Aboriginal painter", as White described them – was also an early model for the ideals of multi-culturalism.[55] "[A] great many ignorant native-born Australians," he wrote in 1960,

> go out of their way to encourage New Australians to drop their own standards in favour of the dreary semi-culture which exists here [but] there are also a great number of civilised Old Australians who are hoping that the migrants ... will bring something of their own cultures with them.[56]

This embrace of difference looks unremarkable now but was, for its time, extraordinary. *Riders in the Chariot*, while maintaining a form of realism, and certainly of social critique, also represents Australian life as having a spiritual dimension. It is, as Carole Ferrier has pointed out, "White's simultaneous engagement with the 'dun-coloured' and the metaphysical that gives his texts ... their peculiar force."[57]

This is certainly true of *The Solid Mandala* (1966), perhaps the most "dun-coloured" of White's novels despite the mysticism of its central mandala symbol and the presence of what had by this time become some of his trademarks: the pair of contrasting siblings, the "outsider" figure, the racially exotic characters, the magpie borrowings from religious, mystical and psychoanalytic systems and schemas, and the social comedy and critique of his by now well-established fictional Australian suburb, Sarsaparilla.

White's next two novels, *The Vivisector* (1970) and *The Eye of the Storm* (1973), mark one noticeable change in his work: his social critique – much of which had begun to look strident, dated, and less and less accurate in its aim – begins to give way to more complex and ambivalent characterisations. One-dimensional satirical representations of the hated 'suburbs' with their bakelite telephones and pink chenille bedspreads likewise disappear and are replaced by a far more complex set of representations of urban Sydney.

White's entire *oeuvre* is marked by what Simon During calls his "rejection of community as a starting point for ethical and spiritual values as well as his emphasis on *individual* genius"; while his novels from *The Vivisector* onwards are indeed preoccupied with one or both of these issues, the first half of this observation is debatable.[58] As is emphasised by the contrasting of European with Australian characters in many of his novels and stories, an *absence* of any coherent sense of community in ordinary Australian life is one of the targets of White's social critique.

But for the most part, his last five novels – *The Vivisector, The Eye of the Storm, A Fringe of Leaves* (1976), *The Twyborn Affair* (1979) and *Memoirs of Many in One* (1986) – do all focus on questions and problems to do with individual subjectivity and individual consciousness, and with the transcendence of various forms of socialisation and cultural difference. White's preoccupation with class difference and with the triumph of individual genius or virtue over class origins, for example, impels him to rewrite *Cinderella* three times in a row: first in *The Vivisector*, then in *The Eye of the Storm* and finally in *A Fringe of Leaves*. In all of these novels the main characters are pulled free of humble class origins by mediocre people of a higher class who sense, and want to possess by marriage or adoption, their superior qualities.

Although his work abounds with artist figures, *The Vivisector* is the only one of White's novels that tackles the *Künstlerroman* genre head-on. *The Vivisector, The Eye of the Storm* and to a lesser extent *The Twyborn Affair*, all in different ways, deal with a morally ambiguous and highly egotistical central character. The odd novel out here is *A Fringe of Leaves*, in which by way of his comparatively humble heroine White looks both forward and back: back to the "good and evil" preoccupations of *Riders in the Chariot* and forward to the theme of self-construction and self-deconstruction that is more fully explored in *The Twyborn Affair*.

The Twyborn Affair, apart from the afterthought-like novella and *jeu d'esprit* that is *Memoirs of Many in One*, is White's final novel. In *The*

Twyborn Affair the fragmentation of subjectivity with which White experimented as early as *The Aunt's Story* is now treated with more directness and detail, with the main character split into three separate identities in the course of his/her life. It is also, as During argues, the first novel in which White "comes out of the closet" and treats the subject of male homosexuality in, again, a direct and detailed way.[59] Although the idea of "gay liberation" was not one that appealed to White, it was inevitable that both his life and his work would be changed by the changing politics of, and around, homosexuality.

OTHER VOICES

Three prolific bestselling writers from this period who tended to be dismissed by their "serious" peers and by later literary historians as middle-brow are Ion L. Idriess, whose popularity stayed high all through the 1930s, 40s and 50s, and the near-contemporaries Jon Cleary and Morris West, who both began publishing fiction in the 1940s and went on doing so into the 1990s. West lived away from Australia from 1955 to 1980; his novels, internationally popular, engage on an international scale with the institutions of public life – usually to do with politics and religion – and the moral dilemmas they pose for the individual. Cleary, among other things an adventure writer, crime novelist and scriptwriter, is also sufficiently "literary" a writer to have won a number of prestigious awards and prizes, including the Australian Literature Society's Gold Medal in 1950.

"Why Idriess," wrote Nettie Palmer to Leslie Rees in November 1934,

> in a list of significant writers? He has wonderful material, certainly, but he almost always debases and falsifies it. His presence in a list dilutes the whole. People have come to take him seriously because he makes a good living: but he won't do, will he?[60]

Idriess' books – some fiction, some non-fiction, and all very popular – were grounded in historical fact and documentary realism and usually set in the most exciting parts of the Australian landscape, the outback and the tropics. The Palmers' problem was that in using what might be thought of as nationalist material and certainly nationalist sentiments to write in the genres of adventure and romance, Idriess seemed to be invading and trespassing upon two of the things that were most important to them: nationalism was being "debased and falsified" and high culture was being ignored.

There are three otherwise very different writers whose work stubbornly resists categorisation but cannot go unmentioned here: Norman Lindsay, Martin Boyd and Kenneth "Seaforth" Mackenzie. Lindsay, best known as a visual artist, was also the author of eleven novels, essays, sketches, stories, autobiographical writing, and the children's classic *The Magic Pudding*. He features prominently in histories of Australian literary production largely because two of his best-known novels were banned for almost thirty years: *Redheap* (1930) and *The Cautious Amorist* (1932).

Martin Boyd's *The Montforts*, published under his early pen-name "Martin Mills", won the inaugural Australian Literature Society's Gold Medal for 1928 and is the only novel to get a whole essay to itself in the authoritative *Essays in Australian Fiction* by M. Barnard Eldershaw ten years later. This novel was an early rehearsal of material that Boyd would go on reworking for the whole of his career: a family chronicle based on Boyd's mother's family and their aristocratic forebears. He is now best known for *Lucinda Brayford* (1946) and the Langton tetralogy, four novels following the fortunes of various outcrops of the Langton family over several generations: *The Cardboard Crown* (1952), *A Difficult Young Man* (1955), *Outbreak of Love* (1957) and *When Blackbirds Sing* (1962).

The Langton novels, especially *The Cardboard Crown* and *Outbreak of Love*, explore one aspect of Australia's historical relationship with Britain through their representation of the Langton family's geo-cultural restlessness, something that might be read now as marking the approach to the "postcolonial turn". Boyd has fallen out of critical favour in recent years, his novels seen as little more than an expression of nostalgia for a vanished way of life and his technical skills less valued than twenty years ago, but there is much in his fiction and in his biography to engage contemporary critics in the fields of postcolonial theory, gender studies and Queer theory.

The development of Queer theory and the concomitant new critical interest in gay and lesbian writing has also precipitated renewed interest in the work of Kenneth "Seaforth" Mackenzie, particularly his best-known novel *The Young Desire It* (1937), one of the earliest Australian novels to treat explicitly and in detail the subject of male homosexual love and desire.

Of the several other fiction writers whose work came to prominence in the 1960s, three are important figures in the history of the Australian short story. Hal Porter wrote three novels and seven collections of stories as well as *The Watcher on the Cast-Iron Balcony*, the first volume of his autobiographical trilogy and the book for which he is best known. Peter Cowan, like Porter, began publishing in the 1940s and has produced seven collections of stories and several novels. Dal Stivens published eight story collections between 1936 and 1979; his experiments with genre and departure from the realist conventions of his peers look forward to the new short fiction of the 1970s.

The rapid growth of Australian literature after the establishment of the Australia Council in the early 1970s and the easing of censorship restrictions around the same time has meant that 1970 tends to be regarded in contemporary literary historiography as a turning point in Australian writing. As the title of Ken Gelder and Paul Salzman's *The New Diversity: Australian Fiction 1970–1988* (1989) suggests, given the exponential increase in literary production, the only way after 1970 to generalise about Australian fiction and fiction writers is to stress their differences from each other.

NOTES

1 Susan Sheridan, "'Temper, romantic; bias, offensively feminine': Australian women writers and literary nationalism", 1986; reprinted in her *Along the Faultlines: Sex, Race and Nation in Australian Women's Writing* (Sydney: Allen & Unwin, 1995), pp. 27–35. See also Susan K. Martin, "National Dress or National Trousers?" in Bruce Bennett and Jennifer Strauss, eds, *The Oxford Literary History of Australia* (Melbourne: Oxford University Press, 1998); Fiona Giles, "Romance: An Embarrassing Subject" in Laurie Hergenhan, gen. ed., *The Penguin New Literary History of Australia* (Melbourne: Penguin, 1988), pp. 223–237.

2 John Bannon, "Fears of Inconvenience: Adelaide as the 1897 Convention Host", *The New Federalist: The Journal of Australian Federation History*, 1 (June 1998), pp. 6–15. Quoted in Brian Matthews, *Federation* (Melbourne: Text Publishing, 1999), p. 79.

3 John Barnes, *Henry Lawson's Short Stories* (Melbourne: Shillington House, 1985), p. 33.

4 William H. Wilde, Joy Hooton and Barry Andrews, *The Oxford Companion to Australian Literature*, 2nd ed. (Melbourne: Oxford University Press, 1994), p. 820.

5 Henry Lawson, Preface, *My Brilliant Career* by Miles Franklin (1901; Sydney: Angus & Robertson, 1986), p. v.

6 Franklin, *My Brilliant Career*, p. 231.

7 Robert Dixon, *Writing the Colonial Adventure: Race, gender and nation in Anglo-Australian popular fiction, 1875–1914* (Cambridge: Cambridge University Press, 1995), p. 24.

8 Wilde, Hooton and Andrews, *Oxford Companion to Australian Literature*, p. 305.

9 Joseph Furphy in a letter to A.G. Stephens, 4 April 1897, in Joseph Furphy and A.G. Stephens, "On Publishing a Novel: A Correspondence" in John Barnes, ed., *The Writer in Australia: A Collection of Literary Documents 1856–1964* (Melbourne: Oxford University Press, 1969), p. 117.

10 Dorothy Green, *Henry Handel Richardson and her Fiction* (Sydney: Allen & Unwin, 1986). See, for example, pp. 249–50 and pp. 313–16.

11 Vivian Smith, ed., *Nettie Palmer* (St Lucia: University of Queensland Press, 1988), p. 30.

12 Patrick White, *Voss* (1957; London: Penguin Books, 1980), p. 443.

13 Quoted in Drusilla Modjeska, *Exiles at Home: Australian Women Writers 1925–1945* (Sydney: Angus & Robertson, 1981), pp. 140–1.

14 Patrick Buckridge, *The Scandalous Penton: A Biography of Brian Penton* (St Lucia: University of Queensland Press, 1994), p. 198.

15 Ken Goodwin, *A History of Australian Literature* (London: Macmillan, 1986), pp. 83, 84.

16 Miles Franklin in a letter to Lucy Spence Morice, 10 August 1936. See Jill Roe, ed., *My Congenials: Miles Franklin and Friends in Letters: Volume One 1879–1938* (Sydney: Angus & Robertson, 1993), p. 338.

17 Marjorie Barnard in a letter to Jean Devanny, 31 July 1945. See Carole Ferrier, *As Good as a Yarn With You: Letters between Miles Franklin, Katharine Susannah Prichard, Jean Devanny, Marjorie Barnard, Flora Eldershaw, and Eleanor Dark* (Cambridge: Cambridge University Press, 1992), p. 128.

18 Judith Wright, "The Upside-Down Hut" in Barnes, ed., *The Writer in Australia*, pp. 332, 334.

19 Carole Ferrier, "Fiction in Transition" in Bennett and Strauss, eds, *Oxford Literary History of Australia*, p. 206.

20 *The Middle Parts of Fortune* was published anonymously in 1929 and republished in an expurgated version in 1930 as *Her Privates We* by "Private 19022". The full text, under both its original title and the full name of its author, was not published till 1977.

21 The unexpurgated version of Tennant's 1953 novel, *The Joyful Condemned*.

22 For detailed discussion of this see Richard Nile, "Literary Democracy and the Politics of Reputation" in Bennett and Strauss, eds, *Oxford Literary History of Australia*, pp. 131–36.

23 Henry Lawson, "'Pursuing Literature' in Australia" in Barnes, ed., *The Writer in Australia*, p. 78.

24 Modjeska, p. 1.

25 M. Barnard Eldershaw, *Essays in Australian Fiction* (Melbourne: Melbourne University Press, 1938).

26 Geoffrey Serle, *From Deserts the Prophets Come: The Creative Spirit in Australia 1788–1972* (Melbourne: William Heinemann Australia, 1973), p. 123.

27 Serle, p. 123.

28 For the various permutations of friendship among this group of women see Modjeska, *Exiles at Home*, and Ferrier, *As Good as a Yarn With You*.

29 Modjeska, *Exiles at Home*, p. 2.

30 Maryanne Dever, "'Conventional Women of Ability': Barnard Eldershaw and the question of women's cultural authority", Maryanne Dever, ed., *Wallflowers and Witches: Women and Culture in Australia 1910–1945* (St Lucia: University of Queensland Press, 1994), pp. 135, 137.

31 Christina Stead, *For Love Alone* (1944; Sydney: Angus & Robertson, 1982), p. 188.

32 See, for example, Susan McKernan, *A Question of Commitment: Australian Literature in the Twenty Years After the War* (Sydney: Allen & Unwin, 1989); Fiona Capp, *Writers Defiled* (Melbourne: McPhee Gribble, 1993) and David Carter, *A Career in Writing: Judah Waten and the Cultural Politics of a Literary Career* (Toowoomba: Association for the Study of Australian Literature, 1997).

33 Both letters quoted in Ferrier, *As Good as a Yarn With You*, pp. 245, 247.

34 David Carter, "Documenting and Criticising Society" in Hergenhan, gen. ed., *The Penguin New Literary History of Australia*, p. 381.

35 Jennifer Strauss, "Literary Culture 1914–1939: Battlers All", *The Oxford Literary History of Australia*, pp. 124–25.

36 Carter, "Documenting and Criticising Society", p. 373.

37 See, for example, Adam Shoemaker, *Black Words, White Page: Aboriginal Literature, 1929–1988* (St Lucia: University of Queensland Press, 1989); Stephen Muecke, *Textual Spaces: Aboriginality and Cultural Studies* (Sydney: New South Wales University Press, 1992); and Susan Sheridan, *Along the Faultlines: Sex, Race and Nation in Australian Women's Writing 1880s–1930s* (Sydney: Allen & Unwin, 1995).

38 Susan Sheridan, "'Wives and mothers like ourselves, poor remnants of a dying race': Aborigines in Colonial Women's Writing" in Anna Rutherford, ed., *Aboriginal Culture Today* (Sydney: Dangaroo Press, 1988), p. 86.

39 Sheridan, *Along the Faultlines*, p. 143.

40 Sheridan, *Along the Faultlines*, p. 145.

41 Quoted by John McLaren, in a review of the 1990 Imprints edition of *Capricornia*, *Australian Literary Studies*, 16.1 (1993), p. 119.

42 Quoted in Modjeska, *Exiles at Home*, p. 138.

43 Nettie Palmer in a letter to Ida Wilmot, 9 August 1929. See Vivian Smith, ed., *Letters of Vance and Nettie Palmer 1915–1963* (Canberra: National Library of Australia, 1977), p. 53.

44 Quoted in Kay Torney, "Filling *Terra Nullius*: Bony in the Deathspace" in Caroline Guerin, Philip Butterss and Amanda Nettelbeck, eds, *Crossing Lines: Formations of Australian Culture* (Adelaide: Association for the Study of Australian Literature, 1996), p. 110.

45 Torney, "Filling *Terra Nullius*", p. 110.

46 Torney, "Filling *Terra Nullius*", p. 109.

47 Stephen Knight, *Continent of Mystery: A Thematic History of Australian Crime Fiction* (Melbourne: Melbourne University Press, 1997), p. 159.

48 Knight, *Continent of Mystery*, pp. 158–59.

49 Sheridan, "Wives and mothers like ourselves", p. 80.

50 Marjorie Barnard, "The Four Novels of Patrick White", *Meanjin*, 35.2 (1956), pp. 156–70.

51 Patrick White in a letter to Marjorie Barnard, 15 June 1956. See David Marr, ed., *Patrick White: Letters* (Sydney: Random House, 1994), p. 103.

52 Simon During, *Patrick White* (Melbourne: Oxford University Press, 1996).

53 Quoted in David Marr, *Patrick White: A Life* (Sydney: Random House, 1991), p. 310.

54 Patrick White, "The Prodigal Son", *Australian Letters*, 1.3 (1958), pp. 37–40.

55 Patrick White in a letter to Ben Huebsch, 11 May 1959. See Marr, ed., *Letters*.

56 Quoted in Marr, *Patrick White: A Life*, p. 369.

57 Ferrier, "Fiction in Transition", p. 193.

58 During, *Patrick White*, p. 55.

59 During, *Patrick White*, p. 71.

60 Smith, ed., *Letters of Vance and Nettie Palmer*, pp. 106–7.

5

RICHARD FOTHERINGHAM

Theatre from 1788 to the 1960s

THE THEATRE OF AUTHORITY

The predominantly English culture which invaded and settled in Australia in the late eighteenth and nineteenth centuries was steeped in performance as a means of asserting control over people and property. The official theatre of authority produced its first symbolic and theatrical act in the flag-raising ceremony by which Britain on 26 January 1788 convinced itself that it had legally taken "possession" of an entire continent already inhabited and controlled by hundreds of Aboriginal communities with quite different ritualised understandings of law, relationships to land, and performance. From that time forward the adventure and military dramas of colonisation and Empire provided understanding of actual historical events and processes, and were explicitly deployed in other quasi-theatrical displays. Military parades, naval pageants, staged battles and mock invasions displayed international political strength and threats as the Empire understood them. In the individual colonies rituals of public order ranging from civic ceremonies to the reading of the riot act laid out the boundaries of acceptable public behaviour and the hierarchies of authority within that community. Rituals of land division and acquisition established rights of lease and freehold title, and the growth of cities produced areas where ritualised public behaviour was not only allowed but expected. Such sites included not just theatres and public halls but also major thoroughfares, military parade grounds, public squares, points of embarkation and debarkation, historical sites, and other places which came to have symbolic significance in the overall mythology of nation-building.

Inevitably many public activities became more overtly theatrical, particularly as the colonists produced a history which could be mythologised and dramatically re-enacted. In 1866 representatives from all the seven Australasian colonies met for the first time in Melbourne during that city's Intercolonial Exhibition, by which time civic celebrations had begun to develop symbols of national identity. For the opening ceremony the English poet and playwright (and then Australian resident) R.H. "Orion" Horne and the composer and conductor Charles Edward Horsley combined to present *The South-Sea Sisters*, a recited and sung celebration of eighty years of "The Genius of Australia". Their "masque" was staged in the main exhibition hall, among allegorical exhibits and under "a tastefully designed canopy, surmounted by a stuffed eaglehawk in the centre, flanked by a similarly prepared kangaroo on his right and emu on his left side".[1] Native animals and the recurring symbols of the wealth of the nation-to-be, wool and gold, were incorporated into British designs for coats of arms, images from classical myth, and ostentatious displays of material achievement.

Such naive dramatised assertions of problem-free national and imperial progress as history in the making continued for another century, though by the 1938 sesquicentennial intellectuals and Aboriginal groups were beginning to voice their opposition. No such doubts were recorded during the Federation ceremonies in January 1901 however. These included a re-enactment of the "Great Historic Event" of the landing of Captain Cook at Botany Bay. A large number of invited guests travelled in eight trams and then by ferry across Botany Bay to the site, where they watched a group of twenty-five Aboriginal people brought from Queensland applying red and white "war paint" and other decorations to their bodies. The official party then lunched in comfort in a large timber and canvas pavilion erected for the occasion, drank wine and champagne, and listened to speeches including one from the New South Wales Minister for Works, E.W. O'Sullivan, who suggested they should treat the "classic soil" on which "they trod" with the same reverence "they would walk the halls of Westminster Abbey". At 3 pm actors dressed as Cook, Joseph Banks and Daniel Solander, and the comedian Sam Poole as the Tahitian chief "Tupia", arrived from a barque anchored offshore, where they were met by the Aboriginal men who, as rehearsed, rushed down to the beach shouting "yells of defiance" and took up poses with their spears "poised in the air":[2]

> Tupia, in the bows of the boat, is endeavouring to make the Natives understand: by Cook's orders he is offering them emblems of peace in the shape of coloured ribbons and beads. The warlike attitude of the Natives indicates that they will maintain an obstinate resistance and act on the defensive; Cook orders a marine to discharge a Musket over the heads of the Natives, but this does not have the desired effect. Finding it necessary to become more severe, he directs the marine to aim at the legs of the foremost Native. He is wounded on the legs and retreats, leaving the coast clear for a landing.[3]

The actors then gave their prepared speeches, including one by Miss Lillian Bethell of the Hawtrey Comedy Company as "Australia (nymph)". Finally, the Aboriginal people gave boomerang-throwing demonstrations and, as such groups had done since the earliest years of white contact and would be pressured to go on doing almost to the present day, performed a decontextualised corroboree for the benefit of the visiting white dignitaries.

Even in the context of such a defining moment of nationhood, there were other ways of understanding an event such as this which emphasised its performativity. Several newspaper accounts represented it as an embarrassing farce, noting the comic-opera nature of the proceedings, with costumes out of *The Pirates of Penzance* rather than history, and that the uninvited crowd, estimated at five thousand, had decided to stage their own carnival during the long delay before the ceremony began. After waiting impatiently in the sun for up to four hours without toilet facilities, and doubtless with many urinating discreetly on O'Sullivan's classic soil, they took the best viewing positions and refused to give them up in spite of a large police presence, disrupted the proceedings by climbing on to the official platform, fired skyrockets "and inflated things of fantastic shapes and bright colours" into the sky. They also cheered the mock battle charge of the Aborigines, who understood perfectly the theatrical nature of the re-enactment and at the conclusion disconcerted many by joining the other actors lined up behind Captain Cook to receive their share of the applause.[4] The carnival of Federation at Botany Bay was undirected; a product of boredom and perhaps a general sense that the wider community was being shut out of the pomp of nation-making. It was not anti-British nor seriously anti-authoritarian, but the *Town and Country Journal* called the event a "parody" and a "distressing affair", and nine years later the Reverend Yarrington, author of the dialogue spoken by the actors and of the "Commonwealth Hymn" sung to the tune of the "Old Hundredth", was obliged to publish his text at his own expense, the official commemorative committee having neglected or decided not to do so.

For the sesquicentennial celebrations in 1938 Captain Arthur Phillip's landing in 1788 was restaged at Farm Cove, but attracted surprisingly few viewers. Yet even here carnival bubbled up: as Governor Phillip (the professional actor Frank Harvey) gave orders for the flag to be raised:

> Steamers far and wide across the harbour set their sirens going in a wild chorus of exultation. The clamour went on and on. In fact from the histrionic point of view it continued too long; for Governor Phillip tried to propose the toast of "His Majesty King George III, the Queen, the Prince of Wales, and success to the new colony," but he could not make a word heard. In desperation, one of the seamen turned to the harbour and raised a hand, like the chairman at a public meeting appealing for fair play. King Canute on the seashore would have had a greater chance of success.

Far more popular was a pageant, "Australia's March to Nationhood", which moved through the city streets, ending at the showgrounds in Moore Park. It included a float representing "the aborigines' camp, with boomerangs to add to its realism, and early aborigines' carvings and drawings decorating the apron of the vehicle".⁵ (Not surprisingly, elsewhere in Sydney, Aboriginal groups organised the first national "Day of Mourning and Protest".⁶) An estimated one million people watched the parade, and the next day the *Sydney Morning Herald* congratulated the public: "Unpractised though they may be in attending public ceremonies, Australians, as exemplified by the crowds which packed the city, proved themselves models of good behaviour", being "appreciative but not loudly demonstrative", "orderly", "good-humoured", and "above all ... keenly interested and thoughtful". This was in spite of a report on the same page that, during the day, over 5,000 people had to be treated by the St John Ambulance volunteers, 250 collapsed in Martin Place and 600 in George Street, children had been knocked down and trampled on at Moore Park where an estimated 250,000 people so exceeded expectations that an extra 500 police had to be rushed to the site.⁷

For the authorities in colonial and federation Australia therefore the power and potential value of theatrical performance was not the issue. All public gatherings, of which formal stage entertainments were from 1833 by far the most numerous and regular, were potentially both celebratory and subversive, orderly and disorderly. What was of concern was unruly physical and vocal behaviour by some audience members, their possibly derisive, non-consensual interpretations of texts, and the likelihood that without strict state control such inflammatory attitudes would be directly encouraged among audiences lacking familiarity with "proper" codes of public behaviour.

In the early colonial period the authorities did have legitimate grounds for concern, related to questions of public order and safety. Playhouses, then the largest public buildings available, were used for political meetings such as those in the 1840s opposing further transportation of convicts. Sometimes stage performances themselves aroused passions, and a few led to street violence. On at least one occasion the disorder had sectarian origins: a group of Catholics vigorously protested the alleged staging of the Mass in *The Jewess* in Melbourne in 1844, in spite of the fact that, as the *Port Phillip Herald* pointed out, what was being represented was the Jewish Passover ceremony.⁸ However, professional performers were not always innocent of deliberately staging inflammatory material. They learnt quickly to negotiate with anti-authoritarian prejudices by parodying local political personalities and intrigues, often with considerable satirical success, and dramatised public grievances, as in the plays about bushrangers which were popularly acclaimed and sometimes banned, particularly between 1880 and 1930.

Nevertheless, comparisons with both England and the United States suggest that theatre in Australia was a relatively well-behaved phenomenon, for the most part actively involved in uncontroversial national and imperial myth-making. W.M. Akhurst's popular 1869 pantomime *The House That Jack Built* was possibly the first of many that included as one scene an extended pageant of European-Australian progress (*tableau vivant* apotheoses, such as several to the lost explorers Burke and Wills, had been staged even earlier). Australian theatre history records no class-based or nationalism-inspired riots of the order of the old-price protests at Covent Garden or the Astor Place tragedy in New York. No Australian audience ever drove the greatest British actors of the day out of the country, as happened in America to Kean in 1825 and Macready in 1848. The arrival in Australia of every English star (and not-so-star) performer was greeted with near-universal grovelling.

In part these differences arose because theatre, on the mainland if not in Tasmania, emerged from a system of strict government control. Until 1832 this was by direct gubernatorial yea or (mostly) nay, then by a system whereby the Colonial Secretary, Edward Deas Thomson, licensed places of performance and censored all locally written plays. Among those he banned was *Life in Sydney* (1843), an often defamatory account of thinly disguised local personalities, and the Melbourne-written *Jackey Jackey the N.S.W. Bushranger* (1845). Deas Thomson also recognised with concern that plays licensed in London such as J.B. Buckstone's highwayman drama *Jack Sheppard* (1839, the probable model for *Jackey Jackey*) could be "locally objectionable". This system fell apart around 1850 when Victoria separated from New South Wales and new legislation was enacted. From this time forwards, rather than licensing play texts as the Lord Chamberlain in London did, colonial governments controlled only the places of performance and the atmosphere within them, through restrictions on where and when liquor could be sold and through public health and safety regulations. This effectively imposed self-censorship: if audiences behaved badly or inflammatory plays were staged, the theatre manager risked losing his or her right to present plays at all, and could not pass the blame for an allegedly subversive or obscene play back to the authorities who had licensed it. It may also explain some significant differences between English and Australian theatrical culture, in particular the fact that music halls never became established in the colonies as viable alternative sites of less structured lower-class performance. The few that began in the 1860s seem to have run foul of the bans on providing both liquor and entertainment at the same time, so variety entertainers were obliged to use the same formally licensed theatres and halls as other stage artists.

In addition, the second half of the nineteenth century saw English-speaking theatre in general move towards more middle-class and family-oriented genres of plays. In the USA the native-born actor-manager Edwin Forrest had from 1820–1850 staged locally written plays which appealed to young American male fantasies and anti-British prejudices. But by the time quasi-equivalent figures emerged in Australia, such as George Darrell, author of *The Sunny South* (1883), and Alfred Dampier, co-author of stage versions of *For the Term of His Natural Life* (1886) and *Robbery Under Arms* (1890), the theatre as an institution was becoming characterised by more luxurious auditoria where the houselights were lowered to try to induce reverential silence and where orchestra stalls replaced the old pit and banished the working classes to the gallery "gods". By the late 1880s even this last male bastion was starting to be invaded by the "gallery girls", signifying the beginning of the end for one kind of theatre and its gradual replacement by another more feminised entertainment culture. Darrell and Dampier (both British-born, both pro-Imperial) were pale echoes of the mid-century possibilities for a more aggressively male and national stage.

Censorship in this new milieu moved from questions of public order to public morals. When controversy appeared, as with Ibsen in the 1890s and then in the amateur theatres from the 1930s, it was not the behaviour of audiences but what was said and done on the stage which caused concern and occasionally calls for intervention to preserve public decency. Nora's motherhood-rejecting exit in *A Doll's House* caused alarm but no intervention, as did the theme of miscegenation in George Landen Dann's *In Beauty It Is Finished* in 1931. Communist propaganda in the plays of the New Theatre Leagues from the 1930s to the 1960s led to police raids and bans by newspapers on advertising and/or reviewing their productions, while obscene language in *Rusty Bugles* in 1948 and in the larrikin Australian drama from the late 1960s also attracted police attention. More subtly, controversial subjects such as Alan Seymour's *The One Day of the Year* (1960), which examines the Anzac legend, and stylistically challenging plays on "serious" subjects such as Patrick White's *The Ham Funeral* (1961), saw those plays rejected by the 1960 and 1962 Adelaide Festivals of the Arts respectively. It was not until the 1970s that theatre broke free of the direct censorship of the state and, in the alternative theatres at least, from the more powerful control of respectable, politically conservative and fashionable audiences, though economic censorship continues to shape and reshape the work that is taken up for wider exposure. While censorship by governments is no longer a major factor, that by state and commercial entrepreneurs continues powerfully to frame most of the formal performance activities in Australia.

MAPPING AUSTRALIAN THEATRE

Any attempt to account for the diversity of activity which might be claimed as part of formal theatre in Australia must recognise three major economic boundaries and a number of shifts in the cultural location of different sectors of that work. An immediate limitation must be pointed out: English-speaking theatre was not the only tradition of performance within Australia. Aboriginal ceremonies took place largely unnoticed and unrecorded unless exploitable as "performance" by European entrepreneurs,[9] and even in the colonial period the Chinese, Italian, French and other migrant communities had their own amateur and in some cases professional troupes staging traditional entertainments in their own languages. It is not clear yet to what extent each community kept to itself; perhaps the fact that at present so little is known about those other traditions suggests that quite different cultural histories could be written to foreground the theatre made by and for other immigrant communities.[10] Occasionally these other traditions intersected with the dominant British industry: Adelaide Ristori performed in Italian when touring, and Sarah Bernhardt in French, while the entire genre of grand opera, which W.S. Lyster's companies in particular did so much to consolidate in the colonies from 1861 onwards, became a major part of the annual offerings in all major cities. But the major industry markers, theatre buildings and the plays performed in them, were those of the English theatre in Australia.

Within this English-language theatre three economic shifts divide up the timeline. The first comes in the 1850s, when the gold rush-inspired prosperity of some colonial capitals, particularly Melbourne, rapidly accelerated the desire for a vibrant and diverse performance culture. Touring stars, theatre and opera companies and large and increasingly luxurious playhouses all multiplied many fold, as did circuses, variety entertainments and tent shows. The second boundary comes in 1930 when a number of factors, particularly the start of the great economic depression and the introduction of Hollywood talking pictures, almost wiped out the professional live theatre industry. The third boundary is marked by the beginnings of significant federal and state government intervention in the arts during the 1950s and 1960s, building new theatres and subsidising artists and companies. It serves as an endpoint for the period covered in this chapter.

Cultural factors also shifted the position of different kinds of activities within the field. Shakespeare, always the most performed author, began as a central part of the commercial repertoire, declined into occasional extravaganza versions (of which Oscar Asche's in 1909–10, 1912–13 and 1922–24 were among the last and most spectacular), was taken up by Allan Wilkie and Frediswyde Hunter-Watts as a less lavish government-supported educational experience in the 1920s, and limped through the next fifty years relying on amateur university productions or professional performances for schools which used small casts and abridged texts. At the other end of the cultural spectrum, variety artists moved into radio comedy after the 1930 collapse and twenty years later into television, while "quality" drama also was taken up on radio and TV by the government-funded Australian Broadcasting Commission (ABC; now a corporation). Dramatic performance itself went on; the modes of delivery changed.

Across all sectors a number of controlling beliefs intersected and competed. Entertainment entrepreneurs wanted to maximise profits, which meant imported stars and stories and little allowance for high art or local writing. Australian-based stage artists wanted work and so approved of performing imported proven successes but argued that they should be restaged with Australians in the leading roles. They also wanted their profession to be accorded greater social respect, with themselves being seen as people of intellect and sophistication; if Shakespeare or "a national drama" would deliver this, they would support them, as long as their livelihood wasn't threatened. Playwrights, never part of that "profession", were less enthusiastic about imported plays and saw the discourse of a "national" stage as potentially opening a place for them as professional writers, but what they wrote mattered less than that they were able to write for performance at all. The literati in the audience wanted the British Bard and intellectual theatre and a national drama to place Australia on the world cultural map. They lamented *Rio Rita* and *Getting Gertie's Garter*, however many artists were consequently employed; they supported the *idea* of local playwriting but wanted it to be non-commercial and preferably within the tradition of Shakespearean verse drama.

Each of these agents of influence therefore had at least one set of beliefs in common with another group and one set of fundamental disagreements, while the overall economic system helped to determine which combination predominated. In the commercial environment pre-1930 the intellectuals got short shrift, though Australian artists were the (poorly-paid, non-starring) backbone of the industry and local authors too were making some headway. In the predominantly amateur years of the mid-twentieth century there was little paying work but hundreds of Australian plays and a respectable number of modern British and European classics were staged for short, poorly-attended amateur seasons. After government support began, it was necessary to maintain the discourse that the principal reason for subsidy was the encouragement of high art and the national drama. Meanwhile the profession covertly went about re-establishing a viable industry with comedies, theatre restaurants and club acts. The industry continued to be very strongly London-oriented; but the national theatre had to be allowed. It was Shakespeare now who missed out; the 1980s probably saw fewer productions of his plays than in any other decade (and fewer theatre-in-education productions). Ironically, they found renewed commercial viability in the 1990s through popular open-air Shakespeare seasons in many major cities; the wheel had to some extent come full circle.

THE ENGLISH THEATRE IN AUSTRALIA

There are two possible moments which could be claimed as the first European theatrical performance in Australia: a staging of an unknown play on the First Fleet ship *Scarborough* on 2 January 1788, seventeen days before it reached Botany Bay, and the presentation eighteen months later, also by convicts, of Farquhar's *The Recruiting Officer* to celebrate the birthday of the reigning British monarch, George III.

This latter is a much mythologised event, with Thomas Keneally's novel *The Playmaker* (1987) and Timberlake Wertenbaker's British play *Our Country's Good* (1988) being two recent retellings of this significant moment of cultural migration: royalist, imitative, offering as Watkin Tench described it an "escape" from the "dreariness and dejection of our situation",[11] yet also inevitably reframed by the new context in which it was performed. One of the performers wrote a new prologue and epilogue which "contained some tolerable allusions to the situation" the convicts and guards found themselves in, and the sixty persons present, including Governor Arthur Phillip, probably realised that the rub between the imagined world of the play and the real world outside the converted convict hut was producing new meanings in the text itself. Their response when Captain Plume tricks the simple Shropshire lad Costar Pearmain into exclaiming "Give me a shilling, I'll follow you to the end of the world"[12] must have been a complex one. And when doubtless some of them left the hut whistling the play's famous recruiting song: "The Queen commands, and we'll obey, / Over the hills and far away", there was surely a new edge there too. Sixty-seven years earlier *The Recruiting Officer* had become one of the earliest plays known to have been performed in New York,[13] perhaps because it was a particular favourite with garrison soldiers, who themselves had a long tradition of performing well-known plays as well as having their own repertoire of military farces which were never presented to the Lord Chamberlain in London for approval.[14] The British armed forces did not merely clear the way for English culture to follow; they were major cultural producers and exporters themselves.

However, in a number of important respects the other event, the shipboard performance about which we have no details other than that it occurred,[15] provides an equally resonant image of the English theatre in Australia. Like a child born at sea which takes its parents' nationality but has no place of birth, theatre became in the nineteenth century a major transnational cultural industry, European in origin but having allegiance principally to its own professional values. Each performance was local, and so often opportunistically appealed to local sentiment,[16] but its genres and stars increasingly aimed at exploiting a grouping of English-speaking populations that included expatriate enclaves in India and Asia, post-revolutionary America, and settler cultures in Canada, South Africa and Australasia. In 1821 Australia's self-styled first poet Barron Field had written that a ship was "sublime" because, while the sea voyage was long, arduous and dangerous, it would allow him to sail away from "this prose-dull land".[17] Thirty years later the sailing ships' land equivalents, theatre buildings which took their paying cargo on imaginary journeys also by the use of canvas, ropes, pulleys and winches, had become ships of the beautiful and even the thrillingly dangerous and sublime; one was nowhere, imagining somewhere else.

From the 1850s onwards many leading British, European and American actors set out on world tours. Charles Kean was in Australia in 1863–64, the younger Charles Mathews in 1870–71, Ristori in 1875, Dion Boucicault in 1885, Bernhardt in 1890, Irene Vanbrugh in 1923 and 1927–28, Sybil Thorndike in 1932, Laurence Olivier and Vivien Leigh in 1948, the predecessor to the Royal Shakespeare Company in 1949 and 1953, to mention only a few at the high-culture end of a spectrum that also included innumerable Gaiety girls, popular singers and variety artists. From the United States there were dozens of blackface minstrels and American circuses and wild west shows from the 1840s onwards, while a young Edwin Booth arrived in 1854. Joseph Jefferson developed his Rip Van Winkle character in the colonies for four years (1861–65) before heading to London and worldwide acclaim, Fred Niblo (George M. Cohan's son-in-law) likewise followed four years in Australia (1912–16) with major success as a Hollywood director, while Joe E. Brown toured in *Harvey* in 1950 and Katharine Hepburn came with *The Taming of the Shrew* in 1955. These and hundreds of other visiting artists brought, as vehicles they could star in, the repertoire of the international entertainment industry: melodramas, Shakespeare, Gilbert and Sullivan, classic drama, popular comedies and farces, extravagantly mounted musicals.

In the context of such global entertainment activity, the citizens of a settler nation like Australia, living before the age of the jumbo jet, were far more likely to experience "culture" in their own theatres than to be able to travel themselves to more "authentic" cultural sites. Consequently it was necessary for the local playhouse to be as close as possible, both aesthetically and functionally, to the edifice it echoed; to be as magnificent, as cosmopolitan, as un-Australian as possible, except perhaps in a few nativist details painted above the proscenium arch. The visiting actor was the primary visible proof that other worlds existed in space/time and not just in representations or objects created in the past, while the customary gauche question by journalists "What do you think of Australia?" revealed the postcolonial fear of being a forgotten land and gratitude at being internationally noticed. Only the far less frequent visits of members of the British royal family, from the Duke of Edinburgh in 1868 to the young Queen Elizabeth II in 1954, or of powerful Americans, from the great white fleet in 1908 to President Lyndon Johnson in 1966, could more vividly realise on Australian shores the existence and importance of richer and more influential nations and cultures. Such events of course brought the theatre of authority to the forefront yet again: pageants, parades and ovals of schoolchildren creating giant visual images of welcome and deference.

The self-enclosed hermeneutic of the theatrical ships of the sublime meant that while plays shared with their audiences the joys and problems of public and private life, taught them etiquette and deportment and courtship rituals and the management of grief, jealousy and desire, and spoke to them as citizens of Britain, of the Empire, and of the English-speaking world, they rarely or only incidentally addressed them as Australians. The major early exceptions to this were the annual Christmas pantomimes of W.M. Akhurst in the 1860s and Garnet Walch in the 1870s, some of which were intensely local in their celebratory and satirical references, but they were one-season successes at best, and usually took traditional English stories as a base. J.C. Williamson, whose entertainment firm dominated commercial theatre from the 1880s to the 1970s, was notorious for not supporting local authors nor ever representing Australian characters or settings. The one exception during his lifetime, the pantomime *Australis; or, the City of Zero* devised for the Federation ceremonies in 1901, was set in a science-fiction Sydney in 2001, used the improbably imagined Jenolan Caves as a variant on the traditional dark scene, and then moved to an equally fanciful Antarctica for the final two acts. Bland Holt, who specialised in Drury Lane sensational dramas and was one of Williamson's few major rivals between 1887 and 1909, was similarly spurred by the creation of the new nation, but only to the extent of making token localisations of English plays. Holt was surprised to find that they became his greatest hits, although critics mockingly noticed the radical disjunction between the flamboyantly Australian visual realism of works like *The Breaking of the Drought* (1902) with its real animal carcases and crows, and the evident British origins of the class-based storyline and characterisation. For others like George Rignold, who built as his Sydney home a mock-Henry V castle to commemorate his greatest role, even such token acknowledgement of national prejudices and differences was unnecessary.

This insistent Anglophilia extended into the post-1930 period, when commercial theatre collapsed. The amateur theatres, overwhelmingly run by women with a background in teaching elocution, were able to secure the amateur performing rights to recent West End successes, and built their companies' fortunes on small-scale and low-cost reproductions of Noel Coward, George Bernard Shaw, Terence Rattigan and others in the British repertory tradition. The better companies occasionally supported local playwrights and also had a literary, European (rather than just English) and intellectual edge, being responsible for the first productions of Osborne, Pinter, Beckett, Ionesco and Brecht in Australia. But virtually all this work was filtered through prior London stagings, theatrical fashions and influences. Delyse Anthony recounts in her history of Brisbane's Twelfth Night Theatre the concern expressed by its artistic director in 1939 who, after returning from a grand tour of Europe, where she discovered that London actors had got rid of "almost all the old superstitions" (they now spoke the last line of the play during rehearsals rather than waiting for first night, for example), called a special meeting of the company to discuss whether they would follow these departures from hallowed tradition.[18] Most "literary" theatre in Australia before 1968 never had any desire to examine at first hand what was happening elsewhere in Europe let alone in the United States, Asia or South Africa; it aped London, dreamt London, and felt anxious when London theatre itself changed even in such absurdly minor ways. It may not be going too far to say that the collapse of the West End theatre of good taste after *Look Back in Anger* in 1956, and the consequent loss of direction this caused, was a major factor during the 1960s in the redefinition of what theatre in Australia could be.

TOWARDS AN AUSTRALIAN DRAMA

The phrase "towards an Australian drama" – with all its resonances of significant cultural achievement in representing the nation and its peoples and of a goal not yet achieved – was used as the title of Leslie Rees' influential 1953 study of plays by and about Australians.[19] From the 1840s to the 1980s it was a nationalist and/or literary-intellectual obsession, involving firstly the selection for review, commentary and publication of particular kinds of plays from a much larger body of work. In any decade in any major city, dozens if not hundreds of plays by local authors were presented. These included work following international genres (such as the enthusiasm for dramatising quasi-Biblical stories c.1895–1910); adaptations of famous English, French and American novels; thinly revised "original" versions of earlier plays; token localisations; domestic comedies which could have been set in any Western city. The motives for such work could be commercial or personal, genuine preference for such genres and subjects, or simply evasion of copyright. As Helen Oppenheim noted in her study of early Sydney theatre, the first surge of local writing for the stage c.1840 was motivated principally by the fact that the English Dramatic Copyright Act of 1833 was beginning to take effect and the supply of printed copies of new British plays had dried up.[20]

British-Australians shared the anxieties of Empire. Both feared the alien abroad and in their midst, hence the curious genres of foreign invasion and white slave-trade plays which circulated in both countries from about 1909 to the end of World War I. Sometimes, though, distance produced local differences. Late nineteenth-century Englishmen feared national degeneracy and prayed that God would make their nation mightier yet, a theme of many of the Drury Lane military melodramas Bland Holt restaged in Australia. But Antipodean settlers also feared their colonies would not become mighty enough quickly enough to withstand enemies, and were infuriated that Britain often undertook foreign diplomatic initiatives which cut across Australian interests and prejudices. Most controversial was the 1902 Britain–Japan Defence Agreement, followed three years later by Japan's imperialist conquest of part of the Chinese mainland. This led to a brief spate of angry anti-British plays such as Randolph Bedford's spectacle-melodrama *White Australia; or, the Empty North* (1909), in which a "degenerate" English-educated traitor assists a Japanese naval invasion of Sydney. Although one of the most chauvinist of playwrights (not surprisingly his play was revised for its only professional season to make it less aggressively anti-British), Bedford's imagined nation of the future was one which had to be passionately concerned with international issues.

Later the amateur movement also produced serious playwrights whose works addressed international themes and subjects, but (probably because many of them were women) had little or only occasional interest in nation-building and alleged national characteristics. A major example which barely mentions Australia at all is Dymphna Cusack's anti-nuclear-testing drama *Pacific Paradise* (1955). Set on a Micronesian island where the inhabitants refuse to be "relocated" to allow nuclear testing to go ahead, it demonstrates how mobilising world opinion can assist such a cause. *Pacific Paradise* was widely performed overseas, being taken up particularly in Eastern bloc countries during the Cold War era, though its Hollywood-influenced view of islander life and romance between a Western scientist and a "native girl" make it a period piece now.

Nevertheless it was not until the late 1970s, when Australian feature films started being noticed internationally and both feminism and the policy of multiculturalism began to undermine the singular concept of a (male) "national identity", that the burden of "writing the nation" passed from the live stage. In the nineteenth and twentieth centuries in some European cultures theatrical works had become powerful weapons in the struggle for national autonomy and in providing international cultural recognition for new nations. Hence both the commercial and amateur theatres in Australia were repeatedly under attack from writers and intellectuals who felt they should be serving the "higher" goal of nation-building and of representing that country to itself as well as (literally) on the world's stages. This was quite explicit in, for example, mid nineteenth-century European opera, with Verdi in Italy, Smetana in Czechoslovakia, and Wagner in Germany working in new nations in highly-charged political circumstances and using librettos with strongly national and/or racial–cultural agendas. Later, in early twentieth-century spoken drama, the Irish national dramatic movement of Yeats, Synge and O'Casey, and the American work of O'Neill, Odets, MacLeish and Wilder, were inspirations for would-be Australian national playwrights like Louis Esson.

Some of Esson's own works were much admired up to twenty years ago, particularly his one-act *The Drovers* (c.1920) with its story of how a group of laconic, emotionally repressed bushmen deal with the accidental death of their leading stockman during a long and dangerous cattle drive. His plays now seem to be attempts to turn Australian story fragments into unconvincing myths of nationalist identity in the style of Yeats' and Synge's symbolist Irish dramas. Esson's earlier urban political comedy *The Time Is Not Yet Ripe* (1912) is clearly indebted to George Bernard Shaw for its structure and Oscar Wilde for the aesthetic socialism of its ineffectual revolutionary hero. But it has energy, a witty role for its heroine (who is the daughter of a conservative prime minister and both political opponent and fiancée of the hero), and a sense of a world Esson knew first hand, when federal parliament was sitting in Melbourne and he was writing occasional political articles for newspapers such as the nationalist *Bulletin*. The Melbourne Repertory Theatre gave *The Time Is Not Yet Ripe* a professionally directed production when it premiered in 1912, and since 1972 it has been republished and occasionally revived by both amateur and professional companies.

The works of the international modern drama movement came to Australia decontextualised and were read as "universal" masterworks with little regard for the geo-political or artistic circumstances that had shaped them. A further consequence of this continuous flow of imported drama meant that few local playwrights read or saw any stage works of other Australians, and even if they did were more likely to ignore them than to participate in the growth of a national school of playwriting. "Towards an Australian drama" implies continuity, growth, and a knowledge of history, but there was no tradition of Australian playwriting. Each new generation of writers looked to current international models.

This was also true of the themes and subject matter of Australian dramas, which often showed an awareness of ongoing international changes and debates but offered individual reactions rather than changing national attitudes to them. An example is the question of protectionism versus free trade, which occupies stage time in many plays. In 1845 Thomas McCombie's novel *Arabin; or, the Adventures of a Colonist in New South Wales* criticised pastoralists who took their profits and went home to England without putting anything back into the local economy, but the 1849 play based on that novel avoided the issue. In Darrell's *The Sunny South* (1883) his protagonists are likewise free to take their colonial fortunes home to England, whereas in Edmund Duggan's *The Democrat* (1891), about the Eureka stockade uprising, the hero's curtain speech reviles those who move profits offshore. This debate continued to rage in Australia at least until the 1973–75 Labor government's disastrous attempt to "buy back the farm", and still could be heard in the flailing protectionism of the One Nation movement in the 1990s, but examination of different attitudes in different plays tells us nothing about any "emerging national sentiment", because no such tradition existed. The dialogue between texts was synchronic, not diachronic; they recognised contemporary contexts but not historical continuities.

The same is true of patterns of characterisation and story motifs, which have always been shaped by pre-existing British and American discourses and narratives. Three of the earliest Australian plays, David Burn's *The Bushrangers* (1829, staged in Edinburgh in Scotland), Henry Melville's *The Bushrangers; or, Norwood Vale* (1834, staged in Hobart and the next year in Launceston), and Charles Harpur's *The Tragedy of Donohoe* (extracts published 1835) were each inspired by documentary facts concerning particular early runaway convict-bushrangers, but each author approached these figures by drawing on different stage genres. Harpur relied heavily on Shakespeare and Schiller's *The Robbers*; Burn also used tortured romantic individualism but placed it within sensational gothic drama; while

Melville drew on domestic melodrama. Unlike Harpur's, Melville's outlaws have no redeeming self-knowledge, although his Aboriginal character is a noble savage, while Burn's are merely savage, and the 1849 play of *Arabin* turned its Indigenous figure into the traditional blackface trickster. While the real-life world undoubtedly affected such works, it did so only indirectly; Melville's play, written in Tasmania by a long-term resident and in other respects keen to name the new world it represents, has its Aboriginal "chief" speak using words from the Sydney Dharuk community a thousand miles away.

Recurrent motifs do exist, such as the appearance in many plays – from Edward Geoghegan's *The Currency Lass; or, My Native Girl* (1844) through the 1907 melodrama *The Squatter's Daughter* to films such as *My Brilliant Career* in the 1970s – of a spirited and independent young woman character who can ride, shoot, and fight (or, in comedy, sing, dance and initiate successful intrigues in the interests of youth and love). Some plays, like Helen Lucy Benbow's 1874 *For £60,000* ("Remember you have no timid English girl to deal with, but an independent, fearless Australian"), constructed the currency lass as nationally different. But the allegorising of the spirit of a nation as a young woman's voice and body is entirely conventional, and the vigorous Australian heroine's dramatic antecedents included English stage characters such as the horse-riding Lady Gay Spanker in Dion Boucicault's *London Assurance* (1844) and the axe-wielding and hero-rescuing Laura Courtland in the American Augustin Daly's 1869 *Under the Gaslight*. As other American examples like Annie Oakley, Calamity Jane, and Cat Ballou suggest, new-land pioneering discourses encouraged such character types.

No Australian plays from the colonial period have re-entered the modern repertoire, although Darrell's *The Sunny South* was revived as a curiosity to launch the Sydney Theatre Company in 1980. Darrell, Walter Cooper (a significant writer in the 1870s of sensation drama with local settings), George Leitch (author of the most successful New Zealand colonial play, *The Land of the Moa*, 1894) and others were primarily actors who wrote plays as vehicles for themselves or for the stars of companies they worked in. The one nineteenth-century figure who went beyond this was Alfred Dampier, who between 1877 and 1904 commissioned and staged plays by many Australian and at least two New Zealand authors, including John Perry's *The Life and Death of Captain Cook* for the 1888 centennial celebrations in Sydney. In 1886 a NSW parliamentarian Thomas Walker provided him with one of the first and probably the most popular stage version of Marcus Clarke's novel of the convict system, *His Natural Life*, and in 1890 Dampier added to his repertoire of national dramas *Robbery*

Under Arms, co-adapted from Rolf Boldrewood's novel of bushranging by the journalist Garnet Walch (a prolific playwright, particularly of pantomime libretti, between 1869 and 1893) and Dampier himself. Walker's play in particular retains considerable power in scenes showing the horrors of the convict system and its wrongful application to an innocent man, juxtaposed with comic scenes designed to appeal to the gallery boys. *Robbery Under Arms*, though even rougher in its construction and surviving only in an unsatisfactory manuscript, turned to another great law-and-order theme of nineteenth-century European and colonial societies: the extent to which the vigilant pursuit and punishment of minor offenders encouraged the abuse of police powers and fuelled resentment which led to greater crimes and widespread sympathy for the criminals. This was the most successful play in Dampier's repertoire and was still being revived twenty-five years later, partly because it drew freely from the example of the Kelly Gang outbreak in 1878–80 which was still fresh in popular memory.

This real-life saga involved the sons of an ex-convict, the legal and administrative persecution of Irish-Australians and poor small landowners ("selectors"), well-documented police corruption and ineptitude, and murderous over-reaction by both sides. Such a confluence of documentary and myth later produced an extraordinary number of successful Kelly Gang dramas, all more or less plagiarised from Dampier's stage *Robbery Under Arms* and from one another, performed all over Australia, particularly in country areas, between 1898 and the 1930s, and which also inspired numerous films in the silent era.

The other major subject of successful popular Australian drama emerged during the Federation period, and involved representing the small property-owning selectors as comic yet also heroic individualists, struggling to build a nation of yeoman farmers against richer and less scrupulous (and usually city corrupted) large landowners. This too had overseas origins in the stories of American homesteaders which had begun to appear on Australian stages early in the twentieth century, but some of these local bucolic farce-melodramas, particularly the first and most successful of them, *On Our Selection* (1912), were viewed and reviewed as unique national utterances. Its sequence of scenes has the impoverished selector Dad Rudd struggle back from bankruptcy in Act One to prosperity and a parliamentary career in Act Four, solely through hard honest work and a refusal to be corrupted. While an old-fashioned melodramatic murder plot linking the scenes is awkward and potentially offensive (the culprit is eventually revealed to be a mentally disturbed farmhand not responsible for his actions), a series of very funny comic sequences and never-say-die heroic speeches made this the most successful Australian stage play of its day. Another worthy of mention is

'Possum Paddock (1919), a charming if slight and childlike romantic bush comedy and the major work of Kate Howarde, Australia's best-known woman actor-manager. These and dozens similar played throughout the country during the 1910s and 1920s, and *On Our Selection* was revived in a 1979 adaptation, published in 1984, and has been produced by many professional and amateur companies since.

The period 1920–60, which straddles the decline and collapse of the commercial drama and the first tentative steps towards a government-subsidised theatre industry, came to be dominated by women writers and artistic directors. Male authority prevailed mainly on ABC radio, where the historical verse dramas of Douglas Stewart (*The Fire on the Snow*, 1941, about Scott's 1912 expedition to the South Pole; *Ned Kelly*, 1942; *Shipwreck*, 1951, about the mutiny on the Dutch ship *Batavia* off the coast of Western Australia in 1629) were for a time seen as best fulfilling national–historical and high-art agendas, though they are largely forgotten today. Attempts to define a "unique" (and singular) national identity remained a major part of the assumed artistic mission for "Australian" dramatists, and this agenda was sustained by the many playwriting competitions (and, in the subsidy period, government grant agencies) which specifically demanded representations of the national as a criterion for eligibility and/or support. A rare early example of a woman playwright who both took on "male" genres and gained professional recognition was Doris Egerton Jones, whose purely commercial detective drama *The Flaw* was taken up by J.C. Williamson's in 1923, with the international star Emilie Polini in the lead. Jones' historical drama *Governor Bligh* (1930), about the arrest of the controversial Governor of New South Wales in 1808, was commissioned and given commercial seasons by the Allan Wilkie Company in Sydney and Melbourne in 1930.

Rather better remembered now are the stage works for amateur companies of Betty Roland and of the novelists Katharine Susannah Prichard and Dymphna Cusack. Roland's *The Touch of Silk* (1928, revised 1955) was popular both with little theatre groups and in radio versions and has been revived by many professional and amateur companies since it was edited and republished in 1974. Its account of a French war bride struggling with the cultural aridity of outback Australia and the war-induced neuroses of her husband possibly resonates more now than at the time of its writing. *The Touch of Silk* offers a remarkable central role for a woman actor and deals sympathetically with European immigrant experiences and the unheroic consequences of war, though it is not kind in its attitudes to what it represents as the intolerance, philistinism and puritanism of country life. Cusack's *Morning Sacrifice* (1942), a girls' school staffroom drama reminiscent of

Christie Winsloe's anti-fascist *Children in Uniform* but informed by Cusack's own work as a Sydney schoolteacher, powerfully examines the crushing of initiative, enthusiasm and sexuality by small-minded and neurotic authoritarianism; it too is revived occasionally.

Prichard's disturbing, unsentimental *Brumby Innes* is perhaps the most challenging and important play of the period. It won a competition in 1927 but was considered too controversial to be staged then, even with blacked-up white actors, and the difficulties of casting its European and Aboriginal roles mean that it has had only one production to date, in Melbourne in 1972. Brumby Innes is a brutal station owner in the north-west of Western Australia who maintains a "stud" of Aboriginal women and roughly seduces (or perhaps simply rapes) a well-bred white city girl and adds her to his "mares". It has been suggested that Prichard was rewriting the legend of Dionysus,[21] but the work's complexity comes from its author's Marxist-inspired sympathy for the conditions in which bush dwellers worked and her relentless social-realist commitment to experiencing at first hand the lives of her subjects and their environment.

It is only since 1970, with the rise of the subsidised professional theatre, and the renewed and ongoing availability of some of these scripts thanks to Currency Press, that such works have been seen as making a significant impact as contributions to a possible Australian dramatic canon. In their own time they were published (if at all) by small regional presses and, if performed, were done by amateurs with minimal production budgets to minuscule audiences. In addition Roland, Cusack, Prichard and many other authors gravitated with greater or lesser enthusiasm to the Australian Communist Party, which virtually alone in this period provided a supportive environment for Australian dramatists. While Roland quickly distanced herself from left-wing causes after hearing of Stalin's show trials in the late 1930s, Prichard and Cusack remained committed party members; Prichard in particular was an unashamed Stalinist to her death. In Australia from the 1930s through the cold-war 1950s such authors were officially shunned and their work ignored where possible.

An even more extreme example of the shutting out of significant work from "respectable" Australian drama is the very successful folk song musical *Reedy River*, which from its first staging in 1953 through to the 1980s kept alive the left-wing New Theatre movement in most major cities and elsewhere in the country. *Reedy River*'s creators, the librettist Dick Diamond and the arranger Miles Maxwell, built on early musicological research into traditional bush and worker ballads, many of which they used in the play. Recordings of the more innocent of these were played on ABC radio but *Reedy River* itself, a dramatised lesson in rebuilding worker solidarity after a disastrous failed strike, has never had a professional production and was long ignored by histories of Australian drama.

During the 1940s reports to the federal Labor government, notably those of the conductor Eugene Ormandy in 1944 and the theatre director Tyrone Guthrie in 1947, considered how the arts could be reinvigorated by government intervention, with one repeated appeal being for the creation of a "national theatre". Guthrie's report in particular, with its proposals for scholarships for Australian actors to go to England and for English companies to tour Australia, was disappointing to those, like the ABC's Federal Drama Editor Leslie Rees, who recognised that this would further marginalise Australian playwriting, and perpetuate a London-dependent mentality where Australian speech and behaviour would be anathema.[22] The election of Robert Menzies' new Liberal Party government in December 1949 provided a new threat, since this conservative coalition was less amenable to government intervention of any kind, but also a new opportunity. By linking a public appeal for arts funding to the tour of Australia in 1954 by the young Queen of England, Elizabeth II, the administrator H.C. Coombs and the head of the ABC, Sir Charles Moses, were able to appeal to Menzies' pro-royalist sentiments. The resulting "Elizabethan Theatre Trust" also resonated with the idea of a new Elizabethan era and re-asserted the part the arts could play in recreating such a mythic golden age. However its theatre program began in 1955 very much in the Guthrie Report mould, with a tour of a Terence Rattigan play starring Ralph Richardson and Sybil Thorndike, followed by the expatriate Judith Anderson in a six-month tour of *Medea*.

One immediate condition in which the new body had to operate was the paranoid early cold-war political environment which the Menzies ministry exploited to stay in office and which meant that left-wing playwrights would be *personae non grata* and government-funded theatre politically cautious if not conservative. As noted, this excluded most of those then working, including two important Sydney New Theatre playwrights, Oriel Gray and Mona Brand. Gray's *Sky without Birds* (1950), a study of prejudice against post-war immigrants, is particularly powerful; Brand's *Here Under Heaven* (1948) looked at the situation of Asian immigrants for perhaps the first time and was another work to find greater favour in communist Eastern Europe than at home. But the Elizabethan Theatre Trust's first executive director, the recently arrived Englishman Hugh Hunt, probably was unaware rather than dismissive of most of the many fine plays already available; his only backward glance was a season of Stewart's *Ned Kelly* in 1956. Other proven plays available, in addition to those mentioned above (and others by those writers), included the commercial musical *Collits' Inn* (1932–33); Max Afford's comedy-thriller *Lady in Danger* (1941), which was also presented commercially and three years later in New York; Dorothy Blewett's *The First Joanna* (1948), a dramaturgically fresh approach to the perennially popular subject of Australian colonial history; and in particular Sumner Locke Elliott's *Rusty Bugles*, perhaps the most remarkable of all plays on the theme of Anglo-Australian male identity. Elliott, a successful stage writer for the Sydney Independent Theatre and radio dramatist, based this intensely realistic sequence of epic scenes on his own experiences in the Australian army, serving at a God-forsaken ordinance depot in the Northern Territory. Each of the many male characters is precisely and sympathetically individualised by physique, language and neuroses, and their emotional as well as physical loneliness, hopelessness in the face of an indifferent bureaucracy and feelings of uselessness and inability to escape are powerfully presented; if it had been written ten years later, *Rusty Bugles* would have been seen as influenced by *Waiting for Godot*. Its premiere at the Independent in 1948 led to its banning for obscene language (then, as in the nineteenth century, the Theatres and Public Halls Act was used to threaten the company with closure), followed by a compromise whereby the offending words were removed (legend has it that they were later quietly and gradually reinstated) which allowed the season to continue and to become a popular success. *Rusty Bugles* was taken up the next year by a commercial management; it played in Melbourne for six months and toured for two years, while a second company went to New Zealand in 1952. Though the offstage women characters, about whom the men dream and try to negotiate with via the one-line telephone, are also strongly individualised, the play's large and all-male cast did not help it find ongoing staging opportunities. Except for two minor productions (1964, 1979) and television versions (1965, 1981), it has disappeared from the national repertoire. As a reading text, however, it still delights with its rich excess of idiomatic language, its sympathy for the plight of all its characters, and it also resonates powerfully as a microcosm of a "nation" both threatened and ignored by a global conflict which it can neither avoid nor influence.

When Ray Lawler's *Summer of the Seventeenth Doll*, winner of yet another playwriting competition, was taken up by the Elizabethan Theatre Trust for a national tour in 1956 and acclaimed as "the birth of Australian drama", the many supporters of *Rusty Bugles* wrote in protest at this return to the pioneering discourse which assumes a cultural wasteland and so devalues Australian cultural history. However, as well as giving the Trust a sense of pioneering achievement and assuaging the Australian cultural cringe by winning the London *Evening Standard* prize as the best play of 1957 after it was performed there (and being made into a less-successful Hollywood movie), the *Doll* is a genuinely outstanding play, still regularly revived both by amateurs and professionally. Interestingly, both Locke Elliott and Lawler worked as comedians in vaudeville before they wrote the plays by which they are remembered; in both the wry and gently comic shaping of seemingly realistic dialogue is central to their success. Reading the *Doll* in the knowledge that Lawler played canecutter Barney in the original production (and in London) is to notice how central that role is, as energiser and comic and thematic counterpoint, in a play more often seen as being about the ageing and failing relationship between a North Queensland canecutter Roo and his barmaid girlfriend Olive, whom he travels annually to Melbourne to see each layoff season. The play's surprise denouement is that, when Roo finally accepts his years of itinerant wandering are over and offers to marry Olive, she rejects him, wanting "what I had before". Some recent feminist scholarship has taken up the complexity of this decision[23] and Lawler once suggested himself that the play was about "an alternative to marriage".[24] The *Doll* might even be seen as an early exploration of two-career relationships, and points to a larger theme of the forced physical separation of men and women by work, war and life-denying institutional bigotries which informs so many Australian plays of the early and mid twentieth century. Barney's casual attitude to sex, relationships and growing old, probably viewed negatively in the 1950s in spite of the character's warmth, fun and generosity, now seems another unremarkable alternative in a world in which the nuclear family is no longer natural or inevitable.

As commentators on both play dramaturgy and cultural policy have noted, it became apparent in later decades that both *Summer of the Seventeenth Doll* and the Australian Elizabethan Trust, which held it up as its proudest achievement towards an Australian drama, were part of the end of one era, whatever claim they might have to be the beginning of a new one. The *Doll* was a well-made play in the old-fashioned English repertory model; its style was often imitated, notably in Richard Beynon's migrant Romeo and Juliet story *The Shifting Heart* (1957, London 1959) and Alan Seymour's critique of the Anzac legend, *The One Day of the Year* (1960, London 1961); both however now seem lesser achievements, and the mini-genre of the "guided tour of Australian working class life" which they represent, gauche and patronising.[25] Only Patrick White's *The Ham Funeral* (1961) transcended the limitations of the subject matter and found a new, expressionistic voice. The Trust for its part was structured on imported British concepts of high art and arts management, seemed unaware of the conflict of interest it generated by having both a subsidising and an entre-preneurial role, and had managed to alienate some of the country's most distinguished artists and arts commentators by ignoring their works and their expertise and by its seemingly lukewarm support for Australian material compared to that for international stars and classics. More mundanely, however, the effort of maintaining a "national presence" meant arduous and expensive touring for artists and logistical difficulties for administrators and technicians, and it was clear by the mid-1960s that both playwriting and the theatre in general were falling far short of the hopes of a decade earlier. New artistic approaches and new institutional structures were needed, and the alleged cultural void would need to be invoked once again.

NOTES

Except as noted, basic biographical information on writers and artists and details of the stage history of individual plays and companies mentioned can be found in Philip Parsons, gen. ed., with Victoria Chance, *Companion to Theatre in Australia* (Sydney: Currency Press in association with Cambridge University Press, 1995), and in Harold Love, ed., *The Australian Stage: A Documentary History* (Kensington, NSW: New South Wales University Press, 1984).

1 *Age* (Melbourne), 25 October 1866, p. 6.
2 *Sydney Mail*, 12 January 1901, p. 50.
3 Rev. W.H.H. Yarrington, *The Landing of Captain James Cook, R.N., Botany Bay, 1770. As produced in connection with the Commonwealth Celebrations at Kurnell, Botany Bay, New South Wales, Australia, on Monday 7th January, 1901* (Sydney: Turner & Henderson, 1909), p. 8.
4 *Town and Country Journal* (Sydney), 19 January 1901, p. 13; *Sydney Mail*, 12 January 1901, p. 50.
5 *Sydney Morning Herald*, 27 January 1938, pp. 6, 14, 16.
6 See Craig Munro, *Wild Man of Letters: the Story of P.R. Stephensen* (Melbourne: Melbourne University Press, 1984), p. 183.
7 *Sydney Morning Herald*, 27 January 1938, p. 6.
8 *Port Phillip Herald*, 6 September 1844, quoted in Love, ed., *The Australian Stage*, p. 39.
9 Stephen Muecke, Jack Davis, and Adam Shoemaker, "Aboriginal Literature" in Laurie Hergenhan, gen. ed., *The Penguin New Literary History of Australia* (Melbourne: Penguin, 1988), pp. 27–46.
10 See for example Elizabeth Webby, "Australia and Europe: Literary and Theatrical Connections 1788–1850", *Quadrant*, June 1983, p. 27; Harold Love, "Chinese Theatre on the Victorian Goldfields", *Australasian Drama Studies*, 3.2 (1985), pp. 47–86; Tony Mitchell, "Italo-Australian Theatre: Multi-culturalism and Neo-colonialism Part One", *Australasian Drama Studies*, 10 (1987), pp. 31–48; Con Castan, "Greek-Australian Plays", *Australasian Drama Studies*, 12/13 (1988), pp. 17–33; Marko Pavlyshyn, "Culture and the Émigré Consciousness: Ukrainian Theatre in Australia 1948–1989", *Australasian Drama Studies*, 20 (1992), pp. 54–69.
11 Watkin Tench, *A Complete Account of the Settlement at Port Jackson, in New South Wales* (London: 1793), p. 25, quoted in Love, ed., *The Australian Stage*, p. 13.

12 George Farquhar, *The Recruiting Officer*, ed. Peter Dixon (Manchester: Manchester University Press, 1986), II.3, pp. 169–70.

13 Don B. Wilmeth and Christopher Bigsby, eds, *The Cambridge History of American Theatre. Volume One: Beginnings to 1870* (Cambridge: Cambridge University Press, 1998), p. 35.

14 Bill Dunstone, "Imperialist Discourses: Amateur Theatrical Performances in Perth to 1854", *Australasian Drama Studies*, 23 (1993), pp. 47–48.

15 The occasion was first noted by Eric Irvin, "Eighteenth-Century Plays on the Early Sydney Stage", *Restoration and Eighteenth-Century Theatre Research* 10.1 (1971), p. 29, citing the manuscript of Private John Easty, held in the Mitchell Library. See Love, ed., *The Australian Stage*, pp. 9, 12.

16 One of the legends that survived the provincial showman Dan Barry was of him giving a speech before the curtain in Wangaratta in Victoria, in which he described the town as the "most charming city on earth". When an audience member interjected that he'd said the same thing the night before about Benalla, Barry quickly replied, "Quite right, sir! … But I had not then seen Wangaratta." (Stanley Grant, "Dan Barry Anecdotes", *Theatre Magazine*, 1 March 1915, p. 48.)

17 Barron Field, "On Reading the Controversy Between Lord Byron and Mr Bowles", *First Fruits of Australian Poetry*, 2nd ed. (1823; facs. ed., Sydney: Edwards & Shaw, 1941), p. 16.

18 Delyse Anthony, "The Early History of Twelfth Night Theatre 1936–1942", BA (Hons) Dissertation, University of Queensland, 1990, p. 14.

19 Leslie Rees, *Towards an Australian Drama* (Sydney: Angus & Robertson, 1953).

20 Helen Oppenheim, "Colonial Theatre. The Rise of the Legitimate Stage in Australia", n.d. (c.1960), typescript with handwritten annotations, ML MSS 3266, Mitchell Library, Sydney, pp. 407–08.

21 D. Biggins, "Katharine Susannah Prichard and Dionysus: *Bid Me to Love* and *Brumby Innes*", *Southerly*, 43.3 (1983), pp. 320–31.

22 "Leslie Rees Replies to the Guthrie Report", quoted in Love, ed., *The Australian Stage*, pp. 197–99.

23 Imré Salusinszky, "What's Bugging Olive? A New Reading of 'The Doll'", *Southerly*, 50.2 (1990), pp. 170–81.

24 "Interview: Ray Lawler Talks to Alrene Sykes", *Australasian Drama Studies*, 3.2 (1985), p. 22.

25 Alrene Sykes, "Theatrical Events 1950–1965 and the Rise of Subsidised Theatre" in Love, ed., *The Australian Stage*, p. 208.

6

DAVID McCOOEY

Contemporary poetry: across party lines

'68 – '79 – '99

Contemporary Australian poetry has often been viewed in terms of factionalism (in which revolutionary forces opposed reactionary ones), followed by a period of pluralism. This model relies on secondary oppositions: internationalist/nationalist; experimental/traditional; urban/rural; modernist/anti-modernist; anti-formalist/formalist; political/non-political. The opposing positions are occupied by the young poets who appeared in the late 1960s and early 1970s, known as the "Generation of '68" (or, more generally, the New Australian Poetry), and an "establishment" or "humanist" wing made up of older figures (such as A.D. Hope) and younger writers (such as Les Murray and Robert Gray).

This literary history is relatively convincing, and poets have employed it themselves, but it does not always reflect the actual state of affairs. Oppositional models can also mask anxieties, such as whether contemporary poetry could be said to *have* a history, whether Australian poets fully engage in contemporary practices, and what constitutes *Australian* poetry. The '68ers were often the most vocal, but not the only, poets to question matters of style, subject matter, influence, audience and a national poetry, in response to the changing status of writing, technologies and markets with(in) which poets worked.

To view contemporary Australian poetry as an upsurge of opposition subsiding into pluralist recognition of difference is a partial account, ignoring differences within and connections between "factions". The Generation of '68 *was* rhetorically oppositional. But it was also heterogeneous in its aims and poetics, something that has become more visible, significant and historically interesting through time. Such heterogeneity is best approached through some of the group's antecedents.

Francis Webb's *Collected Poems* of 1969 had considerable impact on younger poets. Indeed, Webb's mixture of intensity and obscurity seemed more responsive than the poetry found in Shapcott and Hall's anthology, *New Impulses* (1968), the restraint, irony and scepticism of which seemed linked to an earlier poetry.[1] That such "new" impulses were to date so quickly (especially after Shapcott's *Australian Poetry Now* of 1970) suggests something of the telescoped generationalism then developing. Australian poetry of the 1960s began to be found guilty by association with the 1950s, a period derided as culturally arid, a time of reaction against the modernism glimpsed by Ern Malley and other poets of the late 1940s (such as Webb).

This association led to distorting views of individual poets, such as A.D. Hope. The '68ers' historiographical model required Hope to be an arch-reactionary, and Michael Dransfield's sarcastic image of him as one of the "Official Poets", "whose genteel / iambics chide industrialists / for making life extinct", shows how unable they were to read his poetry.[2] But a notable trend in current Australian cultural history is the revision of the 1950s. In Dransfield's day it would have been unthinkable for two literary historians (James Tulip and Chris Wallace-Crabbe) to compare Hope with the '68er John Forbes, but recent theoretically-informed readings make such a comparison possible.[3]

While Webb was symbolically important to the younger poets, he proved a difficult model. Instead, Bruce Beaver is seen as the godfather of the Generation of '68. His *Letters to Live Poets* (1969) heralds younger poets' concerns and techniques. But "establishment" poets were also freeing up. The autobiographical lyrics of *Surprises of the Sun* (1969) heralded the end of James McAuley's impersonal, public aesthetic, while David Campbell's *The Branch of Dodona* (1970) grappled with topical techniques and issues, showing that opposition to the Vietnam War was no longer restricted to the young.

A key "non-aligned" figure of this time was Bruce Dawe. His popularity was achieved through his skilful use of colloquial Australian but did not stop him from criticising his own groups (such as Australia and the Roman Catholic church) or being pessimistic about his characters' ability to render meaning out of their struggles. But while life's meaninglessness may be expressed in poems such as "Enter Without so Much as Knocking", his poems also show compassion for the individuals involved. Dawe's demotic idiom is matched by a rhetoric and seriousness apposite for his ethical-satirical intentions. And related to Dawe's interest in voice – his best poems are dramatic monologues – is his rendering of Australian suburbia, which poets had long ignored, derided or satirised. Dawe found a voice to represent suburbia as a site of significance and authentic experience. This turn to suburbia is a feature of the period, seen in other Melbourne poets from the 1960s such as Wallace-Crabbe and R.A. Simpson.[4]

But these mainstream developments were not enough for the emerging Generation of '68. Their revolutionary rhetoric and commitment to alternative forms of publication (and poetic culture generally) were attended to in stylistically diverse ways, from Nigel Roberts' comedy, to Vicki Viidikas' confessional meditations on subculture, and Kris Hemensley's use of numerous poetic techniques. Named after the year of student and worker militancy overseas, the "Generation of '68" claimed a cultural revolution, based on taking risks and freeing up. As Livio Dobrez, the group's historian, puts it, "The sixty-eighters *can say it.*"[5] Dobrez presents their poetry as a literature of sensibility, valuing frivolity, immediacy and a disregard for proprieties (pp. 64–69).

Such a model determined the early readings of the group as a kind of "new romanticism", James Tulip's term for the younger poets included in *Australian Poetry Now.*[6] This description is significant, given the attention the absence of an Australian romantic movement has received. For Paul Kane this historical absence led to a preoccupation with romanticism that was "grounded in absence or negativity".[7] Marginality and belatedness led to "the concern not so much with genius (the assertion of originality), as with genesis (the constitution of the self), the originating self-authorisation that marks the poet as a poet experientially" (p. 32). This is discernible in the autogenetic rhetoric of the Generation of '68 and their numerous self-referential poems. Kane does not directly address the "new romanticism", but one of his tropes of negativity is relevant, given the movement's emphasis on American and modernist models: "Often the imitation of other writers or styles involves a rejection of the problematic of Australian romanticism and an attempt to substitute some other program or project in its stead." This, as Kane points out, confronts similar problems of belatedness, non-indigeneity, and originality (pp. 45–46). So, did the Generation of '68 simply repeat the pattern of belated romanticism inscribed through tropes of negativity? In the '68ers' case such tropes included social transgression, aporia, indeterminacy and post-humanism.

These tropes suggest the role of modernism. The tension between romanticism and modernism illustrates the fact that the '68ers' project (if it could be said to have one) was self-contradictory. The rhetoric of 1968 was of political engagement and activism, while many of the literary models used by the '68ers were anti-expressivist and autotelic, emphasising the work of art as a thing in itself. Poets such as Dransfield and Charles Buckmaster were generally working with romantic-expressive ideas of the poet, while John Tranter, John Forbes and John A. Scott de-emphasised subjectivity, and argued against poetry's ethical and expressivist purpose. The movement, then, represents a split between late-Romantic modernism and early forms of postmodernism.

Like the old, the new romanticism rejected received ideas about diction and subject matter. Free verse, concrete poetry and self-conscious use of typography flourished under the sign of experimentation (something that detractors viewed as merely conventional). Today, the aesthetic may indeed appear predictably modernist: a Zeppelin standing in for a revolution in travel, perhaps. But this is partly accounted for by Hemensley's description of the new poets as an "illiterati".[8] And despite the emphasis on utopian politics and collective cultural production, the individual poet remained the locus of poetic expression (a common romantic tension). While the death of the romantic subject was gestured towards, pragmatic attempts to effect this were rare (examples are the importance of Ern Malley; John Tranter's work with computer-generated poetry; and some collaborative works).

The American influence was indeed pronounced, especially from the Black Mountain and New York Schools, groups covered in Donald Allen's influential (once banned) *New American Poetry* (1960). Like the Americans, the '68ers equated formal freedom with political freedom. Tranter writes that they desired "freedom from conscription ... bureaucracy and capitalist exploitation, freedom to experiment with drugs, to develop a sexual ethic free of hypocrisy and authoritarian restraints, and freedom from the hand-cuffs of rhyme and the critical strictures of the university English depart-ments".[9] Such a convergence today looks willed, reductive and faintly absurd.

The *idea* of the Generation of '68 marks a materialist turn in criticism. Tranter, for instance, posits in *The New Australian Poetry* (1979) four factors for the group's rise: demography (the baby boomers' access to higher education and "the new rock music"); technology (especially cheap print-ing); illegal drugs; and the American influence.[10] To these we can add the contemporaneous dissolution of censorship, and the convergence of high and popular culture. The former affected *what* could be written without fear of prosecution: "The sixty-eighters *can say it*" because they *could* say it. The latter brought about changes in popular culture that raised the poet's role in youth consciousness. Rock music briefly gave poetry new cultural capital: one thinks of Mick Jagger reading Shelley at the Stones' Hyde Park concert; the Beatles including the lyrics with *Sgt Pepper's* and *The White Album*; rock opera; John Lennon's books; and of course Bob Dylan (who named himself after a poet).

As supporters and detractors quickly noticed, this aesthetic was one of productivity, seen in the period's numerous collections, little magazines such as *The Great Auk* and *Free Poetry* (with some, including *Makar* and

Rigmarole of the Hours, spawning small presses), and countless ampersands, verbless sentences and unclosed parentheses. One effect of this aesthetic, along with the briefly touted belief that "anyone can be a poet", was that poetry need not strive for deathlessness, leading to the aesthetic of impermanence. One thinks again of the Beatles with their short-lived Zapple label (for "paperback" records); street theatre; "happenings" (did they really happen?); and the underground press. But while impermanence and spontaneity were valued, small magazines, like anthologies, quickly became contested sites of power. In 1969 a "coup" at the Poetry Society of Australia saw the poet Robert Adamson and the critic Carl Harrison-Ford take over *Poetry Magazine* (which was daringly retitled *New Poetry*).[11]

The '68ers shared not so much an aesthetic as an opposition: academic and establishment notions of poetry and cultural production. This is seen in the "anthology wars" (another American import) and polemical essays, as much as the poetry. Their programmatic stance led to accusations of bad faith, such as Richard Packer's description of them as "epigones": mimic poets viewing "real" artists as elitist.[12] Polemic led to parody, a late example being Peter Goldsworthy's "The Great Poet Reconsiders The Generation of '68": "He looks back over the gravestones / and his eyes grow misty again: / We Did It Our Way, boys, he thinks / oh, and you two girls".[13] This makes two valid points: the originality was arguable, and the movement patriarchal in structure. The gravestones signify literal as well as symbolic deaths.

Buckmaster's and Dransfield's early deaths seem patently romantic (Forbes saw Dransfield's death as allowing him to be packaged as "the Keats of smack and hippydom").[14] Though Dransfield and Buckmaster presented themselves as *poètes maudits* they quickly received mainstream acceptance (as in Shapcott's notorious description of Dransfield as "terrifyingly close to genius"),[15] and it is now commonplace to view Dransfield's technique as superficially avant-garde. These poets illustrate the tension among '68ers between autotelic and politically committed writing. Their work tends towards the latter, but is attracted to an aestheticism indebted to *les symbolistes* and their tropes: the elliptical style; the *poète maudit*; "the derangement of all the senses"; radical otherness ("JE est un autre"); and anti-bourgeois behaviour. The figure who mediates the romantic and postmodern arms of the Generation of '68 is Robert Adamson, whose early work figures drug use, institutional life, fast cars and ambiguous sexuality, as well as exercises in "romantic" postmodernism, such as "The Rumour". At the same time, the natural world has figured largely in his poetry. Adamson's style ranges from the postmodernism of *Waving to Hart Crane* (1994) to the ultra-romanticism of *Crossing the Border* (1977) and minimalist realism of *Where I Come From* (1979). Despite the latter's flat diction and unromantic landscape, an interest in origins, primitiveness and marginalised characters implies a romantic sensibility, Adamson's most consistent feature.

Adamson's and Tranter's attraction to poetic autonomy tended to corrode political engagement.[16] In addition, the movement's emphasis on personal freedom led to a model of the (male) poet's desire that ironically downplayed the autonomy of others, especially women.[17] One of the few radically political '68ers was also one of the movement's few women: Jennifer Maiden. Her early work, though, is exceptionally elliptical political writing. "The Problem of Evil" (1975) (set in a war zone both allegorical and realist) is narrative poetry almost obscured by metaphor. But, like "The Trust" (1988), this work is principally concerned with the ethical imperatives of linguistic representation. Later poems, such as those on the Gulf War, offer similar concerns, but in a less abstract mode.

J.S. Harry, who has been strangely ignored by (those who defined) the Generation of '68, is also concerned with philosophical issues. As Maiden points out, Harry's poetry works through "miscegenation of ideas".[18] Harry's miscegenetic imagination produces unsettling, sometimes violent, graftings upon the world, effected by coupling of divergent modes, as in "The Little Grenade", which fuses children's literature with the self-reflexive lyric. This is seen most ambitiously in "Peter Henry Lepus" (1995), which concerns the parodic, ludic adventures of Beatrix Potter's rabbit in a philosophical wonderland.

The place (or non-place) of such writing in the Generation's poetics suggests the contradictory and unresolved nature of its project, especially between expressive and autotelic models of poetry. One of the most consistently anti-expressive writers, Tranter, was also the most stylish proponent of a poetry both "absolute" and suspicious of metaphysical art claims. But by the late 1970s the *poésie pure* of *The Alphabet Murders* (1975), *Crying in Early Infancy* (1977) and *Dazed in the Ladies Lounge* (1979) had played itself out without clearly offering a solution. The tension between such writing and the romantic arm of '68 illustrates the impossibility of revolution, something Tranter's polemical essays of the time wrestle with. Dismissing Dransfield and Buckmaster as soft rebels needing middle-class approval, Tranter argues in "Four Notes on the Practice of Revolution" that

> Rebellion for its own sake belongs to the selfish rhetoric of adolescence, and once the opposition has been badly damaged enough, it's time to stop. We are all poets, after all, facing a society hostile to the very idea of the poetic life. It occurs to me sometimes that we were all united once in our opposition to a common enemy; and that we are now perhaps our own enemies.[19]

Such writing ironically employs the rhetoric to which it is opposed, and calls for pragmatic consensus at the moment of welcoming the next revolution (p. 134).

While such contradictions and tensions within the Generation of '68 could not be expected to "resolve", by the end of the 1970s they were sufficiently clear to make the movement redundant. By then the Generation's force was dissipated, partly through what we might call "discursive exhaustion", and partly through the increasingly dominant positions the postmodern arm of the movement was taking. As such, a number of postmodern-formalist poets can be viewed productively as a group. Taking the date of Tranter's anthology (conterminous with the Generation of '68) as our cue, we can describe Tranter, Forbes, Laurie Duggan, Alan Wearne and John A. Scott as "the Generation of '79". While these poets may find membership of another generation a dispiriting thought, there is some cohesion: they have known each other (Wearne, Scott and Duggan were active at the Monash University readings in the late 1960s), and have written about, dedicated poems to, and parodied one another. In addition, the 1980s saw postmodern theories achieving something like hegemony in the academy and, while these poets were not easily incorporated into academic interests and canons, they received considerable attention because of their postmodern aesthetics and techniques.

A key feature of the Generation of '79 is that they wrote what could be termed "vernacular formalesque": their postmodern-formalist interests are expressed in an idiom recognisably Australian and demotic (even true of the relatively hieratic Scott). This stylistic hybridity illustrates a new approach to the issues of nationalism and identity: both deconstructing and reinvigorating those terms' discourses. Its formalism also shows that the '68ers were only ever partially anti-formalist. Though none of the '79ers is much interested in metrical verse, their emphasis on textuality expresses itself through interest in form: in Tranter's sonnets, and many nonce forms; Wearne's (often stanzaic) dramatic monologues; Scott's prose poetry and *livres composés*; the narrative poetry of those three; Forbes' raiding of classical forms (the ode, elegy, abaude and pastoral); and Duggan's promiscuous use of forms from epigram, anagram and haiku to verse-autobiography, satire, epic (*The Ash Range*) and anatomy (*Memorials*). Attending to language, dramatisation and form these poets are variously anti-romantic, parodic, post-humanist and ironic.

Forbes' poetry – with its intermingling of "high" and "popular" culture, arresting similes, laconic humour and unpredictable endings – rewrites cultural clichés into something both artful *and* suspicious of art claims. While sometimes viewed as a worshipper of language or a comic poet, Forbes is not only concerned with the surfaces of language. His poetry, ambivalent as a bathroom, acknowledges both the body's pleasures and incompetencies. His poetry is difficult because both abrasive and caring; detached and involved; highly wrought and politically charged. The political critique of "Love Poem", for instance, is wedged, like an unexploded bomb, into the lyrical subjectivity of love poetry.

The Generation of '79 shows that postmodernism is not inherently antipathetic to questions of national culture. Forbes presents the category as a matter of style (as in "Antipodean Heads"), which is relatively benign, or produced by the cacophony of history, which is not. In "On the Beach: A Bicentennial Poem" the poet's vocation – 1988, after all, was a year for odes – is, in Australia, absurd and vaguely shameful. The relaxed, laconic Australian style is imperilled by – while defined by – violence. Forbes' concern with vocation and nation suggests the early Australian poets, especially Wentworth. His epideictic style, odes and public poems evoke and parody the project of originating a nation poetically.

Though Wearne and Duggan are both interested in the quotidian, Duggan is less concerned with narrative than "moments", found texts and bricolage. His autobiographical musings offer a kind of realist, rather than confessional, aesthetic. Duggan is also a major parodist and satirist of Australian poetry, tempering satire with self-directed irony. His use of bricolage is most ambitious in *The Ash Range* (1987), a history of the Gippsland which uses newspaper reports, diaries and histories. Technically indebted to Pound and Black Mountain poetry, the approach is Duggan's, emphasising oddity and figures ignored by conventional history.

Duggan's liking for poems as "accessible and difficult as films"[20] highlights the importance of the filmic imagination to the '79ers, something noted by critics of individual members of the group. For example, Philip Mead sees the "cinematism" (rather than pictorialism) of Tranter's *The Floor of Heaven* as part of a postmodern project of reclaiming narrative to expand poetry beyond expressive lyricism.[21] This is similarly true for Scott, whose reworking of his own material, interpolations of "prose" into "poetry", and deconstruction of genre further such a program.

St Clair (1986/90) represents both the fruition of Scott's reworkings and a farewell to narrative poetry. As this work shows, Scott (among the '79ers) is the most stylistically extravagant, the most concerned with writing's obsessive nature, and the most taken with the idea of a free play of meaning in literary texts. But, despite his interest in different forms of textuality, he is also sometimes filmic in his pronounced stylisation. "Run in the Stocking" and "St Clair" parody the thriller and dystopian genres in elliptical ways. The interest in violence, sexual obsession and identity (key filmic themes) does not suggest that Scott is divorced from ethical interests. Indeed, one critic sees him as healing the division between the ultra-aestheticism of Nabokov and the ultra-moralism of Solzhenitsyn.[22]

Wearne's milieu is less exotic, but his work no less ambitious. "Out Here", probably the most sustained poetic consideration of Australian suburbia, rejects satire and the mock-heroic to emphasise suburban complexity. *The Nightmarkets* (1986) focuses upon Melbourne, and – as in "Out Here" – plot is secondary to voice and characterisation. Ten long monologues are realised within Wearne's idiosyncratic style, giving the work the paradoxical effect of being both many voices and one voice. *The Nightmarkets* is also paradoxical in being a factitious, formalised kind of naturalism. The stories about sex, politics and work are naturalist in that, like autobiographical narratives, they are interconnected but eschew teleology. Like Duggan, Wearne illustrates a strong documentary tendency within a formalist aesthetic.

In the 1980s and 1990s Tranter remains an important figure. The relatively conventional, communicative lyrics included in *Under Berlin* (1988) were met with some (understandable) critical suspicion. But the poet views these Australian tableaux with both an indulgent and satirical eye, and their emphasis on nostalgia and surfaces remains Tranteresque. They illustrate how much Tranter's internationalism is rooted in an interest in Australian myths and idioms. More obviously postmodern are the verse tales of *The Floor of Heaven* (1992), which render long-standing concerns: ekphrasis, parody, intertextuality and violence (the excessiveness of which suggests the graphic comic-violence of recent film-makers). Like the portmanteau films voguish in the 1960s, *The Floor of Heaven* is an extended exercise in style, self-consciously taking on the features of its "host" genres, as if narration itself could lead to meaningful narrative, as when "Rain" worries over coherence and closure (though this also may be parodic). But the tale's trick ending radically undermines our reading of it, suggesting the instability of all narration (especially when confessional). After thirty years as a "difficult" poet, a number of Tranter's interests are discernible: childhood, popular culture, violence and the poetic sequence. What has become increasingly clear is how these interests are styled through an idiom both demotic and highly aestheticised. Each of the '79ers, then, developed their own form of "vernacular formalesque" in response to both local and international influences.

If the Generation of '79 (save Tranter) does not often appear professionally ambitious, their work is poetically ambitious. Their book-length collections are all generically heterodox, as if redefining contemporary poetry. However, they lack neither antecedents (Duggan's *Memorials*, for instance, owes something to Kenneth Rexroth's *The Phoenix and the Turtle*), nor continuities. Gig Ryan, John Kinsella, Anthony Lawrence, Alison Croggan, Coral Hull, John Mateer and Adam Aitken could all be described as post Generation of '68 (or '79) poets. Ryan's stylistic minimalism, for example, should not blind us to its romanticism, seen in the poems' lack of rationality, "excessive" instances and emotions, and angry indictments of the conditions of women. Such features can also be seen in Hull's poetry, which is even more tortured and violent.

Dorothy Porter's often witty and sensual poetry is also concerned with violence and sexuality. In *Akhenaten* (1992), *The Monkey's Mask* (1994) and *What a Piece of Work* (1999) she develops the period's growing interest in narrative poetry, and illustrates a '68er interest in giving poetry the appeal of popular culture, something realised in the success of *The Monkey's Mask*, which adds parody, erotic poetry and metaphorical inventiveness to the genre of lesbian detective fiction.

Violence is also present in work by Kinsella, probably today's most productive and energetic poet. Kinsella's move to England (where he is a fellow at Churchill College, poetry editor of the *Spectator* and co-editor of *Stand*) has not radically changed his poetic interests. Kinsella has most successfully mixed the lyrical mode with avant-garde experimentation. His post-68er status can be seen in his productivity, fondness for book-long sequences, the long poem and collaboration. Kinsella also maintains links with the pastoral (or anti-pastoral) tradition in Australian poetry, as it is landscape that connects his lyrical and avant-garde projects.

The violence and difficulty of such work is partly a function of these poets' ethical purpose. For instance, Hull's anatomical gaze makes explicit moralising redundant. Similarly, poets such as Aitken complicate the world to lay bare the economic and political bases of the symbolic realm. The post-68ers grew up not only with television but also Foucault, Derrida, Said and Spivak, and their almost ubiquitous deconstruction of binary oppositions suggests another neo-Romanticism, a form of imaginative apocalypse that – like that of the original Romantics – seeks to unify opposites, most notably an ethical poetic with a view of language as autonomous. The '68ers' problem has become the post-68ers' aesthetic.

MATERIAL CHANGES

How does the New Australian Poetry's activity compare with today's? A pessimistic view might compare the hopes and energies of the 1970s with recent events such as the retreat from poetry by Angus & Robertson, University of Queensland Press (UQP) and Penguin. But dynamism is still apparent. Changes in publishing have also seen the rise of smaller publishers, such as Duffy & Snellgrove, Brandl & Schlesinger and Black Pepper, while Hale & Iremonger, Pariah (a collective press) and regional presses like Fremantle Arts Centre continue to be important. In addition, Leros Press publishes poetry in translation, and a number of bi-lingual anthologies and collections have appeared in the last two decades. While newspapers have almost abandoned poetry, *Cordite*, a poetry-dedicated tabloid, was launched in 1997, and literary journals remain strong supporters of contemporary poetry, from established journals such as *Southerly, Overland* and *Meanjin* to newer titles like *Ulitarra, Sligo* and the internationally oriented *Heat* and *Boxkite*. The rise of ethnic minority writing has been seen in journals such as *Outrider* and non-English publications such as *Otherland*, the Australian Chinese-language literary journal edited by Ouyang Yu.

Poetic series were important in the development of a new mainstream in the 1970s. The Paperback Poets series (UQP, 1970–81), mostly edited by Roger McDonald, published numerous new poets well known today. UQP also produced the "Poets on Record" series (1970–75), edited by Shapcott. The "Poets of the Month" booklets (Angus & Robertson, 1976–80) published a mixture of new and established names, while from 1990–93 the National Library's "Pamphlet Poets" series published established poets. Other developments included Penguin's experimentation of multi-collection volumes during Judith Rodriguez's editorship there (1989–97). Ron Pretty, who administers the Scarp/Five Islands Press "New Poets" series (1993–), is one of a number of poet-publishers who continues the merging between writer and producer that characterised the Generation of '68. Others include Adamson (Big Smoke and Paper Bark); Kevin Pearson (Black Pepper); Kinsella (Folio); and Ian Templeman (Molonglo). With Hemensley's Melbourne bookshop, Collected Works, they represent (despite difficulties) an active, independent spirit in Australian poetry publishing and bookselling.

Changes in technology are obviously important. Home computing, desktop publishing and the internet have made self-publication easier than ever, though costs can be prohibitive and cultural capital is more likely to reside in music, video or computer art. The internet has also produced electronic poetry magazines, such as Tranter's stylish *Jacket* (1997–), and the all-poetry *Divan* (1998). Increasingly, poets develop personal web pages themselves (again, Tranter being notably active in this area), with the web site of the performance poet Komninos ambitiously engaging with hypertext. Internet discussion groups – like "Austlit" and Kinsella's "poetryetc" – also allow easy interaction, while "OZpoet" offers a resource and showcase for contemporary Australian poetry.

Not all interaction is virtual. The New Australian Poetry made poetry readings central to poetic culture: at Friendly Street (Adelaide), La Mama (Melbourne) and later at Harold Park (Sydney). Readings have now become ubiquitous for Australian poets. Performance poetry, however, is a minority within a minority, partly because of the difficulty in making work accessible. ΠO's *Off the Page* (1985) anthology includes a record to this end. A number of poets (such as Ania Walwicz, Joanne Burns, ΠO and Kevin Brophy) have also shown that the distinction between performance and "print" poetry is not absolute. The CD and CD-ROM seem ideal for performance poets, though they have so far failed to make an impact. A CD of work by the performance poet Jas Duke was released after his death in 1992, and a CD-ROM of Slessor's "Five Bells" was recently produced. Some poets have used computers to prepare different textual constructions on the page, such as Philip Salom, whose *The Rome Air Naked* (1996) includes "concurrent" poems in which disparate texts are manipulated by computer into one space.

Some, such as Barry Humphries, Michael Leunig and John Clarke, have smuggled poetry into different kinds of performance. Poems in Leunig's cartoons can be satirical, cloying, moving, or surreal. While parody is common to the era (Jan Owen's are particularly effective), the most extended attempt is *The Complete Book of Australian Verse* by the writer-actor-comedian John Clarke, which reinvents English and American poetry as Australian. Such poetry is more or less "public", thanks to its distribution, but Australia, other than for the promotion of sport, rarely calls for public poetry (Britain and the United States have poets laureate).

The current context suggests then that the 1970s laid many of the patterns of production and reception. Poetry, however, is increasingly a minority art, despite the development of organisations such as the Poets Union (1977–). It is true, though, that poetry is no less marginalised in Australia than in comparable countries. For most readers, poetry is to be studied, usually in an anthology.

DEVELOPMENTS

Contemporary with the Generation of '68 was a different kind of international, philosophical poetry. The "Canberra school" of poets (Kevin Hart, Alan Gould, Mark O'Connor and Geoff Page) was so named because its poets were young, gathered (briefly) in Canberra and were writing differently from the '68ers. Like them, though, they used alternative publishing ventures (*Canberra Poetry* and the Open Door Press). While factionalism is seen in Hart's and Gould's mock-epic "The Harrowing of Balmain" (a reference to the '68ers' Sydney address), and Murray's championing of them as "younger" poets, their poetry collections are relatively free of overt literary politics. Their internationalist concerns were distinct from the '68ers': they offered a "return to Europe", and wrote about nature, both elements seen in O'Connor, whose interest in science produces an unsentimental and original view of the natural world. For Gould, history and natural history are linked, as seen in the ambitious, high rhetoric of "The Great Circle" and his long-term interest in the sea and sailing. While not interested in being cryptic, a number of Gould's poems, such as "The Calms", are concerned with the plurality of meaning: "The ocean just above my line of sight / will glitter with its fragments, its glimpses / of what might be, and what might also be".[23]

Hart's poetry is even more concerned with negativity and absence, emanating from quiet, domestic scenes. Though inhabiting a recognisable world, such poems are fundamentally metaphorical. Hart's poetic is one of extreme clarity inhabited by darker, metaphysical concerns, a duality supported by his battery of archetypal images: clocks and hands, water and stone, sun and moon, the north's heat and the south's cold. In addition, Hart is an elegiac poet with a strongly erotic impulse. All these features inhabit Hart's autobiographical evocations of Queensland. In "Her Name", for instance, an adolescent gift speaks of both the profane and sacred: "A picture of Our Lady: on the back / A scarlet lipstick kiss signed 'You Know Who'".[24] For Hart, plurality is central to poetry itself: "while a poem is invariably a wrangle, and while it tries to comprehend the real, it does not necessarily have an unequivocal and undivided aim".[25]

Page is less interested in metaphysics, but the domestic concerns of his poetry are informed by war and its effects on Australians. One of Page's most characteristic effects is to fuse the historical and quotidian. In "Smiling in English, Smoking in French", crucifixes by a French roadside suggest the nineteenth century, "some time of / cleric revival. / The tractors pause / and then roll on, / hardened in their / own survival".[26] Page, then, is an exegete of the ordinary, seen especially in his quiet anatomies of rural Australian families, such as those in *Collected Lives* (1986).

Another international, philosophical poetry can be seen in work by three women poets: Rosemary Dobson, Fay Zwicky and Jennifer Strauss. The latter two, born in 1933, were older than the '68ers when their first books were published in 1975. Both have published sparsely, and written poems out of their experiences as academics. Their ethically concerned poetry (often related to gender politics) is informed by wide historical and cultural knowledge. Zwicky, as others have noted, often expresses a tension between speech and silence, and poems such as "Kaddish" and "Ark Voices" present an ambivalent attitude to social obligation.[27] The more overtly personal poems of "China Poems 1988" and the hospice poems of *Ask Me* (1990) show that expression, though necessary, remains double-edged. Like Harwood, Zwicky is attracted to variety, demi-comic figures, parody and satire. To these *The Gatekeeper's Wife* (1997) adds a new plain, archetypal style, reminiscent of the late Dobson, where plainness adds a new pressure on poetic discourse.

Since *Over the Frontier* (1978), Dobson has moved from her earlier interest in painting to an interest in cultural artefacts generally as part of a search for essentials, a stylistic paring back seen in the blank canvases of the late "mortality" poems of *Collected Poems* (1991). Such poems are concerned with a dialectic between continuity and impermanence, the theme of Dobson's major poem, "The Continuance of Poetry: Twelve Poems for David Campbell". This elegy, simultaneously limited and ambitious, connects not only different modes of artistic endeavour, but also different times and places. The intertextual use of ancient Chinese poetry reinvigorates elegiac commonplaces and allows an emotional reserve in the elegiac process, balancing the claims of poetic presence with a recognition of absence.

Dobson's poem is a kind of pastoral elegy. Pastoral itself has a strong, sometimes disturbed, continuance in contemporary Australian poetry, something that confounds the Generation of '68's anti-pastoral program. While naive, celebratory versions of pastoral have been abandoned, it remains extraordinary how many poets have (re)turned to the country. The rural landscapes of Craig Sherborne, Anthony Lawrence, Martin Harrison, Philip Hodgins, John Foulcher and Philip Salom are often violent and not easily contained by literary conventions. Such a list notably lacks women. While Jennifer Rankin, Jennifer Harrison, Judith Beveridge and Sarah Day are among women poets attracted to pastoral, they have not taken on Wright's or Harwood's pastoral–elegiac concerns with the same emphasis.

Viewed as theme, rather than convention, contemporary pastoral is an ambivalent, self-critical mode. This is so even with the poet most associated with rural Australia. Les Murray is unavoidably aligned with metaphors of largeness: his linguistic facility is vast, he writes fluently, his imagination is capacious, his use of ideas prodigal. Murray's large claims for poetry – and his polemical attitudes – have attracted much praise and censure. Despite some recent Australian critics' belief that his best work was done in the 1970s, in the 1990s Murray's international reputation has exceeded that of any other living Australian poet.

The pastoral is central to Murray's development of an authentic Australian tradition. In his essay on Peter Porter's poem "On First Looking in Chapman's Hesiod", Murray posits a postcolonial distinction between Athens (representing the urbane, imperialist and fashion-conscious) and

Boeotia (representing the traditional, rural and "small holding").[28] This pastoral theme is expressed in poetry where the land represents connection, repetition, and living culture. Where it concerns loss, the poet's bardic function allows a rhetorical healing, as in the elegy for Murray's father, "The Last Hellos". Here individual death is social loss. Despite the description of the collective mourning that this engenders, the poem ends on a note of division: "Snobs mind us off religion / nowadays, if they can. / Fuck thém. I wish you God".[29] This opposition is characteristic, suggesting a tension in Murray's position. Boeotia *requires* a threatening Athens, despite Murray's stated hopes for reconciliation between urban and rural.

Ambitiously nationalistic, Murray attempts to fuse rural, urban and Aboriginal strands of Australian culture. But this unifying project has a concomitant concern with division, seen in the dualism of *The Boys Who Stole the Funeral*; the divisions of self and society (sometimes controversially) imaged in *Subhuman Redneck Poems* (1996); the divided character of Fredy Neptune; the divisions of history (Enlightenment and pre-Enlightenment world views); and Murray's concepts of "wholespeak" and "narrowspeak", "poems" and "poemes". Murray's clearest attempt to heal divisions is his fusing of poetry and religion. For him, "Religions are poems".[30] Murray's "sacramental view of poetry" and "poetic view of religion" is seen in *Translations from the Natural World* (1992) where intense focusing on the natural unveils the numinous, producing a nature poetry cosmic in interest, from "Animal Nativity" to "Cell DNA" ("life's slim volume / spirally bound").[31]

The scale of Murray's project produces a strain. Violence seems structural, inherent in the wrenched syntax and metaphysical imagery (heterogeneous ideas "yoked by violence together", as Johnson defined it). Murray's style is heroically paratactic; seen in ellipses, lack of conjunctions, portmanteau words. Fusion (or violence) can also be seen in opposing poetics. "Bats Ultrasound" owes as much to Kurt Schwitters as to Celtic mouth music. But Murray has sought the widest audience for poetry, seen for example in the narrative poems of *Dog Fox Field* (1990) and his editing of *The Oxford Book of Australian Verse* (1986), which includes light verse, ballads and folk songs. This suggests a persistent Murravian paradox: Murray's anti-modernist belief in a general readership, and the continued validity of poetry to vernacular culture, alongside his original poetic idiolect and deep knowledge of twentieth-century poetics.

Murray's interest in violence is related to a sacramental imagination, where incarnation and grace are connected to sacrifice. This relationship is seen in Murray's long narrative poems: *The Boys Who Stole the Funeral* (1980) and *Fredy Neptune* (1998). The former is a technically stunning and well paced narrative, made up of 140 heterogeneous sonnets. It is also ideological and dualist in nature, and concerns two boys, Kevin and Reeby, who steal the body of an old digger to give him a fitting rural burial. It ends with Kevin's rebirth and Reeby's violent death. Modernity is represented by effeminate men, masculinised feminists, and decadent loss of belief. Such inversion is symbolised most egregiously when the feminist Noeline Kampff pours a bucket of blood on Reeby, a perversion of the legitimate blood sacrifice of the Mass.[32] The work's "blood theology" here is orthodox: through Christ's blood there is forgiveness of sin. More idiosyncratic is the vision of "the Common Dish" which contains "work, agony and laughter" (p. 46), a "difficult food" that some choose not to eat and that affects Kevin's redemption.

Less tendentious is *Fredy Neptune* (1998), Murray's heroic poem for an unheroic age, comedy for a tragic world, and search for "benign" nationalism in the shadow of nationalism's worst phase. Friedrich Boettcher, a German-speaking Australian, loses bodily sensation after witnessing the burning of a group of Turkish women during World War I. This loss of sensation makes him a peripatetic strong man, experiencing the century's violent events: war and Depression. Like other contemporary long poems, *Fredy Neptune* is both aware of literary antecedents and free of strong generic determination. Sometimes phantasmal, sometimes a classic Australian pioneer, Fredy is Odysseus-like, a picaro, a trickster. The poem's violence is a conscience for the artistic act: "How good's your poem? / Can it make them alive again after dancing in the kerosene?".[33] Fredy's condition suggests that of the artist, shocked by the imagery of violence. Ultimately, the work attempts to deconstruct one of this century's most pervasive myths: that violence is stylish.

Pastoral's persistence is also indebted to Robert Gray, Philip Hodgins, and some urbane poets like Geoffrey Lehmann and Peter Kirkpatrick. Gray's Zen-inspired world view produces a realist, imagistic poetry. Increasingly attracted to "loosened form", Gray's attitude to style implies an ethical aestheticism, seen in his nature poems such as "Dharma Vehicle", which represents a physical retreat into nature but also into the world of "those old Chinese / who sought the right way to live".[34]

Hodgins' poetry also looks far back: to the *Georgics*, and *Works and Days*. Like those works it is unembarrassed by poetry that imparts information, seen in "Three Pig Diseases" and "Second Thoughts on *The Georgics*", a jeremiad on farming that discusses matters like weather broadcasts. Hodgins' affection for country life does not preclude criticism of it, an aspect associated with pastoral's ambivalent content. For Hodgins this is related not simply to death, but the death of the self. Diagnosed with leukemia at twenty-four, Hodgins' first and last books contain self-elegiac poems, notable for their use of artful metaphor and plain speaking, as in "A Palinode": "My half a bucketful of blood / is filled with rumours of an early death".[35]

Vivian Smith represents the continuing belief in "the well-made poem" and self-concealing art. In situating his poems in Tasmania and Sydney, he also represents an early instance of the regionalism that became dominant in the 1980s. Smith's ironic, ekphrastic and elegiac interests (as well as his translations of modernists such as Trakl) show his formal, mimetic art to be underpinned by complicating factors. The pastoral mode, then, is one under strain, and must repetitively be called to re-illuminate the poet's natural surroundings.

Smith is also one of a large number of poets who mixed an academic with a poetic career. Given the rise of tertiary education, it is not surprising that, despite the Generation of '68's attempts to free poetry from academic regulation and traditional forms, the 1970s and 1980s saw a *heightening* of the academy's role, through the sheer number of poets who were university graduates, the continued incorporation of poets into the academy and the intellectual changes that were occurring there. "The Rise of Theory" produced a context sympathetic to new poetics on ideological rather than putatively ethical–formalist grounds (though the distinction is not absolute). Aboriginal writing, ethnic minority writing and women's writing were all affected by concomitant "rises" in the academy.

This is not to say that such writing was determined by academic intervention. One of the period's most striking developments is the rise of Indigenous poets (many of whom have distanced themselves from the academy), including Lionel G. Fogarty and younger poets like Lisa Bellear. Fogarty rejects Standard English for the creole of his Murri people and represents a new radicalism among poets of his generation: "I don't want to be a reconciliation writer or a reformist writer", he states.[36] This turning of the oppressor's language back against itself, a key postcolonial strategy, offers a wide tonal range. Fogarty's poetry moves from anger to the tenderness of "Am I": "Am we lonely these days / Am I grief in the wind / Am us friend to nature" (p. 16).

Having been ignored by the Generation of '68, feminist poets produced their own revolution. Rather than reject the past, it embraced Wright, Harwood and Dobson (the most successful women poets of their generation), renewed interest in poets like Elizabeth Riddell and Margaret Diesendorf, and helped others, such as Barbara Giles and Vera Newsom, to develop reputations relatively late. The first overviews of Australian women's poetry are expressive of the decades in which they were published. As an exercise in inclusiveness and free expression, *Mother I'm Rooted* (1975) could be seen as truer to the original impulses of the Generation of '68 than Tranter's anthology, but its anti-academic flavour has made it less visible in the literary history. *The Penguin Book of Australian Women Poets* (1986) – though inclusive – addresses more of the critical issues of women's poetry. Some of these again suggest those of the Generation of '68, despite the different politics; issues such as the defence of subjective or confessional poetry; anxiety over marginality; formal experimentation as a political necessity; and the need for a radical historiography (with similar influences cited).[37]

Unlike the '68ers, however, feminists of the 1980s could more coherently articulate a radical consciousness, to the extent that in Susan Lever's *The Oxford Book of Australian Women's Verse* (1995) the mainstream position of women's poetry is clear. Amid the heterogeneity of women's writing a number of images are used repeatedly to characterise it: the woman poet as mimic, writing obliquely, and subversively through parody, irony and transformative appropriation, seen in the feminist rewriting of folktales and myths by Diane Fahey, Dorothy Hewett, Kate Llewellyn, Alison Clark and others. On the other side of the spectrum is the fusing of personal and political concerns, as seen in the confessional–forensic work of Rhyll McMaster. Younger poets such as Sarah Day, Judith Beveridge and Jemal Sharah also show that formally decorous (though not mild) lyric poetry retains its authority.

It is notable how many Australian poets have written elegies that are central to their *oeuvres*: Zwicky, Strauss, Dobson, Murray, Page, Tranter, Martin Johnston, Shapcott, Adamson, Eric Beach, Wallace-Crabbe, Harwood, Martin Harrison, Peter Porter and Vivian Smith (while John Blight, Page and Rodriguez have written anti-elegies). David Brooks posits that poets in Australia are good elegists because of "a superabundance of a certain feeling that an elegy allows an expression of – that necessitates the elegy, rather than vice versa. And it may be that a certain cultural situation creates a repository of this kind of feeling."[38] This situation is presumably historical, postcolonial, since loss is central to three major narratives of Australian history: dispossession of Indigenous people; colonial loss of British commonplaces; loss experienced by post-war migrants.

Regarding the latter, Sneja Gunew has noted that "the migrant's speech (rather than writing) is solicited and the more disordered it is the more authentic it supposedly sounds".[39] As Gunew demonstrates in her criticism, such a misconstruction is often parodied by ethnic minority writers who deconstruct simplistic notions of ethnicity and authenticity. These writers include Walwicz and ΠO, whose epic-sized *24 Hours* (1995) centres on

Fitzroy and the speech found there, expressed in idiosyncratic orthography. Interconnections between language, voice, subjectivity and difference are important in ethnic minority writing, but the aesthetics of such are numerous. ΠO's poetic, both maximalist and raw, is distinct from Dimitris Tsaloumas' lyrical evocation of deep traditions, Tom Petsinis' spare, controlled verse, or the minimalist, archetypal aspects of Antigone Kefala's work.

While early discussions of ethnic minority poetry tended to emphasise the work of European-Australians (especially Greek-Australians), greater diversity is becoming apparent. For instance, Ouyang Yu (originally from China) illustrates a number of interests to do with voice, exile and language common to many ethnic minority writers. But he works with an even more anti-poetic idiom than Walwicz or ΠO, and anger is even more central to his poetry.

Ethnic minority writing is also the source of unexpected forms, seen in Tsaloumas' book of epigrams, Timoshenko Aslanides' book of riddles, and calendar of poems, *AnniVersaries* (1998), and David Curzon's midrashim. Petsinis' poems on mathematical concepts again illustrate the limitations of thematic analysis. Alternative themes can be used to chart Australian cultural change, such as the increasing importance of the coast to poets like Andrew Taylor, Forbes, Gray, Ken Taylor, Jennifer Harrison, Lawrence Bourke and Caroline Caddy. An unpredictable thematic development has been in the Roman-satirical style. In 1970 Tulip called for poets to turn to the "Latin style" since it "does not appeal to sanctions beyond a literal and present sense of what is good and what is bad. It is the poetry of humour, feeling, and common sense."[40]

Peter Porter, Lehmann, Duggan, Peter Rose, Hugh Tolhurst and even Gary Catalano, Buckley, Tranter and Tsaloumas have all turned to such a precedent. Lehmann's interest is most developed in *Nero's Poems* (1976), concerned with decadence, sexuality and the body (politic). Nero's image of himself as artist, and his desire to see the world as an extension of himself, shows the ambivalence of Lehmann's ethical purpose. Roman models are racy and pointed while simultaneously offering a mode for the moral censure of others. This is seen in Porter's and Duggan's translations of Martial, both of which take creative liberties. These translations and Rose's "The Catullan Rag" use Roman tropes in a contemporary setting, often to satirise the literary subculture. In Tolhurst's *Filth* (1996) even the Roman names have disappeared, presenting fictional gossip of real figures. If Tulip's call was unexpectedly met, then we should note that his description does not exactly fit such poets, especially with regard to feeling. The appeal to decadence, and the mask of translation, means that feeling in such poetry, if present at all, is usually ambiguous or factitious.

Such writing often satirises, while adverting to the existence of "cultural citizenship", the practices and institutions that allow full participation in a national culture. Four "mid-generation" poets who tell us something about this concept are Shapcott, Hall, Rodriguez and Taylor. They show that successful administrative and teaching careers can accommodate progressive poetics. But the group also stylistically prefigured the Generation of '68, and were partly involved with it, seen in Shapcott's anthologies and "experimental" turn of his poetry; or Hall's editing of poetry at the *Australian* and of Dransfield's work; or Taylor's involvement with La Mama. All have used mythical figures, dramatic monologues, sequences, autobiographical material and the experiences of travel.

These poets represent the connection between the poetic changes of the late 1960s and the development of a national poetic culture through vigorous work by individuals and moderate government intervention. The Generation of '68 made a significant impact on the literary culture but have not occupied comparable positions in administration and teaching. The middle generation also illustrate a point about the continuity of careers, seen also in the figures of Beaver, Porter, Wallace-Crabbe, Simpson, Dawe and Hewett, all of whom are active poets who published first in the 1950s.

Such diverse poets illustrate a thematic obsession with subjectivity. A defining feature of Beaver's *Letters to Live Poets* as a pre-68 work is its autobiographical content. This becomes most apparent in *The Way it Was...* (1979) and the eponymous poem from *Anima* (1993), detailing the poet's relationship with his wife. But concomitant to this subjective turn is the use of autobiographical revisionism through "disguised" forms such as myth (including self-mythologising), masks, dramatic monologues and dramatisation. This is seen in the work of Dorothy Hewett, which has long intertwined personal and mythical material in a demonstration both of the defining features of subjectivity (sexuality, in particular) and the ways in which subjectivity itself is defined by culture, history and gender. Poems such as "Alice in Wormland" and "Miss Hewett's Shenanigans" trope events both through their self-referential specificity and archetypal qualities. In this respect Hewett's "confessional romanticism", often commented upon by critics, is far from naive, and may account in part for her growing reputation in the 1990s as a poet (rather than a playwright or fiction writer).

Porter and Wallace-Crabbe also illustrate the folly of summing up careers too soon, since both underwent shifts in mid-career: Porter with *The Cost of Seriousness* (1978), and Wallace-Crabbe with *The Foundations of Joy* (1976). The accidental similarity of these titles suggests the shifts made towards more elegiac, self-dramatising personae, seen in Porter's elegies for his wife, especially "An Exequy" – which uses the octosyllabic couplets of

Robert King's poem of the same title and occasion – and in Wallace-Crabbe's elegies for his adult son, such as "Years On", which evokes elegies by Hardy and Jonson.

Such antecedents illustrate both poets' literary awareness, ability to renew poetry through incorporating earlier poetry, and interest in verse form (which has become especially pronounced for Porter). Both poets display a wide cultural and intellectual range, and connections with other art forms (music for Porter and visual art for Wallace-Crabbe), and both have produced books in cooperation with artists (Porter with Arthur Boyd and Wallace-Crabbe with Bruno Leti).

Stylistically they present lexical richness – probably gained from the shared influence of Auden – and the use of colloquialisms and mixed modes within a discursive voice. Wallace-Crabbe is particularly well known for his plurality of registers, writing of the dead, for instance, that "Space-time is no longer their medium; / they inhabit / antipodes of the radiant fair dinkum".[41] This heterogeneity, and skill in the demotic, make their poetic voices both international and recognisably Australian.

Their emphasis on the linguistic construction of the world, however, shows that they do not subscribe to facile or sentimental ideas about what constitutes the authentically Australian. For Porter, Australia tends to be presented through the complicating lenses of history and the expatriate's condition. For Wallace-Crabbe, expatriation is not an issue, but poems such as "Mulga Jack on Swans" and "Puck Disembarks" use European tropes to deconstruct notions of centre and margin, Europe and antipodes. Porter and Wallace-Crabbe suggest an abundant engagement with the world, the self and their transformations. Their knowledge of literary theory's "linguistic turn" makes them attuned to the fragility and provisional status of "reality". But their scepticism about the uses to which such insights have been put illustrates the humanistic nature of their projects undertaken through postmodern techniques. They deconstruct further any simplistic notions of the map of Australian poetry for, despite their differences from both "camps", they mediate between postmodern internationalists and cultural nationalists.

CONCLUSIONS

Writing in 1965, Hope famously lamented the lost ecology of literary forms: the landscape that supported the epic, verse satire and ode, rather than the "spare and monotonous vegetation of the steppe" (referring to the ubiquity of free verse). Such a lament can still be heard today but, as this chapter shows, the landscape is not as depleted as would first appear. Indeed, one of the features of the period is the rise of a new formalism out of an apparently anti-formalist movement. But compared with America (with its "New Formalists" and "New Narrative"), formalism here is less factional. As well as the Generation of '79, it can be seen in work by Jamie Grant, Peter Kocan, Alex Skovron, Stephen Edgar, Kevin Pearson, Robert Harris, Gwen Harwood and Jan Owen. If women again figure less often, it would be wrong to claim that they are more concerned with content. Not only does that propose a spurious dialectic, it also ignores those poets (like Walwicz and Lily Brett) who have a narrow but well-defined formal idiom.

Despite the interest in form, there has not been the interest in rhyme seen in recent English and American poetry, though some have worked notably with it, such as Murray, Wearne, Harwood and Hodgins. This is perhaps because of the greater emphasis on the vernacular. While lyric poetry remains dominant there has been a pronounced narrative turn, not only in long works such as Hodgins' enigmatic *Dispossessed* (1994) and Jordie Albiston's "documentary" verse novels, but also shorter pieces such as Maiden's "Guarding the Cenotaph", or Edgar's "King Pepei's Treasure". And though the tradition of light or comic verse is less pronounced than in England, the irreverent and comic are repeatedly (almost habitually) incorporated into "serious poems".

The emphasis in this chapter on the Generations of '68 and '79 may seem tendentious. It deflects attention from poets with aesthetics less stridently (post)modernist, such as Evan Jones, Peter Kocan, Paul Hetherington or Dennis Haskell, as well as poets harder to define in terms of movements, such as David Malouf, Gary Catalano and Alex Skovron. Catalano, along with Simpson and Brooks, represents a minimalist arm of contemporary Australian poetry that does not fit with the maximalist aesthetics of either Murray or the '68ers.

However, an emphasis on the Generation of '68 is currently useful, as it addresses a movement previously marginalised, politicised or ghettoised in the literary history. In addition, historians have rarely considered its aftermath: the "Generation of '79"; the influence of the '68ers on younger poets writing today; and the continuing material effects on the production and reception of Australian poetry. One of the ironic features of this historical importance is that today the Generations of '68 and '79 have largely ceased to exist. Dransfield, Buckmaster, Johnston, Duke, Forbes and Viidikas are dead; Duggan appears to have abandoned poetry; Scott writes prose; Wearne's large projects mean long silences; and numerous poets have simply lost their earlier visibility. Tranter maintains the standard, a kind of older John Kinsella, increasingly internationalised through publishing and the internet.

The Generation of '68 may have caused anxiety for putatively radical politics and poetics but, as later developments illustrate, part of their literary significance lies in their emphasis on writing as a pathological and obsessive activity, a tapping of the unregulatable unconscious. Poets, unlike media people, do not talk about "the industry", but Australian poetry is nevertheless increasingly intersecting with institutions. Both these points suggest a way of concluding, for both are relevant to Kevin Brophy's account of the institutionalisation of creative writing: "We are moving, in one view of this journey, from Freud's perception of creativity as expression-of-illness to an institutionalised view of creativity as professional, educational and healthy".[42] It is not surprising that this development has met with tension and anxiety from creative artists. But as Brophy notes, the relationship between institutional ideologies and (the ideologies of) creativity is not utterly unequal. The tension between control and lawlessness found there is not only an image for the creative writing workshop, but also for the development of Australian poetry over the last thirty years. Part of this tension involves ideas of national culture. Murray may be right when he states that "we are a colloquial nation / most colonial when serious",[43] but the proliferation of voices in recent years does not allow any overdetermined idea of *Australian* poetry. Proliferation and excess (of voice, influence and form) can be seen working in a context both positively and negatively postcolonial. Australian poetry is a worldly poetry, both celebratory of and anxious over the idea of an "Australian inflection".

NOTES

1 See Livio Dobrez, *Parnassus Mad Ward: Michael Dransfield and the New Australian Poetry* (St Lucia: University of Queensland Press, 1990).
2 Michael Dransfield, *Collected Poems* (St Lucia: University of Queensland Press, 1987), p. 79.
3 See Kevin Hart, *A.D. Hope* (Melbourne: Oxford University Press, 1992).
4 See David McCooey, "Neither Here Nor There: Suburban Voices in Australian Poetry" in Andrew McCann, ed., *Writing the Everyday: Australian Literature and the Limits of Suburbia* (St Lucia: University of Queensland Press, 1998), pp. 101–14.
5 Dobrez, *Parnassus Mad Ward*, p. 62.
6 The term is used by James Tulip, "Contemporary Australian Poetry: II Transition and Advance", *Southerly*, 32.3 (1972), p. 76, but McAuley had already seen evidence of neo-romanticism in 1968. See *A Map of Australian Verse* (Melbourne: Oxford University Press, 1975), p. 303.
7 Paul Kane, *Australian Poetry: Romanticism and Negativity* (Cambridge: Cambridge University Press, 1996), p. 5.
8 Kris Hemensley, "Beginnings – A Note on La Mama" in Robert Kenny with C. Talbot, eds, *Applestealers: Is a Collection of the New Poetry in Australia*

Including Notes, Statements, Histories on La Mama (Melbourne: Outback, 1974), p. 17.

9 John Tranter, "Anaesthetics: Some Notes on the New Australian Poetry"in Joan Kirkby, ed., *The American Model: Influence and Independence in Australian Poetry* (Sydney: Hale & Iremonger, 1982), p. 104.

10 John Tranter, ed., *The New Australian Poetry* (St Lucia: Makar, 1979), pp. xvi–xvii.

11 See John McLaren, *Writing in Hope and Fear: Literature as Politics in Postwar Australia* (Cambridge: Cambridge University Press, 1996), p. 185.

12 Richard Packer, "Against the Epigones", *Quadrant*, 29.3 (1975), p. 68.

13 Peter Goldsworthy, *This Goes With This* (Sydney: ABC Enterprises, 1988), p. 40.

14 John Forbes, "Two Cheers for Michael Dransfield", *Scripsi*, 5.1 (1988), p. 215.

15 Thomas Shapcott, ed., *Australian Poetry Now* (Melbourne: Sun, 1970), p. xvi.

16 Susan McKernan also points out how the socialist movement became increasingly intolerant of conservative workers. *A Question of Commitment: Australian Literature in the Twenty Years after the War* (Sydney: Allen & Unwin, 1989), p. 226.

17 See John McLaren, *Writing in Hope and Fear*, p. 197.

18 Jennifer Maiden, "When Worlds Collide: A Brief Response to One Aspect of the Work of J.S. Harry" in Ivor Indyk and Elizabeth Webby, eds, *Poetry* (Sydney: Angus & Robertson, 1992), p. 97.

19 John Tranter, "Four Notes on the Practice of Revolution", *Australian Literary Studies*, 8.2 (1977), pp. 130, 133.

20 Laurie Duggan, "Living Poetry", *Meanjin*, 53.2 (1994), p. 279.

21 Philip Mead, "*Ut cinema poesis*: Cinematism and John Tranter's *The Floor of Heaven*" in Lyn McCredden and Stephanie Trigg, eds, *The Space of Poetry: Australian Essays on Contemporary Poetics* (Melbourne: Melbourne University Literary and Cultural Studies, Vol. 3, 1996), p. 199.

22 Christopher Pollnitz, "John A Scott: On Not Resisting These Poems", *Scripsi*, 4.2 (1986), p. 263.

23 Alan Gould, *Mermaid* (Melbourne: Heinemann, 1996), p. 59.

24 Kevin Hart, *New and Selected Poems* (Sydney: Angus & Robertson, 1995), p. 160.

25 Kevin Hart, "John Ashbery and the Cimmerian Moment", *Scripsi*, 8.1 (1992), p. 281.

26 Geoff Page, *Selected Poems* (Sydney: Angus & Robertson, 1991), p. 100.

27 See Ivor Indyk, "Fay Zwicky: The Poet as Moralist", *Southerly*, 54.3 (1994), p. 34.

28 Les Murray, "On Sitting Back and Thinking about Porter's Boeotia" (1978), *A Working Forest: Selected Prose* (Sydney: Duffy & Snellgrove, 1997), p. 122.

29 Les Murray, *Subhuman Redneck Poems* (Sydney: Duffy & Snellgrove, 1996), p. 78.

30 Les Murray, *Collected Poems* (Melbourne: Heinemann, 1994), p. 267.

31 Paul Kane, *Australian Poetry*, p. 186; Les Murray, *Translations from the Natural World* (Paddington, NSW: Isabella Press, 1992), p. 387.

32 Les Murray, *The Boys Who Stole the Funeral: A Novel Sequence*, 1980 (Melbourne: Minerva, 1993), p. 55.

33 Les Murray, *Fredy Neptune* (Sydney: Duffy & Snellgrove, 1998), p. 263.

34 Robert Gray, *New and Selected Poems* (Melbourne: Heinemann, 1995), p. 76.

35 Philip Hodgins, *Selected Poems* (Sydney: Angus & Robertson, 1997), p. 8.

36 Lionel G. Fogarty, *New and Selected Poems: Munaldjali, Mutuerjaraera* (Melbourne: Hyland House, 1995), p. x.

37 Susan Hampton and Kate Llewellyn, eds, *The Penguin Book of Australian Women Poets* (Melbourne: Penguin, 1986), pp. 2, 3, 7.

38 David Brooks, untitled review, *Heat*, 6 (1997–98), p. 199.

39 Sneja Gunew, "Ania Walwicz and Antigone Kefala: Varieties of Migrant Dreaming" in David Brooks and Brenda Walker, eds, *Poetry and Gender: Statements and Essays in Australian Women's Poetry and Poetics* (St Lucia: University of Queensland Press, 1989), p. 205.

40 James Tulip, "The Australian–American Connection", *Poetry Australia*, 32 (1970), p. 49.

41 Chris Wallace-Crabbe, *Selected Poems: 1956–1994* (Oxford: Oxford University Press, 1995), p. 102.

42 Kevin Brophy, *Creativity: Psychoanalysis, Surrealism and Creative Writing* (Melbourne: Melbourne University Press, 1998), p. 201.

43 Les Murray, *Collected Poems*, p. 106.

7

DELYS BIRD

New narrations: contemporary fiction

Contemporary Australia, with its escalating population, greater social and political complexity, widening economic structures and marked cultural diversity, has provided a fertile ground for novelists. The New Left radicalism of the late 1960s, followed by the politics of women's liberation, led to freer cultural attitudes, enabling literary experimentation and allowing much greater licence in what fiction could speak about.[1] Rapid changes also occurred in the material and institutional structures of Australian literary culture, with increased public funding for writers and publishers and the consolidation of teaching and research in Australian literature. This conjunction of cultural and material factors contributed to a "massive increase in the production of Australian fiction" after the early 1970s.[2] A new recognition that Australian society was not homogeneous, but made up of many groups with competing interests and political claims, each seeking a cultural space, influenced the fictional preferences of publishers and readers. This chapter is interested in the effects of such social and cultural changes on the field of contemporary Australian fiction. While it is structurally convenient to refer to dates and decades, the explanatory force of such chronologies is often inadequate and sometimes misleading, especially in relation to the complex social and institutional contexts of contemporary fiction. Modes of writing constantly escape the boundaries which such chronologies propose (realism in the 1940s and 1950s, modernism in the 1960s and 1970s, and so on), and there is much overlap and movement between apparently convenient period divisions.

Expansion of government funding for writing and publishing in Australia from the late 1960s had perceptible effects, both in the volume of fiction published, and in new possibilities, even prescriptions, for so-called "innovative" writing.[3] By 1968 the old Commonwealth Literary Fund had been replaced by the Literary Arts Board, reconstituted in 1973 by the newly elected Whitlam Labor government as the Literature Board (since 1996 the Literature Fund) of what was first the Council of the Arts, then the Australia

Council. The Fund's major function is to award grants to individual writers, publishers and literary magazines.[4] While there is always dissension about the need or worth of such a system – about whether it rewards a predictable kind of writing, or produces a stable of "protected" writers, or promotes what may be invidious competition – it has assisted a flourishing Australian literary culture. State government literary funding is now also part of the arts grants structure, and there is a range of state and privately funded writers' prizes. Writers' festivals have proliferated in Australia over the last couple of decades too. Several major city festivals, as well as numerous regional weekends and other gatherings where writers read and speak about their work, are held each year. Intense public interest in writers' lives ensures that the books of those who give innumerable interviews, appear at writers' festivals, undertake publicity tours and above all are attractive to the public, will be likely to sell well.

Yet although Australian fiction publishing has been extremely active, especially since the 1980s, there has been little real increase in markets or readerships for that fiction. While national opportunities for writers expanded, and deregulation of the international book industry resulted in global publishing and marketing of serious fiction, the small internal market has become more intensely competitive.[5] Shifts in the extent of foreign interest in and ownership of Australian publishing, first from the United Kingdom and by 1990 from the United States,[6] also mark this period. As a consequence, the fortunes of the small independent publishers established through the 1970s, whose role in publishing new fiction helped change the character and range of the national literature, have been hazardous since the mid-1980s. It is notoriously difficult for an Australian publishing industry to compete with the UK and the USA, and many independent as well as mainstream publishers have been taken over by multinational publishing groups.

A global publishing economy invites questions about how we may use a category such as "Australian fiction" in the future. If writers seek to participate in a world market, arguably their writing will be shaped if not determined by the demands of that market. For some expatriate Australian writers the connection between their writing and their national allegiance is irrelevant. Shirley Hazzard has lived outside Australia, mostly in the USA and Italy, since her late adolescence; still she is claimed, uneasily, as an Australian writer. Yet her novel, *The Transit of Venus* (1980), is her only major work to use Australian as well as other settings and characters. For other writers, resident much of the time in Australia and implicated in its literary culture, the issue is more complicated. David Malouf's international reputation and sales owe something perhaps to his having a UK publisher, but also to his transnational style. Malouf's prose is urbane, poetic and classically allusive; the themes and settings of his work are often Australian, but their concerns are universal and humanist. Thomas Keneally's publishing history is different. His early prose fiction dealt with Australian topics, among them convict history in *Bring Larks and Heroes* (1967) and the history of Aboriginal dispossession in *The Chant of Jimmie Blacksmith* (1972). Latterly, his fictional topics have had international significance, such as holocaust history in *Schindler's Ark* (1982), later the enormously popular film, *Schindler's List*. At the same time as he has achieved a considerable international reputation, however, Keneally is marketed around the world as an Australian writer.

The tensions between the national contexts and traditions of Australian fiction and the world book market are thus not solved merely by being able to say that one writer's work is more "European" or "American" than another's. Peter Carey has lived for some years in New York and achieved a respectable international reputation with fiction that is Australian precisely in its continuing preoccupation with movements between the "new world" Australian culture and others, variously American and European. For Carey, expatriation binds him more closely to Australian history, which he fictionalises as one characterised by failure and defeat. An emigrant writer like Elizabeth Jolley is a hybrid; her fiction refers to her European literary and intellectual background but is also inscribed with her Australian experience. And for many Australian writers their primary claim to recognition in an international market is precisely their "Australianness". This phenomenon has been particularly evident in recent interest in North America and Europe in Aboriginal creative work.

ESTABLISHED WRITING

Several major novels and collections of stories by well-established writers appeared during the early 1970s, including Patrick White's *The Eye of the Storm* (1973), *The Cockatoos* (1974) and *A Fringe of Leaves* (1976), Xavier Herbert's *Poor Fellow My Country* (1975), Frank Hardy's *But the Dead are Many* (1975). Each writer represents an important aspect of Australian literary history, which, until the new fiction challenged earlier critical conventions, had been understood as a simple dualism of traditional realism and modernism, often reconstructed in Australian terms as the dualism of nationalism and internationalism.[7] Hardy and Herbert are realist, nationalist writers despite their different styles and preoccupations; White had revived and redefined nascent Australian modernism, and his writing has been a diffuse and ongoing influence on contemporary fiction.

With his near-contemporary, Christina Stead, White is one of the major writers in twentieth-century Western fiction, though Stead's reputation remains relatively minor despite recent critical accounts of its extraordinary range, of style and genre as well as theme. Her formally adventurous first work, *The Salzburg Tales* (1934), is structured through the related tales of different characters, prefiguring Frank Moorhouse's use of similar techniques in the 1970s, hailed as avant-garde, which he called "discontinuous narrative". Like Patrick White's last novel *The Twyborn Affair* (1979), Stead's posthumous *I'm Dying Laughing* (1986) presents a bleak catalogue of the breakdown of pre- and post-war Western civilisation. Their scope and imaginative scale as well as their continuing social and literary relevance give both novels a pre-eminent contemporary status.

In the 1970s, the publication of a number of critical works on the Australian novel signalled the beginnings of an institutionalised literary critical tradition in Australia, coinciding with a perception that Australian fiction had a history and a place in a larger world literature. In 1973 White became the first Australian writer to win the Nobel Prize for Literature, giving Australian fiction international recognition. Subsequently, Keneally won the Booker Prize for *Schindler's Ark* in 1982, followed by Carey for *Oscar and Lucinda* in 1988, while in 1995 Malouf was awarded the first Impac Dublin Literary Award for *Remembering Babylon*. A handful of other Australian novelists have gained international sales and reputations, including popular writers such as Colleen McCullough, Morris West and Bryce Courtenay. Some, like Sally Morgan, Helen Darville, Justine Ettler and Mark Henshaw, have had international sales of one book, while a few, among them Elizabeth Jolley, Helen Garner, Tim Winton, Robert Drewe and Drusilla Modjeska, have achieved modest international reputations. Many of these writers' works are now translated into foreign languages.

Christina Stead and Thea Astley were the only women writers regularly cited as worthy of mention by the new critics of the 1970s, although little attention was given them. Astley is a prolific writer who has been publishing since 1958; *Drylands* (1999) is the latest of sixteen novels and two collections of stories. Patrick White's influence on her work is notable; acknowledged directly in *The Acolyte* (1972), written in response to White's *The Vivisector*, and indirectly in her often savage social satire and her highly elaborated style. In the first couple of decades of her publishing career, Astley's relationship to the male-dominated canon of Australian fiction remained ambivalent, and when a feminist rewriting of that canon began in the late 1970s her position in relation to the new "women's writing" was equally marginal. Despite her numerous literary prizes over the years, only recently has serious critical attention been paid to her work as a whole, and to its place in the field of Australian fiction. Astley's novels and stories typically present a sceptical view of social relationships among ordinary people, one often coloured by her former Catholicism, and directed through the struggles of her self-conscious protagonists to find an expressive space within their uncongenial surroundings.

Jessica Anderson has been publishing over roughly the same period as Astley, yet her reputation too remains undeservedly small. Only the coincidence of the publication of *Tirra Lirra by the River* (1978) with the new awareness of women's writing as a lucrative publishing category and the beginnings of a feminist critical industry gained her a modest national reputation. In her seven novels and one collection of stories Anderson is always concerned with domestic issues, of family structures and relationships, female identity and the possibility of self-realisation. Young Cecily Ambruss, the narrator of *One of the Wattle Birds* (1994), summarises the position she has reached at its end as "Only conception is pure".[8] Suggesting a kind of Forsterian fictional consciousness – Anderson's writing owes much to early European modernism and Henry James is a major influence[9] – it shows too the desire of all Anderson's fictions to reach some point of equilibrium, however tenuous. Conscious experimentation with narrative form and genre, and a consistent interest in questions of gender, power, female sexuality and experience, give Anderson's work its contemporary significance. Although their writing is very different, she and Astley share these interests, as well as a level of narrative experimentation, particularly evident in their historical novels, Astley's *A Kindness Cup* (1974) and Anderson's *The Commandant* (1975). Set in nineteenth-century Australia, each book investigates the gender and power politics of their fictional social worlds as well as the technical possibilities of writing a woman's history.

Of the younger writers whom the new critics of the 1970s predicted would be the big names of the future, Keneally and David Ireland bridge the gap between the established writing of the 1960s and 1970s and the avant-garde fiction of the later 1970s. Keneally, as a traditional realist writer, exemplifies the earlier side of the divide, while Ireland anticipates the new fiction. Ireland, who acquired a major critical reputation in the 1970s, now somewhat diminished, is one of the eight "liars" of Helen Daniel's 1988 publication of that name. Daniel argued that these writers were at the forefront of literary experimentation in Australia in the 1980s, sharing a capacity to unsettle the mimetic functions of traditional realist writing. Ireland's satiric fictions attack aspects of Australian society: the exploitation of Australian workers by industry and the workers' own exploitation of the system that keeps them captive in *The Unknown Industrial Prisoner* (1971); Australian pub culture in *The Glass Canoe* (1976); the corruption of

Australian resources by a capitalist consumer economy in *Woman of the Future* (1979), and so on. Ireland acknowledges the influence of Laurence Sterne and the nineteenth-century South American magic realist writer, Machado de Assis; his work is also indebted to the traditional Australian yarn and to Australian realist fiction as a socially aware, politically active discourse centred in working-class life. Ireland's fictions are remarkable for their fragmented structures, brilliantly inventive language and sharp comic irony; however, the values they propose are often reactionary and misogynist.

Two other writers, Christopher Koch and Randolph Stow, who began publishing in the 1950s, have become significant names in contemporary Australian fiction. In Christopher Koch's first novel, *The Boys in the Island* (1958), the island is Tasmania, where Koch grew up, and he returns to this setting for his latest novel, *Out of Ireland* (1999). Stow, a precociously talented writer, left Australia in 1960 and has lived in the UK since 1969. His third novel, *To The Islands* (1958), published when he was twenty-three, marks the beginning of his remarkable output of mature fiction, characterised by its metaphysical, poetic qualities, and serious themes. Even his children's novel, *Midnite* (1967), the story of a rather stupid boy bushranger and his gang of animals, which has become a minor Australian classic, was written, he explains, "to teach them [adults and children] something about the world they live in".[10] Considered Stow's most important novel, *Visitants* (1979) brings together the preoccupations of all the earlier fiction. Its protagonist, a New Guinea patrol officer born in the Solomon Islands, cannot claim England or Australia as home. He is a visitant, a stranger in the culture where he lives and works and in his increasing state of alienation – caught in the trap of colonialism – he comes to believe that a visitant is haunting him.

EARLY EXPERIMENTATION/NEW DIRECTIONS

Peter Cowan's publishing history indicates the ways social and ideological contexts can shape both writing and a writing career. Affected by the deeply conservative anti-modernist literary climate and the punitive censorship laws of the 1940s and 1950s, Cowan published little until the social changes of the 1960s allowed a "new freedom of expression and subject ... in Australia".[11] *Drift* (1944), Cowan's first collection of stories, was influenced by Ernest Hemingway well before American modernist fiction became known in Australia. Cowan's sparse modernist prose is very different from the sexy, flaunting narrative experiments of the 1970s new wave Balmain writers, or Patrick White's often lush modernism and social satire, and in its vernacular reserve, focus on ordinary people and flat irony, has affiliations with the Australian tradition of realism he rejected. Another writer who began publishing short fiction in the 1930s, Dal Stivens, drew on fable, fantasy and fairytale traditions. Alienated by realism, Stivens published mainly outside Australia until Wild and Woolley, one of the new independent small publishers, produced a collection of his stories in 1976. The influence of international modernism is also discernible in Hal Porter's symbolic style and his use of elaborately metaphoric prose to explore his characters' psyches. While his major achievement in short fiction was recognised by the publication of his *Collected Stories* in 1971, Porter is today most admired for his autobiographical writing; Cowan's reputation is minor and Stivens remains little known. These and other writers were experimenting with the techniques and potential of new fictional modes during those decades when the notion of life-like social realism was entrenched in the literary culture and resistant to challenges.

The literary iconoclasm of the 1970s had its nearest antecedents in fictions ranging from Peter Mathers' brilliant satire on racism, *Trap* (1966), with its radical originality of form and preoccupation with the complacence of middle-class Australian society,[12] to more predictable challenges to contemporary social values and manners in humorously satiric works like David Martin's *The Hero of Too* (1965), and Barry Oakley's four novels. This latter fiction can be seen as part of a trend made popular in Barry Humphries' satiric writing and stage work in the early 1960s. Such developments indicate a society newly capable of a degree of self-mockery; one prepared to interrogate some of its most entrenched mythologies, among them the sanctity of male rituals in sport, the significance of suburban life, the seriousness of religion and the mythology of Australian anti-authoritarianism. Yet Humphries' attack on the assumed conservative mediocrity of suburban Australia is itself ultimately conservative, just as the amiable tone of Oakley's fiction has a reactionary rather than a revisionary effect.

As Australia moved away from its traditional reliance on Britain and Europe towards America, Australian literary culture underwent a similar shift, with American and Latin American as well as avant-garde European writing becoming more widely and easily available. Ironically, while Australia's involvement in the Vietnam War brought it into the international political arena, it also generated one of the few periods of national division in Australian history. That social upheaval was matched by what has been claimed as an absolute shift in Australian literary historiography, a "gulf ... between what had been appearing before and the new writing that has appeared since".[13] This self-styled new writing emerged from the climate of the anti-war movement, sharing its consciousness of radical change. A journal, *Tabloid Story*, was established in Sydney by Frank Moorhouse, Carmel Kelly and Michael Wilding in 1972 to publish the new fiction. Their aims were to promote literary innovation, provide an outlet for work not acceptable to established journals and publishers, foster innovative short fiction, and professionalise Australian writing by paying writers Australian Society of Authors' rates. More flexible modes of production, available through new offset printing technologies, encouraged such small, alternative publishing groups.

Now often criticised as misogynist and sexist, the new fiction challenged restrictive censorship laws and prevailing social and literary conventions. Stories unpublishable in established journals appeared in so-called girlie magazines, and Moorhouse's first collection, *Futility and Other Animals* (1969) had such a publisher. *Days of Wine and Rage* (1980), his collection of prose writings from the 1970s, describes in its title the hedonistic politics shared by writers whose revolutionary ambition was dedicated to the self-conscious revision of what they saw as an archaic tradition of bush realism in Australian fiction. The new fiction would include explicit sex and engage in technical innovation: "no more formula bush tales, no more restrictions to the beginning, middle and end story, no more preconceptions about a well rounded tale".[14] However, although the focus on sex by many of the Sydney fringe writers who became known as the Balmain Group derived from a political impulse, that focus disabled its potential engagement with a broader politics. On the other hand, public recognition that sex could be a topic of fiction encouraged erotic writing, now well established and often written from a gay or lesbian perspective.[15]

The Most Beautiful Lies (1979), title of the first anthology of stories by five of the new writers, suggests the ways this fiction unyoked itself from realism. The opening story, Murray Bail's "The Drover's Wife", establishes both a playful connection with and rejection of the literary and cultural past. Sharing its title with Henry Lawson's classic story, its immediate frame of reference is Russell Drysdale's equally iconic painting, "The Drover's Wife", used as a visual prompt for the new story. Bail, Carey and Wilding all developed forms of surrealism to negotiate the restrictions of formal realism. Carey's stories, later collected in *The Fat Man in History* (1974) and *War Crimes* (1979), were first published in *Tabloid Story* and other periodicals. Brilliant fables of contemporary Australian life, they are disturbing in their capacity to distort only to the extent that the precisely and comically observed "realities" they evoke are both bizarre and horribly familiar. Accepting the nightmare of their lives, the social failures of the stories are depicted as usually hapless victims of a powerful system that degrades its members. Carey's vision is at its sharpest and most convincing in his short fiction; in the novels published since, the most telling narrative moments occur in the internal stories, those of Harry Joy in *Bliss* (1981), for example, or when realism moves into surrealism and then fable in the futuristic *The Tax Inspector* (1991).

Michael Wilding has an important place in Australian writing, not only as a writer of short fiction and novels but as a critic, editor and publisher. In his inventive fictions, Wilding draws on a variety of modes. One of the persistent themes of his writing is the subject of *The Short Story Embassy* (1975), where a group of characters tell the stories that bring their lives into being. Less well known than these members of the male-dominated Balmain Group, Vicki Viidikas used fantasy in a way as disturbing as Carey's surrealism, often as a politicised comment on the secondary position of women in both society and literature, in her only collection of fiction, *Wrappings* (1974).

The contemporary influence of America in Australian culture is recalled in the ironically affectionate title of Frank Moorhouse's *The Americans, Baby* (1972) which deals through a series of linked stories with the ambiguous politics of American/Australian relations. One of Peter Carey's early stories is the equally ambivalently titled "American Dreams". Moorhouse is currently writing a trilogy about the establishment of the League of Nations in Europe in the 1920s and its ultimate failure. Continuing his interest in the intersections of sex and politics in both their public and private manifestations, *Grand Days* (1993), the first volume, focuses on a young Australian woman bureaucrat's experience of the beginnings of the League of Nations as an organisation. She brings the world of international politics into her bedroom while sexualising the political intrigues of the boardroom. Unlike Moorhouse's earlier work, typically series of linked stories or short novels, *Grand Days* is a long realist novel which has been compared to the work of Stendhal and Zola.

LATER CONTEMPORANEITY AND DIVERSITY

A tendency to irony is often said to be a defining characteristic of Australian writing and satire is an important generic influence. Sustained prose satires are rare, however; with Ireland, David Foster is one of the few contemporary prose satirists. Foster's epic narratives draw on comedy and pathos; they are poetic and vulgar, ironic and farcical, excessive and carnivalesque. His style requires readers as quick-witted as he, as well read in music and science and mythology, in Greek and Latin classical literatures as well as others, as linguistically astute, who will take as much pleasure in the fictions' range of allusions, techniques, and modes of reference. In common with the classical satirists who provide his models, Foster places great value on the conceit of the inspiration of art and of the writer as social prophet; his disordered narratives represent a disordered society, where only the voice of the poet can restore sanity and order. Fierce, extended and often ludicrously elaborated arguments between characters are used to define the satirist's values. Jason Blackman's description in *Plumbum* (1983) of the proper role of literature also describes Foster's literary method: "It's the *shattering* of ... preconceptions that forms the basis of all Art".[16]

Foster's satires expose and condemn all forms of material pretension and spiritual humbug while celebrating those who stand out against the prevalence of human folly. The central character of *Dog Rock: A Postal Pastoral* (1985) and *The Pale Blue Crochet Coathanger Cover* (1988), postman D'Arcy D'Oliveres is also the narrator of *The Glade within the Grove* (1996), winner of the 1997 Miles Franklin Award. D'Oliveres espouses idiosyncratic views on topics as diverse as the right way to start a stalled truck on the side of a hill in virgin forest, to the right path to civilisation which can only be achieved by the removal of all trees from a landscape. The good nature as well as the masculine activities of the timber-felling MacAnaspie family in this novel reflect Foster's fondness for the simple, politically reactionary qualities he attributes to such people. Patrick White believed that Foster would be "the Australian novelist most likely to inherit his mantle".[17]

The term "speculative fiction" covers a variety of fictional modes widely used in contemporary Australia. Avant-garde in the 1970s, forms of speculative fiction are now more commonplace. Archie Weller's *Land of the Golden Clouds* (1998), a sprawling, epic narrative with an intricate plot and huge cast of characters, is a recent major example of the genre, seriously engaged with its possibilities but also subversive of them. Set in an Australia 3,000 years in the future, where the land has been blasted by radiation after a 1997 global nuclear holocaust, and various tribes are warring with one another, the narrative recounts the heroes' often bloody and sometimes fatal encounters as they journey through it. After his earlier realist works, science fantasy may appear a surprising direction for Weller's fiction, but his writing exemplifies the formal experimentation and eclecticism Adam Shoemaker claims for contemporary black Australian fiction.[18] In common with other black writers, Weller is preoccupied not just with the survival of a form of Aboriginal culture, but with the politics of a reconciliation that respects difference, articulated in the utopian Epilogue of *Land of the Golden Clouds* by one of its journeying heroes who tells the "many different people" who have helped him: "Let us embrace our enemy and all be friends and I will lead you out of our dark world!"[19]

While many of the fictions discussed in this chapter could be called speculative, Gerald Murnane, whose elliptical, introspective prose is not designed for popular acclaim, consistently uses what might be termed a speculative mode. He is another of Helen Daniel's eight "liars", and although his novels have recognisably Australian settings, their landscapes take on fantastic aspects, and his work owes more to the modern European tradition that includes Kafka, Camus and Beckett, more recently Robbe-Grillet, than any Australian influences. From his first book, *Tamarisk Row* (1974), through *The Plains* (1982) and *Inland* (1988) to *Velvet Waters* (1990), Murnane has constructed a level of "imagistic coherence"[20] among his fictions, which share a central concern with the relationship, often anguished and always alienated, of an individual mind, through which each fiction is focused, to its surrounding reality. This exploration of the question of what is interior and what is exterior to the mind, of solipsism, is recounted through the musings of those consciousnesses in a deliberately monotonous style.

A recent revival of the historical novel, initiated perhaps by Patrick White's *Voss* and *A Fringe of Leaves* and Thomas Keneally's early novels, may suggest that towards the end of the millennium writers have turned to the past to invest a chaotic present with some order and invoke a communal memory. Roger McDonald's first novel, *1915* (1979), combined domestic with war history. His later fictions characteristically use an aspect or a subject of Australian history; the latest, *Mr Darwin's Shooter* (1998), extends his range to include English intellectual history and its interpellation with Australia's. Contemporary historical fictions often interrogate traditional notions of history and speculate on the nature of history as a genre. Peter Carey's *Oscar and Lucinda* (1988) has been read as both a reconstruction of a European history of Australian settlement and a deconstruction of the potential of historical fiction to serve as nationalist myth,[21] while his life history of Dickens' convict character Magwitch from *Great Expectations*, *Jack Maggs* (1997), is metafictional. Rodney Hall's important three-volume work, *The Yandilli Trilogy* (1988–93), explores and unsettles the meanings of settlement of the Australian colonies and their colonial links to Britain. In *It's Raining in Mango* (1987), Thea Astley's discontinuous structure fragments the conventional saga of four generations of a settler family, allowing other histories, especially that of the genocide of Aboriginal peoples, a narrative space. David Malouf endorses the patri-archal myth of land possession as a right that informs traditional white

Australian history in *Harland's Half Acre* (1984), yet *The Great World* (1990), ostensibly epic war history, focuses on the experiences of a group of ordinary men. *The Conversations at Curlow Creek* (1997) takes the form of a personal meditation, reminiscent in style and tone of his early novel *An Imaginary Life* (1978). It juxtaposes two "histories" – the hanging of an escaped convict in the new world, and the memories of life in the old world of the soldier who must carry out his hanging.

Several historical novels were published around 1988, the so-called Australian Bicentennial year. As a marker of a colonising history, that moment has come to represent a fracturing rather than a consolidation of Australian nationhood, so that such fictions are often interested in whose voice makes history and what that voice has left out. Kate Grenville's *Joan Makes History* (1988) narrates a parodic counter-history of two hundred years of European settlement in Australia through a woman's voice. More recently, Debra Adelaide's *Serpent Dust* (1997) retells the history of the arrival of the white settlers from several perspectives, one of them that of an Aboriginal woman who speaks her other, Indigenous history. No "history" is privileged above any other, and the layers of narrative voices are interspersed with supposed journal extracts. In *The Service of Clouds* (1997), Delia Falconer constructs a female family history, while the politics of white Australian history are implicated in the title of Andrew McGahan's *1988* (1995), a bleak narrative of the failure of a young man's journey to induct him into adulthood.

REGIONAL PUBLISHING/WRITING

A contemporary interest in regions as locations of literary difference is matched by regional identification arising from the shared socio-economic problem of publishing from marginal locations. Western Australia has an energetic contemporary literary culture; a high proportion of the anthologies of contemporary Australian fiction published over the past couple of decades have come from the West. Randolph Stow in his early novels, Elizabeth Jolley, Peter Cowan, Dorothy Hewett, Tim Winton, Robert Drewe and Fay Zwicky are Western Australian writers who use landscapes, evoking space and distance, not just as descriptive settings but as a narrative presence in their work. The trajectory of Elizabeth Jolley's discovery and establishment as one of Australia's major writers is paradigmatic of regional politics. For many years, Jolley's work was regularly rejected by publishers. When Outback Press, one of the new, alternative small publishers, agreed to publish *Palomino*, it was another four years before it came out in 1980, in part perhaps because its story of a lesbian relationship between an older and a younger woman was unusual for that time. Jolley's writing also refers to a European cultural tradition not accessible to a wide Australian readership in the 1960s and 1970s. What are now admired as the postmodern features of her work – motifs repeated within and between novels and short stories, self-reflexivity and open-endedness – were not acceptable then. Recognising what made her writing "undesirable" – its stylistic infelicities and "unAustralianness", as well as the problem of her regional location in Western Australia – Jolley wrote what became her award-winning and widely anthologised story "A Hedge of Rosemary" to a carefully worked out formula.

Fremantle Arts Centre Press, established in 1975 to publish and promote Western Australian writing, published Jolley's first book, *Five Acre Virgin and Other Stories* in that year, then another story collection, *The Travelling Entertainer and Other Stories* (1979) and a short novel, *The Newspaper of Claremont Street* (1981). Jolley moved to another regional publisher, University of Queensland Press, with her next book, *Miss Peabody's Inheritance* (1983), then to Penguin who published *Mr Scobie's Riddle* (1983), her first national literary award winner. Jolley's publishing history indicates the complex network of influences that shape a writer's reputation. It also raises the question of the importance of regional publishers, and the tensions that exist between them and national (now multinational) publishers as well as between writers and their regional publishers when they move to a larger press. Latterly, the survival of the smaller regional publishers has been threatened by the buying and marketing power of the larger multinationals.

The phenomenon of Elizabeth Jolley's remarkable reputation remains a matter of interest. A writer with an idiosyncratic and a distinctive, multifaceted style, best expressed in her perfect late novella, *The Orchard Thieves* (1995), Jolley's success owes something to the 1980s awareness of "women's writing". It can perhaps best be explained, however, by an unusual mixture in her work of late twentieth-century modernism, intellectually interesting to many contemporary readers, and a neo-nineteenth-century humanism, thematically satisfying to others. Ultimately paramount in Jolley's writing, humanist values provide the solace the narratives seek. Towards the end of *The Georges' Wife* (1993), third in Jolley's trilogy of semi-autobiographical novels, the disassociated narrator says: "To the questions, is there a Balm and is there a Physician? my answer is yes. There is trust, there is courage and there is kindness … And anyone can be the Physician."[22] Such sentiments also provide solace for readers whose equilibrium may be threatened by Jolley's deracinated wit and uncanny narrative techniques.

Fremantle Arts Centre Press's policy to publish only Western Australian writers has been criticised as parochial, yet it has fostered important Western Australian writers, with Albert Facey's *A Fortunate Life* (1981) and Sally Morgan's *My Place* (1987) enjoying unprecedented national success. Another major regional publisher, University of Queensland Press, has been a significant presence in the construction and maintenance of Australian literature. As a region, Queensland figures strongly in contemporary writing, tending to be represented with either hostility, or nostalgia, as in David Malouf's first novel *Johnno* (1975) and his autobiographical fiction *12 Edmonstone Street* (1985). Janette Turner Hospital's characters often shuttle, as she does, between Brisbane and other places; suburban Brisbane is the evocative space of growing up in Jessica Anderson's interlinked *Stories From the Warm Zone* (1987), while the settings and populations of Thea Astley's novels and stories in small towns in northern Queensland are distinctive.

WHITE ANGLO-CELTIC MALE NO MORE[23]

The invisible orthodoxy of the early 1970s was that Australian fiction was a masculine territory. Women writers of the past were largely ignored, as was their contemporary presence. Although feminist critics had begun the work of recuperating a history of Australian writing by women and delineating their contemporary standing,[24] neither was paid much attention in the new critical works, which also failed to recognise the vigorous social debates about repressive gender ideologies and sexist social structures being generated by feminist politics. Defining the field in those critical works is done from a male perspective and the writers dealt with are overwhelmingly male. *Studies in the Recent Australian Novel* (1978) discusses sixteen novels of which only one, Christina Stead's *The People with the Dogs*, is by a woman, and the Foreword fails to recognise gender as an element in its politics of choice, mentioning only that "Thea Astley is one name which there was general agreement might well have been included".[25] In Astley's well-known statement that she was "spiritually neutered by [her sexist] society", she refers to her assumption that writing and narration were both male activities.[26] This recognition and her invention of a female narrative voice were made possible by the feminist consciousness of the late 1970s. Critical ignorance of the ways gender functions in writing, publishing and reading was radically revised in the early 1980s. By the late 1980s the landscape of Australian fiction was thoroughly gendered, and at the century's end women writers are a significant and well established presence in Australian literature.

The emergence of women's writing as a category in the 1980s was matched by the increasing visibility of other previously disregarded groups: the so-called migrant writers, Indigenous writers, and gay and lesbian writers. This cultural heterogeneity marks a shift from what had in earlier decades been understood as an homogeneous national literary landscape, one enabled by similar shifts in social structures, by new critical discourses and by readers with particular interests and allegiances; also by the presence of small, often specialist – for example feminist, or Indigenous – publishers. Both the history of the opening up of the terrain of Australian fiction to differences of all kinds, and the claims of those other voices, have been the subject of much critical scrutiny, including questioning what constitutes categories such as woman, or multicultural, or Indigenous writer and their writing; the ways we might speak of it; and how such stories are to be told.

FEMINISMS AND "WOMEN'S WRITING"

Some of the new writing by women is overtly radical in its themes and narrative techniques, and often polemical; these feminist fictions are purposeful in their representation and critique of gender ideologies. Entering into masculine literary territories – of genre or modernist fiction or postmodernism – theoretically sophisticated and socially radical feminist writers subvert them from within. In her thriller *A Gap in the Records* (1985) and her crime fiction *Only Lawyers Dancing* (1992), Jan McKemmish deconstructs the masculine conventions of these genres by adopting postmodern techniques of pastiche and maze-like, unfinished narratives to interrogate social corruption and violence. Finola Moorhead also practises genre politics: a large group of women, each named for a letter of the alphabet, construct the web-like narrative structure of *Remember the Tarantella* (1987); the young female detective of *Still Murder* (1991) discovers that the crime she seeks to solve is part of an institutionalised chain of violence.

Janine Burke's *Speaking* (1984) uses four women's voices to convey both a postmodern concern with the provisionality of discourse and a feminist concern with finding spaces for woman's speech and representing its multiple, interactive nature; *Second Sight* (1986) recalls contemporary theories of specularity as the female narrator discovers her own way of seeing. Marion Campbell's novels, *Lines of Flight* (1985), *Not Being Miriam* (1988) and *Prowler* (1999), illustrate the potential as well as the problems of using contemporary theory and poststructuralist techniques in the service of a feminist politics. Campbell's intellectually demanding writing presents feminist art practice as a process of negotiation between the pleasure of formal innovation (authorised by male thinkers) and the ethics of feminist politics (that critiques and subverts masculine systems). Among others consciously using feminist theories in their fiction, Carmel Bird employs irony, humour and gothicism. Sue Woolfe explores the female dilemma of being both subject and object in *Painted Woman* (1989), and relationships between mothers and daughters as well as issues to do with women's intellectual ambition in *Leaning Towards Infinity* (1996). Gail Jones' two collections of short fiction, *The House of Breathing* (1994) and *Fetish Lives* (1997), are playfully and self-consciously postmodern in the serious cause of the liberation of women – and fiction – from the oppressions of realist conventions and sexist institutions.

Lesbian fiction, a small but important body of writing, is radical in its expression of woman-to-woman sexuality. *All That False Instruction* (1975), Elizabeth Riley's dismal *bildungsroman* of a young girl's maturation, compromised and complicated by her lesbianism, was marketed as "a novel about lesbian love", and is often claimed as the first Australian feminist novel; this claim is also made for Helen Garner's more commercially successful *Monkey Grip* (1977), a novel of heterosexual love. Writing the lesbian body, Mary Fallon in *Working Hot* (1989) represents the challenge of that body to hegemonic heterosexuality through an excessive, eroticised and often apparently meaningless narrative pastiche. The problem of readability is politicised – some bodies/texts are rendered illegible in a culture that only reads what is acceptable to it – as Fallon transgresses formal linguistic and discursive codes, bringing together fragments of conversation, song, jokes, advertising, drama, film script, poetry, in her multivocal narrative.

Much contemporary fiction by women is preoccupied with the ways gender difference structures power inequities. In Beverley Farmer's early work, *Alone* (1980), *Milk* (1983) and *Home Time* (1985), female characters may be subject to memories and experiences of rape and male violence. Straightforward representations of sexual politics become more subtle narrative resistances to masculine power in her later work. Challenging and stretching generic boundaries – Farmer says a novel depends "on how you define [it]"[27] – *A Body of Water* (1990) signals the direction of her later fiction. Consisting of five complete stories, sections from other works, her own notebook entries, and jottings of all kinds, it tests the potential of "feminine" writing, often defined by organicism and fluidity. Farmer's style is poetic and meditative, but her presentation of forms of domestic violence is confrontational and realist. *The House in the Light* (1994) depicts the physical, emotional and psychological conflict between Bell and her Greek ex-mother-in-law, disrupting what is often an idealised view of female bonding. The experiences and meanings of female sexuality are central to

Farmer's fictional concerns. Such writing still attracts negative criticisms: one reviewer of *A Body of Water* speaks for the "ordinary reader" whom he says will not want to read about "intimate details", such as female orgasms and menstruation.[28]

Helen Garner is the major representative of a new mode of domestic realism that has been strategically central in women's contemporary fiction. *Monkey Grip* was marketed as the book that would change women's lives, and eagerly read by many: Garner's writing always calls on an identificatory reader politics. At the same time it was criticised for its formlessness, and apparently personal recounting of experience, a critique based in a simplistically comparative formula: male writing is artful if it is fragmentary; women's writing artless if it is diary-like. Now the style of this mode of women's writing has been recoded as distinctively "anecdotal".[29] Garner's writing is deceptively simple, rhythmically evocative of the minutiae of domestic life and the endless, many-layered quality of female conversations. Part of the new wave of the 1970s, her fiction explores women's desire and the gendered power structures within which female sexuality is experienced, marking her distance from the experimental male writers. Her focus is predominantly on forms of family relationships and the complex negotiations women undertake between their own needs and the demands made on them, for love and sex, motherhood and independence. *Monkey Grip*, *Honour and Other People's Children* (1980) and *The Children's Bach* (1984) present women trying to find alternatives to living in traditional family structures; *Cosmo Cosmolino* (1992) describes the desolation of those without families. Commenting on adverse reactions to the attention paid in *Cosmo Cosmolino* to spiritual experience, Garner describes shifts in style and content as necessary renewals of her writing practice: "to talk about things like redemption, and the soul ... you've got to find a new way to write".[30] Mixing her major writing modes of fiction and journalism in *The First Stone* (1995), her bestselling account of a case of sexual harassment at a college of Melbourne University, Garner initiated an ongoing, sometimes virulent public debate among feminist readers and critics, often based on generational politics, and one that extended to questions of the ethics of fictionalising "real" characters and events.

In her numerous short novels, from *The Albatross Muff* (1977) until her premature death in 1991, Barbara Hanrahan established her unique style of gothic realism, although Carmel Bird's work bears resemblances to it. Interested in the very odd lives of very ordinary women, usually in families, in the oppressive milieus of late Victorian England and suburban Adelaide from the 1880s to the 1950s of her own growing up there, Hanrahan juxtaposes calculated narrative naivety with the menacing sexualised brutality and belittling conventionality to which these women's lives are subject. Kate Grenville achieves a similar level of banal gothicism in prose more energetic, comic and experimental than Hanrahan's. *Lilian's Story* (1985) is concerned with the ways women's stories are subsumed within or controlled by grand masculine narratives of imperialism and nationalism. Lilian, subject to male power, and Australia, subject to imperial power, are both represented as colonised bodies in *Lilian's Story*, which is widely allusive and generically plural. An increasingly grotesque hero, Lilian is emblematic of female protest against the social ordering and control of women's bodies, deliberately making herself fat as an emancipatory device. Grenville's later *Dark Places* (1994) is a bleak mirroring of Lilian's story as it takes up the perspective of her father, Albion.

Supported by independent women publishers, McPhee Gribble and Sisters, later Sybylla and Spinifex, as well as by mainstream publishers, particularly Penguin, contemporary women writers have experimented with narrative form to find ways to tell women's stories. Among such novels are Jean Bedford's *Sister Kate* (1981), a rewriting of the Ned Kelly story from his sister Kate's perspective; Amanda Lohrey's novels, particularly the last, *Camille's Bread* (1995); *Westblock* (1983), Sara Dowse's fictionalised account of aspects of the public service in Canberra and the tension between that public realm and women's private lives; Helen Hodgman's expressionist novels with their savagely comic dissection of the supposedly benign spaces of women's existence; the last three of Georgia Savage's four novels, each with widely differing settings and narrative impulses but all dealing with issues particular to women's lives; Margaret Coombs' wickedly satiric investigations of the way public men control women's private lives. In the work of these and many more women writers, the domestic realm and what had been regarded as the unimportant details of the private sphere are made public, using a variety of often complex and subversive narrative modes.

NEW REALISM

A new interest in social realism "as political, as activist",[31] was part of the new wave writing of the 1970s. In her consistent exposure of social and economic injustices, Olga Masters, who began publishing fiction in the 1980s after a long working life as a mother and journalist, shared the concerns of earlier socialist realists, writing as they did about ordinary people in small country towns and rural communities suffering economic depression in the 1930s. But Masters' collections of linked stories and two novels centre on home life with a new intensity: her sexual frankness, observation of idiosyncratic detail and comic irony illuminate the apparently inconsequential events, conversations and feelings of her characters' lives, revealing the rigid social constraints and petty meannesses of those lives as well as celebrating the occasional joys. Amy Witting also came late to fiction writing. An early story, published pseudonymously in *Tabloid Story* 8, dealt ironically with the explicitly sexual nature of other *Tabloid Story* fiction. In a double irony, numerous outraged readers complained about its obscenity. Witting's comic style and interest in the sometimes unconscious impulses that provoke the actions and structure the relationships of the ordinary people in her stories and novels has been called Chekhovian.

Realism is the fictional mode most characteristic of Indigenous writers and writers from non-English speaking backgrounds. At odds with the dominant culture that has denied them a public voice and a cultural space, such writers use their fiction as a vehicle through which to protest their exclusion – and that of their people – from literary and social recognition. Technical innovation is less important than the story that needs to be told, and the fictional form chosen by so-called migrant writers of the first generation is more often that of the short story than the novel. Developed within an urban, literate, Western culture, the novel is an uncomfortable genre for many Aboriginal writers, and other kinds of writing – autobiography as well as drama and poetry – are more often used as literary tools in the struggle for recognition of Aboriginal rights and voices. Archie Weller's *Day of the Dog* (1981) and collection of stories, *Going Home* (1986), are more than powerful social realist narratives; his rich use of language and metaphorical patterning convey what Weller calls a "new dreaming". *The Kaidatcha Sung* (1990), Sam Watson's only novel, a searing narrative of the invasion of Brisbane by black tribes, employs fantasy and magic realism as well as Aboriginal myth. Very different in its approach and impact, Kim Scott's *True Country* (1993) represents the scattering of an Aboriginal fringe group and the unreason of racism in its fragmented narrative structure. A second novel, *Benang* (1999), explores the racist stereotype of whiteness as a superior "skin" through three generations of a settler/ Aboriginal family, using a mixture of extracts from historical documents and multiple, fictional family memories.

One of the effects of the powerful autobiographical writing of Indigenous writers and those from non-English speaking backgrounds has been its imaginative and political influence on contemporary fiction. A recent enormously popular fiction of post-war migrant working and family life, Richard Flanagan's *The Sound of One Hand Clapping* (1997), may prefigure the integration of that experience into Australian fiction. The narrator of Eva Sallis' first novel, *Hiam* (1998), a Vogel Award winner, is an Arabic woman whose alienating view of Australian society is a reminder that multiculturalism should not mean the obliteration but the recognition of cultural differences. Contemporary literary scandals involving writers who have adopted an Indigenous or an ethnic identity – Helen Darville/ Demidenko's claim to be the daughter of Ukrainian immigrants apparently authenticated her award-winning *The Hand That Signed the Paper* (1994), as did B. Wongar's earlier claim to tribal Aboriginality – have raised issues to do with writerly authenticity, particularly important in relation to marginal groups, and of the politics of writing and reading across race and ethnic boundaries.

Robert Drewe's several novels are typically based on an historical or contemporary event. His characters are idealists, confused by the events in which they are enmeshed, their lives characterised by failed sexual and emotional relationships as well as ambition. *The Drowner* (1996), an intricate narrative that moves between Britain and the Swan River Colony and among a large cast of characters, is Drewe's most ambitious and publicly successful novel. Drewe's influential reinscription of the beach as a more significant cultural space for most Australians than the bush takes place in the linked stories of *The Bodysurfers* (1983). A late twentieth-century realist, Drewe treats the public and private politics of Australian life with comic irony. A different kind of narrative distancing characterises the rather sardonic and often satiric later novels of Nicholas Hasluck, which concentrate on aspects of history, often of Western Australia's colonial past. His fictions are intricately plotted and politically informed by their interest in corrupt social structures. Amanda Lohrey's political fictions are also based in real events; they are complex narratives interested like Hasluck's in political corruption, but also in issues of gender and sexual politics. The ironic title of *The Morality of Gentlemen* (1984) sets the tone of the novel, centred on a Hobart waterfront dispute in the 1950s and concerned to reveal the gap between political events and their public interpretation. *The Reading Group* (1988), target of a libel action that raised strong protests from the literary community, is a dystopic fiction tracing the disintegration of a group of left-wing idealists. Its members' capitulation to materialism and self-interest is made allegorical of the political apathy of middle-class Australians.

FICTIONALISING ASIA

Contemporary Australia's growing recognition of its location in South-East Asia has been reproduced in its fiction. First generated in the late 1970s by Australian writers exploring aspects of what is or might be Australia's (and Australians') relationship with Asian countries, this fiction is characteristically focused through an Australian who goes to an Asian country as a journalist or a public servant. At its best, it explores the tensions arising out of a European-Australian fascination with Asian countries as exotic, feminised locations, and develops a postcolonial narrative awareness that positioning Asia as at once the seductive and threatening other of the West is itself a colonising activity. Christopher Koch's *The Year of Living Dangerously* (1978) is the best known of his novels that take up the story of Australians in Asia. Its protagonist is an Australian journalist in Indonesia, one of a group awaiting Sukarno's 1968 deposition, who remains outside the culture he makes some attempts to understand. *Highways to a War* (1995) uses Vietnam as the primary location of the story of the search for a lost war photographer. The central character in Robert Drewe's *A Cry in the Jungle Bar* (1979) is an Australian scientific adviser based in the Philippines. Paternalistically interested in its culture, he remains oblivious to its volatile politics, and even less sensitive to its women. Blanche d'Alpuget has written two novels set in Asia, *Monkeys in the Dark* (1980) and *Turtle Beach* (1981). In the latter, a female journalist observes the breakdown of political order in Malaysia. Tony Maniaty's ethnic background brings another dimension to *The Children Must Dance* (1984), which tells the story of a mysterious death in a Portuguese island colony to the north of Australia and a struggle between revolutionary forces and its occupiers. Alex Miller's *The Ancestor Game* (1992) explores links between Australia and China, including the masculinist biases of both cultures.

Latterly, a number of diasporic writers, most notably Asian-Australian, have rewritten these narrative politics. Their use of hybrid narrative forms brings fictional modes from their cultures of origin into conjunction with contemporary Australian narrative traditions. Brian Castro is the best known such writer, and his six distinguished novels, from *Birds of Passage* (1983) to *Stepper* (1997), defy easy categorisation, shifting as they do between past and present, among different characters with a range of voices and cultural perspectives, to suggest the instability of categories of identity and nation as well as the problematical status of contemporary storytelling, issues that are central to diasporic politics. In *The Crocodile Fury* (1992), Beth Yahp explores the narrative potential of mixed cultural heritages such as her own to tell the intersecting stories of a grandmother, mother and daughter. Fontini Epanomitis, a first generation European-Australian writer, constructs a fabulous narrative out of a series of stories arising from the myths, superstitions and rituals of a Greek village in *The Mule's Foal* (1992). Other Australian writers of the diaspora include Dewi Anggraeni, Satendra Nandan, Don 'o Kim and Arlene Chai.

GENRE FICTION

Peter Corris, Australia's most successful crime writer, began the contemporary revival of crime fiction, currently a flourishing industry, with *The Dying Trade* (1980). Its central character, Cliff Hardy, fits the type of the typically cynical, tough private investigator of hard-boiled detective fiction. Said to be the best known character in Australian fiction, Hardy figures in one of the three series Corris now publishes. There are many varieties of Australian crime fiction. Robert G. Barrett's extremely popular novels rely on the genre's potential violence and sexism for their effect, while in Shane Maloney's crime writing, broad comedy and political satire are more important than murder. His *Nice Try* (1998) anticipates the Olympic Games corruption scandals of early 1999. Garry Disher, well known as a short story writer, has begun a crime fiction series that may rival Corris', with a professional thief as its central character.

The renaissance of Australian crime fiction coincided with the 1980s decade of the woman writer, and several women became prominent in the field, where their writing is often subversive of the genre's misogynisms. Marele Day's very successful Claudia Valentine series upsets the gendered conventions of crime fiction: not only is Valentine a woman, she is a competent professional in the hard-boiled tradition, and sexually and economically independent. Among less consciously oppositional writers are Susan Geason, whose several very witty crime novels feature a bumblingly inept private eye, Syd Fish; Jennifer Rowe, whose amateur female detective, Verity Birdwood, solves crimes in the Agatha Christie tradition; Kerry Greenwood, whose elegant, escapist fiction recreates a 1920s Wodehouse atmosphere for her glamorous hero, the Hon. Phrynne Fisher; and Gabrielle Lord, whose thrillers fictionalise topical events.

Science fiction has also undergone a renaissance since the mid-1970s. One of several major writers in the field, George Turner was established as a writer of mainstream fiction, winning the Miles Franklin Award for *The Cupboard Under the Stairs* (1962), before becoming a leading science fiction practitioner. *The Sea and Summer* (1987), his best known novel, has a frame story in which a far-future historian produces an historical novel, "The Sea and Summer", set in near-future Melbourne, where ecological and economic problems remain unresolved and have reached disastrous proportions. Greg Egan, whose work is sophisticated and ambitious, has published numerous short stories and five novels, and become Australia's most popular science fiction writer. The leading Australian theorist of the genre, Damien Broderick, is also one of its major writers. Among many others, Rosaleen Love is important as a feminist writer of wry satiric fables informed by her former academic experience in the philosophy of science. Describing himself as a "fantasist", Terry Dowling's fiction is infused with an awareness of cultural difference. Younger writers include Sean McMullen, Sean Williams, Mark Shirrefs, John Thompson and others, while Jack Dann, already an established sf writer in the US, has migrated to Australia and is a new influence in the national community of science fiction writers and readers.

The range, volume and popularity of genre fiction being published in Australia at present is striking. Romantic fiction is currently enjoying a revival and mainstream publishers like Random House, Penguin and HarperCollins all have major romance lists. Blockbuster romance writer, Di Morrissey, publishes regularly and commands large readerships; Bryce Courtenay has become another phenomenally successful writer of Australian historical romance. His *The Potato Factory* (1995) is concerned with convict life, while *Jessica* (1998) is set in the early twentieth century and deals with Indigenous issues among others. Formerly, writers of middle-brow romantic fiction like Colleen McCullough and Morris West had to publish overseas in order to find a readership; now such fiction is extremely lucrative for publishers in Australia. What seems to be a concurrent phenomenon, related perhaps to this market drive, is the presence of romance in recent literary fiction; the romance of storytelling is central to several, among them Murray Bail's *Eucalyptus* (1998) and Brenda Walker's *Poe's Cat* (1999), while Kate Grenville's *The Idea of Perfection* (1999) has as one narrative thread the story of the middle-aged love of two homely people.

THE NEW PROFESSIONALS

Tim Winton is one of the few Australian writers solely supported by his publishing. He was an early graduate of the university creative writing courses now proliferating across the country. Immediately successful with his first, student novel, *An Open Swimmer* (1982), a Vogel Award winner, Winton has also won the Miles Franklin Award twice, for *Shallows* (1984) and *Cloudstreet* (1991). His work is closely tied to the coastal areas of southern Western Australia where he grew up and lives. Influenced by American writers of the South and West, Winton's fiction is also informed by the rhythms and loose narrative structures of the yarn.[32] It has a strong vernacular line, is subtly allusive, preoccupied with family and sexual relationships, interactions between people and their environments, and with an other than rational dimension of life. The title of *That Eye the Sky* (1986) suggests this transcendent order of "faith" or the "numinous", which becomes dominant in *Cloudstreet*. A story of the generational lives of two families, each inhabiting half of an old house on Cloud Street in suburban Perth, the novel invites Jungian analogies. Not wanting to write either realism or "1970s fabulism" but to "include both realms because I feel that this is true realism", Winton also avoids the label of "magic realism": for him, the "weird things that happen in my books aren't devices".[33]

Grunge became the new fiction of the 1990s, labelled in this way to appeal to the youthful reading audience to whom it is marketed. The province of young writers, often products of writing schools, whose explicit, sometimes relentless focus on sex, drugs and life on the margins of society makes the new fiction of the 1970s look timid, 1990s grunge fiction may also be preoccupied with generational conflict with authority figures. Christos Tsiolkas' *Loaded* (1997) is confronting in its depiction of a young, first-generation Greek-Australian man's sexual and cultural alienation, concerns which recur in his *The Jesus Man* (1999). Justine Ettler's *The River Ophelia* (1995), the best-known example of the genre, can be read as potently pornographic or as subverting pornography. Andrew McGahan's *Praise* (1992) and *1988* are interested in the political and personal implications of grunge living, giving his writing a dimension this fiction often lacks. John Scott's sexy, dream-like poetry-fictions, including *What I Have Written* (1993), and Rod Jones's controversial *Julia Paradise* (1986) were perhaps forerunners of this fiction's interest in explicit, often alternative, sexual experience.

Unlike grunge, which exists on the margins of Australian fiction, Murray Bail's Miles Franklin winner *Eucalyptus* (1998) brings together and alludes to many of the preoccupations and techniques which have shaped Australian fiction since the 1970s. Set in the country, it refers to earlier bush realism, is a version of family history, and constructs a fable of Australian life, as do David Foster's or Elizabeth Jolley's very different narratives. Concerned with a father's ambition to plant every known species of eucalyptus, then to give his daughter in marriage to the man who can name all of them, it is interested in what an Australian story might be, and is self-consciously fictive. There are several storytellers, the father and daughter and especially a mysterious stranger (the writer?) whose narratives are more powerful than any other's. In the late twentieth century, a multiplicity of fictions call on Australian and other readerships. *Eucalyptus* provides only a temporary coda to the ongoing narrative of Australian fiction, where the contemporary interest in the stories of history and the modes of biography and autobiography as bases of fictional narratives indicate what may be a new hybrid novel form in the future.

NOTES

1 See Bruce Bennett, "Literary Culture Since Vietnam: A New Dynamic", in Bruce Bennett and Jennifer Strauss, eds, *Oxford Literary History of Australia* (Melbourne: Oxford University Press, 1998), p. 239.

2 Ken Gelder and Paul Salzman, *The New Diversity* (Melbourne: McPhee Gribble, 1989), p. 1.

3 Susan Lever discusses the "premium on innovation" encouraged by the competitive system of the Literature Board/Fund of the Australia Council in "Fiction: Innovation and Ideology" in Bennett and Strauss, eds, *Oxford Literary History of Australia*, p. 310.

4 For a fuller discussion, see Susan Lever, "Government Patronage and Literary Reputations" in Delys Bird, Robert Dixon and Susan Lever, eds, *CanonOZities, Southerly*, 57.3 (1997), pp. 104–114.

5 In *Books – Who Reads Them? A study of borrowing and buying in Australia*, Hans Hoegh Guldbert argues that "the smaller the nation, the smaller is the market share of publications published in the country itself" (Sydney: Australia Council, 1990), p. 201.

6 Bennett, "Literary Culture Since Vietnam", p. 245.

7 Patrick White, "The Prodigal Son", *Australian Letters*, 1.3 (1958), p. 39.

8 Jessica Anderson, *One of the Wattle Birds* (Melbourne: Penguin, 1994), p. 192.

9 Elaine Barry, *Fabricating the Self: The Fictions of Jessica Anderson* (St Lucia: University of Queensland Press, 1996), p. 7.

10 Randolph Stow, "Learning Through Nonsense", *Journal of the School Library Association of North Queensland* 1.3–4 (1968), p. 4. Cited in Anthony J. Hassall, ed., *Randolph Stow* (St Lucia: University of Queensland Press, 1990).

11 Peter Cowan, "Author's Statements", *Australian Literary Studies*, 10.2 (1982), p. 196.

12 Mathers' second and last novel *The Wort Papers* (1972) is equally startling. He has also published a collection of short stories and written numerous plays.

13 Michael Wilding, "The Tabloid Story Story", in Michael Wilding, ed., *The Tabloid Story Pocket Book* (Sydney: Wild & Woolley, 1978), p. 306.

14 Wilding, "Tabloid Story", p. 302.

15 See Robert Dessaix, ed., *Australian Gay and Lesbian Writing: An Anthology* (Melbourne: Oxford University Press, 1993).

16 David Foster, *Plumbum* (Melbourne: Penguin, 1983), p. 187.

17 Cited in Geoffrey Dutton, "David Foster: The Early Years", *Southerly*, 56.1 (1996), p. 27.

18 Adam Shoemaker, "Tracking Black Australian Stories" in Bennett and Strauss, eds, *Oxford Literary History of Australia*, pp. 332–347, 346.

19 Archie Weller, *Land of the Golden Clouds* (Sydney: Allen & Unwin, 1998), p. 368.

20 Imré Salusinszky, *Gerald Murnane* (Melbourne: Oxford University Press, 1993), p. 8.

21 Gelder and Salzman, *The New Diversity*, p. 140.

22 Elizabeth Jolley, *The Georges' Wife* (Melbourne: Viking/Penguin, 1993), p. 180.

23 This phrase was coined by Elizabeth Webby in a review article, "Short Fiction in the Eighties: White, Anglo-Celtic Male No More?", *Meanjin*, 42.1 (1983), pp. 34–41.

24 See Sue Higgins, "Breaking the Rules: New Fiction by Australian Women", *Meanjin*, 34.4 (1975), pp. 415–20; Susan Higgins and Jill Matthews, "For the Record: Feminist Publications in Australia Since 1975", *Meanjin*, 38.3 (1979), pp. 321–33.

25 K.G. Hamilton, ed. (Brisbane: Australian Studies Centre of the University of Queensland, 1978).

26 Quoted in Jennifer Ellison, *Rooms of Their Own* (Melbourne: Penguin, 1986), p. 57.

27 Beverley Farmer, quoted in Kristin Hammett, "Beverley Farmer: A Retrospective", *Southerly*, 56.1 (1996), p. 97.

28 Geoffrey Dutton, "Return What is Hungrily Given", *Australian Book Review*, 119 (1990), p. 11.

29 Paul Salzman, "Talking/Listening: Anecdotal Style in Recent Australian Women's Fiction", *Southerly*, 49.4 (1989), pp. 539–552.

30 Cited in Kerryn Goldsworthy, *Helen Garner* (Melbourne: Oxford University Press, 1996), p. 63.

31 Wilding, "Tabloid Story", pp. 305–306.

32 Winton has said "[w]e do have a strong oral tradition in Australia, and that is a tremendous advantage to us as storytellers", in David Butstone, "Spinning Stories and Visions", *Sojourners*, 21.8, 1992, p. 21.

33 Beth Watzke, "'Where Pigs Speak in Tongues and Angels Come and Go': A Conversation with Tim Winton", *Antipodes*, December (1991), p. 97.

8

MAY-BRIT AKERHOLT

New stages: contemporary theatre

THE SHAPING OF A THEATRE

As the German philosopher G.W.F. Hegel said, "those who don't know the past are bound to repeat it". A great body of Australian drama has been written in the last two centuries, but the repertoire of Australian plays is still relatively small, partly because the dramatic canon is rarely revived. Theatres have instead been encouraged by audiences and funding bodies constantly to renew themselves. This has led to a tendency to stage a catalogue of productions without any sense of the traditions to which the plays belonged, or the larger context in which they were written. Australian drama has kept re-inventing itself without forging a theatrical culture.

But before there is a repertoire there has to be a tradition. First of all, Australian theatre had to be invented. The task of chronicling a country, a psyche, an identity from an apparent *tabula rasa* was an intimidating one, as the poet Judith Wright points out. She also argues that the perception of living in an "upside-down hut" caused a sense of disconnection which stifled creative development through "death by apathy".[1] That the language of drama was that of British and American theatre did not help the feeling of inferiority from which the phrase "cultural cringe" was coined. This inherent suspicion of inadequacy is brilliantly satirised in David Williamson's *Don's Party*: "[My prick] isn't small. I just think it is."

A handful of plays, and particularly Ray Lawler's *Summer of the Seventeenth Doll* (1955), marked the end of the well-made play modelled on a British template, and the rise of a drama uniquely Australian in its theatrical language. The immediate and enduring success of the *Doll* proved it was possible to write a local drama with characters as worthy of being mythologised as any Willy Loman. The play's structure and form may be in the tradition of British naturalism, but language and characterisation embody an Australian idiosyncrasy: the immense potential for fertile imagination in conflict with a fear of expressing it. The language dramatises the fusion of irony and understatement, laconic tone and colourful idiom, which defines the vernacular. The unexplored possibilities of language, and the perils of ignoring them, become virtually another "character" in the *Doll*.

Thus a contemporary Australian drama was born out of the British traditions it had so long emulated, borrowing only what was needed to create a tradition of its own. Playwrights have continued to cultivate forms of what may be called "heightened naturalism" and "symbolic realism" in the theatre. The Australian film industry owes much to this tradition. From David Williamson's social satires to Louis Nowra's distilled comedies and Hannie Rayson's domestic dramas, its various strengths have been exploited on the screen. Williamson, Australia's most popular playwright for more than three decades, has written screen versions of a series of his dramas, including *The Club, Travelling North, Emerald City* and *Brilliant Lies*, as well as other film scripts. Nowra's plays *Così* and *Radiance*, and Rayson's *Hotel Sorrento*, became award-winning films, as did Gordon Graham's *The Boys* and the group-devised *Strictly Ballroom*.

The Australian film director Bruce Beresford once said, "A country has to portray itself. Otherwise, what are we?" The big question in Australian drama in the 1960s was not only what but *who are we*? The end of the decade spawned a critical yet celebratory theatre which sought to explore Australian identity and build a new confidence by suggesting that we might, after all, live in a "right-side up hut". The Vietnam War reinforced that we were no longer an idyllic island in the South Pacific, a colony succoured by a European monarch and her government. Playwrights and other theatre artists created works which, directly or indirectly, probed the effects of world events on Australian society, and set their country in a historical and political context.

The search for a more diverse theatrical scene was encouraged by several significant developments. One of the most important was the New Wave movement, a group of theatre workers mostly associated with the Australian Performing Group (APG), first at La Mama and then at the Pram Factory, two converted factory venues in the Melbourne suburb of Carlton. Born in the late 1960s out of opposition to a culturally conservative theatre, the New Wave provided an alternative drama which exploited the vernacular and experimented with forms and structures in an in-your-face exploration of Australian myths and rituals. They created a political and popular drama, consciously, deliberately histrionic. Writers took up the traditions of Commedia dell'arte and pantomime and, like Patrick White before them, borrowed from vaudeville and music hall. They took to the streets with their shows during the Vietnam moratoria, and performed in factories and other workplaces to reach new audiences. The creative cooperation between playwright, director and actors took a significant turn, and young theatre artists were able to cut their teeth on new works and ambitious performance projects.

Two other factors played a major role in changing the face of Australian theatre. One was the increasing contribution of writers from non-English speaking backgrounds, and the theatre companies formed to present their work. The other was the beginnings of an Aboriginal and Torres Strait Islander theatre, written, directed and performed by Indigenous artists, who developed a unique theatrical language to present Aboriginal concerns, traditions and cultures. Whereas before everything had been fitted into the same straitjacket of theatrical conventions and expectations, our drama now began to reflect a more complex and diverse society. By the end of the twentieth century, Indigenous and multicultural drama were part of mainstream theatre and also had their own national festivals.[2]

Other events shaping the arts were the major international arts festivals held in Adelaide, Perth, Melbourne and Sydney, accompanied by the fringe festivals' more risky and radical programming. Another major arts affair, the Sydney Gay and Lesbian Mardi Gras Festival, offers a month of theatre, exhibitions and other entertainments culminating in the famous, or for a vociferous few, infamous, Mardi Gras Parade and Party. After growing up on a monotonous diet of Terence Rattigan and Noel Coward, within a relatively short time Australian audiences were being offered a disparate, challenging and at times even exotic fare.

Few Australian works had been performed overseas before the *Doll* won the London *Evening Standard* prize for best play in 1957. Since the 70s, international touring has played an active part in the development of a confident Australian theatre. David Williamson's *The Removalists*, in a Royal Court production, repeated the *Doll*'s achievement by taking out the *Evening Standard* award for most promising playwright in 1973. Williamson's *Don's Party* was also performed at Royal Court (1975), by an Australian cast directed by Michael Blakemore. *The Elocution of Benjamin Franklin* by Steve J. Spears, one of the first "gay plays" to achieve mainstream status, had a six-month season in London after it toured Australia in 1976. It also played in Los Angeles and New York, where Spears won an Obie for best play in an off-Broadway production, Gordon Chater took out the Obie for best actor and Richard Wherrett for best direction. A number of Indigenous works have also been seen internationally. Robert Merritt's *The Cake Man*, the first Aboriginal play to be published, was performed by the Australian Aboriginal Theatre Company at the World Theatre Festival in Colorado in 1982. Fittingly, Mudrooroo's *The*

Aboriginal Protesters Confront the Proclamation of the Australian Republic on 26 January 2001, in which an Aboriginal theatre ensemble performs Heine Müller's *The Commission – Memory of a Revolution*, travelled to Germany in 1997.

CHANGES IN INFRASTRUCTURE

Institutions

Evolutions in infrastructure and support systems were crucial to the development of a contemporary Australian theatre. The most important of many initiatives was the formation of the Australia Council in 1968, the federal government's arts advisory body which displaced the Australian Elizabethan Theatre Trust as the main funding organisation for the performing arts. OzCo, as it is affectionately known, was welcomed as an official acknowledgement that we needed people with imagination and creativity to tell our stories and mythologise our lives; or, more importantly, to redefine the no longer valid myths of a white colonisation and create new myths out of the old. Government support at federal and state levels meant that writers, actors and directors could become professional rather than part-time practitioners, and that an increased number of playwrights could write for a living. It invigorated a theatre culture riding on a merry-go-round of British well-made plays and popular overseas entertainments. Most importantly, it gave theatre practitioners licence to take artistic risks, to experiment, and to fail and try again.

The foundation of drama schools also played a major role in fostering a theatre performed, directed, designed and produced locally. However, students were taught to speak with a neutral British accent, acknowledged as the only acceptable stage language, even in Australian works. It was not until the late 1960s that actors could start using their natural voices on our stages, and resistance to this from conservative factions went on for some time.

Australia's first professional theatre school, the National Institute of Dramatic Art (NIDA), was established in 1959 with funding from the University of New South Wales. An interesting connection was made with the profession when NIDA's founding father, Professor Robert Quentin, established the Old Tote Theatre Company on campus, which functioned as a "state" theatre company until 1978 and gave employment to a large number of NIDA graduates. In 1966, Quentin and NIDA teacher and later director John Clark set up Jane Street Theatre which operated as an alternative space until 1981, premiering a series of works by Australian playwrights. Famous graduates include Mel Gibson, Geoffrey Rush, Cate Blanchett, Baz Luhrmann, and Judy Davis, who played Juliet to Gibson's Romeo in an acclaimed 1976 student production.

NIDA is still considered the national drama school, but has serious competition from the Victorian College of the Arts (VCA), founded in Melbourne in 1976, and Perth's Western Australian Academy of Performing Arts (WAAPA, 1979). All offer a three-year degree course in acting, while other courses, such as design, technical production, playwriting and directing, differ in length and structure in each institution. WAAPA is the only school with a degree course in Musical Theatre.

In 1969, translator, teacher and director Rex Cramphorn founded the Performance Syndicate, a research and performance organisation devoted to helping actors develop and refine their skills. Operating until 1975, it played a pivotal role in stimulating the growth of Australian theatre and motivating theatre artists to seek out new challenges. Persistently pushing boundaries and experimenting with style, form and theatrical expression, Cramphorn taught and inspired a whole generation of theatre workers, as well as researchers and scholars through his relationship with Sydney University's French Department and Centre for Performance Studies.

Publishing Australian plays exclusively, Currency Press (1971) is the enterprise of the eminent critic Katharine Brisbane and her late husband, academic, dramaturg and theatre historian Philip Parsons. Their commitment, devotion and tenacity have been instrumental in the creation of a vital and confident Australian theatre. Not only were plays made more readily available to companies, performing artists and a reading public, but they were perceived as worthy of being published, sold in bookshops, read, performed. Currency Press stimulated interest in the history of Australian drama and contributed to the increase in productions of local work. In 1996 the company launched its crowning effort, the *Companion to Theatre in Australia*, edited by Parsons with Victoria Chance.

Another crucial event occurred in May 1973 with the inaugural National Playwrights' Conference at the Australian National University in Canberra; among the founding members were Katharine Brisbane and the Aboriginal actor and director Brian Syron. Since then, the annual Playwrights' Conference has played a significant role in the fostering and promotion of new Australian drama. A considerable number of playwrights have had their work developed at the Conference, which also offers intensive writing workshops and craft seminars. The Australian National Playwrights' Centre (ANPC) was established in 1989 to run the Conference and offer year-round dramaturgy programs, playwriting courses, and special projects for young writers.

Theatre companies

With writers and other theatre artists increasingly becoming an established part of the nation's cultural life, federal and local governments became more alert to the fact that non-commercial theatre gave employment to a large number of people and could even boost the tourist and hospitality industries. There was clearly a need for more subsidised companies, and for buildings to house these companies. "Serious" theatre, not just commercial blockbusters and imported comedies, had become big business, and was given the equipment to operate as such – professionally, albeit still frugally. The growth of state theatre companies paralleled the building of larger cultural centres. Australia's oldest state theatre organisation, Melbourne Theatre Company (MTC from 1968), performed in older city venues until it became the "resident" company of the new Victorian Arts Centre from 1984, with use of The Playhouse and the George Fairfax Theatre.[3] The State Theatre of South Australia (STSA, 1965) was invited to perform in The Playhouse and The Space in the Adelaide Festival Centre from 1974. Queensland Theatre Company (QTC, 1970) produced their work in the large SGIO Theatre in the central business district and later opened the new Cremorne Theatre before moving into the Queensland Performing Arts Complex in 1993. In New South Wales, the Old Tote became the resident company in the Drama Theatre of Sydney Opera House in 1973. When it ceased operations, the Sydney Theatre Company (STC, 1980) was established, with Richard Wherrett as its first Artistic Director. In 1984, the STC moved into its own building, The Wharf, a converted shipping warehouse on the other side of the Harbour Bridge from the Opera House. By the late 1990s, STC was the largest company in the country, with 20,000 subscribers to its annual seasons of plays.

MTC has premiered a large number of new Australian works, including *Summer of the Seventeenth Doll* and the *Doll Trilogy* (the *Doll*, *Kid Stakes* and *Other Times*), and was the first to demonstrate the commercial as well as artistic success of our own drama. QTC's Aubrey Mellor (Artistic Director 1988–1993) adopted a policy of presenting fifty percent Australian works in each season, including one by a Queensland writer. In Wherrett's first ten years at the STC, over forty percent of the company's work was Australian.

A variety of smaller companies and theatre spaces sprang up in the late 1960s and early 1970s, offering an alternative to the established theatre. One of the first important venues was La Mama, which has nurtured, motivated and inspired a great number of theatre artists since it was founded in 1967 by the legendary Betty Burstall. Based on the principles of New

York's La Mama, it provided a space for innovative and experimental shows, and offered an environment free of the burdens of box-office and critical reception. La Mama encouraged an effective collaboration between playwrights, directors and actors which changed the perception of hierarchy in the theatre and fostered a more collaborative approach. Run by the long-standing director Liz Jones, it is still home to numerous productions of new works every year, presented by cooperative companies or teams.

The Nimrod Theatre Company was founded on similar principles in 1970 in an old stable in Sydney's Kings Cross. It presented challenging and innovative theatre which soon drew larger audiences than the tiny Stables could accommodate; four years later the company moved to a renovated salt factory in Belvoir Street, Surry Hills. The company's role in the evolution of a confident Australian theatre was far reaching. It was dedicated to a strong repertoire of new Australian works, a radical re-interpretation of the classics, and to supporting emerging theatre artists in the development of their art and craft. It established a writer-in-residence scheme, offered young directors professional opportunities, and was active in the actors' struggle to use their natural accents rather than having to play everything in an artificial Queen's English.

When Nimrod moved to the larger Seymour Centre[4] in 1984, the profession rallied to save their old premises for the arts. A syndicate of more than 650 shareholders created Company B at the Belvoir Street Theatre. Neil Armfield was appointed Company B's first Artistic Director in 1995. Through exploring a variety of forms of theatrical storytelling and presenting a balanced program of small-scale and epic productions drawing on diverse cultural influences, Company B has built a nation-wide reputation for the quality and daring of its productions.

The tradition of theatre ensembles has never taken root in Australia, mainly for financial reasons. Since 1995, Company B has endeavoured to establish a core ensemble of theatre artists for its productions. Armfield has fought for this since becoming part of Jim Sharman's Lighthouse Company, the name the State Theatre of South Australia was known by from 1982–84. Sharman established a dynamic ensemble of twelve actors working with a small group of writers, directors and other theatre artists. Lighthouse gave young directors such as Armfield the opportunity to stage major works in a creative and supportive environment; it commissioned new Australian translations of foreign plays; and fostered new works which have contributed significantly to the Australian repertoire.

Another company working with a core group of artists was Australian Nouveau Theatre (Anthill, 1981–92), founded by French immigrant Jean-Pierre Mignon at a small converted church in South Melbourne. He developed a non-naturalistic style of performance, scheduled new Australian plays of a poetic or stylised nature, and "re-invented" the classics with theatrically imaginative interpretations. His expressionistic version of *Summer of the Seventeenth Doll*, a work epitomising Australian naturalism, was a landmark; it enhanced the play's themes by revealing their symbolic nature and emphasising what the characters fail to say or do. Its author Ray Lawler is said to have stated that this production exposed the play's true nature.

Smaller but significant companies concentrated on new Australian plays exclusively. In the early 1980s, Rex Cramphorn revived the flagging fortunes of Victoria's Playbox Theatre Centre with a bold program which brought audiences back to the theatre. Playbox has become the second major company in Melbourne through the consistent work of Carillo Gantner and his successor Aubrey Mellor. Griffin Theatre Company in Sydney and La Boite Theatre in Brisbane premiered a number of works throughout the 1980s which have since entered our repertoire. All three companies run regular public readings of plays in development, and put resources, energy and professionalism into fostering new works for performance.

The most successful professional Aboriginal theatre company is Kooemba Jdarra Indigenous Performing Arts in Brisbane, which has produced a series of Indigenous works under the leadership of Wesley Enoch and his successors Lafe Charlton and Nadine McDonald. Enoch directed the acclaimed one-woman show *7 Stages of Grieving*, which he co-wrote with the work's performer Deborah Mailman. It toured nationally for nearly two years and was performed at the 1997 Edinburgh Festival. In 1999, Kooemba Jdarra co-produced *Romeo and Juliet* with La Boite, with white actors performing the Montagues and black actors the Capulets, "to symbolise reconciliation as a process and not just an act".[5] Another company of note is Yirra Yaakin Noongar Theatre (Artistic Director David Milroy), formed in Perth in 1993 to provide training programs for Aboriginal artists in key decision-making positions, and to present a program of professional Indigenous theatre each year.

Other companies established with a specific agenda include the Per-for-mance Space in Sydney, with a credo to support and present visual, sound and movement-based projects rather than texted drama. Melbourne Workers' Theatre (1987) functioned initially as a link between theatre and trade unionism; its program was extended to include a wider community, with productions of Aboriginal plays, and plays written for and by prisoners and sex workers. Vitalstatistix was founded in Adelaide in 1984 to cater for women's writing and has been instrumental in training female directors, designers and lighting designers as well as writers. Despite some opposition to the idea of a subsidised company which exclusively performed non-

Australian works, actor and director John Bell founded the Bell Shakespeare Company in 1991. The company has steadily prospered, with Bell directing (and often acting in) the majority of the productions. However, it is now also attracting guest directors of the repute of Jim Sharman, Steven Berkoff and Barrie Kosky.

PUTTING A COUNTRY ON THE STAGE

Patrick White, Australia's only Nobel Prize winner in Literature, had four plays produced between 1961 and 1964. His drama influenced a number of the playwrights and directors who were to shape our theatre in the next two decades. Having already caused some controversy by showing Australians disturbing images of themselves in his novels, White created a symbolic, ritualistic and satirical theatre which exposed the Australian way of life as a Procrustean bed where everything was measured against the known, tried and accepted. He became the first playwright to seriously challenge the strong traditions of Australian conventional theatre, and dignified and celebrated the Australian vernacular by transforming it into a fertile, vigorous and imaginative stage language.

The Ham Funeral was written in London in 1947, but remained unproduced until John Tasker directed it for the Adelaide University Theatre Guild in 1961.[6] European influences are evident in the play's extensive use of expressionistic devices to portray inner states, with the characters' thoughts and visions taking living, verbal forms. White's fondness for music hall and vaudeville is expressed in the Scavengers, two tattered, eccentric choric figures of tarnished splendour and dignified gutter existence who devour life from dustbins. The four Relatives are a more sinister chorus; funeral ham-eaters who have come to have a "dig at the livin'". Despite an enthusiastic reception, The Ham Funeral did not come to life again in the mainstream theatre until Neil Armfield directed an acclaimed production for Sydney Theatre Company in 1989.

Within a year of The Ham Funeral, White had written his second full-length play. The Season at Sarsaparilla (1962) is an ironic exposure of the sterile patterns of Australian suburban life, with the characters existing in a Beckett-like predicament in Mildred Street's near-identical boxes.[7] Jim Sharman's neo-surreal 1976 revival in the Drama Theatre of Sydney's Opera House created a renewed interest in White's dramatic works. White showed his enthusiasm by writing his first play for thirteen years, Big Toys (1977), a dark comedy of radical manners.

Sharman and Neil Armfield were together responsible for the renewed popularity of White's drama and for his picking up the theatrical pen again.

Sharman's revival of *A Cheery Soul* (1963) broke all box-office records in the Drama Theatre in 1979. In a memorable entrance, Robyn Nevin as the cheerful do-gooder exploded down the stairs leading to the stage from the back of the auditorium in a flurry of suitcases, her cackling laughter breaking the serenity of the Custances' kitchen. In 1996 Armfield re-staged *Night on Bald Mountain* (1964), White's effort at an Australian tragedy in a classic form. The caustic humour, melodrama and tragic events of the play were all performed to the hilt in a production which exposed the raw emotions and the high stakes of the characters.

The Lighthouse Company presented two world premieres of White's plays, *Netherwood* (1983) and *Signal Driver* (1982). Armfield directed three productions of the latter in different states, each incorporating new ideas and changes which created fascinating shifts of perspective. The story is told over thirty years at a bus-stop, where a husband and wife, the Vokes, repeatedly try to leave each other, but somehow never manage to signal the driver. In dramatising the rituals and rites we fill our lives with and the worship we offer up to meaningless "gods", White's plays are wonderful satires on the voices we refuse to listen to, the visions and dreams we ignore. They convey some of White's grave concerns about the apathy of Australian society and our responsibility as citizens of the world, in their inherent warnings about the danger of world politics, the misuse of power, and the threat of nuclear war.

Playwright, poet and novelist Dorothy Hewett was strongly influenced by White's drama as well as New Wave writers. She created a fertile and colourful theatre, full of poetry, song and music, and with characters who challenge society's restrictions and conventions. In 1971 *The Chapel Perilous* confronted audiences with a questing female Sir Lancelot, who not only wants to "walk naked through the world", but does it. The text combines poetic with colloquial language, is full of songs and poems, and includes giant authoritarian masked figures, caricatures of insular and bureaucratic minds. The play provoked a range of responses, from praise to outrage, but its critics tended to overlook that, while the protagonist Sally Banner is drawn with passion, conviction and celebration, there is also a deal of irony in the characterisation.

The Chapel Perilous was first produced by the New Fortune Theatre in Perth, but was soon banned in Western Australia.[8] Ironically, a few years later Perth's National Theatre commissioned Hewett's most popular work, *The Man from Mukinupin* (1979), for the sesquicentennial celebrations of Western Australia. It is an abundant epic celebrating a dried-out wheatbelt town "east of the rabbit proof fence" through folk songs, dance, mythical rites and a profusion of literary allusions. Heroine Polly of the "vieux rose" bedroom is the epitome of an Australia entrenched in European culture and decorum. Polly's Aboriginal half-sister Touch of the Tar (played by the same actress), a displaced person in her own country, is both the song and the colour of the nation, and its conscience and guilt. But she is a double figure in herself. While Touch of the Tar holds out her arms to the rain "like a fertility rite", she also puts up a ragged social parasol to ward off the fertile forces of nature.

Like Hewett, many writers in the New Wave movement were stimulated by White's challenge to conventional theatre. The New Wave aimed to create a drama that was "rough, relevant and ribald ... a theatre of accessibility that is above all Australian in theme and substance, a theatre of the populace that deals with legendary figures and events, perennial and idiosyncratic rituals, mythically implanted in the nation's consciousness".[9] A theatre was born which not only embraced relevant and large, even epic, issues but searched for new forms in which to express them.

John Romeril's *Chicago, Chicago* (1969) is an evocative, surreal piece dramatising an American society rushing towards self-destruction and insanity. It established him as one of the key figures of the New Wave, and especially the Australian Performing Group, which operated on Marxist principles in which the "collective imagination" of the theatre workers was shaped and articulated through the specific skills of the playwright. Romeril's interest in Asian theatre and Australia's relationship to the South Pacific region has resulted in several plays, including *The Floating World* (1974) in which Les Harding, a former prisoner of war of the Japanese, and his wife Irene embark on the "Women's Weekly Cherry Blossom Cruise" to Japan. The work's adventurous structure and imaginative form skilfully frame and support the story of how the two countries have dealt with the aftermath of war. In the original Pram Factory production, the audience was seated in a big wire cage within the performance space. They were unable to distance themselves from Les Harding's steady spiralling into madness, his wife Irene's comi-tragic unawareness, the ship entertainer's stand-up comedy acts, and the invasive, persistent rituals of ship routine. A more glamorous production with added demons in Kabuki costumes was co-directed by Richard Wherrett and Wayne Harrison for Sydney Theatre Company in 1986. Performed on the wide Drama Theatre stage, the audience was connected to the characters and the "ship" by a gangway leading into the auditorium.[10] Romeril is one of the few New Wave writers who continue to contribute significantly to the contemporary theatre. Later works include *Love's Suicide* (1997), another excursion into Australian–Asian relations, and *Xpo – The Human Factor* (1998), which explores how the international 1988 Expo in Brisbane engulfed people's lives and changed the city.

The critic Eunice Hanger claimed that, while traditionally theatre has always been searching for the hero, "it is traditional in the nature of the 'typical Australian' (if he exists) that he should prick the bubbles of the pretentious and so tumble what could be tragedy into the mood of laughter".[11] This is closely linked with another "tradition": the suspicion that eloquence and the articulation of emotion are synonymous with insincerity (as dramatised in the *Doll*) and authoritarian figures (historically the "enemy" of Australian principles and way of life). These are contributing factors to the penchant for the ironic and aggressive treatment of language, a dominant element of Australian theatre since it stopped imitating the British.

Nowhere is the "anti-hero" more prominently and fondly characterised – and satirised – and the Australian vernacular so eloquently displayed than in the work of Jack Hibberd, who was also a major player in the Australian Performing Group. His dramatic dialogue is both exuberantly vulgar and defiantly sophisticated. His eye for spotting the ludicrous in social rites is given full range in the robust wedding farce *Dimboola* (1969), and the now classical mono-drama *A Stretch of the Imagination* (1972). Its character Monk O'Neill lives as a hermit in a dilapidated shack on One Tree Hill, a metaphor for a barren Australia made vigorous through the character's imagination and versatile language. Monk himself is opinionated, prejudiced, garrulous, with a proclivity for telling tall stories.

Although David Williamson's first plays grew out of the New Wave movement, he quickly withdrew from what he felt was a stifling, anti-creative ideology of group decisions and "Maoist power play". His output has been prodigious, with a new work nearly every year for more than three decades, a number of films and several television series. His social satires soon gained enormous popularity and by the mid-1970s they were performed nationally and internationally. Williamson's work, especially the early plays, captures the rhetoric of the middle class and punctures the pretentious with accuracy and irony. He defines and exposes his characters with startling clarity, but refrains from judging them, and his satire is thus less uncomfortable than that of White and Romeril.

In 1971, Williamson produced two key works. *The Removalists*, a hard-hitting black comedy about abuse of power on domestic and institutional levels, premiered at La Mama, was picked up by Nimrod Theatre Company, and toured nationally for several months before it opened in London. *Don's Party* is a contemporary comedy of manners set on the eve of the 1969 federal election. The characters are thirty-something professionals who retain the leftist jargon of their youthful idealism while indulging in middle-class affluence. As they group and re-group in infantile sexual games, Williamson unmasks their affectations, illiberal antics and indifference to the political nature of the evening. It had productions at the Pram Factory, NIDA's Jane Street Theatre and the Parade, followed by national and international tours.

Each new Williamson play is scheduled by two or three companies before it is even written, with box-office returns virtually guaranteed. For instance, *Dead White Males* (1995), a send-up of contemporary critical theory in which William Shakespeare makes a guest appearance, enjoyed an extended season in Sydney's Opera House before it toured the country, only to return to Sydney for another season of packed houses. But despite his success, Williamson has fought a constant battle with the critics, claiming there is an unaccountable division between critical reception and audience popularity.

Alex Buzo achieved great popularity as a satirist in the early days of his career. He exulted in dissecting the foibles and vanities of his society, cruelly exposing the rhetoric and affectations of social *poseurs*. His first play, *Norm and Ahmed* (1968), is a chilling and timely two-hander dealing with the complex issues of xenophobia. It was followed by *Rooted* (1969), a savage exposition of an immoral society which discards its best elements, and *The Front Room Boys* (1969), a ruthless comedy about office culture. *Coralie Lansdowne Says No* (1974) depicts an affluent middle class whose code of speech and behaviour isolates and alienates them, finally also from their own selves.

THE SECOND SURGE

As Australian society grew more complex and less isolated, writers began to explode the borders of Australia, setting the country in a larger geographical as well as historical context. Romeril's *The Floating World* inaugurated a contemporary theatre which became increasingly preoccupied with the past – distant and recent – and with other worlds and cultures. This is reflected in the early works of Louis Nowra, who came to prominence with *Inner Voices* in 1977, a parable of Australian contemporary life set in eighteenth-century Russia. Its main character Ivan VI has spent his life in isolation without the opportunity to develop reasoned argument. When proclaimed King, his only voice is one echoing a pair of scheming opportunists – outer voices. In the end, Ivan is again alone, listening to a mixture of his own inner voices and a cacophony of outer sounds.

After two more plays with international settings, Nowra turned his attention directly to Australia in *Inside the Island* (1980). While the action takes place in 1912, the play's main preoccupation is the devastating effects of two centuries of colonisation on Nowra's contemporary society. In a striking theatrical metaphor, soldiers, crazed from wheat poisoned by the landowner's greed and indifference, embark on atrocious acts of self-mutilation and destruction. They burn down property and crops, rape and murder the landowner's daughter (youth and future), and kill a musician (creativity and art). Nowra maintained this focus in *The Golden Age* (1985), based on the alleged discovery in the early 1940s of a group of white Europeans lost for three generations in the Tasmanian wilderness. Suffering from genetic degeneration and using a bastardised form of dialect, they are interned in an asylum, as the authorities fear they will add fuel to Hitler's racial theories. Exposed to the destructive science and patronising benevolence of the twentieth century, the group, inevitably, dies out.

Stephen Sewell arrived as an angry and politically passionate playwright in 1977 with *The Father We Loved on a Beach by the Sea*, a family play with an overt and ambitious political argument. But, like Romeril and Nowra, Sewell extended the question "who are we" to "who and what are we in the world?" and turned his considerable powers as a writer towards a larger world with his next play, *Traitors* (1979). First performed at Melbourne's Pram Factory, *Traitors* had six productions during the following year, including one in London. Set in Leningrad and Moscow in 1927, it explores the disintegration of the Russian Revolution and the rise of Stalinism, and asks how "ideological splits ... could lead to such a deadly and systematic betrayal of the struggle for social change".[12] *Welcome the Bright World* (1982) takes place in post-war Berlin, but the themes of the effects of science on contemporary society, from governments to the individual, are of universal relevance and a warning to Australians that their isolated position offers only illusionary protection against world affairs.

From then on, however, Sewell became involved with events at home. One of Australia's most powerful contemporary plays, *The Blind Giant is Dancing*, was commissioned and performed by the Lighthouse Company in 1983. It exposes corruption at different levels of government through the eroding effects of pragmatic politics and the right-wing push in the Labor Party on principles of truth, and on an individual level, the betrayal of love and loyalty. A sell-out revival of the play at Belvoir St. Theatre in 1996 proved its continued relevance and enduring nature.

Part of the strength of Sewell's political plays is the vitality with which he portrays the more intimate family scenes and integrates them with the larger political themes. In *Hate* (1988) the family takes centre stage in a story in which passionate and tortuous characters inexorably damage themselves through elaborate games of manipulation. In its furious emotions, *Hate* is reminiscent of the plays of Eugene O'Neill, as is *The Sick Room* (1999) which, inspired by a Munch painting, explodes family myths through the conflicts which arise at the deathbed of a young girl.

The early 1980s was a time of consolidation of past achievements and, with it, an increasing faith in the future. However, while Australian theatre continued to grow, the "cultural cringe" was still operating as a negative force on the creative imagination. Michael Gow's *Europe* (1987), a deceptively simple two-hander about an affair between an Australian man and a European actress, is a complex examination of Australian attitudes towards a continent steeped in centuries of tradition and confident in its cultural values and significance. During 1986–87, Gow wrote three major plays, *Europe, On Top of the World* (1986) and *Away* (1986), in a short and intense burst of creativity. Together with the novelist David Malouf's only play, *Blood Relations* (1987), and works by Alma De Groen, *Away* made an assured transition into a local drama which borrows from other sources and genres, experimenting with intertextuality and postmodernist structures. The richness of the text, its subtext and resonances, and its examination of contemporary local issues through the use of *King Lear* and *A Midsummer Night's Dream*, created a sophisticated work that lends itself to a variety of interpretations.

Alma De Groen's theatre creates "other" worlds through the use of innovative forms and heightened language, although always formalised and controlled in structure and expression. *Rivers of China* (1987), which dramatises contemporary society in the context of other eras and cultures, has achieved the status of a modern classic. The play is an experiment in dramatic dialogue and composition in its juxtaposition of past, present and future, and historical and fictionalised characters. *The Woman in the Window* (1998) explores a future time in which literature, indeed most art, is suppressed in the name of technology and political control; this world is set in relief with Stalin's Russia through a focus on the poet Anna Akhmatova who lived under house arrest for her "criminal" art.

Another writer whose career steadily rose throughout the 1980s is Nick Enright, who became a household name overnight with an impertinent musical version of Goldoni's *The Venetian Twins* (1979). It was followed by a series of plays exploring the influence of a Catholic upbringing, and a light comedy, *Daylight Saving* (1990), whose success, according to Enright, allowed him to write as he really wanted. The award-winning *Property of the Clan* (1992) is based on the rape and murder of a teenage girl during a youth party on a Newcastle beach. *Blackrock* (1995), the "adult" version of the play written for Sydney Theatre Company, lacks the strong focus and convincing characterisation of *Property*, but did extremely well and was adapted to film by the author. Enright's musical *The Boy from Oz*, about the life of Australian singer and performer Peter Allen, and with characters including Liza Minnelli and Judy Garland, had long seasons in Sydney and other major cities in 1998–99.

Unlike those of Enright, Daniel Keene's plays are rarely performed by commercial and state companies. However, Keene has had considerable influence on developments in Australian theatre since the 1980s. Most of his works have had multiple productions, being performed in all major cities, with several produced overseas. He is a versatile writer whose themes range from the highly personal, in claustrophobic, intense dramas such as *The Hour Before My Brother Dies* (1985) and *Low* (1992), to the strongly political in *Because You Are Mine* (1994), a harrowing piece on faith, courage and loss set in war-torn Bosnia. Among his best work is *Cho Cho San* (1984), based on the themes of Belasco's *Madame Butterfly*. First produced by Handspan Visual Theatre in Melbourne before touring to most states, the story is told through dialogue and music and performed by a mixture of actors and puppets.

TOWARDS THE BICENTENARY

By the time Australia got ready to celebrate its Bicentenary in 1988, the country had grown into a society of contradictions which could no longer be defined by the clichés and stereotypes of a few decades earlier. Three areas of theatre had developed rapidly as part of social and political changes, and played a role, if not in causing change, at least in influencing it.

Multicultural theatre

A number of writers with multicultural backgrounds were exploring Australian stories from new perspectives and often in the context of other countries and cultures. *Too Young for Ghosts* (1985) by Janis Balodis was produced by three state theatre companies within a short space of time. An intriguing story about a small group of Latvians who emigrate to Australia from the war camps of Europe, the action moves back and forth between two continents, and takes excursions into a past Australia by juxtaposing the trials of the explorer Leichhardt with the Latvian story. It forms *The Ghosts Trilogy* (published 1997) with *No Going Back* and *My Father's Father*.

Multicultural companies were beginning to attract audiences and interest beyond their cultural groups. Teresa Crea, founder of Teatro Doppio in Adelaide, presented a series of works based on Italian stories, with the use of bilingual dialogue forming part of the meaning as well as the concept of the performances. Teatro Doppio has continued to be a strong force in Australia's theatre, touring performances of Anglo-Italian works from its base in Adelaide. In the late 1980s Polish-born and raised Bogdan Koca began producing plays, often written, directed and designed by himself, on a cooperative basis with a small group of performers of diverse backgrounds, developing a particular "European" production style suited to his works. He founded Sydney Art Theatre in 1998, a company mostly presenting foreign-language plays rarely seen in Australia.

Aboriginal theatre

A significant achievement of the 1980s was the consolidation of an Indigenous drama. Although Aboriginal performance builds on tens of thousands of years of traditions and rituals, text-based theatre was a relatively new art form – the first written Aboriginal play, Kevin Gilbert's *The Cherry Pickers*, appeared in 1968. As late as 1990 the writer and critic Mudrooroo claimed that there was still no escape from the standard realism and limitations of the conventional European theatre into a theatre of Aboriginality which "utilises the Aboriginal environment of ceremony to recreate a symbolic drama drawing heavily on traditional structures".[13] However, there is no doubt that Aboriginal theatre has developed a form which explores its own voice and separateness of vision. Indigenous writers merge Western forms of theatre with Aboriginal spirituality, ceremony and rituals to create highly idiosyncratic storytelling which uses a mixture of Australian English, Aboriginal English and expressions from the writers' tribal languages.[14]

In 1975 actor and director Bob Maza led a team at the National Black Theatre in Sydney's inner-city suburb of Redfern in developing and presenting Robert Merritt's *The Cake Man*. This production continued to evolve and, in 1982, the Australian Aboriginal Theatre Company performed it at the World Theatre Festival in Colorado to an enthusiastic reception. That year, Jack Davis, poet and playwright, truly put Indigenous writing for performance on the theatrical map with *The Dreamers*, set in the 1970s kitchen of an Aboriginal family and dealing with the poverty and confusion created by their sense of displacement and the clash of cultures. It forms the second play in the poignant and profoundly moving trilogy *The First-Born*, which opens with *No Sugar* (1985), whose action portrays the forced removal of Aboriginal Australians from their lands to supervised native settlements during the depression of the 1930s. The third play, *Barungin (Smell the Wind)* (1988), is an Aboriginal *J'accuse* about the poverty, alcoholism and deaths in custody caused by white treatment of black Australia. It is ironically and deliberately set in the Bicentenary year of 1988, when most Aborigines mourned 200 years of white colonisation. That was also the year the Perth-based Marli Biyol Theatre Company embarked on a national tour with the trilogy. In Melbourne, it was performed in an inner-city town hall with the audience surrounding the set on all sides, and moving to different locations with each play. The sense of being included in the stories, even participating in the characters' lives, made it impossible to feel distant from the action and resulted in a strong political as well as theatrical event. While Davis' work is conventionally Western in structure and characterisation, it achieves a distinctly Indigenous theatrical style through the use of Nyoongah language and Aboriginal symbols, rituals and dance.

In 1990, Perth's Black Swan Theatre Company premiered the first Aboriginal musical, *Bran Nue Dae* by Jimmy Chi and Kuckles, followed in 1996 with *Corrugation Road* by the same team.[15] Both works have toured major cities and, more importantly, a large number of country centres and small towns throughout Australia, where they reach new audiences. The Introduction to the published version of *Bran Nue Dae* suggests its highly political nature: "This is a story of how someone found his uncle and a whole lot besides. Since white settlement of the country, Australians have looked on while bureaucracy ripped, religioned, cajoled and legislated black children away from their families, mothers from their children, fathers from their roles. This was called Assimilation. If it had succeeded, a culture would be extinct, and a unique identity lost."[16] However, the work also shows that satire is far more effective than didacticism. It not only pokes fun at grievous issues, but does it in rousing celebratory tunes: "There's nothing I would rather be, than to be an Aborigine, and watch you take my precious land away."

Classics, translations

By the 1980s Australian theatre was appropriating the classics rather than emulating the British model which now seemed more and more distant and foreign. We were writing new translations for our own productions, interpreting foreign works in light of ourselves, and creating a unique theatrical language from our own culture and experiences. Directors such as Aubrey Mellor, Richard Wherrett and Neil Armfield played a significant role in the re-interpretation of the classics and modern European works by insisting on commissioning new translations by local writers.

These directors have also been instrumental in bringing new perspectives and a new stage language to our theatre. Armfield's productions of *Hamlet* and *The Alchemist* in the 1990s were in a sense as Australian as his staging of Australian works. Critics and audiences alike commented on the profound cultural experience of his *Hamlet*, with its utterly Australian theatricality and sensibility. While the play was distinctly Shakespeare, the performance was redolent of our own society and its shame, commitment, guilt and culpability.

Armfield was also responsible for STC's production of Gogol's *The Government Inspector* (1991). A new version, completely designed around the production concept and the cast, was written by Armfield, the production dramaturg May-Brit Akerholt, and the actor Geoffrey Rush (Khlestakov), from a literal translation by Lech Mackiewicz. The translators tailored the speeches around the cast, knowing the unique flavours that the performers' idiosyncrasies and acting styles would add to their characters and language. Armfield and Rush had already tackled Gogol in 1989, in an adaptation of *Diary of a Madman* by David Holman. The production, which also featured the Aboriginal actor Lydia Miller, toured to Moscow and St Petersburg where it met with rapt enthusiasm from audiences mesmerised by Rush's physically and mentally agile performance.

A new version of Rostand's *Cyrano de Bergerac* (1980) by Louis Nowra provided a distinct Australian sense of irony and an anti-heroic flavour in a production directed by Wherrett. John Bell played a Cyrano magnificently and tragically in love. Wherrett also commissioned a new translation from Akerholt for a production of *Hedda Gabler* (1986) with Judy Davis in the title role in one of her few stage appearances after graduating from NIDA in 1977. Davis created a contradictory Hedda; brittle, scheming, vulnerable, it was a complex and compelling performance in a production which brought out the sharp irony and poetic resonances of Ibsen's play.

TOWARDS THE MILLENNIUM

The 1988 Bicentennial celebration had its share of critics. The cultural program was boycotted by many theatre artists (including Patrick White) who refused to have their work performed in a year celebrating two centuries of white invasion of another race's country. But extra funding for celebratory projects also saw a new injection of life into the theatre. Six Years Old, a company formed under the auspices of Sydney Theatre Company with assistance from the Australian Bicentennial Authority, offered a group of young artists the opportunity to play major roles in the evolution and realisation of three works. The Artistic Director was Baz Luhrmann, who had participated in a group-devised project at NIDA in 1984 called *Strictly Ballroom* when he was an acting student. Luhrmann re-worked and presented the play in Six Years Old's program in 1988; many of the members went on to participate in the award-winning film, a direct result of the stage play's success and the company formed for the Bicentenary.

The Bicentenary year coincided with the Tenth Birthday Season of STC, which opened with Katherine Thomson's bitter-sweet musical *Darlinghurst Nights* (1988), based on the light verse of Kenneth Slessor about the many colourful characters in Sydney's bohemian Kings Cross. It was a fitting celebration for a city which prides itself on being the leader in both cultural and hedonistic pursuits. Most of Thomson's work is strongly located in the ethics of working people and the ramifications of political and industrial conflict for those caught up in it. Her ear for the vernacular creates a pungent dialogue which, although peppered with dry wit, gives her characters dignity and imagination. Her most enduring work, *Diving for Pearls* (1991), set in the industrial city of Wollongong, dramatises the effects of corporate greed on the hopes and dreams of battling people. One of the characters is a mentally impaired young girl who functions a little like a Shakespearean fool in pointing out the truths (and the possibility of love) hidden behind rhetoric and false images.

While the 1980s fostered plays exploring Australian political systems and social structures, there was a strong trend in the early 1990s towards a dramatisation of the intensely personal. Interestingly, this was accompanied by productions of Shakespeare's late plays *The Winter's Tale*, *Cymbeline* and *The Tempest*, as well as the drug-induced fantasy *A Midsummer Night's Dream*, in Australia and overseas. The Polish critic and scholar Jan Kott has claimed that Shakespeare's plays are revived according to the way they reflect a particular society or time, so that, at certain periods, some works become more contemporary than others.[17] Perhaps these trends were reflections of the "New Age" and its fascination with the dark inner self, of a need for the mystical and the enigmatic which defy rational explanation, of the power of art as creation and the artist as creator. Plays such as Gow's *Furious* (1991) and Timothy Daly's *Kafka Dances* (1993) explore the personal lives of writers and, through that, the art of writing and the writer's or the artist's role in the family and in a larger community whose materialistic and moralistic attitudes clash with the creative imagination. Nowra's semi-autobiographical *The Summer of the Aliens* (1992) and *Così* (1992) are written from a highly personal perspective, as is Sewell's intimate piece *Sisters* (1995).

Beatrix Christian's work marks in some ways the transition into a new decade. It tackles large political issues through individual conflicts in works which are on the edge of theatrical conventions, exploring worlds whose structures are becoming fractured and chaotic. Each of her plays is extremely different in form, structure and content, but her language clearly distinguishes her writing. She creates a non-naturalistic dialogue which is at once incisive and rich, enigmatic and illuminating, its heightened quality arising out of its sparse, rhythmic character. *Blue Murder* (1994), set on a rock in Sydney Harbour, is a contemporary thriller which takes the medieval Bluebeard story as a springboard in its examination of archetypal male/female conflicts. *The Governor's Family* (1997) is based on a case from 1887 when six men were hanged for the rape of an Aboriginal girl. Written at the time of Eddie Mabo's fight for Native Title in the High Court, *The Governor's Family* "is, more than anything else, about acknowledging the past in order to deal openly and honestly with the present and the future".[18] *Fred* (1999) is a piercing comedy of contemporary manners; its ironic treatment of a group of friends who find an unknown corpse in their garden – and that is only the beginning of a surfeit of corpses – is suffused with darker questions of death and loss and their inherent capacity to bring new life as well as devastation.

The 1990s consolidated the trend of a "director driven" theatre, with directors often taking an active hand in "writing" the whole production, including the text. The young director Barrie Kosky first attracted critical interest with his reworking of the old Jewish story *The Dybbuk*, performed by his Gilgul Company in Melbourne in 1991. The second play *Es Brent* appeared the next year, followed by *Levad*. They formed *The Exile Trilogy*, presented together for the first time at Belvoir St. Theatre in 1993. Kosky's work for theatre and opera is histrionic, saturnalian and with deliberate Judaic touches. His highly farcical suburban version of Molière's *Tartuffe* and his fervent production of O'Neill's *Mourning Becomes Electra* could scarcely be more different in expression, tone and style, but both had the distinct Kosky stamp of inventiveness and high passion. In 1998, Kosky presented a surreal interpretation of *King Lear* for the Bell Shakespeare Company; it toured to major cities and country centres, and despite out-raged reactions to some of its more vaudevillian aspects, enjoyed sell-out and extended seasons. Kosky was only twenty-six when appointed Artistic Director of the 1996 Adelaide Festival, one of Australia's most prestigious arts positions. He has created considerable waves with his dismissive attitudes to what he feels is the irrelevance of most established theatre. This has not stopped him, however, working for the main companies. Kosky's answer to his critics is always yet another controversial theatre or opera production, inevitably with good box-office returns.

Australia does not have a strong tradition of adapting novels for the stage, but the 1990s have seen a sharp rise in theatrical versions of prose works, partly due, perhaps, to the director's increased involvement in shaping the text. Curiously enough, most of the successful stage adaptations have been of works by Western Australian authors, including Tim Winton's *Cloud-street*. A family saga of enduring love and commitment, tenacity, generosity, crushing disillusions and stubborn hope, *Cloudstreet* has become a major theatrical event. In Sydney it played in a warehouse whose huge sliding doors opened at the end of the performance to reveal the city lights glinting on the harbour waters, into which the actor playing Fish took a running leap, disregarding sharks and pollution. A line from the novel sums up why audiences flocked to it and wanted more at the end of the five-hour evening: "And you can't help but worry for them, love them, want for them." The production had a successful national and international tour in 1999.[19]

CONCLUSION

Going into the new millennium, Australian theatre is a paradox. On the one hand, the subsidised companies are expected to increase their income from box-office and corporate sponsorship, and are thus edging closer to Broadway's commercialism and neon slickness through cautious and conservative programming. And the need for more economically scheduled seasons inevitably dictates the nature of the playwrights' vision and passion. The bulk of scripts received by most large companies are small in scale and unadventurous in structure and form.

Simultaneously, the theatre is experiencing a shift towards artistic exploration of larger issues which have a profound effect on us all. The 1990s saw an increase in plays and productions challenging the status quo of the mainstream theatre, especially from collectives of young writers, directors and actors who created works on a collaborative basis. These smaller companies, and the fringe festivals, are presenting risky, diverse and adventurous programs, confirming our unique position in the development of a language of theatre that will draw naturally on influences from hundreds of cultures. Like Patrick White's Scavengers, Australia has a wonderfully tasty dustbin from which to scavenge theatrical food in order to stay healthy and strong. For what is theatre if not vital sustenance for the spirit and the heart?

> Are you for magic? I am. Inadmissible when we are taught to believe in science or nothing. Nothing is better. Science may explode in our faces. So I am for magic. For dream. For love. That pervasive dream which becomes more real than reality if we have faith in it. If we can resist abusing them, all our dreams can amount to a world faith.[20]

NOTES

1 Judith Wright, "The Upside-down Hut", *Australian Letters*, 3.4 (1961), pp. 30–34.
2 The Indigenous Festival of Dreaming was the first of four arts festivals leading up to the 2000 Sydney Olympics. Carnivale is a multicultural arts festival which has existed since 1976.

3 MTC was founded in 1953 as the Union Repertory Company by John Sumner, who ran the company for more than thirty years. Like Sydney's Old Tote, it was established in cooperation with a university, the University of Melbourne.

4 An arts complex with three theatres at Sydney University.

5 Nadine McDonald, *Australian*, 21 May 1999, p. 12. Ironically, also in 1999, Kooemba's first Artistic Director Wesley Enoch directed a black–white touring production of *Romeo and Juliet* for the Bell Shakespeare Company, with black Montagues and white Capulets.

6 The Guild produced *The Ham Funeral* after it had been rejected in a much publicised and controversial decision by the Board of the Adelaide Festival.

7 If *The Ham Funeral* had been written the year it was first performed rather than fourteen years earlier in 1947, much critical space would have been taken up analysing Beckett's influence on White's drama.

8 *The Chapel Perilous* is still banned in Western Australia, and the published play carries a sticker to that effect. Hewett's first husband, who lives in WA, has threatened legal action if the play appears in any form in that state.

9 Jack Hibberd's notes to the Australian Performing Group program for the 1970 Perth Festival, quoted in "Pramocracy: the Alternative Theatre in Carlton", 1974 (unpublished).

10 For a discussion of this production, including drastic changes to the text, see co-director Wayne Harrison's article "Maintaining the Rage" in Peter Holloway, ed., *Contemporary Australian Drama*, 2nd edn. (Sydney: Currency Press, 1987).

11 Eunice Hanger, "Forebears of 'The Doll'", *Southerly*, 18 (1957), p. 33.

12 Julie Rose, Introduction, Stephen Sewell, *Traitors* (Sydney: Currency Press, 1983), p. 8.

13 *Writing from the Fringe* (Melbourne: Hyland House, 1990), p. 27. Mudrooroo agrees, however, that symbolic statements in Aboriginal plays are "integral parts pointing to the polysemic nature of Aboriginal drama". See "Black Reality" in Jack Davis, ed., *Barungin* (Sydney: Currency Press, 1989), p. ix.

14 Aboriginal English is a legitimate dialect, not an uneducated form of English.

15 The Black Swan Theatre Company in Perth, a non-Indigenous company, is funded primarily to produce plays by Western Australian writers, but also to support Indigenous playwrights.

16 Peter Bibby, Introduction, Jimmy Chi and Kuckles, *Bran Nue Dae* (Sydney and Broome: Currency Press and Magabala Books, 1991), p. vi.

17 Jan Kott, *plays INTERNATIONAL*, March 1991, p. 14.

18 Neil Armfield, in the program for the production of *The Governor's Family*.

19 Adapted by Justin Monjo and Nick Enright, directed by Neil Armfield and produced by Belvoir St. Theatre and Black Swan Theatre Company for the 1998 Sydney and Perth Festivals. In 1999 it toured to Zurich, London and Dublin, and won the award for Best International Production at the Dublin Festival.

20 Daniel Shepherd, in Patrick White's last play, *Shepherd on the Rocks* (1987).

9

GILLIAN WHITLOCK

From biography to autobiography

For many readers, critics and writers, Australian literary biography and autobiography are rich and complex domains. In this chapter the texts themselves will be used as points of departure, and anchors of a series of cross-sections which will stress the importance and energy of this writing from the very beginnings of European settlement, although the focus will remain on contemporary examples. One of the pleasures of these books is their ongoing interrogation of ways of writing about the self and subjectivity; some of the best critiques of biographical and autobiographical writing occur in the primary texts themselves. Another pleasure, and further reason to modify a chronological approach, is that nineteenth-century Australian life-writing remains very much alive, and continues to emerge anew in the present. The past is not settled. Extensive bibliographical and critical work continues to challenge Australian literary history by revealing hitherto "invisible lives" in nineteenth-century materials, so bringing a much larger volume of autobiographical writing into bibliographical records. Furthermore, the recent work of critics who draw on the methods of feminist criticism, deconstruction and/or new historicism has produced re-readings of many nineteenth-century texts. So, for example, in the wake of Paul Carter's *The Road to Botany Bay* (1987), the writings of explorers like Sturt and Mitchell, or Watkin Tench's journals, previously categorised as "descriptive writing", may now be read as autobiographical acts, allowing insight into the historical, cultural and social contexts which shape the autobiographic subject. Lucy Frost's *A face in the glass. The journal and life of Annie Baxter Dawbin* (1992) also uses a nineteenth-century journal as the basis of a biographical study of Annie Baxter, weaving together the autobiographical journal and a contemporary biographical account. Similarly, Deirdre Coleman's edition of *Maiden Voyages and Infant Colonies. Two Women's Travel Narratives of the 1790s* (1999) works with late eighteenth-century texts in an innovative way. By bringing together the journals of Mary Ann Parker and Anna Maria Falconbridge, she produces a comparative study which explores synchronicities between these two quite different yet contemporaneous accounts.

The complexities and richness of Australian biographic writing are, in part, due to the establishment of a settler colony here. The early years of settlement produced an extraordinary amount of writing: diaries, journals, letters and memoirs. The absence of "Literature" was lamented in the colony; as in other settler colonies it was a struggle to establish literary institutions in Australia, and yet a great deal of writing went on, much of it auto-biographical. Emigration and colonisation profoundly challenged notions of self and place, so that a sense of estrangement became a recurrent feature of white writing, both then and now. The legacies of colonisation – the displacement of Indigenous peoples, ongoing immigration from Europe and (recently) Asia, the idea of Australia as peripheral to European centres, the desire to establish a distinctive national culture and identity – remain important in reading contemporary Australian life writing. This is not to suggest that Australian life-writing remains trapped in a time warp. How-ever, it is to reiterate that our past is not settled. The postcolonial location of Australian literature emerges in such seemingly diverse ways as thematic interpretations which focus on "the uncertain self", concerns that Australian autobiographical writing is almost obsessively concerned with manhood and masculinity, the issue of expatriatism and identity and, more recently, the pre-eminent place of biography and autobiography as a means of fore-grounding Indigenous resistance.

Because the forms of literary biography and autobiography are inter-dependent and interactive, this writing can be imagined as a spectrum, a linkage of separate yet related forms, beginning at one end with the "grand portraits", the biographical studies of Australian writers and artists, where biographer and subject remain discrete; moving across to those texts which exploit the interdependencies of writing about self and other, where the con-tours of biography and autobiography come together; and then concluding with texts which are more traditionally autobiographical, where the con-fessional, truth-telling "I" anchors the text. This spectrum organises the following discussion, which suspends a chronological or thematic approach in favour of a traverse across Australian literary biographic writing where the points of departure are the texts themselves. This traverse cannot be definitive, but it is designed to be indicative, inclusive and (perhaps) provocative.

GRAND PORTRAITS

In Sydney in 1969 Patrick White invited Christina Stead to lunch at his Martin Road house. They discussed the characters in their fiction. Stead said hers were all people she had known, and she didn't believe White's assertion that his characters, the important ones anyway, "are latent bits of myself". White gave her some books and advised her to think carefully before returning permanently to Australia. He loved Stead's novel *The Man Who Loved Children* in particular, although he also thought *For Love Alone* a remarkable book. For her part, Stead was embarrassed that she had read so little of White; although she found *Riders in the Chariot* "consoling" she couldn't get beyond the first few pages of *The Vivisector*. She did greatly admire White's skills as a host and his delightful home, and remarked "his cooking is also perfection".

We know something of the different perspectives these two eminent writers brought to their encounter because each has been the subject of a particular style of literary biography, the grand portrait mode. David Marr's *Patrick White. A Life* (1991) and Hazel Rowley's *Christina Stead. A Biography* (1993) are highly acclaimed. Both Stead and White lived extraordinary lives, and Rowley and Marr chart these in all their complexity and ambiguity. In doing so, they raise questions about what Australian life and Australian literature might be, for both White and Stead pursued modernist and European modes in their fiction. Stead was an expatriate; White spent extensive time in Europe and the United States, and remained attuned to European affairs. Marr's *Life* and Rowley's *Biography*, like Axel Clark's *Henry Handel Richardson* (1990) and *Christopher Brennan* (1980), and Brenda Niall's *Martin Boyd* (1988), bring to literary studies insights which have been important in recent historical writing, such as Alan Atkinson's *The Europeans in Australia* (1997) and David Walker's *Anxious Nation. Australia and the Rise of Asia* (1999). These studies stress the variety which has always prevailed in interconnections between Europe and Australia, and Australia and Asia, connections which are more complex, subtle and ongoing than the traditional metaphors of centre and periphery suggest.

Two elements of White's identity interest Marr in particular, and explain his empathy with his subject. The first is notions of Australianness. Marr's biography foregrounds an understanding of Australianness where it isn't a contradiction to be both a jackaroo in the Snowy Mountains and then a Cambridge undergraduate. White did both these things. This pattern continued. In the 1950s and 1960s White farmed a small property just outside of Sydney with his lover Manoly Lascaris; yet they also frequently travelled to Europe and remained in close contact with intellectual, cultural and political events there. From White's very first fiction, *Happy Valley* (1939), his work did not sit well with the assumption that the great Australian novel would emerge from the realist and rural tradition of writing about the bush. It was always evident that White's writing about Australian landscapes and character would draw its energies from European and American modernism.

The other issue is of course White's sexuality. In Marr's biography homosexuality, like nationality, is one of the complications fundamental to White's life as an artist: "White saw himself as a sufferer: as an asthmatic, homosexual, foreigner and artist."[1] Sexuality and nationality cannot be held apart for, as White wryly points out in his autobiography *Flaws in the Glass* (1981), poofters and artists are equally "unAustralian". Masculinity has been one of the central obsessions of Australianness, and homophobia its base note. Although White was unaware of the haunts and lifestyles of homosexual Sydney in his youth, his biographer is not; Marr takes the opportunity to establish the importance, longevity and vivacity of this sub-culture. Later generations of Australian intellectuals, such as Marr, David Malouf and Robert Dessaix among others, are free to write about manliness and to imagine themselves as Australian men in ways not available to White and earlier generations. As Marr remarks, homosexuality was lived and not debated by White. In telling the life, Marr likewise refuses the polemics and debates about sexuality in favour of presenting the long marriage of White and Lascaris as an important emblem of stability and happiness for homosexual men.

The grand portrait style of biography tends to draw direct relationships between the fiction and the life. For example, Marr suggests an organic relationship between the two, observing "Like *Voss*, the fiction … grew from this life" (p. 16). The fiction permeates the biography, with Marr locating not only the origins of characters in the life but also of phrases, accent and grammar. The contact between the life and the art suffuses Marr's vision of Patrick White, they are integral one to the other, so the shift from the life to the fiction is embedded: "Ruth suspected Manly was rather common: servants swam and made love on the sand under cover of darkness, and simple country folk like Stan and Amy Parker came here for holidays" (p. 49). The recent attention to structuralism and poststructuralism in literary criticism has made this kind of suturing of life and text problematic; as we shall see, other styles of biography are inclined to "search" for the life rather than grasp it whole.

In her biography of Christina Stead, Hazel Rowley relishes the "grand portrait" tradition of biography: the organisation of the narrative is chronological, beginning with the childhood and ending with death. This biography too stresses the interdependency of life and art, the fiction is read as autobiographic. Rowley presents the characters in Stead's major fictions – Louisa in *The Man Who Loved Children* and Theresa in *For Love Alone* – as Stead's fictional alter egos. Like Marr, Rowley takes the opportunity to present an Australian life which opens onto European contexts and intellectual histories. This biography too focuses on a life which was unconventional: both marriage and motherhood were abortive affairs for Stead; her life with William Blake was peripatetic and increasingly aimless; she was unrecognisable as "Australian" in the terms of local literary networks because of her interest in modernism and admiration for Joyce's writing in particular. Stead's books have been appreciated in retrospect; at first publication the response was almost always ambivalent, in Australia and elsewhere.

The "grand portrait" of the eminent individual has always been the dominant mode of Australian biographical writing. As one critic has remarked, this empiricist, positivist tradition seizes whatever "lives and times" have to offer and puts its faith in extended chronological narrative and the power of a good story to seduce the reader.[2] Others have called the preference for detailed description and narrative, and the shape of the "whole" life in Australian biography and autobiography, a "sociographic" impulse.[3] Given the flowering of Australian biographic writing since the 1980s, literary biographies of individual subjects in the sociographic mode now comprise an Aubusson carpet where complex patternings, intersections and designs emerge; these work their way through individual lives but are characteristic of wider social, cultural and historical patterns. Other "grand portraits" of literary biography include Craig Munro's *Wild Man of Letters: the Story of P.R. Stephensen* (1984); Garry Kinnane's *George Johnston* (1986); Brenda Niall's *Martin Boyd* (1988); W.H. Wilde's *Courage a Grace. A Biography of Dame Mary Gilmore* (1988); John Barnes' *The Order of Things. A Life of Joseph Furphy* (1990); Michael Ackland's *Henry Kendall* (1995), Bruce Bennett's *Peter Porter* (1991); Geoffrey Dutton's *Kenneth Slessor* (1991), A.T. Yarwood's *From a Chair in the Sun. The Life of Ethel Turner* (1994) and *Jock. The Life Story of John Shaw Neilson* (1999) by Cliff Hanna.

This profusion needs to be related to the opportunities and institutions available to the literary intelligentsia. Large literary projects require substantial funding; the recognition of Australian literature and writers as appropriate research topics has been fairly recent. Secondly, biographic projects require publishers, and in turn a reading public to secure their legitimacy. Again, these thresholds have only recently been achieved. Melbourne University Press and the University of Queensland Press have now established series for Australian biographical writing; developments of this kind help shape an active research culture on literary biography.

As the Marr and Rowley biographies suggest, the grand portrait can achieve a wide readership, well beyond the literary intelligentsia, and an enthusiastic critical reception at one and the same time. Innovations within the frame of the grand portrait may be less enthusiastically received. For example, Veronica Brady's *South of My Days. A Biography of Judith Wright* (1998) is not radical in a formal way. It is however radical in its attempt to prioritise the spiritual dimensions of Wright's life. Reviewers have criticised this biography for Brady's empathy with her subject, her refusal to focus on the poetry in detail, her attention to Wright's career as an environmentalist and activist. Like Marr she stands accused of lack of critical distance.[4] This is to miss Brady's pursuit of a more holistic sense of her subject, whose religiosity regards poetry, politics and the familial as deeply interdependent. The Brady biography follows its subject into a domain where the secular, analytic and confidently rational mode is superseded by more intuitive, mythical and bodily kinds of knowledge. Similarly, there has been resistance to psychobiography as a mode of biographical writing in Australia. One of the few examples of literary psychobiography is Frances de Groen's *Xavier Herbert, A Biography* (1998), which is concerned with the inner life and understanding Herbert's motivation and desire. De Groen is interested in how exploring this writer's identity involves larger national issues related to gender, sexuality and race. Cassandra Pybus' speculations about desire, masculinity and the psyche in *The Devil and James McAuley* (1999) have been equally contentious.

CAUTION: BIOGRAPHER AT WORK

Expatriatism, travel and migration recur as themes across Australian biography. At times, departures assume the proportions of exodus. Ian Britain's biographic study of a group of eminent expatriates, *Once an Australian* (1997), takes a more collective approach, representing Germaine Greer, Barry Humphries and Clive James as examples of a generation of intellectuals who left in the 1960s to establish brilliant careers elsewhere – ironically as professional Australians. Others, for example Shirley Hazzard, Jill Ker Conway and Robert Hughes, departed for the United States around the same time. Relations between Australian and American letters have received little attention. In his biographic study of the American critic Hartley Grattan, *No Casual Traveller. Hartley Grattan and Australia–US Connections* (1995), Laurie Hergenhan uses the model of the conversation to grasp not just the diversity of Grattan's career as a journalist and academic but also the ongoing yet fluctuating interaction between Australia and the USA. Both Britain and Hergenhan alert us that certain subjects – not just lives but also particular themes and issues – might well require that the grand portrait mode be dispensed with in favour of other kinds of biographic writing, where the life and the story fragment.

Much recent biographic writing has striven to generate a more complex sense of Australian cultural life and connections. The discussion of literary nationalism in general, and (in particular) approaches to the 1890s and writers celebrated by the Australian legend, is an important issue. Biographies which take up the lives of Australian writers, critics and journalists who chose to stay home tend to replace the idea of a consistent, uniform literary nationalism with a more dynamic view of Australian cultural institutions. This approach is attuned to regional difference, political contexts, different literary institutions and the diversity of print culture. Patrick Buckridge's *The Scandalous Penton. A Biography of Brian Penton* (1994) is written with the expressed purpose of bringing back into view the life of a journalist and novelist who came to embody behaviours and attitudes which seemed undesirable, unmanly and unAustralian to his peers: "Penton managed, at one time or another, to stand for just about every kind of non-Australianism Australians could think of."[5] Buckridge's biography reminds us that the national culture is always a site of contestation and difference, although his work also suggests how difference is incorporated or obscured in the records. Focusing as they do on modernist writers who were in their own way scandalously unAustralian, Marr and Rowley elucidate complex connections between Australia and Europe; however they are inclined to overestimate the power, authority and uniformity of the "dun coloured realism" school of Australian letters. We can glimpse this in Rowley's contrast between Stead's "internationalist perspective" and Nettie Palmer's attitude, which "seemed narrow and provincial by comparison". However Rowley also points out that Nettie Palmer read French, German and Greek and believed it essential for Australian writers to keep in touch with the larger world, while also championing "a distinctive Australian national culture, one that was no longer passively responsive to British and European influences".[6] In their biography *Eleanor Dark. A Writer's Life* (1998), Barbara Brooks and Judith Clark argue that the word "nationalist" needs to be used carefully, for it means different things at different times, or can be put to various uses within different discourses. Their remark relates to a discussion of P.R. Stephensen in particular, and Stephensen's own biographer would concur.[7] The argument has more widespread relevance, however. In writing the life of Eleanor Dark, Brooks and Clark are careful to mark their tracks as biographers very clearly. Although they proceed to narrate the life in its entirety and in chronological order, they foreground Dark's life as part of a larger Australian history – of women, of writing, and of social and political change – and they suggest parts of this life eluded capture, "there are places where a history we know can be seen as if through the holes in a net".[8] In her biography *Jean Devanny. Romantic Revolutionary* (1999),

Carole Ferrier examines the implications of political radicalism in Devanny's life with a similar sense of the elusive connections between public and private domains. *Jean Devanny*, she suggests, is a "heteroglossic interplay" of voices and stories, with particular emphasis on relations between voice, story and history.

The complexities and ambivalences of Australian literary culture are foregrounded in biographical works which cluster together a number of subjects. Here there is no intention to capture the whole life of any single individual but rather to understand a milieu, family, place or intellectual formation by weaving together disparate lives. Peter Kirkpatrick's *The Sea Coast of Bohemia. Literary Life in Sydney's Roaring Twenties* (1992) is a fine example of this. Kirkpatrick argues that bohemianism can be understood not in terms of a single embodiment of rebellion and unconventionality, a creative genius, but through an inquiry which draws on social and cultural history to understand an aesthetic which motivated a group of very different individuals. Integral to this bohemianism is a place and a time: Sydney in the 1920s. Kirkpatrick evokes the sights, sounds and smells, what the bohemians were reading, seeing, wearing. He brings to light a number of literary careers which would be lost to view in the biography of an eminent individual writer. Other examples of group biography include Britain's study of the expatriates, discussed earlier, and Joanna Mendelssohn's *Letters and Liars. Norman Lindsay and the Lindsay Family* (1996). The group biography is used here not to challenge the idea of the singular creative genius of Norman Lindsay – Mendelssohn subscribes to that orthodoxy – but to examine how the myth of Lindsay as artistic hero emerged as a creation facilitated and sustained by his intimate circle. A final example of the group biography, with a different rationale again, is Peter Fitzpatrick's *Pioneer Players. The Lives of Louis and Hilda Esson* (1995). This is a particularly interesting example of group biography for two reasons. Firstly, the milieu of the theatre, and the fact that the Essons founded the nationalist theatre group Pioneer Players, means that writing about a company rather than an individual is appropriate, and Fitzpatrick always keeps this dimension in view. Secondly, this is a dual biography; it focuses on a marriage, and Fitzpatrick approaches this relationship with an interest in how appropriate roles for men and women in marriage are determined in part by history and in part by the individuals themselves. Familiar issues arise here – for example, the passion to develop an Australian culture and identity and the difficulties of cultural nationalism. However, the historical interest in the emotional life of the couple, and their gendered roles within marriage, is distinctive.

These group or cluster biographies challenge some of the orthodoxies of the grand portrait, moving away from the singular creative genius as the centre of the biographic display. Other biographies depart from the grand portrait in reminding the reader that a biographer is at work. Here the biographer becomes an uncertain angler, unsure whether the gauge of the line is just the one for their catch, aware of the potential for escape, or, perhaps worst of all, conscious that if they do manage to bring this fish to the surface it will lose all the lustre and grace they glimpse as it remains submerged. Forms of biographic writing which indicate the tenuousness of the project can be seen to move across the spectrum towards autobiography. Why do biographers make this shift? In some cases it is initiated by their subject and/or its milieu, as in the case of the Hergenhan, Ferrier, Fitzpatrick and Kirkpatrick books. Some literary careers take the biographer away from the "grand portrait" into different styles of writing where the vicissitudes of such careers, and the biographer's search for the subject, are brought into the reader's view. In other contexts we find the biographer is disinclined to present the relations between biographer and subject in terms of discourses of individualism and realism.

Sylvia Lawson's *The Archibald Paradox. A Strange Case of Authorship* (1983) is, in part, a biography of J.F. Archibald, editor of the *Bulletin*; this is the first of a series of contemporary biographies which focus on journalism. Lawson eschews the word "biography" for "story" and writes with a sharp sense of how self and text merge in the "print circus" of journalism: "Archibald's own story disappears into the *Bulletin*'s ... [his] authorship was vital, but it was not about a signature, nor about personal expression as that is generally understood."[9] Lawson argues that a definitive biography of Archibald is neither possible nor relevant; she isn't interested in the kind of biographical plenitude which chronicles what was said when Archibald lunched with Sidney and Beatrice Webb. The method of *The Archibald Paradox* pursues a different understanding of the subject of biography; the pieces of the life are not pulled together into coherence, rather the idea of the single life as in a constant process of change, in need of careful contextual biographic work, is dominant. Lawson's idea of journalism in general, the 1890s and the *Bulletin* in particular, as a "print circus", suggests that to capture her subject and his milieu required an innovative biographical approach. The 1890s and writers associated with the bush myth have long been represented as fundamental to Australian literary studies and the national psyche more generally. Sylvia Lawson's study shows how understanding of this period may be furthered by formally innovative kinds of biographical writing. We can now also compare a series of very different biographical studies of Henry Lawson to understand their different effects in the representation of the life and times of this icon of Australian writing.[10] Richard Fotheringham's study of another writer of the bush school, *In Search of Steele Rudd* (1995), takes up an extreme example where author, pseudonym and characters (Arthur Hoey Davis, Steele Rudd, and Dad and Dave respectively) came adrift to assume a life independent of each other. Fotheringham's is an important study of the ongoing appropriation, reworking and revitalising of writers and writings associated with the Australian legend, a process which occurs in both high and popular cultural forms.

It is the career of his subject (or subjects!) and their history in literary and other media which takes Fotheringham into this poststructuralist utopia rather than any theoretical predilection on his part. David Carter's speculations about careers in writing are similarly produced by the nature of his subject, in his case the Jewish-Australian writer Judah Waten. Both Fotheringham and Carter deal with the fetishisation of an image of Australianness in a man and a writer, although for very different reasons. "Steele Rudd" is one of the makers of the Australian legend, alongside Lawson, Paterson and Furphy. He has assumed a remarkable posthumous life. On the other hand, Waten was Jewish, an immigrant, a communist intellectual and writer, the first to write "from the inside" about non-English speaking migrants in Australia.[11] Like Buckridge, Carter has to begin by resuscitating his subject, and arguing why Waten should be rescued from obscurity. *A Career in Writing. Judah Waten and the Cultural Politics of a Literary Career* (1997) is not strictly a biography; however Carter's speculations about the literary career are useful: what shapes a literary career, and under what terms might this career be recognised as "Australian" and/or as significant for Australian letters?

Biographic writing confirms eminence in the dominant culture, and yet it has also been a means of redefining and rethinking what constitutes significant lives, and how these life stories are told. Biography is a significant form of writing by and about Aboriginal Australians. It has been suggested that biographic writing allows Aboriginal Australians to represent what they have witnessed, that it stands as a form of testimony. This perhaps obscures the debates about how Aboriginal Australians gain access to biography, and how the production of biographic narratives about Indigenous men and women become entangled in complex interracial relations. There has been a long tradition of ethnobiographic writing about Indigenous Australians – for example Douglas Lockwood's *I, The Aboriginal* (1962), Bruce Shaw's *My Country of the Pelican Dreaming* (1981) and Diane Bell's *Daughters of the Dreaming* (1983). The latter has been the subject of rigorous critiques by Jackie Huggins (1998), Aileen Moreton Robinson (1998) and Mudrooroo (1997). *Gularabulu* (1983), by Paddy Roe and Stephen Muecke, is an experimental interracial text which takes a different approach

by foregrounding the different perspectives and voice of the white inter-
mediary and the Aboriginal inhabitant. Patsy Cohen and Margaret Somerville's *Ingelba and the Five Black Matriarchs* (1990) uses another biographical
format, focusing on the generational and regional identifications which are
important in Indigenous communities. Here too the problems of interracial
collaboration in the production of a biographic text about Indigenous
Australians are evident. Until 1970 ethnobiographic representations of
Aboriginal Australians by far exceeded autobiographic writing; since then
there has been a decisive shift so that the latter is increasingly dominant,
indeed overwhelmingly so by 1985.[12] The changing presence of Indigenous
peoples in biography and autobiography is an important indicator of an
ongoing process of cultural exchange where appropriation and decolonis-
ation co-exist and contest in the aftermath of invasion and settlement. Here
the politics of who is authorised to speak, and who becomes the subject(s) of
biographic writing, and when and where and why, are brought to light.

EQUATORIAL ZONES: WHERE LOUISA MEETS
POPPY AND RITA

Rather than a clear line where we move from biography to autobiography,
there is an equatorial zone of biographic writing where the two commune.
Here I will use Brian Matthews' *Louisa* (1987), Drusilla Modjeska's *Poppy*
(1990) and Rita and Jackie Huggins' *Auntie Rita* (1994) to transit from the
biographical into the autobiographical. *Louisa* offers samples of all the
varieties of biographical writing: it is in part a work of historical scholarship
centred on the life of Louisa Lawson, it is also speculative about the problems in documenting this life, and it is absorbed in the problems of writing
biography. In Matthews' book there is the scrupulous and scholarly biographer who desires to work in the grand portrait manner. There is, too, his
alter ego, "Owen Stevens", who calls into question the conventions of
beginning with the birth of Louisa Lawson née Albury on Guntawang
Station in 1848. Stevens and "the biographer" struggle for control of the
biographical narrative, and in so doing foreground the theoretical debates
which circulate around biography. *Louisa* presents a biographical portrait
of Louisa Lawson even as it questions the capacity of the biographer and his
text to capture the life.

Drusilla Modjeska's *Poppy* also began as biography: "my intention was
to write a biography of my mother and I expected that I would keep to the
evidence. In the writing of it, however, I found myself drawn irresistibly into
dream, imagination and fiction. The resulting *Poppy* is a mixture of fact
and fiction, biography and novel."[13] Modjeska's point reminds us that the

borderlands of biography and autobiography also abut on those of fiction, and both Matthews and Modjeska range among these forms. As a daughter, Modjeska writes about a life entwined with her own, and the character Lalage is clearly autobiographical. As an historian Modjeska is trained to keep to the evidence which attaches the life to history, and yet this leaves out so much of the everyday life she wishes to capture. She offers readers a metaphor for the feminine discourse she seeks to write: the braided twine which Poppy weaves from threads and scraps, a thread which invokes the mythical subtext of Ariadne, and which ties together the diaries and letters the daughter/biographer brings back to Australia from England. Or does it? *Poppy* is dedicated to "my mother who died in 1984 and never kept a diary". The method of *Poppy* proclaims itself as both feminine and Antipodean. Lalage, Poppy's biographer in the text, places herself in the "messy brilliance" of Sydney in contrast to the "stately centres" of Europe. Australia for Lalage is a new world, "not exile so much as a new way of living" where she is able to re-make old myths and knowledges. Place, then, is fundamental to this innovation in writing. Modjeska's interest in innovative ways of writing about women's lives is also evident in *Stravinsky's Lunch* (1999), a biographical study of two women artists.

Negotiations between biography and autobiography, and a heightened sense of the adjacency of narrating subjects, emerge with different resonances in Aboriginal writing. These tensions are foregrounded in Jackie Huggins' biography of her mother, *Auntie Rita* (1994). As Huggins points out in the Foreword: "[This] is not a fashionable story of how she suddenly found her 'Aboriginal identity'".[14] Elsewhere Huggins is critical of the recent stereotypes which white Australia has applied to Aboriginals, such as the expectation that they be deeply spiritual and mystical: "this is especially necessary for the new-ageist agenda".[15] To some extent Huggins' biographical project is familiar. Like Modjeska's *Poppy*, it is a biography of her mother which becomes autobiographical; a project which calls the daughter's knowledge and academic learning into question; a book which focuses on the relational, interdependent making of identities, and the force of memory. But Rita and Jackie Huggins are not English or Anglo-Australian, like Poppy and Lalage, they are Aboriginal, members of the Bidjara and Birri Gubba Juru people, and in the wake of their dispossession and dispersal, filiation, knowledge and memory are transformed. *Auntie Rita* pursues an Indigenous discourse which foregrounds the different tongues of mother and daughter. Jackie Huggins has no desire to translate her mother's history into her own, nor to obliterate the regional and social codings and meanings which are the locality of the story, nor to lose the specific history of racism as it occurred in Queensland. The stakes are high.

Anne Brewster argues in her discussion of Aboriginal women's autobiography that identity is a shifting, changing and relational thing, it is contingent and constructed according to historical circumstance and political strategy.[16] Autobiography has been a resource whereby Indigenous writers have taken responsibility for defining themselves. In so doing they challenge fundamentally the politics of identity which underwrote policies of assimilation and protection in Australia.

Poppy, *Louisa* and *Auntie Rita* eloquently dramatise debates about the production and reception of fiction, biography and autobiography which emerge in critical discourse too. There have been four monograph-length studies of Australian autobiography: John Colmer's *The Personal Quest* (1989), Joy Hooton's *Stories of Herself When Young* (1990), David McCooey's *Artful Histories. Modern Australian Autobiography* (1996) and Rosamund Dalziell's *Shameful Autobiographies. Shame in Contemporary Australian Autobiographies and Culture* (1999). McCooey engages in an extensive and useful discussion of the relations between biography, autobiography and fiction. He turns to history rather than literature to understand autobiography, arguing that a distinction between fiction and autobiography needs to be sustained. From this perspective, autobiographies are read as social documents, both artful and historical. It is, he suggests, a legitimate question to inquire "what happens after?" of an autobiography, whereas this is always an illegitimate question to ask of fiction. McCooey makes a distinction between "autobiography" as an intended narrative account and "autobiographical" as an unintended or related product of another form of writing (usually fiction).[17] This relegates books such as Miles Franklin's *My Brilliant Career*, Henry Handel Richardson's *The Getting of Wisdom*, Christina Stead's *For Love Alone* and George Johnston's *My Brother Jack* trilogy into the category of "fiction". By comparing Kinnane's biography of George Johnston with the *My Brother Jack* series, McCooey argues for the differences between autobiographical and fictional intent; in his view the writer of autobiography and biography is accountable to history, and responsible to others, in ways which do not hold for fiction. As a consequence, the muster of texts discussed in *Artful Histories* is not coextensive with the collection selected for my anthology of contemporary Australian autobiography, *Autographs* (1996). Following feminist and post-colonial critiques, *Autographs* courts the "disobedient subjects" (like *Poppy* and *Louisa* and *Auntie Rita*) which play on the boundaries between biography, autobiography and fiction. John and Dorothy Colmer's *Penguin Book of Australian Autobiography* (1987) is more wide ranging again, both chronologically and methodologically.

The critic who has established the foundations of much contemporary work on Australian autobiography, Joy Hooton, is also eclectic in her approach to these equatorial zones where fiction, biography and autobiography meet. Her two-volume annotated bibliography *Australian Autobiographical Narratives* (1993; 1998) vastly expands the archive of texts available for scholarly work. Here Philippe Lejeune's working definition of autobiography as a retrospective prose narrative, written with a focus on the author's individual life and personality, is used to include memoirs, travel writings and other hybrid forms of life writing.[18] Hooton's anthology *Australian Lives* (1998) similarly celebrates the many diverse forms of Australian autobiographical writing. The monograph *Stories of Herself When Young. Autobiographies of Childhood by Australian Women* (1990) suggests the influence of feminist scholarship on Hooton's work. Here she draws on feminist psychoanalytic theory to suggest the importance of a relational perspective in women's writing, and to argue that the neglect of much autobiographic writing is due to a gendered and exclusive view of what life writing should be. Hooton claims women's life writing characteristically presents the self as related; defined through interaction with intimate others, and/or the community, this writing stresses the importance of the private and domestic sphere, and is inclined to narrative structures which are discontinuous, or open ended. Hooton's inclusive and eclectic approach sets out to explore the spaces beyond narrowly defined and normative ideas of Australianness and the "literary"; she argues that women's life-writing dissolves notions of an homogeneous culture: "collectively they establish Australia as an exotic amalgam of alternative cultures".[19] In his *Career in Writing* (1997), David Carter takes up Hooton's argument to slightly different ends. He finds her work useful in foregrounding questions of positionality, suggesting ways of approaching the work of disempowered writers more generally. So, for example, a writer such as Judah Waten, who is not part of the dominant cultural understandings of masculine Australian identity, might use the autobiographical in ways Hooton typifies as "feminine", to express an ambivalent relation to language and cultural institutions. In this way feminist theories of autobiography have significance beyond the domain of women's writing, and relate to issues of authorisation and empowerment in biographic writing more generally. For example, the influence of this work by Hooton and Carter is evident in my comparative study *The Intimate Empire. Reading Women's Autobiography* (2000).

Critics and students of literary biography and autobiography organise the numerous and diverse texts they work with in quite different ways. One method is chronological. Another is comparative. Another is thematic.

David McCooey uses a series of themes to organise his study of literary autobiography: Childhood, Death, Education, Voice, for example. Rosamund Dalziell, on the other hand, argues that shame is a theme which characterises contemporary Australian autobiography. A fourth approach would use identities such as gender, race, generation, sexuality to organise the field. The fifth, a formalist approach, has been used in this chapter to foreground the relational nature of this writing. Aboriginal autobiography can be incorporated into each of these models. A chronological approach would remark on the proliferation of Indigenous autobiography in the 1980s. A thematic approach would find plenty of material in Aboriginal autobiography, for it frequently narrates childhood and death. An identities approach would foreground the importance of this writing in the politics of resistance, and the fact that Aboriginal autobiography has been deeply implicated in exploring the politics of gender and race. The formalist approach of this chapter can incorporate Sally Morgan's *My Place* (1987) and *Auntie Rita*, for instance, among those autobiographies which stress multiplicity of voice in autobiographical narration. Others, such as Ruby Langford Ginibi's *Don't Take Your Love to Town* (1988), might appear as "self-portraits".

And yet Aboriginal autobiography is the thread which, when pulled, causes thematic, chronological, formalist and identity-based approaches alike to unravel. Where does Aboriginal autobiography "fit"? Should it be taken up as political biography? Its effects are certainly profoundly political, and many of its writers are not "literary" as that is conventionally understood. Yet the fact remains that the institutions and intelligentsia of literary and historical studies have been the main media through which Aboriginal autobiography has emerged and circulated, and which it has, in turn, transformed. Furthermore, Indigenous texts like *My Place*, *Auntie Rita* and the series of biographical writings by Ruby Langford Ginibi reflect critically upon how Australian lives can be written about biographically and auto-biographically. Aboriginal lives don't quite "fit" into the forms, themes and categories which organise thinking about literary autobiography because their experience of childhood, death, or education, for example, is marked by race, and produced by systemic and systematic racism. So to incorporate the textual innovations of *My Place* or *Auntie Rita* alongside those of, say, *Poppy* is to perform a critical sleight of hand which hides from view the reasons why *My Place* splits into different stories, and why certain things are not spoken of. To put the narration of childhood in *Auntie Rita* along-side that of Jill Ker Conway's *The Road from Coorain* (1989), for example, is to turn aside from the fact that childhood as it is traditionally under-stood in Western biographic writing as a time of innocence is non-existent in Aboriginal autobiography.

The politics of race unravel and disturb conventional ways of reading autobiographical writing, suggesting some different questions. Who is authorised to speak in any one place and time? And on whose behalf? Why did Aboriginal autobiographies emerge with such force in the 1980s, and what have been the political effects? How does biographic writing relate to the racial politics which shape Australian lives, black and white? How have Aboriginal biographers and autobiographers engaged with the politics of whiteness? White too is a racial identity, socially and culturally produced: what role has biographic writing played in its construction?

As is evident from this very brief overview of current debates, a number of issues circle in these equatorial zones where biography, autobiography and fiction come into play. The boundaries between literary and political biography, and between primary and secondary writings about biography and autobiography, are friable. One way of navigating through this is to introduce another player altogether: the reader. Readers might need to take one step back and become conscious about how they read *for* the life in writing. For example, the reader might choose to step aside from reading biographically, where the life is assumed to be reflected in the text, and where protagonist, narrator and author are assumed to be one and the same, to examine the different ways that the self is staged in texts. As Carter suggests, to "read for autobiography will be to read across both fictional and non-fictional texts for inscriptions, stagings or emplotments of the self – not just self-portraits – which may be concentrated and dispersed in character, anecdote, plot or narrative sequence, perspective and voice".[20] Here boundary disputes are approached with a sense of the *relational* nature of genres of biography, autobiography and fiction. The question of "what is autobiography" is replaced by a series of questions about when and how it is possible to read autobiographically. Equally, it suggests that the reader needs to question how writers and critics approach these issues too, to understand the artfulness and the historicity of both literary and critical discourses.

With these equatorial currents behind us, we can now proceed to look at literary autobiography in terms of various styles of autobiographic writing. The remainder of this chapter first discusses self-consciously autobiographic texts which locate themselves close to debates which problematise relations among the author/narrator and protagonist. It will then proceed to autobiographers who appeal to the reader by using more confessional, truth-telling and transparent modes of writing. These "self-portraits" are the autobiographical equivalents of "the grand portrait" of biography, for they too assert the integrity of the small personal voice in the text.

THE FLAWED GLASS

Feminism, poststructuralism, postmodernism and new historicism have problematised textual relations which realist and humanist aesthetics present as relatively straightforward. In so doing they have produced circumstances where autobiographic writing proliferates, and writers explore the conditions and limits of autobiography. Hal Porter's *The Watcher on the Cast-Iron Balcony* (1963) did not begin Australian autobiography; however it did originate a modernist, self-conscious style of contemporary autobiography here. *The Watcher* pre-dates the "isms" listed above, and suggests these discourses have merely accentuated a tendency towards more self-conscious and experimental forms of literary autobiography. Chris Wallace-Crabbe ponders the historical causation of *The Watcher* and suggests overseas examples of self-conscious modernist autobiography and Porter's own theatrical talents as important considerations; throughout the *The Watcher* the self is conceived not as a stable ego but a theatre in which all sorts of possibilities are played out.[21] *The Watcher* is recognisably modern, with its uncertain narrator who discovers "as I write these words that my autobiography, at this period, is my mother's biography".[22] The narrator refuses any unification of past and present selves or the idea of a seamless narrative; he delights in refractions of the self into a series of subjects: the remote watcher, the biographer, the child, the adult confessor.[23] The constructed nature of the self, and the multiplicity of selves created by time and language, are presented to the reader again and again. Porter's autobiography has been read as an inscription of the collective national psyche, an exemplar of the insecurity of the Australian male psyche, an expression of the themes of "the uncertain self", and Romantic individualism. This tells us little about *The Watcher*, but a good deal about the ongoing desire to find some collective national ethos and coherent subjectivity reflected and authenticated in autobiographical writing. In fact Porter, like Donald Horne and Bernard Smith, uses irony and explores third person narration in autobiography to suggest the constraints of national stereotypes of masculinity. In *The Boy Adeodatus. The portrait of a lucky young bastard* (1984), Smith turns to classical myth and legend, to politics, to art history and to religion as alternative mythographies for a life which is Australian, although not stereotypically so. Like Donald Horne in his trilogy of memoirs, Smith stands back, deploys irony, and rehearses or imagines various styles of narrating his career, beliefs and desires.

Porter's autobiography can be read as a harbinger of the intense interest in more experimental forms of autobiographical writing which have proliferated since the 1960s. The title of Patrick White's *Flaws in the Glass: A Self*

Portrait (1981) is indicative, for this is a "portrait" in the modernist style, asserting the rejection of autobiography as a dependable form of historical writing and signalling its place in the exploration of subjectivities and literariness. And yet that White chose to "come out" publicly as a homosexual in his autobiography indicates that, for the writer, autobiography retained elements of referentiality absent from fiction. The popularity of autobiography in contemporary Australian writing grows from its many uses and capacities: to allow meditations on language, writing and reading, to include the discussion of representational capacities of literary language, and to rehearse the problematic identification of the self in relation to larger intellectual, social and historical issues such as national identity, sexuality, ethnicity and race. The expansion of this type of autobiographic writing, its publication and its enthusiastic readership, signals changes and diversification in Australian literary intelligentsia and culture more generally. Writers of some of the most interesting autobiographical projects work in diverse cultural institutions: public broadcasting, journalism, art, academia.

Just as Porter's theatrical career fed into the tone and style of *The Watcher*, so too these other media affect the consciousness of voice, language, positionality and address in the text. For example, Eric Michaels' training as an anthropologist affects his representation of identity and authenticity in *Unbecoming: An AIDS Diary* (1990). Michaels embraces with relief the idea of the individual as a social/cultural construct and uses this perspective to discuss the development of his homosexual preferences in terms of quite specific social, cultural and historical determinations. Drusilla Modjeska's academic credentials affect *Poppy*. Modjeska has taught textual studies professionally and uses the autobiographic to speculate at length on the relationship between language and representation, and the limitations of academia. Robert Dessaix, an eminent and accomplished broadcaster, also uses autobiographic writing to reflect on gendered and sexual identities. In *A Mother's Disgrace* (1994), an autobiographical account of his life as an adopted child and his eventual meeting with his natural mother, Dessaix addresses the reader openly, and gives plenty of warning that he will lie, exaggerate and confuse. In his later *Night Letters* (1996), he is similarly aware of the narratee, and the ways his narration will be received. Both Beverley Farmer and Helen Garner have explored different ways of writing about the self which are influenced by feminist thinking. Although Farmer classifies *A Body of Water: A Year's Notebook* (1990) as fiction, this notebook of a writer's life, which discusses the writing process, is highly autobiographical. So too is the "new journalism" of Helen Garner's controversial *The First Stone. Some Questions About Sex and Power* (1995). This analysis of a sexual harrassment case, Garner's first non-fiction book, includes intimate and revealing details about Garner's own experience which are directly autobiographical.

Formally innovative styles of autobiographic writing tend to have features in common, as the examples above suggest. They refuse the coherent consistent singular narrative of a life and turn to the more episodic forms of the diary, journal, essay and notebook. They openly court the inconsistencies and lacunae of language, and are inclined to address the reader directly and intimately to rupture any illusions about the capacity of language to tell a whole story. There is a self-consciousness about language and subjectivity, and also a sense of play, performance and virtuosity, that can be facilitated by some styles of autobiographic writing. Writers are drawn to these self-conscious uses of language in autobiography to address certain issues about identity, such as sexuality, or ethnicity. In *Jump Cuts* (1996) Sasha Soldatow and Christos Tsiolkas describe their dialogues about masculinity, sexuality and politics as "an autobiography"; in *In Full View* (1997), a series of intimate autobiographic essays by expatriate Lily Brett, the implications of being Australian and Jewish are written on and about the body. Although the tendency to assume that migrant writing is inherently autobiographical is to be resisted,[24] ethnic minority writing has long been an influence in establishing styles of autobiographic writing which focus on language and representation. For example, Rosa Cappiello's autobiographic fiction *Oh Lucky Country* (1984) and Ania Walwicz's prose fragments, collected in *writing* (1992), draw attention to the gaps between the spoken and written word, between what is said and what is heard, between signified and signifier.

These styles of autobiographic writing foreground the reader, and recall the earlier suggestion that to read for autobiography is to pursue various inscriptions, stagings or emplotments of the self – not just self-portraits. Writers may be drawn to styles of writing which are deeply personal and revealing whilst refusing to sanction the identification of author and textual "I" – perhaps because of the very literal, sometimes prurient, types of reading which the classification "autobiography" can produce. As the "flaws in the glass" metaphor suggests, autobiography is not necessarily "show and tell" or a form of historical writing. To the contrary, it can be used to court and explore artifice, literariness and debates about language and subjectivity.

Again these techniques emerge to different effect in Indigenous auto-biography. We can see why this is so by focusing on one of the most popular contemporary Australian autobiographies, *My Place* (1987). How, when and where questions are important here too. Like its precursors, Morgan's text was carefully edited to produce the effects of authentic first person narration.[25] It models quite brilliantly a process of discovering Aboriginality through identification, as the narrator delves into her family history. It displaces genetic understandings of Aboriginality ("blood" markings such as half-caste or quadroon) through an enactment of the process of identification by an urban Aboriginal family and the acceptance and recognition of this identity by their tribe of origin. Morgan's book deploys various tropes and discourses of autobiographic writing to extraordinary effect. There is, for example, the quest motif, which becomes almost a detective story. The "Chinese box" structure allows the narrator's story to incorporate first person narrations by earlier generations, Arthur, Gladys and Daisy Corunna, so that different dimensions of Aboriginal resistance and dispossession come into play. Finally, this structure also addresses what cannot be said, and how both silence and speaking out are part of the politics of resistance. *My Place* is controversial.[26] It has also been translated into a variety of forms to access different readerships – there is a pictorial edition, for example – and it is a mainstay of the secondary school curriculum.

Ruby Langford Ginibi has written a series of biographic texts in a style quite different to *My Place*. In *Don't Take Your Love to Town* and *Real Deadly* (1992) it is evident that Langford Ginibi is never in any doubt about her racial identity. Her autobiographic narrator in *Don't Take Your Love to Town* is not in a process of discovering her Aboriginality, although her story is about the metamorphoses of this identity across time and place – between urban and non-urban lifestyles, for example. Langford Ginibi's autobiography reverses the anthropological gaze – where the Aborigines are "explained" to the white reader – and shows the "colour" of the dominant culture. For example the "privilege" of being allocated a space in the suburbs, and the pressure to assimilate to the suburban Australian way of life in the 1950s, is presented from an Indigenous perspective to profoundly unsettling effect. The element of mystery and detection which is fundamental to the dynamics of *My Place* is absent. Furthermore, Langford Ginibi's autobiographic narrator "fails" to meet certain expectations that an autobiographical subject will be realised in the text.[27] She does not marshal the incidents of a life into an easily intelligible pattern; we have to work harder to see the coherence of Langford Ginibi's book, and the effort delivers a more uncomfortable knowledge than *My Place* imparts. It may well be, as Tim Rowse suggests, that *My Place* created a new space within Australian literary culture: a space for the discovery of Aboriginality and for repudiation of all that obliged its invisiblity and silence. The question which arises for subsequent biographical and autobiographical writing by and about Indigenous Australians is to what extent that space is familiar and prescriptive to the point of becoming a constraint, a limitation policed by the tastes and expectations of a white readership and publishing industry.

SELF-PORTRAITS: "OPENING MY HEART"

As the dominant style of Australian biography is sociographic, so too most autobiographers choose to trust the medium of the word, a first person narrative voice, a singular narrative focal point, and a consistent chronological order. These narrators invite trust, and their narrations entice empathy. A.B. Facey's *A Fortunate Life* (1981) is a prime exemplar of this in recent Australian autobiography. A number of reasons have been suggested for its extraordinary popularity: it taps into an Australian oral narrative tradition in its usage of tropes and motifs, and a simple moral vocabulary. Although it focuses on the life of an individual, it operates in terms of group mythos at the same time, incorporating elements at the heart of Australian nationalist thinking: the bush, and Anzac; it lends itself to social, historical and literary readings; it stresses the narrator's reliability and the text's authenticity.[28] *A Fortunate Life* appears quintessentially Australian, a celebration of mateship, bush life and the pioneering tradition. The ongoing attraction of the pioneer battler in the bush is evident not just in Facey's success but also the popularity of autobiographical series by Sara Henderson and Patsy Adam-Smith. And yet it also invites interracial comparison with Indigenous autobiographies such as Ruby Langford Ginibi's *Don't Take Your Love to Town*, Sally Morgan's *My Place* or Jack Davis' *A Boy's Life* (1991) for its depiction of the poverty which sanctioned the intervention of welfare into family life.

That Facey's recollection of pioneering life and Anzac should appear so recently underscores the span of "living" memory in Australia. Certain phases and domains of social and cultural life are richly chronicled through self-portraits which verge on the memoir. Russel Ward's *A Radical Life* (1988), Roger Milliss' *Serpent's Tooth* (1984), Dorothy Hewett's *Wild Card* (1990), Ric Throssell's *My Father's Son* (1990), Betty Roland's autobiographical quartet *An Improbable Life* (1989), and Bernard Smith's *The Boy Adeodatus* (1984) reflect on experiences of left-wing politics in the post-war era, recalling a profound sense of the individual being caught up in larger historical forces and social change.[29] Vincent Buckley recounts the same period with a different political and spiritual commitment in *Cutting Green Hay* (1983). The dominant "Australian way of life" in the post-war period – white, middle-class and relentlessly suburban – sparks quite different autobiographical responses. For example, there is the satiric Barry Humphries' *More Please* (1992), Clive James' *Unreliable Memoirs* (1980) and the comic *Over the Top With Jim* by Hugh Lunn (1990). We see what it was like to arrive as a migrant in the very class-conscious utilitarian post-war society from Andrew Riemer's *Inside Outside: Life Between Two Worlds* (1992), the first of an autobiographical series by him which reflects on migration and dislocation; in Morris Lurie's *Whole Life: An Autobiography* (1987), Mary Rose Liverani's *The Winter Sparrows: Growing Up in Scotland and Australia* (1975), and Amirah Inglis' *Amirah: An Un-Australian Childhood* (1983). Germaine Greer, Jill Ker Conway, Kathleen Fitzpatrick and Dorothy Hewett attest to the stifling constraints which women faced in the 1950s. For young intellectual women like Conway and Greer, expatriation seemed the only option, although Kathleen Fitzpatrick's *Solid Bluestone Foundations and Other Memories of a Melbourne Girlhood, 1908–1928* (1983) presents a quite different perspective on the experiences of Australian intellectual women in prestigious universities overseas. For Dorothy Hewett (like Jean Devanny) commitment to social change was a necessity for personal survival and integrity. Finally, some autobiographers use recollections of a post-war childhood to develop a regional perspective, and to reflect upon a profound attachment to place. Glimpses of Brisbane emerge from a series of very different autobiographical representations, for example David Malouf's *12 Edmonstone Street* (1985) and Jessica Anderson's *Warm Zone* autobiographic stories (1987), which focus on unique spaces within and under the Queensland house as constitutive of the self. Both Malouf and Anderson – like Barbara Hanrahan in her recollections of an Adelaide childhood in *Iris in Her Garden* (1992) – are interested in using the child's perspective to explore a poetics of space, an identification which is profoundly local and personal, and which incorporates exquisite detail.

As this brief summary suggests, a surge in autobiographic self-portraiture in the past twenty years has led to various snapshots of post-war Australian life as a time of childhood and adolescence. Autobiography is generically attached to childhood however, early memories are more poetical than historical.[30] What are the effects of this in the construction of social memory? To be more precise, what does it mean that the conventions of self-portraiture represent and organise a generational experience of childhood and/or young adulthood in memoirs of post-war Australia? Tom Keneally's *Homebush Boy* (1995) is representative: "this is not an exhaustive tale of boyhood but of one reckless, sweet, divinely hectic and subtly hormonal year".[31] As suggested above, different allegiances, histories, languages and identifications emerge in these self-portraits due to differences in ethnicity, gender, political affiliation and place. Stylistically there are also variations – *More Please, 12 Edmonstone Street* and *Wild Card* are very different autobiographies. Nevertheless, a particular period of Australian social and cultural life, a phase of assimilation and protection in social and cultural policy in "the lucky country", is represented autobiographically in a mode where the dominant note is innocence rather than history. By "history" here I mean knowledge of difference, desire and danger, an awareness of how profound historical constructions of the self, sexuality, and relationships are, a grasp of identity as shifting and above all relational. This knowledge is fundamental to social responsibility and agency.[32] Autobiographers such as Eric Michaels and Drusilla Modjeska write with self-consciousness of these issues; on the other hand, self-portraits are inclined to be innocent of the frame which surrounds, contains and displays the self in the text.

For many autobiographers and readers the sense of "opening my heart to readers" and drawing on universal human experience, as Ruth Park suggests in *Fishing in the Styx* (1994), is fundamental to the pleasures of the genre. It suggests intimacy, confession, and a direct communication between author and reader, unmediated by language. This kind of autobiography is on the borderlands of the memoir, and is an important resource in social, intellectual and national histories. The self-portrait takes autobiography towards a kind of historical writing. The question is just how aware such autobiographers are of the relational, historical nature of subjectivity? What are the politics of innocence? What are the complicities between the genre of self-portrait autobiographies and processes of assimilation? These questions are raised by Indigenous autobiographical writing, which tells a very different story of post-Federation Australian history, and which frequently calls into question the assumption that to speak autobiographically is to speak of the individual subject. Dick Roughsey's *Moon and Rainbow: The Autobiography of an Aboriginal* (1971), Jack Mirritiji's *My People's Life: An Aboriginal's Own Story* (1978), Robert Bropho's *Fringedweller* (1980), Ruby Langford Ginibi's *My Bundjalung People* (1994) and *Haunted by the Past* (1999), Doris Pilkington's (Nugi Garimara's) *Follow the Rabbit-Proof Fence* (1996) and Ruth Hegarty's autobiographical account of being a "dormitory girl" at Cherbourg in *Is That You Ruthie* (1999), are just a few examples of the self-portrait as a form of testimony, speaking on behalf of other Aboriginal Australians, with a deeply felt sense of community and the "shared story" which is told through forms of auto/biographical writing. The importance of this as a style of reportage is nowhere more evident than in the autobiographical accounts gathered as part of the Report of the National Inquiry into the Separation of Aboriginal and Torres Strait Islander Children from Their Families, entitled *Bringing Them Home* (1997). In the Preface to an edition of some extracts from this, *The Stolen Children. Their Stories* (1998), Ronald Wilson (like Ruth Park) turns to the heart: "[These] are words which were spoken from the heart to the heart. The Report must be read with an open heart and mind, and with a willingness to listen, and to listen intently."[33] This draws on the power of autobiographical genres to promote empathy and understanding in new and important ways. It signals the place of these genres in the process of reconciliation in Australia, which came to a new boundary through these testimonies by Indigenous men and women.

This chapter has moved from biography to autobiography, from grand portrait to self-portrait, and then beyond to Indigenous writing and testimony which exceeds the bounds of literary biographics as it is traditionally understood. The politics of race has yet to affect how we think about Australian lives in any fundamental way, unlike the politics of gender and sexuality. However, this chapter has suggested that biographical writing is in the process of altering how we think about ourselves and our community in germinal ways. We have yet to recognise the politics of whiteness in our portraiture. Whiteness remains a transparency which we perceive in literary biography and autobiography as an occasional shimmer or disturbance. This spectrum of writing has been impervious to colour. In his linked lectures *Writing Asia and Auto/biography* (1995), Brian Castro suggests that Australians must begin to lose themselves – that is, imagine themselves as something other than national subjects, and absorb cultural and linguistic change, multiplicity and social critique. He argues that auto/biographical forms have the transgressive potential to serve these ends, to exceed "sclerotic cultural myths", and yet to do so the genre will need to exceed generic boundaries which have also been used as racial boundaries.[34] The writing discussed in this chapter will continue to be part of the illness and the cure, a medium for both complicity and resistance, obedience and transgression, in thinking about national subjects and subjectivities. Australian readers and writers will continue to find themselves in biography and autobiography. But critics, writers and readers can no longer claim innocence. The uses of these genres and inventions of the self are ethically, morally, socially, politically held to account, and at the heart of ways Australians respond to their unsettled past.

NOTES

1 David Marr, *Patrick White. A Life* (Sydney: Random House, 1991), p. 311. Further references to this edition in text.
2 James Walter, "Biography, Psychobiography and Cultural Space" in Ian Donaldson *et al.*, eds, *Shaping Lives. Reflections on Biography* (Canberra: Humanities Research Centre, 1992), p. 261.
3 John Colmer, *Australian Autobiography: The Personal Quest* (Melbourne: Oxford University Press, 1989), p. 154.

4 Andrew Riemer, "Brady on Wright", *Australian Book Review*, 201 (1998), p. 9.

5 Patrick Buckridge, *The Scandalous Penton. A Biography of Brian Penton* (St Lucia: University of Queensland Press, 1994), p. 310.

6 Hazel Rowley, *Christina Stead: A Biography* (Port Melbourne: Minerva Australia, 1993), p. 174.

7 Craig Munro, *Wild Man of Letters: the Story of P.R. Stephensen* (Melbourne: Melbourne University Press, 1984).

8 Barbara Brooks with Judith Clark, *Eleanor Dark. A Writer's Life* (Sydney: Macmillan, 1998), p. 12.

9 Sylvia Lawson, *The Archibald Paradox. A Strange Case of Authorship* (Melbourne: Allen Lane, 1983), p. x.

10 Manning Clark, *In Search of Henry Lawson* (Sydney: Macmillan, 1985), republished as *Henry Lawson. The Man and the Legend* (Melbourne: Melbourne University Press, 1995); Denton Prout, *Henry Lawson. The Grey Dreamer* (Adelaide: Rigby, 1963), Colin Roderick, *The Real Henry Lawson* (Adelaide: Rigby, 1982).

11 As the work of Graeme Davison, Richard White and others makes clear, Lawson and Paterson, like many of the 1890s "bush writers", were urban intellectuals too. However they did not celebrate the intellectual life of the city or cosmopolitan circles, and they did not court associations with European intellectual circles, although European and American influences were important in their thinking about a national culture and literature.

12 On this point I am indebted to Christine Watson for access to her PhD dissertation "'My Own Eye Witness': Australian Aboriginal Women's Autobiographical Narratives", University of Queensland, in progress. This includes a bibliography of biographical and autobiographical writing by and about Indigenous men and women in Australia.

13 Drusilla Modjeska, *Poppy* (Melbourne: McPhee Gribble/Penguin, 1990), p. 317.

14 Rita Huggins and Jackie Huggins, *Auntie Rita* (Canberra: Aboriginal Studies Press, 1994), p. ix.

15 Jackie Huggins, *Sister Girl* (St Lucia: University of Queensland Press, 1998), p. 86.

16 Anne Brewster, *Reading Aboriginal Women's Autobiography* (Sydney: Sydney University Press, 1996), p. 15.

17 David McCooey, *Artful Histories. Modern Australian Autobiography* (Cambridge: Cambridge University Press, 1996), p. 7.

18 Joy Hooton, Preface to *Australian Autobiographical Narratives. An Annotated Bibliography*, Vol. 2 (Canberra: National Library/ADFA, 1998).

19 Joy Hooton, *Stories of Herself When Young. Autobiographies of Childhood by Australian Women* (Melbourne: Oxford University Press, 1990), p. 374.

20 David Carter, *A Career in Writing: Judah Waten and the Cultural Politics of a Literary Career* (Toowoomba: Association for the Study of Australian Literature, 1997), pp. 219–20.

21 Chris Wallace-Crabbe, "Autobiography" in Laurie Hergenhan, ed., *The Penguin New Literary History of Australia* (Melbourne: Penguin, 1988), p. 564.

22 Hal Porter, *The Watcher on the Cast-Iron Balcony* (London: Faber & Faber, 1963), p. 62.

23 Vaughan Prain, "Forging Selves and Salvaging Forms: Reading Australian Autobiographical Fiction", *Meridian*, 13 (1994), p. 44.

24 Sneja Gunew, *Framing Marginalities* (Melbourne: Melbourne University Press, 1994).

25 See Delys Bird and Dennis Haskell, eds, *Whose Place? A Study of Sally Morgan's "My Place"* (Sydney: Angus & Robertson, 1992).

26 See for example the debates in *Australian Historical Studies*, 99 (1992) and 100 (1993).

27 Tim Rowse, "The Aboriginal Subject in Autobiography: Ruby Langford's *Don't Take Your Love to Town*", *Australian Literary Studies*, 16 (1993), pp. 14–29. See too Jo Robertson, "Making Sense", *Hecate*, 18 (1992), pp. 117–130.

28 Joan Newman, "Reader-response to Transcribed Oral Narrative: *A Fortunate Life* and *My Place*", *Southerly*, 48.4 (1988), pp. 376–389.

29 See David Carter, "History was on our side: memoirs of the Australian Left", *Meanjin*, 46:1 (1987), pp. 108–121.

30 McCooey, *Artful Histories*, p. 27.

31 Tom Keneally, *Homebush Boy. A Memoir* (Melbourne: Minerva, 1995), p. 1.

32 It may seem contradictory to include Ward, Hewett and other communist activists who campaigned with a profound sense of social responsibility and connection between the individual and historical forces in these remarks. However Stalinism and the growing yet resisted awareness of evil in Soviet Russia ensures tropes of innocence and knowledge are central to these personal histories of communist commitment. See Roger Milliss' *Serpent's Tooth* and Dorothy Hewett's *Wild Card* in particular.

33 Carmel Bird, ed., *The Stolen Children. Their Stories* (Sydney: Random House Australia, 1998), p. xiii.

34 Brian Castro, *Writing Asia and Auto/biography. Two lectures* (Canberra: Australian Defence Force Academy, 1995), p. 32.

10

DAVID CARTER

Critics, writers, intellectuals: Australian literature and its criticism

INTRODUCTION

More than once in recent times literary criticism has found itself in the unfamiliar circumstance of being front-page news in Australia. Controversies about the ethical and historical responsibility of literature and criticism, and a series of high-profile scandals about the identities of some celebrated authors, have brought into the public domain debates about literary theory that might otherwise have remained within the university.[1] There have been echoes of American "culture wars" about political correctness and the destruction of the canon. We have become familiar with talk about a crisis in literary studies. In the pages of the higher journalism, the universities have been accused – in one sense correctly – of having abandoned literary values and tradition for theory, ideology or pop.

Literary criticism in the universities has undergone dramatic changes over the last two decades. There has been a new confidence in the relevance of literary studies to broader issues of cultural and political importance, such as questions of ethnicity in the nation's history. But the changes in literary studies have also been driven by anxieties about the point of literary criticism in a postmodern or "post-media" world. Literary studies has typically become a kind of *cultural* studies. This has increased its scope and worldliness, but perhaps, too, its sense of significant cultural dynamics that exist beyond traditional notions of the literary.

Outside the universities there are prominent independent critics such as Peter Craven who publish regularly in newspapers and magazines, probably with a more direct influence than academic critics on publishers, readers and editors. Academic literary criticism nonetheless dominates the reception of Australian literature, especially its shaping into histories. At the same time, it is often attacked as both too specialised and too politicised. Such concerns have been at issue in the remarkable increase, in the 1990s, in debate over the role of "public intellectuals" in Australia. The public intellectual is distinguished from the academic specialist (the literary theorist, say) by his or her ability to step outside a narrow, professional field and address issues of general cultural concern. Whereas literature was once central to public intellectual life, now literary theory and political correctness, the argument goes, have corrupted contemporary criticism. Many commentators have remarked on the decline of the public intellectual and the shrinking space for serious debate as the media monopolies close in and academics retreat behind jargon. But the discourse surrounding public intellectuals is itself unprecedented; and in many ways the public presence of Australian literature is booming, for example in literary festivals or the cinema, or in books of essays aimed at the educated general reader, a new phenomenon in the marketplace.[2] All the talk about a crisis in public intellectual life might indicate that the public intellectual is in fact flourishing; but also that the nature of cultural authority, especially the authority of the literary critic, is undergoing profound change.

These debates remind us that the meanings and institutional sites of literary criticism and so the ways of being a critic in Australia have undergone significant shifts, especially since the mid twentieth century. At different times the authority of criticism has been concentrated in literary associations of educated gentlemen, in newspapers and periodicals, in informal networks of writers and critics, and in professional practice within the academy. While the history of ideas would suggest strong lines of continuity and influence, for example in the recurrence of romantic, evolutionary metaphors describing the national literature, a focus on institutional changes indicates rather the discontinuities in the meaning and function of literary criticism in Australia. It would be difficult to write the history of Australian criticism around a series of seminal books or an evolving tradition of major critics, not because of the quality of the criticism but because of the inconsecutive nature of its institutional and social contexts. It is tempting nevertheless to tell the story as one of evolutionary progress from simplicity to diversity or from colonial ignorance to postcolonial enlightenment. But one of the effects of recent work in cultural theory and historiography has been a renewed sense of the complexity – and originality – of earlier cultural formations in Australia.[3] The situation of culture in Australia must be understood not merely in terms of insularity or belatedness. Australia has always been a point where a complex pattern of cultural flows converged, and then diverged throughout the structure of local cultural institutions. A model of cultural transference and transformation is more useful in describing this pattern than cultural evolution or "becoming".

Literature and talk about literature have played a central role since at least the 1830s in debates about the status of the national culture. Literary criticism has rarely been about literature alone; at stake has been the nature of civilisation, culture and "character" in Australia and the authority to speak in their name. In the nineteenth century, debates about the national culture turned on its relation to tradition. In the twentieth century they have more often expressed a postcolonial anxiety about the status of the national culture's *modernity*. This in turn has expressed itself as anxiety about the status of the literary critic and, more particularly, the literary intellectual. What kind of critics or intellectuals should the national culture sustain? What was the appropriate relationship between critics and writers? What was the relationship between local culture, and ideas or intellectual movements from elsewhere?

Rather than a broad survey of literary criticism in Australia, the present chapter is structured around the issues outlined above. It traces the significant role of literary criticism in defining attitudes to modernity in Australia and in struggles over cultural authority; the relation of criticism to other public discourses; the shaping of criticism by notions of "high" versus "popular" cultures; institutional changes governing where and how criticism was practised; and shifts in how the critic or intellectual has been conceived; perhaps even the rise and fall of the critic in Australia.

CRITICISM AND THE INCIPIENT NATION

Early twentieth-century critics inherited from the nineteenth century a set of beliefs about national literatures that would remain influential in Australian criticism until the 1970s. Perhaps most revealing is the recurrence over a century or more of the critical judgement that the *beginnings* of a national literature could be discerned but that it had not yet fully arrived. Frederick Sinnett, in 1856, found "some small patches" of the potentially vast fiction fields that had "been cleared, and fenced, and cultivated". Two decades later, Marcus Clarke found in Adam Lindsay Gordon's verse "something very like the beginning of a national school of poetry". Two decades more, and H.G. Turner could claim only that "Australian literature begins to assume some definiteness of form". A.G. Stephens, no friend to the critical views of Clarke or Turner, saw in Lawson and Paterson "something like the beginnings of a national school of poetry". Vance Palmer in 1905: "even now the national movement is beginning". P.R. Stephensen in 1935: "we are on the threshold of Australian self-consciousness, at the point of developing Australian nationality, and with it Australian culture". And Vincent Buckley in 1957: "we are still not quite modern ... yet we are on our way to being mature". The national literature or culture was always emerging but never fully emerged. As Miles Franklin remarked, "Native literature remained chronically incipient".[4]

The recurrence of this judgement suggests the lack of continuity in local literary institutions. It also reveals how widely shared was a particular notion of literature and its relationship to nation, race and civilisation. As Brian Kiernan has argued, the concept of a national literature emerged well before the political nationalism of the late nineteenth century.[5] From the 1830s, the idea of an Australian literature was connected to the social and moral development of the nation. A neo-classical view of literature as the index of a society's level of civilisation was absorbed in romantic theories of literature as the expression not merely of individual genius but of the genius of the nation or race, its essential spirit or character. In setting the model for Australian literature, Nettie Palmer wrote, in 1929, "it is Shakespeare that proves England a nation".[6] In what kind of literature, then, would Australian nationality be proved?

Literature had this exalted role before any of the other arts because of its seemingly more "organic" relationship to place and race: it was "the basis, the soil of the arts".[7] Behind such arguments lie evolutionary ideas regarding the influence of environment on national character. Kiernan refers to the specific influence of Taine's *History of English Literature* with its "scientific" approach to literature as determined by race, environment and epoch.[8] In a country "without history" such as Australia it followed that the environment would be most influential. Literature would adapt to the environment; the environment would express itself through a literature "racy of the soil".[9] Despite Marcus Clarke's famous speculation that the "dominant note of Australian scenery" was "Weird Melancholy", evolutionary thinking generally suggested a more optimistic view of the national character which became fundamental to both nationalist and imperialist attitudes: "the great body of our nascent literature is *cheerful and vigorous*, as becomes the pioneer writers of a young and hopeful country".[10] The idea that Australia was pioneering a literature often led to the romantic notion that it should be a literature of pioneering. Such evolutionary assumptions generated the constant search for the emergence of the national literature, while the recurrent sense that it had not yet fully emerged was inevitable given that it was expected, impossibly, to express the whole "national life and character".

It is, however, easy to underestimate the level and complexity of colonial literary activity both in the spread of its institutions – by mid-century there was a thriving if volatile newspaper and magazine market – and its intellectual range, as the English tradition was defined through classical, continental, romantic and religious knowledges, and then again through knowledge of the local. While there were few books published on local literature, criticism flourished in newspapers and magazines.[11] Essays on literature were part of a more general field that included writings on moral, philosophical and religious subjects. Discussions of the national literature participated in a wider discourse about the progress of civilisation in the colony. Criticism was not a matter for literary experts – there were in this sense no literary critics – but rather a field for all cultivated men and very occasionally women. If the ideal was that of the man of letters, few other than journalists saw themselves as professional writers, let alone full-time literary critics.

It is also easy to underestimate the *contemporaneity* of colonial culture. Imperialism carried its own kind of internationalism. The imperial connection did not mean only that local culture was provincial. It could also mean cosmopolitanism, a sense of contemporaneity with literary and intellectual issues in London, Europe and America. Towards the end of the century, however, these cosmopolitan links became less rather than more important in elite literary circles. A narrower form of British affiliation came to dominate official culture as the new imperialism flourished and as romanticism settled into Victorian moral hygiene. Even for an enthusiast such as H.G. Turner, the "service" of Australian literature was "to *supplement* and perchance in *minor* departments replace the magnificent body of writing to which our lucky stars destined us to be heirs".[12] Turner was bemused by the popular success of Paterson and Lawson, for he could not see their modernity. Cosmopolitanism re-emerged in a more populist, nationalist and anti-imperialist cultural formation, particularly around the Sydney *Bulletin*.

THE RISE OF THE CRITIC

The *Bulletin* was a distinctively modern phenomenon in the 1880s and 1890s. It addressed a new kind of citizen and consumer; it identified the public or national interest against established interests; its city was a place of energy and spectacle; it was ironic; it spoke for the here and now.[13] Its nationalism was a statement of its modernity, a way of placing Australia in the contemporary world. Its work in literature had similar effects, democratising and modernising the relation between writers and readers and helping to bring a new kind of writer and writing into being. The *Bulletin* was central in the widespread feeling that "something like the beginnings of a national school of literature" had emerged by the century's turn. Australian literature could be seen to have its own time and place, no longer merely as a "supplement" to English literature. This development was understood in evolutionary terms but we can understand it now in terms of institutional changes: a new class of readers, the rise of popular journalism, the professionalisation of writing careers, an inner-city literary "bohemia".

What was new about A.G. Stephens' work on literature, as critic and editor of the *Bulletin*'s literary section, the Red Page, was not a new literary theory but the way he modernised the business of criticism. This was the effect of literary realism overlaying the late-Romantic heritage but also of Stephens' journalistic context. The *Bulletin* was a popular commercial weekly, not a literary magazine. This format demanded a local, contemporary focus and delivered a new kind of audience to Stephens which he made his own even if it lacked traditional forms of cultural capital. His criticism was almost wholly focused on contemporary writing or the contemporary "force" of earlier writers.[14] He wrote not through populist identification with his readers or fellow writers but as one engaged in the same cultural enterprise, criticising in order to educate, entertain, improve and exemplify "the possibilities of work in literature" in Australia.[15] The *Bulletin* provided him with evidence of thousands of readers and writers "quickening" across the continent, and Stephens defined his role in relation to this burgeoning national movement.

If Stephens was Australia's first professional literary critic, institutionally he was a professional journalist whose authority to talk about literature – and a wide range of other subjects – was general and amateur rather than specialist.[16] The profession of critic was still in its earliest stages. Stephens was the most original figure in a vigorous public culture of literary journalism perhaps best represented in its witty and biting theatre criticism. In this commercial sphere the literary and the journalistic, the popular and the high, inhabited the same public space. Stephens had a journalist's sense of the craft of writing alongside an elevated, ideal sense of the literary. This enabled him to give the idea of a national literature a more popular meaning, and, at the same time, to "elevate" popular reading and writing, to give them more national and more *literary* meanings. His modernising literary nationalism was expressed in the radical break he saw between the colonial past and the emerging national present. Stephens shared the common view that literature should be both local and universal, but Australia was no longer a matter of externals, incidental to the permanent truths. For the Australian writer it was the necessary site of the universal, to be embraced not transcended. Thus Stephens' insistence on the "wealth of novel inspiration for the writers who will live Australia's life and utter her message".[17] It was this mix of "high" and popular values that enabled the *Bulletin* and its Red Page to establish, not a new literary elite, but something like a "national literary club" for a new generation of writers.[18]

Stephens' credentials as much more than a "literary nationalist" are by now well established. His focus on the contemporary meant, no less, a focus on the international (this was not the opposite of "national"; "colonial" was). On the Red Page "discussions and printings of Australian literature ran side by side with reviews of Stephen Crane, Kipling, Mark Twain, Gorki, Oscar Wilde, Olive Schreiner, Bernard Shaw, D'Annunzio, Henry James and many others".[19] "Cosmopolitan" was one of his preferred terms of praise, even if his list of writers who were "essentially Australian, yet cosmopolitan" comprised only three rows of asterisks.[20] Critics have also defended Stephens from mere nationalism by showing how he judged Australian literature always on a "universal" scale. Most famously, he celebrated Miles Franklin's *My Brilliant Career* (1901) as "the very first Australian novel" yet judged that it was "not a notable literary performance".[21] But the appeal to universal values is something of a mannerism in Stephens' criticism and it is likely to be the aspect of his writing *least* interesting to readers today. It reveals most clearly the limits of the journalistic sphere, and the orthodox dimensions of Stephens' taste for "artistic emotion" or "ideals of beauty".[22] It was difficult on this scale for realism to make it to the very highest level of literature. Modernism had even less chance, and Stephens' sense of the new would remain in the 1920s what it had been in the 1890s. The same might be said of Christopher Brennan despite his precocious appreciation of French Symbolism.[23]

MODERNISM AND THE NATIONAL CULTURE

The *Bulletin* continued into the twentieth century as Australia's principal magazine of review, producing new offshoots such as the *Bookfellow* and the *Lone Hand*. But by the 1920s its modernity had disappeared into a conservative, patriotic nationalism that was anti-cosmopolitan. Its literary pages were still varied and sometimes contentious – its weekly appearance encouraged conversation and debate on literary matters – but there was little of the creative pressure that Stephens had brought to bear. The Red Page itself was not noticeably nationalist. Essays and reviews covered much the same ground as any middle-brow English magazine. A few essays on art and nationality by Louis Esson and Vance Palmer were just one minor part of the mix and were answered in the predictable way with arguments about universality or individual greatness.[24]

The language of criticism was largely that of the romantic nineteenth century: critics praised writing that was natural, simple, noble and sincere. But that language was increasingly under pressure. The Red Page of the early 1920s worries away at the manifestations of modernity all around it – Cubism, Futurism, Freud, Joyce, Pound, jazz, free verse and free women. America is ubiquitous, for it presented a special kind of problem. While American literature represented all the worst aspects of modernity –

sex-obsessed, feminised and mass-produced – it also showed a distinctly American energy that could suggest just what Australian literature lacked. The *Bulletin* and other magazines that defined the Australian literary scene in the early twenties were on the cusp of a new "modern" understanding of culture. As commercial magazines, most of them, they had a strong sense of their own contemporaneity. They could identify themselves with the world of Shaw, Wells, James, Conrad or Synge. But the "ultra-moderns" – the "neurotic-erotic moderns" – were another case altogether.[25] Modernism was characterised through a sense of *unbalance*: ideas divorced from emotion; style distorting nature; an overload of abstraction, introspection or sex. If one thing defined this moment of extreme modernism for its critics it was the way form seemed to be unhinged from feeling, in violation of the "natural" laws of artistic expression which called for their organic unity. Represented thus, as lacking form or as nothing but form, modernism was unnatural, primitive, pathological; or merely fashionable, artificial, a confidence trick. It was typically the product of literary schools, cults or "isms", not individual vision. By contrast, an optimistic pastoral tradition set the frame for Australian literature.

There was nothing unique about this Australian response to modernism nor were Australian critics "behind the times", for modernism was still marginal in contemporary culture. But the sense of Australia as distant and different confirmed critics in their overwhelmingly dismissive response. Even for critics unenthusiastic about nationalism, Australia could be seen as a refuge from the twin aspects of modernity: the decadence of Europe, manifested in the fractured forms of modernist art, and the degraded modern culture of America, from jazz to cinema. Both were seen as alien to an Australia defined as young, vigorous, cheerful and *manly*, with a culture as wholesome as its climate.[26] Against a modern world divided into "isms", or massed into an anonymous market, Australia was projected as still a "living culture", a classless organic community, a unified nation.

In such terms criticism politely excused itself from having to think its way through the intellectual challenges of modernism. Australia's national characteristics belonged to a pre-industrial pastoral world cleansed even of Henry Lawson's darker notes. These responses were not just ideological but institutional in that, unlike in America and England, there was no fully fledged, distinct class of "literary intellectuals". The bohemian circles of writers that formed in the 1880s–1890s had not developed into a permanent intelligentsia. Literature was reviewed in numerous papers but the mode was genial amateurism rather than intellectual authority. The magazines were broad in their contents and readership; even a dedicated journal of arts and letters such as the *Lone Hand* was proudly middle-brow. The universities had little to do with contemporary Australian literature. There was virtually no place within mainstream Australian literary culture where modernism – as a set of ideas, a movement – could be given an intellectual response. A partial exception was the virulently anti-modernist *Vision* magazine.[27] A fragmentary intelligentsia existed in more political domains, in socialist or rationalist movements for example, but these were marginal. Ideas of the nation as an ideal, democratic community did not encourage the concept of a separate class of intellectuals.

THE NATIONALIST PROJECT

It was against this background that literary nationalism – and the career of the nationalist intellectual – achieved its modern form, most prominently in the work of Vance and Nettie Palmer and P.R. Stephensen.[28] Although they inherited romantic, evolutionary notions of culture and shared with conservatives a belief in Australia's essential vitality, their nationalism was defined by a distinctly modern sense of social and cultural crisis. Its meaning lay not in celebration of a pastoral tradition but in the problem of modern democracy. Its formative moment was the emerging split between high and "mass" cultures. Nationalism, in this view, was a contemporary movement; indeed, alongside the Irish revival, an *international* movement in which vernacular cultures would underwrite the creation of new, democratic national cultures.

The Palmers applied a general post-war analysis of cultural malaise to the specific situation of Australian culture. Their nationalism was a complex phenomenon: cosmopolitan in its sense of other national literatures, isolationist in its dislike of cosmopolitan modernism; populist but never certain that the public existed; more confident than Stephens about the "deep" origins of a national culture but more pessimistic about its continuity into the present; intellectual in calling for a serious, committed Australian literature, but anti-intellectual in the privileging of literature above abstract thought or modern "isms". Nonetheless, even if its solutions were inevitably more symptom than cure, nationalism between the wars did name an unresolved problem, the problem of colonial identity. Shorn of their organicism and populism, certain aspects of literary nationalism can – once again – strike us as surprisingly modern in their sense of a radical originality in Australian culture: for example, despite its romantic racism, Rex Ingamells' notion that Aboriginality was part of the contemporary meaning of Australian culture.[29]

From the other side of modernism, the Palmers worked the image of Australia's 1890s into a powerful myth of origins in which "conscious literature" and folk culture were fused in the ideal image of an organic national culture. Such a myth "solved" the problems of modernity and colonialism together. The writer should be at one with the reader, the culture, the people – the soil – in a living relationship, an idea linked to the bush where individuality and community could still be imagined democratically together. For Nettie Palmer the key notion was *intimacy*, the evolution of an intimate relation between writer and environment, writer and audience.[30] This was the message of Australia's 1890s, all but lost it seemed in the modernising 1920s. On one side, provincial or colonial attitudes still prevailed; on the other, the new trends of cosmopolitanism and commercialisation threatened what fragile traditions had been laid down. Without its own strong cultural life, Vance Palmer argued, Australia was peculiarly vulnerable to the cheapening (even feminisation) of culture, above all in the rootless cities and standardised suburbs.[31]

The heroic task of the contemporary writer and critic was to resist these forces and bring forth a common culture. Palmer found its modern expression in the *novel*, with Conrad as one model.[32] Against the general elevation of poetry, Palmer's commitment to the novel was symptomatic of the modern form of nationalism and was shared with a generation of literary nationalists who emerged in the 1930s. The novel was the art form, above all others, in which individual and social expression could be fused. In this sense, the ideal form of the novel was an ideal image of the national culture itself.

The modernity of the Palmers' nationalism can also be seen in their "life project" as nationalist literary intellectuals, articulating a new image of the writer and critic, equally, as a public intellectual defined by his or her responsibility to the national culture. They worked to separate the vocation of intellectual from the uncommitted professional literary journalism that surrounded them. But there remained an anxiety, at once structural and ideological, towards the notion of the intellectual as distinct from the "writer". Australia lacked *serious* critics and an "impersonal critical atmosphere". Consequently there was no responsive public for Australian writing. But the notion of a professional intellectual or writing class was foreign to the idea of a national culture in touch with its popular roots. Then again, where the people should have been, there instead was the mass audience "in its promiscuousness, vagueness and lack of any kind of unity". Where, then, did the genuine culture and its "peculiarly Australian kind of democracy" exist?[33] Among the people or only among a small band of intellectuals, in social institutions or only in literature? The nationalist project was driven by these anxieties, alternating between pessimism at what had been lost or ignored and optimism that despite everything a distinctive culture persisted at the core of our national character, almost by definition, because it *was* the national character.

While mid-century nationalism extended Stephens' understanding of the national culture, it also represented a *narrowing* of what literature in Australia could mean. This was not simply a matter of the limits of the nationalist critical vocabulary, but an effect of the professionalisation of literary work in Australia in which the Palmers were centrally engaged. Throughout their criticism, they made clear distinctions between "serious" literature and everything else. In doing so they were defining the cultural authority of the critic. The narrowing of the field was in this sense a necessary effect of their efforts to give Australian literature depth and tradition, to make it worthy of intellectual work. But although the Palmers came as close as anyone to the public "life of letters", their careers indicate the uncertain institutional status of the literary critic at least until the 1960s. Their work fell structurally between the professional and the amateur, with a significant degree of cultural authority legitimised through their public roles in literary journalism, but with no secure institutional location. The career of the freelance intellectual was partly choice, partly a virtue made out of necessity.

LITERARY INTELLECTUALS AND CULTURAL CRISIS

Despite the recurrence of nationalist language through to the 1950s it is misleading to see an unbroken nationalist mainstream dominating Australian criticism. Nationalism was crossed by a mix of traditional, vitalist, bohemian and communist tendencies that made up the web of literary conversation. The more "intellectual" forms of nationalism were also internationalist, taking their bearings from European and American models.

Literary nationalism had an ambivalent status, at once commonplace and marginal in the field of culture. That Australian culture had its source in the bush; that it was popular rather than intellectual and cheerful rather than gloomy; that it first took shape in Lawson and Paterson; that environment and national character together made it distinctive: such ideas were widespread. But only rarely were they shaped into a coherent intellectual program or cultural critique. Thus while most discussions of Australian literature assumed a "nationalist" framework underscored by pastoral or post-Anzac myths, the militant nationalism of the Palmers, Stephensen and others was a minority position. As they attempted to distinguish the vocation of the intellectual from occasional literary journalism, nationalist intellectuals occupied one small corner of the literary field while arguing its centrality.

Literary nationalism had yet to find any authoritative statement or institutional identity. The strongest sense among the nationalist intelligentsia throughout the 1930s and 1940s was still of "the inconsecutive nature of our literary life" and the feeling that the nationalist argument needed "stating over and over".[34] The forms of criticism remained ephemeral, their brief lives passing in the weekly or monthly papers. The *Bulletin* offered some continuity, some space for intellectual contestation, otherwise the critical density of periodical and book publication was mostly lacking.[35] Expressions of anxiety about the national culture, its absence, betrayal or unfulfilled promise, were far more common than confident statements of the Australian tradition.

Further, political events in the 1930s – the Depression, international fascism and communism, the Spanish civil war and world war – changed the meaning of democratic and nationalist arguments. These events were not seen as external to Australia (or to literature) but symptomatic of a deep crisis in its national culture.[36] Fascism abroad was linked to censorship and conservatism at home. Nationalism had to be distinguished from the complacent patriotism of the mainstream press and politics. For many writers, literary culture was at once politicised and "intellectualised". The early 1930s saw a number of little magazines influenced by radical political and artistic theories. New writers' organisations were established or, in the case of the Fellowship of Australian Writers, re-organised around a more explicit understanding of the writer's social responsibility. Novelists and critics turned to writing pamphlets on culture, democracy and freedom. The "crisis of civilisation" demanded an engagement with new political and artistic ideas *together*, and in this crossover of aesthetic and political discourses the literary intellectual was called into being.[37]

This was the moment of Stephensen's *The Foundations of Culture in Australia* (1936). "We are," he wrote, "being *forced* into national consciousness."[38] His essay is famous as an aggressive reprise of environmental language but less well known as a call for *intellectuals*. "An act of intellectual self-consciousness, an *act of thought* performed now, by those equipped to do the thinking for this nation, is necessary." Stephensen found no sustaining tradition, no literature of contemporary Australia. He wanted "a finer, less sensational, less journalistic, Australian literature"; in short, a more intellectually sophisticated and modern literature.

THE AUSTRALIAN TRADITION

In 1942 a special "Crisis Issue" of the new magazine *Meanjin* appeared (its name suggests the role Aboriginal culture played in the search for a national sense of belonging which also motivated the Jindyworobak movement).[39] It was symptomatic that in the space of a year or so *Meanjin* had moved from a poetry magazine to cultural politics. By 1943 it had become a quarterly, the form of the most serious reviews and expressive of its distance from "mere" journalism. *Meanjin* was a new kind of magazine in Australia, a magazine for literary intellectuals. Much of its talk was "self-reflexive", discussions on the role of the writer and the magazine itself. Cultural commentary, philosophy, literary criticism, history and anthropology appeared together, alongside verse and fiction, in what seemed like a shared public sphere of liberal values. Editor C.B. Christesen was committed to opening up lines to European literature and philosophy, aligning Australian intellectual life with a "modern tradition" which he understood in terms of an enlarged, humanist realism.

Despite the broad range of its articles, literature remained at the centre of *Meanjin*'s interests as the medium through which cultural values were created and sustained. Christesen saw his magazine as "a literary forum ... a document of our aesthetic development".[40] He wanted it to produce "a core of sound literary criticism". It is important, while recognising the magazine's commitment to nationalist cultural politics, not to underestimate the role it played in sustaining the formal study of Australian literature. Alongside *Southerly*, *Meanjin* enabled the regular publication of extended critical studies. The two quarterlies "virtually introduced the formal critical essay into twentieth century Australian literary criticism".[41]

Perhaps the most important shift to which *Meanjin* contributed was a new confidence in talk about an Australian tradition. The *presence* of an Australian tradition comes to replace that sense of its loss or absence which had produced earlier nationalist arguments. The previous decade had seen a substantial output of new fiction and, later, poetry that seemed both modern and distinctively Australian. M. Barnard Eldershaw's *Essays in Australian Fiction* had, in 1938, taken the unprecedented step of devoting a whole book to individual studies of contemporary novelists. (Women played a much larger part in Australian criticism before its institutionalisation in the universities in the 1950s.) This newly-available density in the literary tradition was underscored by developments in the writing of Australian history which, earlier than literature, had become the subject of a serious body of work, from W.K. Hancock to Brian Fitzpatrick.[42] The late 1940s sees a concentration of articles in *Meanjin* on literature and the democratic tradition, including Manning Clark's first two contributions, on mateship and tradition.[43]

The notion of an Australian cultural tradition received its authoritative statements in a series of major books in the 1950s: Vance Palmer's *The*

Legend of the Nineties (1954), A.A. Phillips' *The Australian Tradition* (1958) and Russel Ward's *The Australian Legend* (1958).[44] These books were historical studies of a social tradition: "the evolving personality and the evolving traditions of the Australian community, as reflected in the works of our writers".[45] Although the socio-political rather than environmental aspects of nationalism now received greater emphasis, the image of the bush contained both meanings at once. Realism and democracy, it was assumed, went together. Australia's unique historical experiences had given rise to distinctively Australian attitudes, democratic, nationalist and popular, manifested at first unconsciously in ballads and folk song and then consciously in the literature of the 1890s. These same ideals *still* defined what was most valuable, and most Australian, in Australian society and culture. That was the point of the argument, sharpened for nationalist intellectuals by their sense of a new struggle between true and false popular cultures and true and false democracies in the Cold War. When *Overland* magazine began in 1954, connected to the Communist Party and the Realist Writers movement, it could name itself heir to a continuous democratic and realist Australian tradition.[46] Communist intellectuals shared the democratic nationalist reading of Australia's literary history but articulated a more politically-conscious working-class tradition within nationalism.[47]

What is easily forgotten is the *newness* of this understanding of the Australian tradition after the war, particularly its radical democratic edge. The sense of a tradition with historical density extending back into the nineteenth century and forward into contemporary literature was scarcely available earlier, to even the most optimistic nationalists, although it had always been foreshadowed. For Phillips, by contrast, there was a "democratic theme" in Australian literature, reflecting the "spirit of the nineties". Its effects could be found in a wide range of contemporary writers as a belief in "the Common Man", a determination to do without the "fripperies" of aesthetic practice – though Phillips could also refer to Furphy's "literary modernism" – and a "preference for revealing the simple verities rather than the sophistications of human nature".[48] Phillips was university educated but like Barnard and Eldershaw wrote as an informed amateur (in the fullest meaning of the word). The amateur critic in this sense was closer to the figure of the public intellectual than was the academic specialist, in a period when the bulk of the criticism of Australian literature was still written outside the university.

The notion of an Australian tradition gave new complexity and depth to nationalist cultural history. But it also simplified and narrowed the *literary* history. The body of a strong democratic and realist tradition immediately produced its shadow, an alternative stream of "Australian literature" which could only be seen as alien, belonging neither to its time or place or to its public, but *there* nevertheless – colonial fiction and verse, Christopher Brennan and, more recently, Patrick White. Underlying the "tradition" was still an organic, evolutionary model of the national culture emerging from colonialism into national self-consciousness and then, soon, on to "unselfconscious" maturity. Ironically, nationalist criticism revealed its limitations most clearly where it also found its strengths, in its understanding of literature as a social phenomenon.

AUSTRALIAN LITERATURE AND THE UNIVERSITIES

Meanjin and *Southerly* went further than any previous journals in bringing together academic and amateur work. One part of the nationalist argument had long been that Australia *had* a literature and it should be studied. Some Australian literature had been researched and taught in universities since the 1920s.[49] This work was uncontroversial because it remained clearly supplementary to the English department's core business. By the 1950s, however, the place of Australian literature in the universities became contentious, first because of the pressure of the newly articulated Australian tradition, second because of changes in the English departments themselves. Lectures sponsored by the Commonwealth Literary Fund were also important, bringing non-academic critics such as Miles Franklin into the universities while giving younger university critics the chance to exercise their professional skills on Australian literature.[50]

In 1954 *Meanjin* initiated a forum on the question of "Australian Literature and the Universities". The academic contributors were not hostile to Australian literature but sceptical about whether it possessed the necessary cultural capital for the real work of English, as a training in critical standards and "sensibility". Only Vance Palmer argued differently, proposing "Australian studies" rather than literature in isolation.[51] Nonetheless the density which now cohered around the Australian tradition was felt by others besides nationalist intellectuals. In the two decades following the war, a new generation of professional critics entered Australian English departments, trained in the modern tradition and armed with the vocation of "English" and its methods of ethico-formalist criticism.[52] Such views intensified the centrality of criticism itself in the literary domain; Australian literature was revealed as a "new" field scarcely touched by modern criticism and demanding its close scrutiny. *Was* there a tradition? Was it a *literary* tradition? Did it coincide with the *best* Australian literature?

The decade from the mid-1950s saw the institutionalisation of Australian literature in that its locus shifted from the ephemeral forms of general magazines, newspapers and occasional books of "amateur" criticism to the university and critical quarterlies. Vincent Buckley's return to the question of Australian literature and the universities, in 1959, summed up a process that had already begun in critical articles, of applying the same "standards" to Australian literature as were applied to English literature. What was needed, Buckley argued, was critical discrimination in forming a properly articulated canon of Australian authors based on "some agreement about their relative value"; and then, more reluctantly, "some link between Australian literature and Australian history or sociology: if only to stop the swamping of our literature by sociological interests and criteria".[53] The latter reference was to nationalist criticism. A work should be analysed, not as an "adjunct" to sociology, but as a "document in the history of Australian attitudes and sensibility": "It would [then] be a *literary* analysis all the way." This slight shift of focus from sociology to sensibility had major consequences in redefining the *autonomy* of both the literary text and literary criticism. The national historical framework remained but it was removed from the centre of properly literary concerns.

The institutionalisation of literary criticism within the universities meant arguing Australian literature back into the mainstream of English or European literature, back into a modern tradition. (Strangely, then, the new criticism was generally very narrow in its own intellectual reference points. It seldom stretched far beyond the reach of Arnold, Eliot, Leavis.) The literary works most highly valued were those seen as aligning Australian reality with European culture in a synthesis of the Australian and the traditional or the Australian and the modern taken to define the *maturity* of Australian literature. Maturity was also figured in terms of emerging "individuality". This approach favoured relatively neglected, complex, "European" writers such as Brennan and Richardson; an extraordinary number of studies of these two was produced from the 1950s to the 1970s.[54] The argument towards maturity was a reflection of the critics' own "mature" institutionalisation.

In the process of revaluation, literary values were discerned less in formal characteristics than in moral, "metaphysical" or "spiritual" questions.[55] These were grasped as universal, in contrast to ephemeral "sociological interests". Discovering literary greatness was not as important as discovering the right kind of "literariness". Brennan's poetry was valued upwards: although a failed *oeuvre*, it was the right kind of failure, compared to Paterson who represented the wrong kind of success. In a series of publications from the early 1950s Australian writers past and present were subject to critical scrutiny.[56] Colonial writing was revalued, especially poetry, because again it showed the right kind of literariness; poetry in general was revalued against the nationalist preference for realist prose. Canonical authors like Lawson were re-interpreted for the metaphysical beneath their social themes.

Re-interpreting the high nationalist moment of the 1890s against "strictly literary standards", G.A. Wilkes concluded:

> Lawson is memorable not for the part of his work ... that reflects the temper of his age, but for the part that transcends it, while Furphy's work is important not for its democratic temper or offensively Australian bias, but for its exploration of issues that are not local, but universal in their reference ... The best poetry written at the time [Brennan] is unrelated to social and political movements, as is the work of the most notable novelist to emerge [Richardson].[57]

Buckley provided a similar revaluation in "The Image of Man in Australian Poetry", the lead piece in his 1957 *Essays in Poetry, Mainly Australian* (the casual authority of the titles suggests the weight of the institution).[58] Brennan, not Lawson, was the pivotal figure, producing "the first genuinely unselfconscious Australian poetry ... representative of the human condition in a way, and with a depth, which makes Lawson's attempt at representative statement appear no more than striking of an average". The notion of poetry shaping Buckley's essays carries within it all the weight of the modern tradition, from Arnold to Eliot.

"Brennan stands like a Colossus between the world of our first nationhood and the world of our modern endeavours." This remarkable figure grounds Buckley's subsequent account, leading to a model of synthesis at once familiar from earlier critics and radically new in the literary history it describes. *Southerly* and the *Bulletin*, especially under Douglas Stewart's editorship of the Red Page (1940–61), had maintained a strand of Australian literature, especially poetry, based on a more vitalist, individualist ideology than the nationalist tradition.[59] Many of the twentieth-century poets featured in the influential 1958 *Penguin Book of Australian Verse* could not be easily accommodated in the nationalist canon, but now became the very definition of Australian literature's modern maturity. Buckley traces a line from Brennan to Slessor and FitzGerald, then to Webb, McAuley, Hope, Wright and Stewart. This was the evolution that mattered, not the democratic tradition. Australian poetry was reaching "spiritual maturity", a "deepening of sensibility to the point where the land is conceived ... in terms which are at once spiritual, moral, sensory, and directed to the drama of human existence". The poets were *individual,* not "in any obvious or insistent way, Australian"; but each had "begun to bring together into a satisfying synthesis the objective and the subjective ... European culture and Australian fact". Buckley insisted that his arguments for "a literature strongly rooted in a local place and atmosphere are not at all the same as the arguments for a nationalist bias and stereotype".[60]

MODERNITY AND MATURITY: PATRICK WHITE AND THE CANON

The nationalist social tradition was rendered superficial in relation to true literary meaning. It was also rendered *obsolete*, as if belonging to an earlier, "immature" moment in the culture's development. The argument with nationalism was partly about redefining the image of Australian modernity. Buckley rewrote the history of Australian poetry to show the contemporary poets as its deepest evolutionary outcome. In another influential essay, H.P. Heseltine rewrote the whole history of Australian literature so that Patrick White emerged as its modernity and its maturity.[61]

Heseltine defined the "literary heritage" (not "tradition") as "that element of our most accomplished literary works which makes known their Australianness"; he thus makes literary standards coincide with distinctive national qualities. Heseltine takes three common versions of the Australian tradition: Phillips' "democratic theme", confrontation with the land, and evolution from colony to nationhood. Each has a point, he argues, but none is adequate to define "the very *centre* of the Australian imagination". Calling on Trilling's notion of "the modern element in modern literature", Heseltine, who had studied in America, modernises the Australian canon by claiming it is this modern element that defines the "Australianness of Australian writing". From the beginning, Australian literature expressed "the terror at the basis of being", from Clarke to Lawson to Hope and White. White's *Voss* (1957) provides the ultimate synthesis, for it "fuses almost all those aspects of Australia's literary heritage which define both its modernity and its Australianness". This was a powerful form of argument that did not reject the nationalist tradition but absorbed it, giving it a new depth and modernity.

The sudden emergence of White's novels *The Tree of Man* (1955) and *Voss* was a major event in the history of Australian criticism. The two novels took themes deeply embedded in nationalist history but treated them in a symbolic or "metaphysical" manner that appeared to contradict the democratic, realist tradition. For some, White was an un-Australian writer, anti-realist and anti-democratic.[62] For a critic like Buckley, by contrast, he was just the kind of writer who might be canonised – another case

of "spiritual maturity" – whether or not his works were totally successful literary achievements.[63] White's fiction seemed to be at once highly
individual, within the modern tradition, and distinctively Australian. Critics
linked him to Hope and McAuley, and to Brennan as precursor, even though
they often remained uncomfortable with his "anti-organic" symbolism and
disdain of the genteel.[64]

For many nationalist critics, White caused a troubled revaluation of the
Australian tradition, already under stress from the weight of critical re-
interpretation. Such was the power of White's canonisation that to reject
him was virtually to announce one's own marginality. White could be
accommodated by broadening the notion of realism to include, say,
"psychological realism" or by changing the grounds of the tradition itself.
Overland shifted its talk from the Australian "tradition" to the Australian
"myth".[65] John McLaren argued that White was "the latest contributor
to a distinctly Australian tradition, which rises from the hostility of the
landscape to man's efforts to tame it". Phillips added a footnote to the 1966
edition of *The Australian Tradition* to the effect that, in *The Tree of Man*,
White had "succeeded in reconciling a sensitive interpretation of Australian
life with a keen feeling for the spiritual mysteries". By the mid-sixties, in
short, the new language of metaphysical depth had won the day even within
nationalism itself.

The redefined Australian literary tradition was confirmed in a series of
books. Buckley's *Essays in Poetry* contained individual studies of Slessor,
FitzGerald, Hope, Wright and McAuley. Grahame Johnston's collection,
Australian Literary Criticism (1962), reprinted Wilkes on the 1890s,
A.D. Hope's seminal "Standards in Australian Literature", plus individual
essays on Brennan, Neilson, FitzGerald, Slessor, Wright, Hope, McAuley,
Lawson, Furphy, Richardson, Boyd, Herbert and White. Geoffrey Dutton's
more generous *The Literature of Australia* (1964) included broader essays,
some in the nationalist vein, but again was dominated by essays on
individual writers in the canon.[66] Wilkes' *Australian Literature: A Conspectus* (1969) drew the orthodox themes into a book-length study. White
in fiction, Hope and McAuley in poetry, provided the culmination of its
story – "the extension of European civilisation, and the assertion of an
indigenous culture" coming together "to produce a literature that is both
distinctive and mature".[67] Despite its different intellectual provenance,
Judith Wright's "Romantic-idealist" study of traditional and environmental
influences in her *Preoccupations in Australian Poetry* (1965) could be
recruited to the cause. It would take another generation before the postcolonial potential of Wright's – or Brian Elliott's – criticism could be
perceived.[68]

POLITICS AND PROFESSIONALISATION

As John Docker has argued, the anti-nationalist tenor of the new academic criticism was not only an effect of its institutionalisation but also of its political context within what Buckley called the "peculiarly Australian intellectual cold war".[69] Literature was a key battlefield in this ideological struggle because of its traditional significance as the bearer of both national and universal meanings. Although, for most critics, the move "beyond" nationalism was a matter of applying appropriate professional rather than political standards in criticism, the influence of the cold-war notion of the "end of ideology" was pervasive. For others, like Buckley and McAuley, there was a more conscious project of wresting the cultural meanings of the national literature away from left-leaning nationalist or communist intellectuals. McAuley's opening editorial in *Quadrant* met point by point the foundational principles of cultural nationalism by redefining the core concepts of Australianness, modernity, democracy, tradition, liberalism and literature.[70] As Susan Lever has argued, the poetry published in *Quadrant*, although apolitical, worked to underwrite the magazine's ideological project.[71] The "ordered, rational, decorous" poetic language spoke eloquently for civilised tradition against the twin evils of nationalism and modernism (communism was a form of both).

To see the cultural field polarised into antagonistic ideological camps dramatises the fact of a fundamental struggle over cultural authority in the 1950s and 1960s among literary intellectuals. It captures the institutional distance between nationalist and "new" critics. But is misleading if it suggests utterly opposed notions of literature or literary criticism. Underlying debates over the meaning of the Australian tradition was a common "expressive realist" aesthetic based on organic form and fidelity to individual experience.[72] Christesen, Phillips and the Palmers shared with the academic critics a belief in literary autonomy, in "disinterested criticism", and in the universal values of great literature.[73] So did communist writers. On the other hand, modernism remained as difficult for Hope and McAuley as for nationalist critics; for others it could be accommodated from an academic distance as a modern tradition. Buckley and Wilkes were as committed to defining the distinctive qualities of Australian literature as were nationalist critics. Some, like Heseltine or Vivian Smith, although within the circle of the new academic criticism, were not anti-nationalist in their wider intellectual sympathies. There was a broadly shared assumption (not shared by James McAuley) about the natural links between literature and the values of liberal humanism.

Interestingly, like earlier commentators, authoritative university critics such as Buckley, Hope and McAuley still derived much of their cultural status from *outside* the university, as poets and therefore as committed "amateur" readers rather than academic specialists. Christopher Lee has described a complex set of sceptical, sometimes hostile responses among writers, literary journalists – and academics themselves – to the professionalisation of the criticism of Australian literature.[74] Institutionalisation brought with it the suspicion that academics were less than adequate to the role of writer or (less commonly) intellectual. Buckley argued that literature was not really a university subject at all in the sense that other subjects were.[75]

As Patrick Buckridge suggests, the commitment by university critics to Australian literature must be understood in positive not merely negative, anti-nationalist, terms.[76] Buckley's commitment to literature was part of a broader commitment to the intellectual life, which saw literature as profoundly expressive of the human condition. Wilkes' criticism was as often scholarly as evaluative or anti-nationalist, as in his studies of Brennan. The new criticism *could* render Australian literary works as complex, morally serious texts in ways that nationalist criticism had rarely managed.

There was also an ongoing stream of "middle-ground" criticism that remained largely unaffected by the intellectual cold war, for example the monumental work of H.M. Green, memorable for its discussions of print culture, or Cecil Hadgraft's regular books.[77] A less narrowly evaluative concern with literary history and scholarship continued alongside ethico-formalist analysis, for example in *Australian Literary Studies*. Novelists, poets and journalists continued to review in the newspapers, although academic critics became increasingly prominent. Nonetheless, despite being a minority position in some respects, the mode of evaluative criticism captured the intellectual high-ground, such that its frameworks came to dominate criticism of Australian literature into the 1980s, to become the "commonsense" of critical practice, and to make *careers* in Australian literature possible, long after the cultural politics of its founding moment had dissolved. Later critics such as Brian Matthews and Brian Kiernan, with no cold-war campaign against nationalism, show its influence: Matthews in his analysis of Lawson as a kind of proto-existentialist, Kiernan in reading the fiction canon through the theme of the "individual and society".[78] The dominant mode of criticism was the formal academic essay on an individual text or writer; concerns with cultural history were pushed to the margins, although they would never quite disappear.

LITERARY CRITICISM AND LITERARY THEORY

Australian literary criticism in the 1970s remained marked by its founding moment as a university study. Australian literature was widely taught although its typical status was as an "option" added to the core English curriculum. More criticism than ever before was being published in a range of established magazines including *Meanjin, Southerly, Overland, Westerly* and *Australian Literary Studies*. The formation of the Association for the Study of Australian Literature (ASAL) in 1977 represented both the culmination of the critical enterprise of the previous two decades and the stirring of new developments beyond its orthodoxy. Australian literature was now academically respectable but many of its younger advocates also wanted it to be more than "merely" academic. Although ethico-formalist criticism remained dominant, Australian literature also became the vehicle for a revised cultural history.

The 1970s saw a period of complex neo-nationalism in Australian culture and politics. In intellectual terms this neo-nationalism was founded in a critique of "old" nationalism, denounced for its racism, sexism and lack of theoretical rigour, most famously in Humphrey McQueen's *A New Britannia* (1970). But the critique was also anti-imperialist, hence predisposed towards new articulations of nationalism. The influence of "new left" neo-Marxism, especially in history and politics departments, was decisive.[79] If there were certain Australian traditions to be rejected, there were others to be reclaimed. A revitalised interest in national histories coincided with new movements in Australian fiction, poetry, drama, journalism and cinema.

Against these movements, the university could look like the last refuge of imperialist attitudes, especially in the English departments. The institutionalisation of Australian literature could appear *too* successful given the dominance of formalist studies. Most of the important books which helped redefine attitudes to Australian literary studies came from outside the English department: McQueen's books, Anne Summers' *Damned Whores and God's Police* (1975), Miriam Dixson's *The Real Matilda* (1976), David Walker's *Dream and Disillusion* (1976), Tim Rowse's *Australian Liberalism and National Character* (1978), Drusilla Modjeska's *Exiles at Home* (1981), Richard White's *Inventing Australia* (1981) and Sylvia Lawson's *The Archibald Paradox* (1983). From within English, John Docker's *Australian Cultural Elites* (1974) expanded the boundaries of literary criticism into a politically informed history of ideas which, among much else, argued the sexist basis of the "Sydney" tradition of vitalist idealism from Brennan to Hope and White.

Feminism and neo-Marxism were linked via the central concept of *ideology* through which accepted versions of Australian history and culture were criticised and politicised. Both radical nationalist and conservative liberal traditions were critiqued. The claims to universal truth or ideological disinterest which had sustained the academic institutionalisation of Australian literature were directly challenged. Still, new theories of *textuality*, structuralist or poststructuralist, had a less immediate effect in literature departments. A radical historiography was not necessarily linked to radical notions of textuality. If literary criticism was slow on the up-take perhaps this was because the one thing structuralist, poststructuralist and neo-Marxist theories shared was scepticism about the autonomy of the literary text – and with that went late-romantic notions of authorship, individuality and organic form which had sustained the critical enterprise.

There was a perception in the 1970s and early 1980s that criticism of *Australian* literature was particularly resistant to theory, as if theory were foreign to the revised or residual nationalist sympathies of Australian studies and to the strictly literary concerns of criticism, still involved in "justifying" Australian literature in the university. A survey of the mainstream critical periodicals nevertheless reveals shifts in the critical agenda. While formal studies of individual texts and authors dominate, feminist terms and notions of "ideology" begin to appear in literary essays. Across all journals, interestingly, race is a recurrent issue (*The Chant of Jimmie Blacksmith* was an important catalyst).[80] Numerous articles indicate that contemporary Australian drama in this period posed unfamiliar questions about genre and ideology. New Australian fiction and poetry demanded similar rethinking beyond the boundaries of expressive realism. Contemporary American literature became a more important reference than the English tradition for contemporary Australian work. Still, explicit theorisation of textuality remained the exception – spectacularly in two articles by Don Anderson which managed to refer to Frye, Marx, Freud, Barthes, Macherey and Lévi-Strauss.[81] Anderson's subjects – Christina Stead and Patrick White – suggest that there remained an inverse relation between an interest in nationalism and an interest in theory.

Outside mainstream literary criticism, however, a flourishing subculture of informal reading groups emerged in the 1970s among students and younger academics, perhaps with some parallels to the writers' associations of the 1930s except that the *literary* no longer dominated. The novelist or literary intellectual was replaced by the "cultural theorist", and before too long careers in "theory" could be pursued. It was precisely the collapse of literary autonomy, and the anti-empirical "excess" of theory, that seemed liberating. New theoretical work was consumed with enormous energy, not surprising when even Northrop Frye could come as a revelation. Williams, Eagleton and Jameson led back to Marx, Lukács, Benjamin, Adorno and Russian Formalism – or to Althusser, Macherey and Foucault; Barthes led back to Lévi-Strauss and Saussure or forward to Derrida and de Man; Lacan and Kristeva led back to Freud. The trajectories closely followed those being pursued in British and North American universities, including the high-tension debates about "foreign theory", but Australian work soon developed its own dynamics, governed in part by its postcolonial situation.

One indicative occasion was the *Foreign Bodies* conference on "Semiotics in/and Australia" held in February 1981, with papers subsequently published by the Local Consumption Collective (the titles are rich in meanings).[82] *The Foreign Bodies Papers* included three essays specifically on literature although perhaps only one which would have been recognised as "literary criticism". The interest, instead, was in the construction of authorship, the authority of critic and teacher, the literary institution, the nature of literary textuality, and textual politics; the references are to Foucault, Barthes, Baudrillard, Lacan, Eagleton, Deleuze and Derrida. This was indeed a foreign world to the earlier post-war generation of critics. The location of the conference and publication outside the mainstream periodicals and other disciplinary forms suggest well enough where poststructuralism stood in 1981.

By the early 1980s some critique of the poverty of theory in Australian literary studies was being voiced within the field itself. The notions of individuality and value which had established the modern canon appeared oppressively moralistic in face of the new literary movements and naive, indeed anti-intellectual, in their understanding of textuality. This was made strikingly clear in the hostile response accorded the 1981 *Oxford History of Australian Literature*. For some of the book's reviewers at least, the ideological bias of its criticism, its unquestioning assumption of authority, and its inability to deal with history or the national culture were almost scandalously evident.[83]

The "arrival" of literary theory was announced controversially, and in one sense prematurely, at the 1982 Association for the Study of Australian Literature conference. Papers included Sneja Gunew on "discourses of otherness", drawing on Foucault and Kristeva; Ian Reid on the status of the literary text and canon, drawing on Marxist, semiotic and reader-response theory; Graeme Turner and Delys Bird on the theorisation of Australian studies alongside cultural studies; and Carole Ferrier on "proletarian fiction", using Marxist and feminist theory.[84] All except Ferrier were then teaching in newer interdisciplinary contexts rather than in traditional English departments. Other papers, although more orthodox critically, introduced feminist categories or Aboriginal literature.

Although it would be the best part of a decade before the full impact of poststructuralist or deconstructive theories of textuality was absorbed into the mainstream of Australian literary criticism, the new tendencies represented by these papers dramatically redefined the field of Australian literature and its criticism over the course of the 1980s. Modjeska's *Exiles at Home* and Reid's *Fiction and the Great Depression* contributed to a positive re-reading of the fiction of the 1930s and 1940s through feminist and Marxist categories. Feminist criticism has had the single greatest influence in reshaping the nature of Australian literary studies, not only in its critique of the masculinism of the nationalist tradition and the established canon, but positively in the rediscovery of mid-century women writers and the recovery of colonial romance and autobiographical genres.[85] These had been invisible or negative examples to both nationalist and "universalist" critics. *Gender, Politics and Fiction* (1986) edited by Ferrier, continued the process of re-reading authors marginalised in the canon on the basis of gender, genre, politics or ethnicity. Communist, social realist and working-class writings have all been the subject of new research.[86]

As early as 1984, Docker could attack the new formalism of High Theory, although the main force of his book, *In a Critical Condition*, was to savage the ideological freight of the "metaphysical orthodoxy" still dominant in Australian criticism. Other works explicitly signalled their debts to structuralist and poststructuralist theory. Graeme Turner's *National Fictions* (1986) examined national traditions and myths across both cinema and literary texts, bringing literary criticism and cultural theory together. The book's impact was muted, perhaps because its literary references were mostly canonical although its method pointed elsewhere. Turner began with the proposition that ideologies or cultures rather than individuals produce meanings: "As the culture produces its texts *it* prefers certain meanings, thematic structures and formal strategies. Within these ... we find the ideology of the culture."[87] Such a proposition could still be scandalous in literary studies, although already commonplace elsewhere. Kay Schaffer's *Women and the Bush* (1988) began from a similar point, this time bringing feminist and psychoanalytical theory to bear on the gendered mythologies of land and identity. Although orthodox in critical vocabulary, Adam Shoemaker's *Black Words, White Page* (1989) helped establish Aboriginal writing as a subject internal to "Australian literature". Mudrooroo's *Writing from the Fringe* (1990) theorised the issue.

These changes in criticism are summed up in Ken Gelder and Paul Salzman's 1989 study of contemporary fiction, *The New Diversity*. It included no chapters on individual authors but was organised around particular genres, including popular genres, and around issues of cultural difference and exclusion – gender and sexuality, politics and history, Asia, regionalism, the migrant experience, and Aboriginality. The book is a study of the relationship between textuality and ideology. Similarly, although its organising principles were looser, the *Penguin New Literary History of Australia* (1988) had no essays on individual authors but instead, among other topics, essays on Aboriginal writing, women's writing, political fiction, children's literature, autobiography, and literary production. The fact that it was only mildly theoretical and aimed at the middle ground makes it all the more significant of changes in the critical institution.

For many in Australian literary studies, structuralist and poststructuralist theories arrived almost simultaneously. One effect of this delayed and compressed arrival was their agglutination into the single category of "theory" which could then be opposed to "normal" practice. A more interesting effect has been the relative importance accorded to the social and political rather than philosophical or linguistic dimensions of theoretical work. The general force of (post)structuralist theory was registered in a framework already defined by feminist and Marxist categories and by the critique of nationalism they provided. While postcolonial criticism has a complex theoretical relation to both feminism and Marxism (which it has to some degree displaced), in practice its critical modes have been largely complementary to them. Thus the notion of "textual politics" has become constitutive of contemporary criticism. Criticism has become critique, "deconstruction" a shorthand for work on ideology. Semiotic play is taken as subversive. While deconstruction and semiology have been influential, the revision of textual analysis and literary history has been weighted towards questions of *gender, race and nation*.[88] We can observe the shift in Robert Dixon's work, from a neutral history of ideas in *The Course of Empire* (1986) to a politically conscious critical history in *Writing the Colonial Adventure* (1995). In the latter, which treats popular genres and journalism alongside high art forms, the influence of Marxist "ideology critique" is overwritten by poststructuralist and postcolonial concerns with representation and subjectivity. Although the focus is on texts – on the narrative shaping of ideologies – the framework is cultural history.

POSTMODERNISM – POST-CRITICISM?

By the late 1980s most literary studies departments included Australian literature courses in an array of options that diluted the traditional core function of English literature. Notions of literary autonomy persist, of course; poststructuralism can be routinised as a new style of "close reading"; teaching and criticism continue to produce canons. But criticism – at least within the academy – has developed a new relation to the process of canon formation. The maintenance of the canon is no longer its governing rationale. On the contrary, criticism is deployed to challenge the process of canonisation, reveal its exclusions, and dissolve it back into (political) histories of production and reception. Simon During's *Patrick White* (1996) is an indicative text. Although in the guise of a single-author study, it pursues its subject not through the individual "vision" but through cultural institutions and "as part of a transitional moment in the emergence of postcolonial Australia". The effect is profoundly non-canonical and the book was controversial among literary journalists and some established critics.[89]

Australian literary history has been thoroughly rewritten since the early 1980s. It is almost impossible now to think "Australian literature" without thinking women's writing, Aboriginal writing, ethnic minority writing.[90] In the 1990s, in what we might call the second wave of theoretical innovation, postcolonialism became increasingly important in articulating notions of identity and difference, in work on colonial and Indigenous writings, and in shifting analysis away from Australia's national distinctiveness to what it might share with other settler colonies.[91] Queer theory has emerged too, but as yet without the same inevitability. "Australian literature" – the construction of Australian literature through the process of canon formation – has come to be seen not as the oppressed space of national identity and freedom, but as the oppressive dominant asserting its power by excluding a range of different voices which it is the task of criticism to argue back into the field.

In some ways the canon has merely been modernised once more, its past re-aligned with its present to accommodate new literary developments such as Aboriginal literature. More profoundly, the sense of an Australian literature or tradition has been dispersed across a wide range of written, oral and visual forms such as autobiography, biography, travel and history writing, journalism, essays, crime, romance, science fiction, cinema and television. The literary is no longer a pure category. Thus, what constitutes "literary criticism" is no longer self-evident: is it something distinct or a branch of cultural studies or history? Recent critical work, for example, has included studies of explorer narratives; representations of "the Centre"; Indigenous narratives across different media; the Eliza Fraser stories; travel writing; even gardening. Those trained in literature might write about media, republicanism or the Aboriginal sacred, while writers from "outside" literary studies such as Stephen Muecke or Meaghan Morris have as much to say to it as those within the field.[92]

Such developments are international, but they can have a particular edge in Australian criticism because of the potential proximity of cultural politics to national politics, for example around issues of race. The cultural dynamics of Australia's place in the world have also shifted. In both positive and negative ways, Australia can now be seen as *exemplary* rather than merely supplementary or antipodean; exemplary, for example, of such post-modern and postcolonial conditions as McKenzie Wark describes when claiming that "the great virtue of Australian culture is its unoriginality – that it borrows shamelessly from all manner of foreign sources, that it adapts and collages".[93] The anxieties about maturity and universal values that drove "modern" criticism in Australia have suddenly disappeared, not because they were solved but because they ceased to pose interesting questions. Australia has become an exporter of work in postcolonialism, cultural studies, feminism, Foucault and more, or rather one point in a circulation network in which import/export metaphors no longer make the best sense.

Inevitably the approaches of the 1980s and 1990s can be represented as a new orthodoxy. Despite their oppositional rhetoric they are, after all, now constitutive of the critical institution. The textual revelation of "transgressive" elements in literary works – the dominant mode of criticism by the mid-1990s – can be as routinised, romanticised and ahistorical as any earlier method. There have, subsequently, been signs of a shift towards a more "positive" cultural history of literary institutions and practices which goes beyond negative critique alone. At least this is one strand in a field that shifts easily from semiotics to sexual politics to sociology – and to scholarship. Contemporary studies in biography and the history of the book, studies of reading, a recent collection on canon formation, and an altogether new *Oxford History* indicate current directions in work on Australian literature.[94]

If literary studies re-asserted its centrality when linguistic and semiotic-based theories altered the nature of studies across the humanities, it did so at the cost of any secure sense of literature as a privileged domain of meaning. Hence the disquiet among some sections of the literary world both inside and outside the academy. Literary criticism in the university has responded in a number of ways, sometimes re-affirming the tradition of modernity, or the avant-garde notion of literature as a permanent opposition; sometimes re-inventing work on texts as discourse analysis; sometimes turning literary into cultural studies or history; sometimes re-affirming the deep significance of textual play. Perhaps after all Vincent Buckley's notion that literature was not really a university subject sufficient to itself has been proven correct – although not at all in the sense he intended.

NOTES

1 Mark Davis, *Gangland: Cultural Elites and the New Generationalism* (Sydney: Allen & Unwin, 1997); McKenzie Wark, *The Virtual Republic: Australia's Culture Wars of the 1990s* (Sydney: Allen & Unwin, 1997). Controversies over identity have involved Helen Darville, Mudrooroo, Roberta Sykes and Paul Radley.

2 See Robert Dessaix, ed., *Speaking their Minds: Intellectuals and Public Culture in Australia* (Sydney: ABC Books, 1998); Robert Manne, *The Way We Live Now: The Controversies of the Nineties* (Melbourne: Text, 1998); Helen Garner, *True Stories: Selected Non-Fiction* (Melbourne: Text, 1996); Peter Craven, ed., *The Best Australian Essays 1988* (Melbourne: Bookman, 1998); Morag Fraser, ed., *Seams of Light: Best Antipodean Essays* (Sydney: Allen & Unwin, 1998).

3 For example: Alan Atkinson, *The Europeans in Australia: A History* (Melbourne: Oxford University Press, 1997); Wayne Hudson and Geoffrey Bolton, eds, *Creating Australia: Changing Australian History* (Sydney: Allen & Unwin, 1997); Tom O'Regan, *Australian National Cinema* (London: Routledge, 1996).

4 Frederick Sinnett, "The Fiction Fields of Australia" (1856) in John Barnes, ed., *The Writer in Australia, 1856–1964* (Melbourne: Oxford University Press, 1969), p. 19; Marcus Clarke, "Preface to Gordon's Poems" (1876) in Barnes, ed., p. 34; H.G. Turner and Alexander Sutherland, *The Development of Australian Literature* (Melbourne: George Robertson, 1898), p. vii; A.G. Stephens, "Henry Lawson's Poems", *Bulletin*, 15 February 1896, reprinted in Leon Cantrell, ed., *A.G. Stephens: Selected Writings* (Sydney: Angus & Robertson, 1978), p. 220; Vance Palmer, "An Australian National Art" (1905) in Barnes, ed., p. 170; P.R. Stephensen, *The Foundations of Culture in Australia: An Essay Towards National Self Respect* (1935–36) (Sydney: Allen & Unwin, 1986), p. 22; Vincent Buckley, "The Image of Man in Australian Poetry" (1957) in Barnes, ed., p. 294; Miles Franklin, *Laughter, Not For a Cage* (Sydney: Angus & Robertson, 1956), p. 217 (published posthumously, based on CLF lectures delivered in 1950).

5 Brian Kiernan, *Criticism* (Melbourne: Oxford University Press, 1974), pp. 11–12.

6 Nettie Palmer, "The Arts in Australia" (1929) reprinted in Vivian Smith, ed., *Nettie Palmer* (St Lucia: University of Queensland Press, 1988), p. 378. Palmer is paraphrasing with approval a lecture by Will Dyson.

7 Nettie Palmer, "The Arts in Australia", p. 377.

8 Kiernan, *Criticism*, p. 9.

9 Turner and Sutherland, *Development of Australian Literature*, p. 30. For this common phrase, combining the meanings of racially characteristic and organically rooted, see also Elizabeth Webby, "Before the *Bulletin*: Nineteenth Century Literary Journalism" in Bruce Bennett, ed., *Cross Currents: Magazines and Newspapers in Australian Literature* (Melbourne: Longman Cheshire, 1981), pp. 3 and 25.

10 "The Characteristics of Australian Literature" (1890) in Barnes, ed., *Writer in Australia*, p. 45. Emphasis added.

11 Ken Stewart, "Journalism and the World of the Writer: The Production of Australian Literature, 1855–1915" in Laurie Hergenhan, ed., *The Penguin New Literary History of Australia* (Melbourne: Penguin, 1988), pp. 174–93; Webby, "Before the *Bulletin*", pp. 3–34; George Nadel, *Australia's Colonial Culture: Ideas, Men and Institutions in Mid-Nineteenth Century Eastern Australia* (Melbourne: Cheshire, 1957), chapters 5–9. Books published were: Turner and Sutherland, *Development of Australian Literature*; Desmond Byrne, *Australian Writers* (London: Richard Bentley, 1896), in Barnes, ed., *Writer in Australia*, pp. 50–61; A. Patchett Martin, *The Beginnings of an Australian Literature* (London: Sotheran, 1898). Earlier, G.B. Barton had published *Literature in New South Wales* and *The Poets and Prose Writers of New South Wales*, both 1866.

12 Turner and Sutherland, *Development of Australian Literature*, p. x.

13 Sylvia Lawson, *The Archibald Paradox: A Strange Case of Authorship* (Melbourne: Penguin/Allen Lane, 1983), chapters 6–7; John Docker, *The Nervous Nineties: Australian Cultural Life in the 1890s* (Melbourne: Oxford University Press, 1991), pp. 26–69.

14 Stephens, "Australian Literature I" (1901), in Cantrell, ed., *A.G. Stephens*, p. 77; "Fashions in Poetry" (1899), p. 52: "Beyond all other verse writers [Tennyson] embodied the spirit of his time. But his time is gone, and the spirit of his time is gone, and with them has gone the force of much of Tennyson's poetry."

15 Lawson, *Archibald Paradox*, p. 171.

16 See H.M. Green's vivid descriptions, *A History of Australian Literature Pure and Applied* (Sydney: Angus & Robertson, 1961), pp. 762–74, especially p. 773.

17 Stephens, "Introduction to *The Bulletin Story Book*" (1901) in Cantrell, ed., *A.G. Stephens*, p. 109.

18 Stewart, "Journalism and the World of the Writer", p. 189.

19 Leon Cantrell, "A.G. Stephens, the *Bulletin*, and the 1890s" in Cantrell, ed., *Bards, Bohemians and Bookmen: Essays in Australian Literature* (St Lucia: University of Queensland Press, 1976), p. 110. Also S. E. Lee, "A.G. Stephens, the Critical Credo", *Australian Literary Studies*, 1.4 (1964), pp. 219–41; Gillian Whitlock, "A.G. Stephens: An Internationalist Critic", *Australian Literary Studies*, 8.1 (1977), pp. 82–90; Lawson, *Archibald Paradox*, pp. 170–77.

20 Stephens, "Australian Literature I", p. 82.

21 Stephens, "A Book of Sunlight", in Cantrell, ed., *A.G. Stephens*, p. 213. Also "Lawson and Literature", p. 228.

22 Stephens, "Literary Criticism of Art", in Cantrell, ed., *A.G. Stephens*, pp. 346 and 348.

23 Christopher Brennan, "Studies in French Poetry, 1860–1900", *Bookfellow*, January 1920, pp. 44–46.

24 Vance Palmer, "Fiction for Export", *Bulletin*, 1 June 1922; "The Missing Critics", 26 July 1923; "The Writer and his Audience", 8 January 1925; Louis Esson, "Nationality in Art", 1 February 1923. Answers include: Wallace Nelson, "Art and Nationality", 1 March 1923; Frank Morton, "Art and Nationality", 5 April 1923. Morton was a powerful, witty critic in his own right, mainly in the pages of the *Triad*. He argued that "The fetich (sic) of Nationality is just as bad and damned a thing in Art as in Affairs ... Art, like true greatness, has no nationality." All *Bulletin* articles from the Red Page.

25 Phrases quoted from Pictor, "The Purpose of Art", *Bulletin*, 13 September 1923; and R.H.M., "A Celt in a Kilt", 20 September 1923.

26 John F. Williams, *The Quarantined Culture: Australian Reactions to Modernism 1913–1939* (Cambridge: Cambridge University Press, 1995), chapter 8. Richard White, *Inventing Australia: Images and Identity 1688–1980* (Sydney: Allen & Unwin, 1981), chapter 7.

27 Humphrey McQueen, *The Black Swan of Trespass: The Emergence of Modernist Painting in Australia to 1944* (Sydney: Alternative Publishing Co-Operative, 1979), pp. 18–20; Peter Kirkpatrick, *The Sea Coast of Bohemia: Literary Life in Sydney's Roaring Twenties* (St Lucia: University of Queensland Press, 1992), pp. 89–91, 205–17.

28 Vivian Smith, *Vance and Nettie Palmer* (Boston: Twayne, 1975); David Walker, *Dream and Disillusion: A Search for Australian Cultural Identity* (Canberra: Australian National University Press, 1976); Drusilla Modjeska, *Exiles at Home: Australian Women Writers 1925–1945* (Sydney: Angus & Robertson, 1981), chapter 3; Ivor Indyk, "Vance Palmer and the Social Function of Literature", *Southerly*, 50.3 (1990), pp. 346–58; Craig Munro, *Wild Man of Letters: The Story of P.R. Stephensen* (Melbourne: Melbourne University Press, 1984).

29 Rex Ingamells, *Conditional Culture* (1938), in Barnes, ed., *Writer in Australia*, pp. 245–65; this was the founding document of the Jindyworobak movement. See Brian Elliott, ed., *The Jindyworobaks* (St Lucia: University of Queensland Press, 1979).

30 Nettie Palmer, *Modern Australian Literature*, in Smith, ed., *Nettie Palmer*, p. 293.

31 For "feminisation": Vance Palmer, "Novels for Men", *Bulletin*, 19 April 1923. For suburbia: Tim Rowse, "Heaven and a Hill's Hoist: Australian Critics on Suburbia" in Gillian Whitlock and David Carter, eds, *Images of Australia* (St Lucia: University of Queensland Press, 1992), pp. 241–44.

32 Vance Palmer, "The Narrative Faculty", *Bulletin*, 5 January 1922; "Fact and Its Proper Place", *Bulletin*, 17 January 1924.

33 Quotations from Vance Palmer, "The Missing Critics"; "The Writer and his Audience"; Rann Daley [Vance Palmer], "Undemocratic Democracy", *Aussie*, 16 August 1920, p. 13. Tim Rowse, *Australian Liberalism and National Character* (Malmsbury, Vic.: Kibble, 1978), pp. 176–87.

34 Quotations from letters by Nettie Palmer (1936) reprinted in Vivian Smith, ed., *Letters of Vance and Nettie Palmer 1915–1963* (Canberra: National Library of Australia, 1977), pp. 135, 138.

35 Kiernan, *Criticism*, p. 27: "it was not until the late fifties that a wide range of journals such as existed elsewhere, or had existed here in the nineteenth century, became available to writers".

36 Ian Reid, *Fiction and the Great Depression: Australia and New Zealand 1930–1950* (Melbourne: Edward Arnold, 1979), pp. 77–84; David Carter, "Documenting and Criticising Society" in Hergenhan, ed., *New Literary History of Australia*, pp. 370–71.

37 John Tregenza, *Australia's Little Magazines 1923–1954* (Adelaide: Libraries Board of SA, 1964); David Carter, "Paris, Moscow, Melbourne: Some Avant-Garde Australian Little Magazines", *Australian Literary Studies*, 16.1 (1993), pp. 57–66; Patrick Buckridge, "Clearing a Space for Australian Literature 1940–1965" in Bruce Bennett and Jennifer Strauss, eds, *The Oxford Literary History of Australia* (Melbourne: Oxford University Press, 1998), pp. 170–86; Modjeska, *Exiles at Home*, chapter 5. Examples of pamphlets/booklets include: P.R. Stephensen, *Foundations of Culture* (1935–36); Frank Dalby Davison, *While Freedom Lives* (1938); the unpublished "Writers in Defence of Freedom" (1939) (see Modjeska, pp. 259–60); Brian Penton, *Think – Or Be Damned* (1941).

38 Stephensen, *Foundations*, p. 8 (my emphasis). Following quotations: pp. 84, 66 (my emphasis).

39 On *Meanjin* see Lynne Strahan, *Just City and the Mirrors: Meanjin Quarterly and the Intellectual Front 1940–1965* (Melbourne: Oxford University Press,

1984); Jenny Lee *et al.*, eds, *The Temperament of Generations: Fifty Years of Writing in* Meanjin (Melbourne: Melbourne University Press, 1990). The 1942 Crisis issue of *Meanjin* published Vance Palmer's "Battle" and "Australian Outlook" by Ingamells.

40 Quotations from a *Meanjin* editorial, "The Wound as the Bow", 10.1 (1951), p. 4.

41 Kiernan, *Criticism*, p. 30. See Stuart Lee, "*Southerly*" in Bennett, ed., *Cross Currents*, pp. 161–71.

42 W.K. Hancock, *Australia* (London: Ernest Benn, 1930). Don Watson, *Brian Fitzpatrick: A Radical Life* (Sydney: Hale & Iremonger, 1979).

43 Manning Clark, "Letter to Tom Collins: Mateship", *Meanjin*, 2.3 (1943), p. 40; "Tradition in Australian Literature", 8.1, p. 16. New books included J.K. Ewers' *Creative Writing in Australia* (1945), Colin Roderick's surveys of fiction (1947 and 1950) and, not least, the republication of Furphy's *Such is Life* (1944).

44 See Phillips, "Cultural Nationalism in the 1940s and 1950s" and Andrew Wells, "The Old Left Intelligentsia 1930–1960" in Brian Head and James Walter, eds, *Intellectual Movements and Australian Society* (Melbourne: Oxford University Press, 1988), pp. 129–44, 214–34.

45 Phillips, "Preface to the 1966 Edition", *The Australian Tradition* (Melbourne, Lansdowne, 1966), p. xxv.

46 David Carter, "Capturing the Liberal Sphere: *Overland*'s First Decade" in Carter, ed., *Outside the Book: Contemporary Essays on Literary Periodicals* (Sydney: Local Consumption Publications, 1991), pp. 177–92. John McLaren, *Writing in Hope and Fear: Literature as Politics in Postwar Australia* (Cambridge: Cambridge University Press, 1996), chapters 2 and 3.

47 On cultural communism see Modjeska, *Exiles at Home*, chapter 6; David Carter, *A Career in Writing: Judah Waten and the Cultural Politics of a Literary Career* (Toowoomba: Association for the Study of Australian Literature, 1997); Jack Beasley, *Red Letter Days: Notes from Inside an Era* (Sydney: Australasian Book Society, 1979); Susan McKernan, *A Question of Commitment: Australian Literature in the Twenty Years After the War* (Sydney: Allen & Unwin, 1989), pp. 23–49; McLaren, *Writing in Hope and Fear*.

48 Phillips, "The Democratic Theme", in *The Australian Tradition*, p. 70.

49 Leigh Dale, *The English Men: Professing Literature in Australian Universities* (Toowoomba: Association for the Study of Australian Literature, 1997), pp. 148–51.

50 Chris Wallace-Crabbe, "Poetry and Modernism", in Bennett and Strauss, *Literary History of Australia*, p. 223. The CLF made grants available for lectures from 1940, while the CLF and publishers Angus & Robertson prepared lists of Australian "classics".

51 *Meanjin*, 13.2–4 (1954), pp. 165–69; 429–36; 591–96. Buckridge, "Clearing a Space for Australian Literature", pp. 186–90; Dale, *The English Men*, pp. 155–60.

52 Dale, *The English Men*, pp. 92ff; John Docker, *In A Critical Condition: Reading Australian Literature* (Melbourne: Penguin, 1984), pp. 86–92; David Carter, "Literary Canons and Literary Institutions" in Delys Bird *et al.*, eds, *CanonOZities: The Making of Literary Reputations in Australia, Southerly*, 57.3 (1997), pp. 29–32. The influence of F.R. Leavis and the New Criticism has been

much debated. See Docker, *In A Critical Condition*, pp. 1–14; 86–92. Dale, *The English Men*, pp. 113–42, 162–64. Andrew Milner, "The 'English' Ideology: Literary Criticism in England and Australia", *Thesis Eleven*, 12 (1985), pp. 120–26. Buckridge, "Intellectual Authority and Critical Traditions in Australian Literature 1945-1975" in Head and Walter, eds, *Intellectual Movements and Australian Society*, pp. 200–202.

53 Vincent Buckley, "Towards an Australian Literature", *Meanjin*, 18.1 (1959), p. 64. Following quotations, pp. 68, 61. An important precursor was A.D. Hope, "Standards in Australian Literature" (1956) in Grahame Johnston, ed., *Australian Literary Criticism* (Melbourne: Oxford University Press, 1962).

54 For example G.A. Wilkes, *New Perspectives on Brennan's Poetry* (1953); Leonie Gibson [Kramer], *Henry Handel Richardson and Some of Her Sources* (1954); Buckley, *Henry Handel Richardson* (1961). For a somewhat other view of Richardson see Dorothy Green, *Ulysses Bound: Henry Handel Richardson and Her Fiction* (Canberra: Australian National University Press, 1973), although Brennan still plays a framing role. The periodicals of the early 1970s reveal a concentration of articles on Richardson and Brennan.

55 Docker, *In a Critical Condition*, pp. 90–107.

56 For example, Buckley, "*Capricornia*", in Johnston, ed., *Australian Literary Criticism*, pp. 169–86; Wilkes, "The Progress of Eleanor Dark", *Southerly*, 3 (1951) and "The Novels of Katharine Susannah Prichard", *Southerly*, 4 (1953), pp. 220–31.

57 Wilkes, "The Eighteen Nineties" (1958) in Johnston, ed., *Australian Literary Criticism*, p. 40.

58 Buckley, *Essays in Poetry, Mainly Australian* (Melbourne, Melbourne University Press, 1957). "The Image of Man in Australian Poetry" in Barnes, ed., *Writer in Australia*; quotations: pp. 273, 275, 283–84.

59 See Thomas Shapcott, "Douglas Stewart and Poetry in the *Bulletin*, 1940–1960" in Bennett, ed., *Cross Currents*, pp. 148–57. John Thompson, Kenneth Slessor and R.G. Howarth, eds, *The Penguin Book of Australian Verse* (Melbourne: Penguin, 1958).

60 Buckley, "The Image of Man", quotations in this paragraph from pp. 292, 293, 295.

61 H.P. Heseltine, "The Literary Heritage", *Meanjin*, 21.1 (1962), pp. 35–49. See Phillips' reply, "The Literary Heritage Re-Assessed", *Meanjin*, 21.2 (1962), pp. 172–80.

62 See Buckridge, "Intellectual Authority and Critical Traditions", pp. 206–208.

63 Buckley, "Patrick White and his Epic" in Johnston, ed., *Australian Literary Criticism*, pp. 187–97. The first positive study of White's fiction was by Marjorie Barnard: "The Four Novels of Patrick White", *Meanjin*, 15.2 (1956), pp. 156–70.

64 But see James McAuley's anti-romantic discussion of White's style as Mannerism: "Literature and the Arts" in Peter Coleman, ed., *Australian Civilization* (Melbourne: Cheshire, 1962), p. 131.

65 Carter, "Capturing the Liberal Sphere", pp. 188–91; McLaren, "The Image of Reality in Our Writing", *Overland*, 27–28 (1963), p. 45; Phillips, *The Australian Tradition*, p. 111.

66 Geoffrey Dutton, ed., *The Literature of Australia* (Melbourne: Penguin, 1964). The revised 1976 edition goes further, dropping some of the broader essays, adding Stead, Webb and Boyd to the canon.

67 Wilkes, *Australian Literature: A Conspectus* (Sydney: Angus & Robertson, 1969), p. 11.

68 Judith Wright, *Preoccupations in Australian Poetry* (Melbourne: Oxford University Press, 1965); Brian Elliott, *The Landscape of Australian Poetry* (Melbourne: Cheshire, 1967). Buckridge, "Clearing a Space for Australian Literature", p. 179.

69 Docker, *In a Critical Condition*, chapters 3 and 4. Buckley, "Unequal Twins: A Discontinuous Analysis", *Meanjin*, 40.1 (1981), p. 9.

70 McAuley, "Comment: By Way of Prologue", *Quadrant*, 1 (1956–7), p. 3.

71 McKernan [Lever], "The Question of Literary Independence: *Quadrant* and Australian Writing", in Carter, *Outside the Book*, pp. 165–76. Also McKernan, *A Question of Commitment*, chapter 2. McLaren, *Writing in Hope and Fear*, chapters 4 and 5.

72 Carter, *A Career in Writing*, pp. 78–90.

73 Quoted phrase from Christesen, "The Wound as the Bow", *Meanjin*, 10.1 (1951).

74 Christopher Lee, "'Sinister Signs of Professionalism'? Literary Gang Warfare in the 1950s and 1960s", in Alison Bartlett *et al.*, eds, *Australian Literature and the Public Sphere* (Toowoomba: Association for the Study of Australian Literature, 1999), pp. 187–93.

75 Buckley, "Towards an Australian Literature", p. 62. See also his essay "Intellectuals" in Coleman, ed., *Australian Civilization*, pp. 89–104.

76 Buckridge, "Clearing a Space for Australian Literature", p. 186.

77 For example: Colin Roderick, *An Introduction to Australian Fiction* (Sydney: Angus & Robertson, 1950); H.M. Green, *Australian Literature 1900–1950* (Melbourne: Melbourne University Press, 1951) and *A History of Australian Literature* (1961); Cecil Hadgraft, *Australian Literature: A Critical Account to 1955* (London: Heinemann, 1960).

78 Brian Matthews, *The Receding Wave: Henry Lawson's Prose* (Melbourne: Melbourne University Press, 1972), with a foreword by Buckley; Kiernan, *Images of Society and Nature: Seven Essays on Australian Novels* (Melbourne: Oxford University Press, 1971). Also Brian Kiernan, ed., *Considerations: New Essays on Kenneth Slessor, Judith Wright and Douglas Stewart* (Sydney: Angus & Robertson, 1977).

79 See Richard Gordon, ed., *The Australian New Left: Critical Essays and Strategy* (Melbourne: Heinemann, 1970).

80 John Frow, "The Chant of Thomas Keneally", *Australian Literary Studies*, 10.3 (1982), which refers to Russian Formalism, Lukács and Barthes. J.J. Healy's *Literature and the Aborigine in Australia, 1770–1975* (St Lucia: University of Queensland Press) appeared in 1978.

81 Don Anderson, "Christina Stead's Unforgettable Dinner Parties", *Southerly*, 1 (1979), pp. 28–45; "A Severed Leg: Anthropophagy and Communion in Patrick White's Fiction", *Southerly*, 4 (1980), pp. 399–417.

82 Peter Botsman *et al.*, eds, *The Foreign Bodies Papers* (Sydney: Local Consumption Publications, 1981) including Tony Thwaites, "Speaking of Prowlers:

Patrick White and Teaching Literature"; Cathy Greenfield and Tom O'Regan, "K.S. Prichard: The Construction of a Literary/Political Subject"; John Forbes, "Aspects of Contemporary Australian Poetry". See Robert Dixon, "Deregulating the Critical Economy: Theory and Australian Literary Criticism in the 1980s" in Bartlett *et al.*, eds, *Australian Literature and the Public Sphere*, pp. 194–201.

83 See reviews listed in Dale, *The English Men*, p. 224 (note 97) and Docker, *In a Critical Condition*, pp. 163–79, David Carter, "The History that is no History", *Helix*, 9–10 (1981), pp. 23–28.

84 Association for the Study of Australian Literature 1982 Conference Program and Abstracts (University of Adelaide, May 1982). See Graeme Turner and Delys Bird, "Australian Studies: Practice Without Theory", *Westerly*, 3 (1982), pp. 51–56.

85 Debra Adelaide, ed., *A Bright and Fiery Troop: Australian Women Writers of the Nineteenth Century* (1988) and Kay Ferres, ed., *The Time to Write: Australian Women Writers 1890–1930* (1993), both in the Penguin Australian Women's Library established in the 1980s; Fiona Giles, "Romance: An Embarrassing Subject" in Hergenhan, ed., *Literary History of Australia*, pp. 223–37.

86 Essays by Buckridge and Ferrier in Ferrier, ed., *Gender, Politics and Fiction: Twentieth Century Australian Women's Novels* (St Lucia: University of Queensland Press, 1986); Carter, *A Career in Writing*; Ian Syson, "Fired from the Canon: The Sacking of Australian Working Class Literature" in Bird *et al.*, eds, *CanonOZities*, pp. 78–89.

87 Graeme Turner, *National Fictions: Literature, Film and the Construction of Australian Narrative* (Sydney: Allen & Unwin, 1986), p. 2 (my emphasis). See Dixon, "Deregulating the Critical Economy", p. 195.

88 Note the sub-titles of Dixon, *Writing the Colonial Adventure: Race, Gender and Nation in Anglo-Australian Popular Fiction 1875–1914* (Cambridge: Cambridge University Press, 1995); Susan Sheridan, *Along the Faultlines: Sex, Race and Nation in Australian Women's Writing 1880s–1930s* (Sydney: Allen & Unwin, 1995).

89 Simon During, *Patrick White* (Melbourne: Oxford University Press, 1996), p. 15. Peter Craven, "The Kingdom of Correct Usage is Elsewhere", *Australian Book Review*, 179 (1996), pp. 36–41.

90 Sneja Gunew and Kateryna O. Longley, eds, *Striking Chords: Multicultural Literary Interpretations* (Sydney: Allen & Unwin, 1992); Gunew, *Framing Marginality: Multicultural Literary Studies* (Melbourne: Melbourne University Press, 1994) ; Bob Hodge and Vijay Mishra, *Dark Side of the Dream: Australian Literature and the Postcolonial Mind* (Sydney: Allen & Unwin, 1990).

91 Bill Ashcroft *et al.*, *The Empire Writes Back: Theory and Practice in Post-Colonial Literatures* (London: Routledge, 1989); a different alignment is argued in Leela Gandhi, *Postcolonial Theory: A Critical Introduction* (Sydney: Allen & Unwin, 1998), pp. 168–70.

92 Simon Ryan, *The Cartographic Eye: How Explorers Saw Australia* (Cambridge: Cambridge University Press, 1996); Roslynn D. Haynes, *Seeking the Centre: The Australian Desert in Literature, Art and Film* (Cambridge: Cambridge University Press, 1998); Kay Schaffer, *In the Wake of First Contact: The Eliza Fraser Stories* (Cambridge: Cambridge University Press, 1995); papers on exploration, space, women and botany in Caroline Guerin *et al.*, eds, *Crossing Lines: Formations of*

Australian Culture (Adelaide: Association for the Study of Australian Literature, 1996); Ken Gelder and Jane Jacobs, *Uncanny Australia: Sacredness and Identity in a Postcolonial Nation* (Melbourne: Melbourne University Press, 1998); Stephen Muecke, *Textual Spaces: Aboriginality and Cultural Studies* (Sydney: University of New South Wales Press, 1992); Meaghan Morris, *The Pirate's Fiancée: Feminism, Reading, Postmodernism* (London: Verso, 1990).

93 Wark, "Media Policy and Law to Suit All", *Australian*, 6 December 1995.

94 Bird *et al.*, eds, *CanonOZities*; Bennett and Strauss, eds, *The Oxford Literary History of Australia*; Bartlett *et al.*, eds, *Australian Literature and the Public Sphere*.

Further reading

REFERENCE WORKS
Historical and general

Australian Dictionary of Biography (Melbourne: Melbourne University Press, 1966–). Currently published to Volume 15, 1940–80, Kern–Pie (2000).

The Australian Encyclopaedia, 8 volumes (Sydney: Australian Geographic Pty Ltd, 1996). Sixth edition of work first published in 1925.

Australians, A Historical Library, 12 volumes (Sydney: Fairfax, Syme & Weldon, 1987–89).

Caine, Barbara, gen. ed., *Australian Feminism: A Companion* (Melbourne: Oxford University Press, 1998).

Horton, David, gen. ed., *The Encyclopedia of Aboriginal Australia*, 2 volumes (Canberra: Aboriginal Studies Press, 1994).

Dictionaries

Delbridge, Arthur, *et al.*, *The Macquarie Dictionary* (Sydney: The Macquarie Library, 1981; 3rd revised edition, 1997).

Moore, Bruce, *The Australian Oxford Dictionary* (Melbourne: Oxford University Press, 1999).

Ramson, W.S., *The Australian National Dictionary: A Dictionary of Australianisms and Historical Principles* (Melbourne: Oxford University Press, 1988).

Bibliographies

Duwell, Martin, Ehrhardt, Marianne and Hetherington, Carol, *The ALS Guide to Australian Writers: A Bibliography 1963–1995* (St Lucia: University of Queensland Press, 1997).

Ferguson, John, *Bibliography of Australia*, 7 volumes (Sydney: Angus & Robertson, 1941–1969). Covers 1784 to 1900, but excludes literary works after 1850.

Johnston, Grahame, *Annals of Australian Literature* (Melbourne: Oxford University Press, 1970; revised edition by Harry Heseltine and Joy Hooton, 1992).

Miller, E. Morris, *Australian Literature from its Beginnings to 1935*, 2 volumes. (Melbourne: Melbourne University Press, 1940). Dated but especially useful for nineteenth-century material.

Further reading

Literary companions and encyclopedias

Benson, Eugene and Conolly, L.W., *Encyclopedia of Post-Colonial Literatures Written in English*, 2 volumes (New York and London: Routledge, 1994). Contains many Australian entries.

Pierce, Peter, gen. ed., *The Oxford Literary Guide to Australia* (Melbourne: Oxford University Press, 1987; revised edition, 1993).

Sage, Lorna, ed., *The Cambridge Guide to Women's Writing in English* (Cambridge: Cambridge University Press, 1999). Contains many Australian entries.

Wilde, W.H., Hooton, Joy and Andrews, Barry, eds, *The Oxford Companion to Australian Literature* (Melbourne: Oxford University Press, 1985; revised edition, 1994). An essential work of reference.

Literary histories

Bennett, Bruce and Strauss, Jennifer, eds, *The Oxford Literary History of Australia* (Melbourne: Oxford University Press, 1998).

Goodwin, Ken, *A History of Australian Literature* (London: Macmillan, 1986).

Green, H.M., *A History of Australian Literature Pure and Applied*, 2 volumes (Sydney: Angus & Robertson, 1961). Although only covering literature published before 1950, remains the most comprehensive historical survey of that material.

Hergenhan, Laurie, gen. ed., *The Penguin New Literary History of Australia* (Melbourne: Penguin, 1988).

Kramer, Leonie, ed., *The Oxford History of Australian Literature* (Melbourne: Oxford University Press, 1981).

General and cultural histories

Carter, Paul, *The Road to Botany Bay* (London: Faber, 1987).

Clark, C.M.H., *A History of Australia*, 6 volumes (Melbourne: Melbourne University Press, 1962–1987).

Day, David, *Claiming a Continent: A History of Australia* (Sydney: Angus & Robertson, 1996).

Head, Brian and Walter, James, eds, *Intellectual Movements and Australian Society* (Melbourne: Oxford University Press, 1988).

Macintyre, Stuart, *A Concise History of Australia* (Cambridge: Cambridge University Press, 1999).

Reynolds, Henry, *The Other Side of the Frontier: Aboriginal Resistance to the European Invasion of Australia* (Melbourne: Penguin, 1990).

Rickard, John, *Australia: A Cultural History* (London: Longman, 1988).

Schaffer, Kay, *Women and the Bush: Forces of Desire in the Australian Cultural Tradition* (Cambridge: Cambridge University Press, 1988).

Serle, Geoffrey, *From Deserts the Prophets Come: The Creative Spirit in Australia*, 1788–1972 (Melbourne: Heinemann, 1973; revised edition 1987).

Smith, Bernard, *European Vision and the South Pacific, 1768–1850* (Oxford: Oxford University Press, 1960).
White, Richard, *Inventing Australia: Images and Identity 1688–1980* (Sydney: Allen & Unwin, 1981).

STUDIES OF PARTICULAR AREAS
Aboriginal writing

Brewster, Anne, *Reading Aboriginal Women's Autobiography* (Sydney: Sydney University Press, 1996).
Gilbert, Kevin, ed., *Inside Black Australia* (Melbourne: Penguin, 1988).
Gilbert, Kevin, ed., *Living Black* (Melbourne: Allen Lane, 1977).
Healy, J.J., *Literature and the Aborigine in Australia, 1770–1975* (St Lucia: University of Queensland Press, 1978; 2nd edition, 1989).
Mudrooroo, *The Indigenous Literature of Australia* (Melbourne: Hyland House, 1997).
Sabbioni, Jennifer, Schaffer, Kay and Smith, Sidonie, eds, *Indigenous Australian Voices: A Reader* (New Brunswick: Rutgers University Press, 1998).
Shoemaker, Adam, *Black Words, White Page: Aboriginal Literature 1929–1988* (St Lucia: University of Queensland Press, 1989).

Autobiography and biography

McCooey, David, *Artful Histories: Modern Australian Autobiography* (Cambridge: Cambridge University Press, 1996).
Walsh, Kay and Hooton, Joy, *Australian Autobiographical Narratives: an Annotated Bibliography*, 2 volumes (Canberra: Australian Scholarly Editions Centre and National Library, 1993, 1998). Covers material published to 1900.
Whitlock, Gillian, ed., *Autographs* (St Lucia: University of Queensland Press, 1996).

Children's literature

Lees, Stella and MacIntyre, Pam, eds, *The Oxford Companion to Australian Children's Literature* (Melbourne: Oxford University Press, 1993).
Muir, Marcie and White, Kerry, *Australian Children's Books: A Bibliography*, 2 volumes (Melbourne: Melbourne University Press, 1992).
Niall, Brenda, *Australia Through the Looking Glass: Children's Fiction 1830–1980* (Melbourne: Melbourne University Press, 1984).
Saxby, H.M., *A History of Australian Children's Literature 1841–1941*, 2 volumes (Sydney: Wentworth Books, 1969, 1971).

Drama and theatre

Fitzpatrick, Peter, *After the Doll: Australian Drama Since 1955* (Melbourne: Edward Arnold, 1979).

Gilbert, Helen, *Sightlines: Race, Gender and Nation in Contemporary Australian Theatre* (Ann Arbor: University of Michigan Press, 1998).
Kelly, Veronica, ed., *Our Australian Theatre in the 1990s* (Amsterdam: Rodopi, 1998).
Love, Harold, ed., *The Australian Stage: A Documentary History* (Sydney: NSW University Press, 1984).
Parsons, Philip, gen. ed., *Companion to Theatre in Australia* (Sydney: Currency Press in association with Cambridge University Press, 1995). Major reference work in the area.
Rees, Leslie, *Australian Drama 1970–1985: A Historical and Critical Survey* (Sydney: Angus & Robertson, 1987).
Rees, Leslie, *The Making of Australian Drama: A Historical and Critical Survey from the 1830s to the 1970s* (Sydney: Angus & Robertson, 1973).
Williams, Margaret, *Australia on the Popular Stage, 1829–1929* (Melbourne: Oxford University Press, 1983).

Fiction

Clancy, Laurie, *A Reader's Guide to Australian Fiction* (Melbourne: Oxford University Press, 1992).
Daniel, Helen, *Liars: Australian New Novelists* (Melbourne: Penguin, 1988).
Dixon, Robert, *Writing the Colonial Adventure* (Cambridge: Cambridge University Press, 1995).
Ferrier, Carole, ed., *Gender, Politics and Fiction: Twentieth Century Australian Women's Novels* (St Lucia: University of Queensland Press, 1985; revised edition 1992).
Gelder, Ken and Salzman, Paul, *The New Diversity: Australian Fiction 1970–88* (Melbourne: McPhee Gribble, 1989).
Hergenhan, Laurie, *Unnatural Lives: Studies in Australian Fiction about the Convicts, from James Tucker to Patrick White* (St Lucia: University of Queensland Press, 1983).
Knight, Stephen, *Continent of Mystery: A Thematic History of Australian Crime Fiction* (Melbourne: Melbourne University Press, 1997).
Modjeska, Drusilla, *Exiles at Home: Australian Women Writers 1925–45* (Sydney: Angus & Robertson, 1981).
Reid, Ian, *Fiction and the Great Depression: Australia and New Zealand* (Melbourne: Edward Arnold, 1979).
Sheridan, Susan, *Along the Faultlines: Sex, Race and Nation in Australian Women's Writing: 1880s–1930s* (Sydney: Allen & Unwin, 1995).
Wilding, Michael, *Studies in Classic Australian Fiction* (Sydney: Sydney Studies, 1997).

Journals and magazines

Antipodes, 1987–
Australian Book Review, 1978–
Australian Literary Studies, 1963–
Meanjin, 1940–
Overland, 1954–

Scripsi, 1981–94
Southerly, 1939–
Westerly, 1956–
Bennett, Bruce, ed., *Cross Currents: Magazines and Newspapers in Australian Literature* (Melbourne: Longman Cheshire, 1981).

Literary criticism

Docker, John, *In a Critical Condition: Reading Australian Literature* (Melbourne: Penguin, 1984).
Hodge, Bob and Mishra, Vijay, *Dark Side of the Dream: Australian Literature and the Postcolonial Mind* (Sydney: Allen & Unwin, 1991).
Kiernan, Brian, *Criticism* (Melbourne: Oxford University Press, 1974).
Ross, Robert L., *Australian Literary Criticism 1945–1998: An Annotated Bibliography* (New York: Garland, 1989).

Multicultural writing

Gunew, Sneja, *Framing Marginality: Multicultural Literary Studies* (Melbourne: Melbourne University Press, 1994).
Gunew, Sneja et al., *A Bibliography of Australian Multicultural Writing* (Geelong: Deakin University, 1992).
Gunew, Sneja and Longley, Kateryna O., eds, *Striking Chords: Multicultural Literary Interpretations* (Sydney: Allen & Unwin, 1992).

Poetry

Brooks, David and Walker, Brenda, eds, *Poetry and Gender: Statements and Essays in Australian Women's Poetry and Poetics* (St Lucia: University of Queensland Press, 1989).
Digby, Jenny, *A Woman's Voice: Conversations with Australian Poets* (St Lucia: University of Queensland Press, 1996).
Duwell, Martin, *A Possible Contemporary Poetry* (St Lucia: Makar, 1982).
Kane, Paul, *Australian Poetry: Romanticism and Negativity* (Cambridge: Cambridge University Press, 1996).
Kinsella, John, ed., *Landbridge: Contemporary Australian Poetry* (Fremantle: Fremantle Arts Centre Press, 1999).
Kirkby, Joan, ed., *The American Model: Influence and Independence in Australian Poetry* (Sydney: Hale & Iremonger, 1982).
McCredden, Lyn and Lucas, Rose, *Bridgings: Readings in Australian Women's Poetry* (Melbourne: Oxford University Press, 1996).
McCredden, Lyn and Trigg, Stephanie, eds, *The Space of Poetry: Australian Essays on Contemporary Poetics* (Melbourne: Melbourne University Literary and Cultural Studies Volume 3, 1996).
Page, Geoff, *A Reader's Guide to Contemporary Australian Poetry* (St Lucia: University of Queensland Press, 1995).
Murray, Les, ed., *The New Oxford Book of Australian Verse* (Melbourne: Oxford University Press, 1991).

Taylor, Andrew, *Reading Australian Poetry* (St Lucia: University of Queensland Press, 1987).
Tranter, John and Mead, Philip, eds, *The Penguin Book of Modern Australian Poetry* (Ringwood, Vic.: Penguin, 1991).
Wilde, William, *Australian Poets and their Work: A Reader's Guide* (Melbourne: Oxford University Press, 1996).

Radio, film, television

Caputo, Raffaele and Burton, Geoff, *Second Take: Australian Film-makers Talk* (Sydney: Allen & Unwin, 1999).
Inglis, K.S., *This is the ABC: the Australian Broadcasting Commission 1932–1983* (Melbourne: Melbourne University Press, 1983).
Johnson, Lesley, *The Unseen Voice: A Cultural Study of Early Australian Radio* (London: Routledge, 1988).
McFarlane, Brian, *Australian Cinema, 1970–1985* (London: Secker & Warburg, 1987).
McFarlane, Brian, Mayer, Geoff and Bertrand, Ina, eds, *The Oxford Companion to Australian Film* (Melbourne: Oxford University Press, 1999).
Murray, Scott, ed., *Australian Film 1978–1992: A Survey of Theatrical Features* (Melbourne: Oxford University Press, 1993).
O'Regan, Tom, *Australian Television Culture* (Sydney: Allen & Unwin, 1993).
O'Regan, Tom, *Australian National Cinema* (London: Routledge, 1996).
Turner, Graeme, *National Fictions: Literature, Film and the Construction of Australian Narrative* (Sydney: Allen & Unwin, 1986).

Index

Page numbers in bold type (e.g. **75–8**) indicate detailed discussion of a topic.